5-9-55

POLISH POSTWAR ECONOMY

STUDIES OF THE RUSSIAN INSTITUTE
COLUMBIA UNIVERSITY

Thad Paul Alton

POLISH

POSTWAR

ECONOMY

1955

Columbia University Press, New York

THE TRANSLITERATION SYSTEM USED IN THIS SERIES
IS BASED ON THE LIBRARY OF CONGRESS SYSTEM
WITH SOME MODIFICATIONS

LIBRARY OF CONGRESS CATALOG CARD NUMBER: 55–5751

COPYRIGHT 1954 COLUMBIA UNIVERSITY PRESS, NEW YORK
FIRST PUBLISHED AS A BOOK 1955

PUBLISHED IN GREAT BRITAIN, CANADA, INDIA, AND PAKISTAN
BY GEOFFREY CUMBERLEGE: OXFORD UNIVERSITY PRESS
LONDON, TORONTO, BOMBAY, AND KARACHI

MANUFACTURED IN THE UNITED STATES OF AMERICA

The Russian Institute
of Columbia University

904559

THE Russian Institute was established by Columbia University in 1946 to serve two major objectives: the training of a limited number of well-qualified Americans for scholarly and professional careers in the field of Russian studies and the development of research in the social sciences and the humanities as they relate to Russia and the Soviet Union. The research program of the Russian Institute is conducted through the efforts of its faculty members, of scholars invited to participate as Senior Fellows in its program, and of candidates for the Certificate of the Institute and for the degree of Doctor of Philosophy. Some of the results of the research program are presented in the Studies of the Russian Institute of Columbia University. The faculty of the Institute, without necessarily agreeing with the conclusions reached in the Studies, believe that their publication advances the difficult task of promoting systematic research on Russia and the Soviet Union and public understanding of the problems involved.

The faculty of the Russian Institute are grateful to the Rockefeller Foundation for the financial assistance which it has given to the program of research and publication.

Studies of the Russian Institute
of Columbia University

SOVIET NATIONAL INCOME AND PRODUCT IN 1937
By Abram Bergson

THROUGH THE GLASS OF SOVIET LITERATURE: VIEWS OF RUSSIAN SOCIETY
Edited by Ernest J. Simmons

THE PROLETARIAN EPISODE IN RUSSIAN LITERATURE, 1928–1932
By Edward J. Brown

MANAGEMENT OF THE INDUSTRIAL FIRM IN THE USSR: A STUDY IN SOVIET ECONOMIC PLANNING
By David Granick

SOVIET POLICIES IN CHINA, 1917–1924
By Allen S. Whiting

UKRAINIAN NATIONALISM, 1939–1945
By John A. Armstrong

POLISH POSTWAR ECONOMY
By Thad Paul Alton

TO

ARDYTH, TEDDY, AND CHUCKIE

Preface

THIS STUDY seeks to appraise the character of Polish economic planning and its success in solving problems of economic development. The inquiry is focused on developments after World War II, especially after 1946; however, for purposes of background and comparison, Polish economic development up to 1939 and the effects of World War II are included. Major portions of the study deal with the evolution and ideology of the postwar government as a determinant of economic policy; the extension of state control over factors of production, sectors of production, and consumers; the administration of the planned economy; and planning and performance in the economy as a whole and in major sectors of activity. An attempt is made to take account of economic changes through 1953 and of economic plans through 1955, the end of the current Polish Six-Year Plan. The study is restricted primarily to comparisons within the Polish economy, but inasmuch as Polish economic organization and planning have been patterned increasingly on the Soviet model, it has been found illuminating to refer at times to the Russian experience.

For the most part the information in this study has been drawn from Polish publications, which in the postwar period were either published directly by state enterprises or otherwise under strict control of the Polish government. In both instances the publications reflect the government's policy of withholding much economic information which would be freely available in countries outside the Soviet sphere. Despite the serious difficulty posed by this restriction, the writer believes that enough information is available to describe the economic system and to analyze its performance in broad outline. The reader will find quantitative information in this volume both in the form of Polish official indexes for sectors of economic activity and as physical measures for selected items. In general, the writer believes that more confidence can be placed in the physical measures than in the value aggregates and that the official indexes for sectors of economic activity must be considered subject to reservation until more is known about their contents, prices, and underlying methodology.

I am greatly indebted to Professors Abram Bergson and Arthur R. Burns for numerous helpful criticisms and valuable suggestions and to Professor Philip E. Mosely for encouragement and advice at the outset of my work and throughout its course. I acknowledge with gratitude a fellowship awarded by the Social Science Research Council for 1949–50, when research for the present study was initiated. I wish to thank also Professor John N. Hazard, Dr. Oleg Hoeffding, and Dr. Nicholas Spulber for reading the manuscript and offering critical comments. My wife was a constant source of encouragement and cheerful assistance in all phases of the work. To many others who have aided me through discussion and comment, assistance in libraries, and in various other ways, I extend my appreciation and thanks. Needless to say, the views expressed in this book are my own, and I alone am responsible for any mistakes or deficiencies.

THAD P. ALTON

New York, N.Y.
February, 1955

Contents

Tables

POLISH POSTWAR ECONOMY

I

Poland's Economic Development Before World War II

UPON her renaissance after World War I, Poland faced the formidable task of establishing political and economic unity after a century and a half of partition. The areas annexed by Russia, Austria, and Prussia had developed strong economic ties with their respective occupying powers. Reestablishment of a Polish state from these areas was difficult because of their differing legal and monetary systems and the poorly integrated transportation network which was designed to connect each of the areas with its former occupying power. Poland's history between the two World Wars reveals a succession of difficulties associated with the problems of war economy and reconstruction, repeated attempts to attain monetary stability, and efforts to achieve economic progress and military strength. These difficulties were complicated by internal maladjustments derived from an earlier period and by external pressures, particularly the revisionist aims of powerful neighbors and the cyclical fluctuation of the world economy. In attempting to solve these problems the Polish government early manifested a tendency toward extensive direct participation in economic activity which increased up to the outbreak of World War II.

Review of Economic History, 1919–39

From 1919 to 1921, Poland was engaged in war with Russia and in attempts to unify the three parts of the country that formerly were ruled by Germany, Austria-Hungary, and Russia. State authorities controlled the prices and distribution of basic consumer goods, regulated foreign trade, and exercised close supervision over banking, finance, and industry. Although many of these controls disappeared at the end of the Russo-Polish War, still a great number

survived. This early experience in a managed economy may be regarded as the basis of the subsequent expansion of the role of the
state in the economic field.

In this early period, the process of unification was furthered in the
fields of customs, money, taxation and fiscal monopolies, and laws.
A unified Polish tariff law was not attained until the fall of 1921.
Monetary unification was completed by the spring of 1920, but effective fiscal unity was not achieved until 1925. Fiscal monopolies
which had formerly been in operation in only one part of Poland
were extended to the whole country, and in this manner the state
acquired five important monopolies, namely, tobacco, alcohol, salt,
matches, and lotteries.[1] Legal unification proceeded more slowly,
and only by the mid-thirties was the process of uniform codification
completed.[2]

The unification of Polish territories was made more difficult by
the extensive destruction of buildings, industries, communications,
and farms during World War I and the subsequent Russo-Polish
War.[3] The expenditures for war and reconstruction resulted in a
great excess of money income with respect to the supply of consumer
goods. In the absence of an effective system of taxation, the inflation
which had begun during World War I increased its momentum.
Price and wage controls were not applied, due partly to an inexperienced administration and partly to peasant parliamentary opposition
to control of agricultural prices and left-wing antagonism to wage
controls. The astronomical inflation which occurred is indicated by
the climb of the dollar rate of the Polish mark from 186 marks in
July, 1920, to 20,000,000 at the end of January, 1924.[4]

During 1924, the Polish government initiated a program of financial reform and temporarily halted the inflation. The Bank of
Poland was founded to act as the central bank and assist in exchange
stabilization, and the mark was replaced by the zloty, a new currency
unit on a gold exchange standard at a parity of 5.18 zlotys per dollar.
The fiscal revenues were buttressed by adding tobacco and matches
to the state monopolies and foreign credits were obtained. At first

---

[1] Ferdynand Zweig, *Poland between Two Wars*, p. 30.

[2] Birmingham Information Service on Slavonic Countries, *Poland: Monograph No. 3, Poland's New Codes of Law.*

[3] For an account of the extent of destruction, see Roman Gorecki, *Poland and Her Economic Development*, pp. 21–22.

[4] Zweig, *op. cit.*, pp. 34–39.

the reform was effective, but by the middle of 1925 increased government deficit financing of investments raised the internal price level relative to world prices. Adverse foreign trade balances rose rapidly, and the central bank's gold and foreign exchange reserves were inadequate at the newly established parities. The tariff war with Germany, which started in the summer of 1925, was one of the chief elements leading to the failure of the financial reform. Foreign long-term credits became practically unobtainable, and the dollar rate of the zloty rose from the initial parity rate of 5.18 zlotys per dollar in August, 1925, to 10.55 in May, 1926.[5]

Beginning in mid-1926 the Polish government took effective measures to balance the budget and stabilize the currency. The prior currency depreciation coupled with the British coal strike and prosperous conditions abroad favored Polish exports and thus facilitated economic recovery. In 1927 the government obtained a stabilization loan of 62 million dollars and 2 million pounds sterling from a group of private American and European bankers and a 20 million dollar stabilization credit from the U.S. Federal Reserve Bank and leading European central banks. Under these favorable circumstances the government issued the Stabilization Plan of October, 1927, with provisions for a new gold zloty, increased capital for the Bank of Poland, and other measures directed at maintaining monetary stability.[6] The plan was successful, and the zloty remained on the gold standard until April, 1936, long after leading world currencies had fallen from it.

Poland's period of high prosperity in 1928–29 was suddenly reversed in the fall of 1929 under the impact of the world economic crisis and the attendant cessation of influx of foreign capital, capital flight, and adverse effects on foreign trade. Polish exports in particular suffered from the drastic fall in world agricultural and raw material prices, while Polish imports of manufactures failed to benefit as much due to the greater rigidity of prices in this sector. In view of the long struggle with inflation up to 1926 and the very recent successful monetary stabilization, the Polish government decided upon deflation of prices and wages in order to restore equilibrium with world prices and keep the zloty on the gold standard. In an endeavor to cope with the maladjustment in foreign trade

[5] *Ibid.,* pp. 34–41.
[6] *Ibid.,* pp. 49–50.

caused by the divergence of the domestic and world price levels, the
Polish government introduced various import prohibitions, quota
regulations, clearing agreements, restrictions on travel abroad by
Polish citizens, and other measures to protect the zloty. The trends
in prices, wages, and employment in the period 1928–38 are shown
in Table 1. Employment in worker-hours in industry began to rise in
1934, but the wholesale prices of industrial and agricultural commodities continued to decline through 1935. Early in 1936, however,
general recovery from the protracted depression was under way.

During the years 1933–39, concurrently with the strengthening of
the executive branch of the government at the expense of the legislative, the controls of the government over the national economy
were augmented by a body of economic legislation.[7] The new Commercial Code of 1933 required registration of large-scale enterprises
and provided for closer supervision over their activities. By the law
of March 13, 1934, control over cooperative associations was transferred from the Council of Cooperative Associations to the Minister
of Finance or his appointee, and cooperatives were required to become members of auditing unions. Under the law of March 16,
1933, creating a Labor Fund for financing public works as an unemployment relief measure, the state enlarged its direct role in the field
of construction and investment. Controls over cartels were specified
in the law of March 28, 1933, and extended by the decree of November 28, 1935, to enable the Minister of Industry and Trade to cancel
cartel agreements and otherwise regulate cartels.

With the fall of the zloty from the gold standard upon the introduction of foreign exchange control on April 27, 1936, the government initiated a new economic policy seeking to guide the national
economy by even more direct measures. In May, 1936, a decree
strengthening state control over foreign trade made all imports subject to special license by a newly created Commission for Trade,
while exports required foreign exchange permits obtainable only
after the Commission was notified. By the following November foreign trade controls were augmented by the establishment of the
Polish Clearing Institute to deal with the execution of clearing agreements. Internal trade was subjected to a large measure of government control in 1938 by laws regulating trade in primary necessities,
such as foodstuffs, clothing, and fuel. The government was entitled

[7] *Ibid.*, pp. 72–76.

to regulate the quality of flour milling and baking, the prices of primary necessities, and storage of these commodities, and to require record keeping and reporting of relevant transactions.

Poland's major industrial planning effort in the interwar period was begun in 1936 and was terminated prematurely by the outbreak of World War II. Although this plan for the industrialization of central Poland [8] was motivated by military requirements, it also aimed at providing an enlarged base of heavy industry, machine building, and related enterprises that would provide employment for the surplus agrarian population both directly and by inducing industrial expansion in the country as a whole. The planners were aware of the external economies inherent in a balanced development and therefore provided for a network of rail and highway transportation, fuel and electric power supply, flood control and improvement of navigation along the rivers, and development of agriculture. Various privileges, tax deductions, and other incentives were offered to induce private investment in the central area to complement the direct effort undertaken by the state.

The plan contemplated an initial three-year period beginning in mid-1936 to be followed by three additional five-year periods extending through 1954, by which time it was anticipated that Poland would emerge unified by a communications network and with a satisfactory balance between agriculture and industry.[9] In the two and one-half years that the plan was in effect an important part of the program was realized. The investment program of the government for the entire country, including the Central Industrial District, amounted to 800 million zlotys in 1937 and about 1,000 million zlotys in 1938, or about 5 percent of the national income.[10] However, the estimated per capita national income of Poland in 1938 was about 160 United States dollars of 1925–34 purchasing power,[11] an extremely low figure which did not afford much surplus over essential consumption. In spite of the planned effort by the state, employment as measured by the total worker-hours in industry in 1938 was still about 9 percent below the pre-depression level,[12] although the

[8] Roughly the present area of southwestern Poland.
[9] Zweig, *op. cit.*, p. 79.
[10] Based on data from Zweig, *op. cit.*, p. 80, and Colin Clark, *The Conditions of Economic Progress*, p. 115.
[11] Clark, *op. cit.*, pp. 19, 115; *Mały rocznik statystyczny—1939* (Little Statistical Yearbook—1939), p. 15.
[12] See Table 1.

Table 1

PRICES, WAGES, COST OF LIVING, AND EMPLOYMENT, 1928–38

Year	General Index of Wholesale Prices	Wholesale Prices of Industrial Goods	Wholesale Prices of Industrial Goods Bought by Farmers	Wholesale Prices of Goods Sold Directly by Farmers	Cost of Living of Workers' Families
1928	100.0	100.0	100.0	100.0	100.0
1929	96.3	98.6	100.7	89.5	100.5
1930	85.5	89.8	98.5	67.6	92.1
1931	74.6	76.8	90.4	59.5	82.8
1932	65.5	67.4	81.0	48.9	74.8
1933	59.0	61.0	72.6	42.6	67.5
1934	55.7	59.4	70.3	37.0	62.6
1935	53.0	56.7	66.3	35.8	60.0
1936	54.0	57.1	64.6	38.7	58.0
1937	59.4	60.9	66.2	49.2	62.0
1938	56.2	57.8	65.0	43.8	60.9

Year	Nominal Wages of Industrial Workers	Real Wages of Industrial Workers	Employment in Worker-Hours in Industry	Real Value of the Sum of Wages Paid
1928	100.0	100.0	100.0	100.0
1929	108.4	108.1	101.1	109.3
1930	108.1	117.4	84.2	98.9
1931	100.9	121.9	71.8	87.5
1932	92.8	124.2	56.9	70.7
1933	85.5	126.6	56.6	71.6
1934	82.0	131.0	63.7	82.2
1935	80.7	134.6	67.5	88.0
1936	80.5	138.8	73.3	98.2
1937	82.8	133.7	84.4	107.9
1938	.... [a]	....	90.9	....

Source: Edward Lipiński (ed.), *Koniunktura Gospodarcza Polski, Miesięczne Tablice Statystyczne* (Economic Conditions in Poland, Monthly Statistical Tables), Special Issue, December, 1938, pp. 20, 22, 32.

[a] .... = not available.

number of employed workers was only 5 percent below the 1928 total.[13] Meanwhile Poland's population was increasing at the rate of about 400,000 annually, so that the surplus agrarian population increased substantially.

[13] *Mały rocznik statystyczny—1939*, p. 261.

Aspects of Economic Development

National income and the occupational structure of the population. Analyses of Poland's national income have been handicapped by the lack of reliable statistical data. The series shown in Table 2 is based on estimates from various sources roughly adjusted for comparability by Colin Clark, with the exception of the 1933 figure which is inserted from Gorecki. This series shows an increase of about one third in the period 1929–38, but according to Zweig, the national income by 1939 had merely recovered to its 1929 level.[14] Detailed information concerning the composition of the national income for the years shown in Table 2 is lacking, except for 1929. In that year an estimated national income of 26 billion zlotys was distributed into percentage shares as follows: urban consumption—48.0; rural consumption—42.3; investment—8.1; government services (education only)—1.6. Despite the crudity of the calculation, it affords an insight into the poverty of the Polish peasantry which composed about 62 percent of the population but consumed less than half of the national income, and of this, nearly three fourths consisted of the peasants' retained production. Of the total savings of about 8 percent of the national income, two thirds represented public savings.[15]

The occupational distribution of Poland's population is shown in Table 3 for the years 1921 and 1931. The low percentages in manufacturing and services are a reflection of the low level of economic

Table 2

NATIONAL INCOME OF POLAND, 1926–38

Year	Amount in Billions of U.S. Dollars at Average 1925–34 Prices	Index
1926	4.21	100
1929	4.21	100
1933	3.56	85
1938	5.59	133

Sources: Colin Clark, *The Conditions of Economic Progress*, p. 115; Roman Gorecki, *Poland and Her Economic Development*, p. 31.

[14] Zweig, *op. cit.*, p. 88.
[15] Birmingham Information Service on Slavonic Countries, *Poland: Monograph No. 4, National Income of Poland*, p. 3.

progress attained in Poland. In Poland's case the high proportions of population engaged in agriculture and extractive industries were not offset very significantly by a high degree of participation in foreign trade, but instead indicated an economy in early stages of industrialization with largely self-sufficient agriculture and handicrafts.

Table 3

OCCUPATIONAL DISTRIBUTION OF POLISH POPULATION, 1921 AND 1931

Category	1921	1931
Total population in millions	27.2	32.1
Percentage distribution by source of livelihood:		
Agriculture, forestry, and fishing	63.8	60.6
Mining and other industry	15.4	19.4
Commerce and insurance	6.2	6.1
Communications and transport	3.3	3.6
Other	11.3	10.3
Total	100.0	100.0

Source: *Concise Statistical Yearbook of Poland, 1933*, p. 11; *1937*, p. 31.

Industrialization. The basic economic problem facing Poland in the interwar period was to provide useful employment for the surplus agrarian population. Although the rate of natural increase per 1,000 inhabitants showed a declining trend from a peak of 17.0 in 1930 to 10.7 in 1938, it remained substantially above the 8.3 and 6.3 per 1,000 for Europe minus the USSR in 1928–30 and 1936–37, respectively.[16] Poland's agriculture showed yields substantially lower per unit area than western Europe in spite of a density of agricultural population nearly twice as great. The possibility of relief through emigration had declined, and intensive development of agriculture for export markets was discouraged by the low world prices on agricultural products during the depression of the thirties. Polish industry failed to reattain the 1929 level of employment even by 1938,[17] much less provide for an annual population increment of around 400,000, even though industrial output increased about 20 percent during the same period.

Table 4 shows the trend of real investment and industrial production in Poland from 1928 to 1938. Industrial production recov-

[16] *Mały rocznik statystyczny—1939*, pp. 45–46.
[17] *Ibid.*, p. 261.

Table 4

INDEXES OF REAL INVESTMENT AND INDUSTRIAL PRODUCTION IN POLAND, 1928–38

Year	INVESTMENT			INDUSTRIAL PRODUCTION			
	Sale of Rolled Products, Pipe, Bricks, Cement, and Lime	INVESTMENT IN MACHINERY		General Index	Producer Goods	Consumer Goods	Other (Electric Energy and Export Goods)
		Industry and Communications	Agriculture				
1928	100.0	100.0	100.0	100.0	100.0	100.0	100.0
1929	92.1	99.0	72.8	101.9	99.5	100.8	107.9
1930	65.4	69.0	42.5	89.7	86.9	90.0	93.5
1931	49.2	48.1	25.6	78.2	73.2	78.0	86.8
1932	34.9	33.7	11.8	63.7	56.6	67.1	69.6
1933	41.4	34.8	14.3	70.0	67.7	71.4	71.4
1934	52.5	40.1	16.1	78.8	79.7	78.6	77.7
1935	58.4	48.4	22.0	84.9	88.0	86.1	77.8
1936	73.8	61.9	30.5	94.3	103.1	93.0	82.2
1937	94.5	82.3	46.0	110.7	127.3	102.7	97.1
1938	105.0	....a	....	119.3	139.8	109.2	103.2

Source: Edward Lipiński (ed.), *Koniunktura Gospodarcza Polski, Miesięczne Tablice Statystyczne* (Economic Conditions in Poland, Monthly Statistical Tables), Special Issue, December, 1938, p. 24.

a .... = not available.

ered more rapidly than investment, while investment in agricultural machinery showed the greatest decline and the smallest recovery among the series shown. After 1936 the expanded public expenditure on rearmament and on the planned industrialization of central Poland was the primary factor in the revival of production and investment.

Among the factors retarding industrialization was the low average per capita national income which was reflected in a low level of demand for consumer goods and small scope for rapid capital formation. The poor communications network was another limiting factor. A greatly expanded network of highways, waterways, and rail transport could have enlarged the internal market very substantially. In foreign trade, the animosity of Germany and the USSR toward Poland and Poland's desire to achieve economic independence from her neighbors generated many difficulties. These were reflected in internal maladjustments, especially in the textile industry of central Poland, which had been oriented toward the east, and the mining and metallurgy of Upper Silesia and the agriculture of Posen and Pomerania, which had close ties to German markets. The world economic crisis of the early thirties brought a curtailment of foreign loans, capital flight, and a drastic fall in earnings from Poland's agricultural and raw material exports, which reduced Poland's ability to import capital goods for investment and raw materials for fabrication. Prices on Poland's agricultural exports fell relatively lower than the prices on capital goods imports. Moreover, the attempts of many of Poland's trading partners to achieve a favorable trade balance through restrictions upon imports further reduced Poland's export possibilities. The deflationary policy which the Polish government applied in its efforts to protect the gold zloty and restore equilibrium in foreign trade introduced a series of maladjustments in the domestic economy which appear to have retarded recovery.

In many branches of Polish industry the high degree of cartelization forced the internal prices above competitive levels and reduced output accordingly. Cartelization was fostered partly by government policy which sought to expand exports by various subsidy arrangements at the expense of the domestic market. In the years 1919–36, the number of domestic cartels increased from 11 in 1919 to a peak of 274 in 1935, followed by a slight decline to 266 in 1936; and at the same time the number of international cartels in which Polish enterprises participated grew from 4 to 106.[18]

Foreign trade. Foreign trade lagged behind the revival of domestic industrial production, as may be seen by reference to Tables 4 and 5. Prior to World War I nearly all of Poland's trade was directed across land frontiers, and even by 1927 only about one fourth of total trade by value was shipped through the port of Danzig, while the role of Gdynia, Poland's other exit to the sea, was insignificant. Increasingly thereafter, partly as a matter of deliberate policy and partly as a consequence of the German-Polish tariff war, foreign trade was routed by sea.[19] In 1938, 63 percent of total foreign trade, by value, was directed via the two Baltic ports, and of the total, the share of Gdynia and Danzig was, respectively, 48 and 15 percent.[20] The rise of Gdynia was but the outward manifestation of the expanding role of the state in the domestic economy. The port was constructed on the initiative of the government largely through public investment.

Table 5

POLAND'S FOREIGN TRADE, 1928–38

Year	Import	Export	Import	Export	Balance
	(Index, fixed prices)		(Million zlotys, current prices)		
1928	100.0	100.0	3,362	2,508	−854
1929	89.6	108.6	3,111	2,813	−298
1930	74.7	113.4	2,246	2,433	+187
1931	62.9	102.3	1,468	1,879	+411
1932	48.9	73.0	862	1,084	+222
1933	52.0	71.2	827	960	+133
1934	53.9	78.4	799	975	+176
1935	58.6	80.3	861	925	+64
1936	61.3	86.8	1,003	1,026	+23
1937	66.5	81.0	1,254	1,195	−59
1938	76.0	78.5	1,300	1,185	−115

Sources: Edward Lipiński (ed.), *Koniunktura Gospodarcza Polski 1928–38*, p. 34; *Mały rocznik statystyczny—1939*, p. 162.

Expansion of the public economy. The role of the state in the Polish economy has always been large, and it manifested itself in

[18] *Concise Statistical Yearbook of Poland—1937*, p. 99.
[19] Raymond Leslie Buell, *Poland: Key to Europe*, pp. 148–49.
[20] *Mały rocznik statystyczny—1939*, p. 165.

various forms ranging from indirect controls to direct regulation and outright ownership and operation of enterprises. In part this role was derived from the partitioning powers, but over the interwar period it expanded greatly under an assortment of influences, while simultaneously the scope for private competitive enterprise diminished.

The demands of war and preparations for defense generally entail an expansion of state participation in the national economy. This factor worked especially strongly in Poland, for in addition to a war economy under the occupying powers up to the end of World War I, the regimen had to be extended to cover the Russo-Polish War. Thereafter, in the interest of national survival, the government took the lead in establishing munitions factories, reconstructing the communications network, and planning the industrialization of central Poland. The scarcity of domestic private capital for industrial pursuits contributed to state intervention and control.

The world depression brought to Poland, as elsewhere, an increase in government financial intervention in the economy. Private banking concerned itself mostly with short-term credit operations, and even in this field it frequently had to seek aid from state banks. Up to 1930, the private banks outranked state institutions in the field of short-term credit, but their role shrank progressively thereafter and by 1938 was definitely secondary.[21] The field of long-term investment credit was almost completely controlled by state institutions. Using the resources of expanded public finance, the state undertook a series of measures to relieve unemployment, carry through needed public works, and otherwise promote economic recovery.

State ownership of properties of all kinds in 1927 was estimated at about one eighth of the total national wealth.[22] Included in state ownership were about 90 percent of all railroads, 95 percent of the merchant marine, 100 percent of commercial aviation, 70 percent of iron production, 30 percent of coal production, 37 percent of the country's forests, the entire potash industry, 50 percent of the metal industry, and the entire armament industry. Moreover, the state participated in a large number of industrial enterprises through joint ownership with private business, cooperatives, and municipalities.[23]

[21] *Ibid.*, pp. 226–27, 233.
[22] Zweig, *op. cit.*, p. 108, citing S. Kruszewski, *The Ownership of the Polish State.*
[23] *Ibid.*, p. 109; Buell, *op. cit.*, p. 158; Leopold Wellisz, *Foreign Capital in Poland*, pp. 175–76.

The state monopolies in salt, alcohol, matches, tobacco, and lotteries have already been mentioned. In addition, the whole area of money and credit was dominated by the state through its ownership of the National Economic Bank, the State Land Bank, and the Postal Savings Bank, and through its direct control since 1936 over the Bank of Poland.

Private enterprise in commerce and industry faced increasingly glum prospects over the interwar period. The field of activities requiring licenses, concessions, or permits was steadily broadened. Cartels, partly under government sponsorship, introduced restrictions on production and marketing, and in some areas state monopolies totally excluded private enterprise. In other areas, competition of state enterprises further reduced the scope for private activity. Foreign exchange controls, government price fixing, and other regulations pointed more and more toward a controlled economy. The successive governments in Poland were motivated by a desire for economic and military self-sufficiency in the presence of powerful neighbors harboring revisionist aims. The environment was neither one in which private enterprise could plan investments with confidence in the future, nor one in which the government could feel that it could depend on private effort to make adequate provision for national security. The result was an increase in the economic role of the state at the expense of the private sector.

Problems in agriculture. The leading problem in Polish agriculture in the interwar period was the excessively high ratio of agricultural workers to land at the existing level of demand for farm products and the status of agricultural science. Measurement of the surplus farm population[24] at best is relative, and the results depend on the standards that are used. If one considers only the total agricultural population and the total agricultural land expressed in "arable-equivalents," [25] the density of agrarian population per square kilometer before World War II was greater in Poland than in most of the other European countries. Such a measure, however, neglects the quality of agricultural land and the output per capita of the farm population. Poland's production per hectare of agricultural

[24] The account in this section is based on Wilbert E. Moore, *Economic Demography of Eastern and Southern Europe,* pp. 56–72.

[25] The method of "arable-equivalents" assumes all arable land to be of equal value and attempts to convert land in other agricultural uses into approximate equivalents of arable land.

land expressed in "arable-equivalents" was considerably below the European average. When both the relatively greater density of farm population and the relatively lower yields per hectare are taken into account, it follows that "surplus" agrarian population was higher than on either count alone.

If the average European per capita product in agriculture is taken as a standard, it can be divided into the total value of agricultural production in a given country in order to obtain a "standard population" to compare against the actual population in agriculture. Such calculations by Wilbert Moore for Polish agriculture around 1930 gave a "standard population" of about 9.4 million. Since the actual population in Polish agriculture was about 19.3 million, the "surplus" by this measure came to about 9.9 million, or more than half the total agricultural population. The "surplus" computed by regions of Poland ranged from about 4 percent in the west to 50 to 62 percent in other regions, being highest in the south and east. Under this kind of measurement the "surplus" population would be smaller if the total output of agriculture were greater. By calculating a hypothetical output for Polish agriculture using the Polish area and assuming French yields per hectare and again dividing the total output by the European average per capita product in agriculture, Moore derived a second "standard" agricultural population for comparison with the actual Polish agrarian population. This calculation showed a "surplus" of about 5.7 million, or 29 percent of the total. It seems clear that by most of the standards employed, prewar Poland had too many farm people for the available farm land. This does not imply that it would have been possible immediately to withdraw a substantial part of the labor force from agriculture without reducing total agricultural production. It suggests, however, that with improved techniques and equipment in agriculture such a transfer could be made.

Feudal survivals in the form of land tenure presented additional difficulties. In the Prussian part of Poland the peasants' scattered plots or strips of land were combined into integrated holdings at the time of the liberation of the serfs. In the other parts of Poland commassation was not effected at the same time that the property settlements for the emancipated serfs were carried out, and the original pattern of mingled plots of land of various owners became more confused through subdivision upon inheritance and upon liquidation of easements.[26] After World War I, the proportion of farms holding arable land in scattered plots ranged from 17 percent of the total number of farms in the western region to 60 percent in the eastern region, and averaged about 47 percent for the country as a whole.[27] Another feudal survival that encumbered Polish agriculture consisted of numerous easements which one farm owner had in the property of another. The village common grounds alone accounted for about 5 percent of the total area of the country and constituted a serious impediment to higher agricultural output. The presence of landless peasants to the extent of about 31 percent of the agrarian population was an important element in social discontent.[28] Large estates of more than 100 hectares in 1921 represented only about half of 1 percent of the total number of agricultural holdings but comprised 45 percent of the total area including forests and 27 percent of the land utilized for agriculture.[29]

Polish agriculture was most highly developed and intensive in the former German areas of partitioned Poland and least intensive in the eastern part of the country, and its market orientation correspondingly diminished from west to east, reflecting the degree of development of the communication network and the general level of economic development. The large estates were primarily market oriented, whereas peasant production was directed toward self-sufficiency. By the end of the interwar period the regional variation in intensity of cultivation was somewhat leveled to the disadvantage of the western districts, which suffered from the loss of protected markets in Germany and had to face the competition of a more extensive mode of production in central and eastern Poland. In comparison with the agriculture of western Europe, Polish production as a whole was more extensive, placing primary emphasis on plant production, although animal production was coming into increasing favor over the interwar years.

State intervention in Polish agriculture manifested itself primarily in policies with respect to agrarian reform, prices, and trade. Agrar-

[26] Easements in Poland consisted of various privileges of use which peasants had in the lands of others, such as rights of grazing, gathering firewood, right of way, and fishing.

[27] V. Lesniewski and W. Ponikowski, "Polish Agriculture," in O. S. Morgan (ed.), *Agricultural Systems of Middle Europe*, p. 263.

[28] *Ibid.*, p. 264.

[29] *Concise Statistical Yearbook of Poland—1930*, p. 14.

ian reform was laid down in principle by the land reform law of July 10, 1919, and placed in effect a year later by another statute. However, not much was accomplished until after a new land reform law was passed on December 28, 1925. Both statutes provided for the creation of self-supporting peasant farms through parcellation of estates larger than 300 hectares in eastern Poland and 60 to 180 hectares elsewhere. The law of 1925 laid down a yearly contingent of 200,000 hectares for parcellation over the succeeding ten years. It exempted highly productive estates and those operating plants for processing farm products up to a total area not exceeding 550,000 hectares and provided for commassation, distribution of common lands, liquidation of easements, and melioration of land. Although the provisions of the law were not fully observed as concerns the pace of parcellation, the total results of the reform were impressive. In the period 1919–38, 2,654,800 hectares were parceled; 5,423,300 hectares were consolidated out of the patchwork holdings; easements were eliminated on 280,500 farms resulting in transfer of 595,300 hectares and 3,889,100 zlotys as compensation; and 548,700 hectares were affected by melioration under the reform.[30] Since the total agricultural land amounted to about 25.6 million hectares, it is clear that the prewar agrarian reform benefited about a third of the total farm area.

The land reform as a measure to cope with the excess agrarian population failed even to keep up with the increase of peasant population, and the average size of peasant holdings declined. The average area parceled annually over the twenty interwar years was about 133,000 hectares, whereas the increase in agrarian population in the same period was about 250,000 annually. At this rate the reform could provide peasant farms of an average size of 5 hectares for little more than one half the additional family units. The basic limitation was the ratio of agrarian population to the total agricultural land. Even if the total of 25.6 million hectares were distributed evenly among the people drawing their support from agriculture, it would have yielded only about 1.2 hectares per capita of agrarian population in 1939. Under the prevailing law for agrarian reform, there remained in 1939 only about 1,000,000 hectares for further division into smaller units, but if 50 hectares per private farm were the maximum permitted, the land reserve for parcellation in 1939 would

[30] *Mały rocznik statystyczny—1939*, p. 70.

have amounted to about 3,000,000 hectares, or little more than had been distributed in the preceding twenty years.[31]

Government trade and price policy with respect to agriculture in Poland reflected the rise in output of farm products. Up to the end of 1927, Polish agriculture had not regained the 1909–13 level of output in principal grain crops, potatoes, and sugar beets. The government desired an adequate domestic supply of food and therefore discouraged agricultural exports by means of export duties, various restrictions, and certain prohibitions. After 1928, the production of rye, wheat, and potatoes rose above prewar levels, and surpluses were available for export. Official policy changed from restriction of exports to protection of domestic production by import tariffs and export subsidies. The domestic and foreign trade policy in agriculture was part of the government's over-all deflationary program to protect the zloty against the effects of the world depression. Other measures affecting foreign trade included a series of rye and wheat agreements with Germany and the USSR to share export markets and to support prices of these products. Internally the state tried to ease the debt burden on agriculture by means of conversion of long-term debts into less burdensome obligations. It attempted unsuccessfully to raise agricultural prices relative to industrial by a campaign against industrial cartels and by measures seeking to support domestic grain prices through state purchases, crop loans to farmers to enable them to store grain after the harvest, and a price subsidy on grain financed by a tax on grain sales. The rail freight rates were a tool toward facilitating the government's policy with regard to marketing of farm produce, the rates being set so as to encourage export of surplus agricultural commodities from districts remote from seaports and the western frontier.[32] The government endeavored to raise the level of agricultural practices by expanding the services of experimental farms, enlarging the veterinary service, and extending agricultural education to a larger group of students. State intervention in agriculture, however, was modest in comparison with its role in industry.

By the eve of World War II, Poland had gone far toward achieving economic unity, assuring monetary stability, and pro-

---

[31] Zweig, *op. cit.,* p. 132.
[32] Lesniewski and Ponikowski, *op. cit.,* p. 281.

viding for economic growth. Progress toward these objectives, however, was hindered by an inexperienced public administration and ineptly chosen economic policies, by the unsettled international political situation which discouraged private investment, and by the incidence of the world depression. In attempting to solve its economic problems the Polish government expanded its role in the management of the economy, both directly in the form of ownership and operation of enterprises and indirectly through regulation of private economic activity. The agricultural problem remained acute in spite of substantial redistribution of land under the agrarian reform, but toward the end of the interwar period its solution was being approached in the framework of planned industrialization. At the same time that the government expanded the state's direct role in industry, it encouraged private enterprise to join in the planned industrialization of the country. The emerging experiment of partnership of state and private enterprise, however, was cut short by the outbreak of World War II. In the postwar period a new ideology was to triumph proclaiming lasting antipathy between the state and private sectors.

II

Economic Significance
of World War II Changes in Poland's
Boundaries and Population

Area and Population

A COMPARISON of Poland's prewar production with its recent postwar output shows that a very substantial expansion has taken place. The increase in production is particularly impressive on a per capita basis, and unless one is aware of the prior changes in production potential and population, the gains may falsely be attributed largely to changes in economic organization under economic planning. On closer examination, it appears that a large part of the Polish postwar economic gains are a direct consequence of the boundary shifts which resulted in the acquisition of a greatly expanded industrial plant and better agricultural land, even though the country's total area was diminished.

The factor of economic planning must not be discounted, however. Increasingly over the postwar years, the factors of production in the Polish economy have been mobilized for the achievement of the goals set forth in the national economic plans. The very extensive direct and indirect controls exercised by the Polish government over economic activity and the martial atmosphere under which the economy operates are of considerable significance in recent developments and certainly must be taken into consideration in any evaluation of progress thus far realized and perspectives envisioned for the future.

Area and boundaries. The Polish eastern boundary was drawn on the basis of the decision of the Yalta Conference which specified that the boundary should follow the Curzon line with some deviations in favor of Poland, in certain regions, of from five to eight kilometers.[1] Subsequently, by the treaty signed in Moscow on February 15, 1951, the Polish-Soviet boundary as established in 1945 was modified by the exchange of 480 square kilometers of Soviet territory in the province of Drohobycz for an equal area of Polish territory in the province of Lublin.[2] Under the Potsdam Agreement, the German territory east of the Oder and Neisse rivers, the city of Stettin, the southern part of East Prussia, and the city of Danzig were placed under Polish administration, with the final status to await a treaty of peace with Germany. These changes resulted in the cession of 69,400 square miles in the east to the Soviet Union, while 38,600 square miles of German territory came under Polish administration. The area of Poland was reduced in the process from about 150,000 square miles to somewhat less than 120,000, that is, a reduction of about 20 percent.[3]

From the very beginning the Polish government has acted on the assumption that the former German lands have become an integral part of postwar Poland, renaming this area the Recovered Territories, and asserting that in past history these lands were Polish. One of the basic aims of the three-year plan of economic reconstruction was the unification of the former German areas with the old territories of Poland.[4] The German population was almost completely expelled, and on January 11, 1949, the separate Polish ministry for the administration of the former German areas was abolished, the territories being incorporated into the general Polish administration.[5] Finally, by the June, 1950, agreement between Poland and East Germany, the latter renounced all claims to the areas incorporated into Poland.[6] It is clear, therefore, that Poland regards the provisional boundary in the west as final, and her economic plans are based on this assumption.

Population. The population of prewar Poland was estimated for January, 1939, at about 35.0 million. Of this number, approximately 11.8 million lived in the eastern areas subsequently ceded to the

[1] *Dziennik Ustaw Rzeczypospolitej Polskiej* (Journal of Laws of the Polish Republic), 1947, No. 35, Item 167. Hereafter cited as *Dziennik Ustaw*.

[2] *Ibid.*, 1952, No. 11, Item 63.

[3] U.S. Department of Commerce, Office of International Trade, *International Reference Service*, V, No. 33, 1.

[4] *Dziennik Ustaw*, 1947, No. 53, Item 285, Art. 4.

[5] *Ibid.*, 1949, No. 4, Item 22.

[6] *Ibid.*, 1951, No. 14, Item 106; No. 17, Item 132.

Soviet Union, and 23.2 million inhabited the area which remained within the Polish boundaries. At the same time the population of the German areas subsequently placed under Polish administration amounted to 9.1 million, making a total population of 32.3 million in 1939 for the area within the present Polish boundaries.[7] In 1948 the population within the same area was only 23.8 million.[8] If one neglects the rise in population that might have occurred if the war had not intervened, the population loss suffered by Poland can be reckoned at approximately 11 million, or, if the postwar area be considered as the base, the reduction amounted to about 8.5 million. Within these totals, the chief components are war-produced excess mortality, migratory losses, and the loss resulting from the exchange of nationals between Poland and the USSR.

Accompanying the reduction in total population were changes in ethnic composition which almost completely eliminated the national minorities. The population of Poland in 1931 had a percentage composition by mother tongue as follows: Polish—68.9; Ukrainian, Russian, and Byelorussian—17.4; Jewish—8.6; German—2.3; and other and those not specified—2.8. However, if these figures are compared with the composition of the population by religious faith, it appears that the Polish component may be somewhat overstated.[9] Under German occupation, the Jewish minority was almost completely destroyed, and many of the Jews that survived later fled from the area. By 1949 it was estimated that only about eighty thousand remained in Poland.[10] In addition to this loss of population, the mutual repatriation and exchange of nationals between Poland and the USSR, repatriation of Poles from other areas, and the expulsion, flight, and transfer of Germans from Poland and the German areas under Polish administration have brought about nearly complete ethnic uniformity in postwar Poland.

The area and population changes brought about by World War II have reduced the average density of population in Poland from about 232 per square mile in 1938 to approximately 198 per square

[7] Polish Ministry of Foreign Affairs, Press and Information Department, *Information on Poland*, p. Bb 1.

[8] *Statistical Yearbook of Poland—1948*, p. 16.

[9] *Mały rocznik statystyczny—1939*, pp. 23, 25.

[10] Eugene M. Kulischer, "Population Changes behind the Iron Curtain," *Annals of the American Academy of Political and Social Science*, September, 1950, p. 106.

mile in 1948. The average density in 1946 varied from 234 per square mile on the old territories to about 130 on the former German provinces as a result of the expulsion and flight of the German population and the incomplete settlement of the area by Poles. One of the objectives of the Polish postwar economic plans is to effect a more uniform distribution of population by encouraging migration of Poles to the new western areas and by settling repatriates in these regions. An immediate consequence of the more than proportionate reduction of population with respect to area was the rise in per capita wealth of the population as regards land and capital. This rise in wealth was of course conditioned by the extent of destruction caused by war.

Changes in Industrial Potential

Losses in the east. The areas ceded by Poland to the USSR were poorly industrialized and were not richly endowed with mineral resources with the exception of rock salt, potash, and petroleum deposits. In 1937, the ceded area, which contained about one third of the total prewar population and about 46 percent of the total prewar area, accounted for about one eighth of the country's total employment in industry and mining.[11] This rough measure of the degree of industrialization overlooks the factors of capital intensity per worker and the value of output. However, these factors very likely would serve to reduce further the industrial importance of the areas ceded in the east, since, aside from the extraction of the mineral resources mentioned earlier, chiefly light industry was located there.

The principal mineral losses in the transfer of territory to the USSR, on the basis of 1937 data, were: (1) reduction of crude oil output by about 72 percent, (2) reduction of rock salt resources by approximately 33 percent, and (3) about a 100 percent loss of potash deposits.[12] While the salt deposits remaining in postwar boundaries appear adequate for Poland's domestic needs, a major part of the requirements for potash and oil products will have to be met by

[11] Estimated from data in *Mały rocznik statystyczny—1939*, pp. 11, 123. The employment data relate to all establishments whose employment in any period exceeded four workers, including in this the owner and members of his family.

[12] Central Board of Planning, *Some Facts Concerning the Polish Economy*, p. 15. See also Table 6.

imports, or in the case of petroleum products, also by synthetic production. The ceded area was particularly backward in the production of electric energy, accounting for only about 5 percent of Poland's 1938 output.[13]

Gains in the west. In contrast with the areas that Poland ceded to the Soviet Union, the German territories placed under Polish administration were relatively highly industrialized, especially in Upper and Lower Silesia and in the vicinity of Stettin. If the 1938 level of industrial production is used as a basis of comparison, then the areas placed under Polish administration had attained an output two-thirds as large as all Poland within prewar boundaries.[14] Even if war damages are considered, it was estimated in 1946 that postwar Poland, including the German areas under Polish administration, had an industrial production capacity one-third greater than prewar Poland.[15]

Comparison of the 1938 levels of production shows that the area of postwar Poland had an industrial output at least one and one-half times as great as the area of prewar Poland.[16] When this is related to the greatly diminished population, it follows that the per capita industrial output of postwar Poland can be more than double that of prewar Poland merely by reattaining the 1938 level of production. Since war devastation was very extensive, it was difficult to apply the existing capacity to immediate production. It was possible, however, for the rate of growth of production to be high initially since many partially destroyed plants could be restored to production with relatively small capital outlays. On the other hand, the inadequate supply of skilled labor and technicians to replace the transferred German population was an important limiting factor in the expansion of production.

A comparison of the 1937 production of coal, coke, and other mineral products within the areas of Poland's prewar and postwar

[13] Estimated from *Mały rocznik statystyczny—1939*, p. 127, taking account of all installations in excess of 100 kilowatt capacity.

[14] Computed from data given in United Nations, Economic Commission for Europe, *Economic Survey of Europe in 1948*, p. 5; 1949 *Survey*, p. 1.

[15] Polish Ministry of Foreign Affairs, *op. cit.*, p. Ea 31.

[16] Calculated from data in United Nations, Economic Commission for Europe, *op. cit.*, 1948 *Survey*, p. 5; 1949 *Survey*, p. 3. A comparison of indexes for industrial production for 1945–46, based on 1938=100, for both present and prewar boundaries given by UNRRA, indicates that the 1938 output in present boundaries was more than twice as great as in prewar boundaries (United Nations Relief and Rehabilitation Administration, *Operational Analysis Papers*, No. 45, p. 12).

boundaries in Table 6 shows that the chief losses due to the shift in boundaries were the total loss of potassium salt deposits and the 72 percent reduction of oil output. The largest gains were in coal, coke, and ores of zinc and lead. If one considers the coal reserves apart from production, the gain is not nearly as great, since the German areas now under Polish administration have added only about six to seven billion tons to the estimated sixty billion tons of reserves on the prewar Polish area.[17] However, the resources of zinc and lead were doubled, and there are increased possibilities for the production of nickel, chromium, uranium, arsenic, and low grade iron ore. Other mineral gains included resources for the production of fireproof materials, quartz and slate, and clays for ceramic production. It is estimated that possibilities for the production of ordinary and technical porcelain have been increased four-fold over the 1939 Polish output, while possibilities for production of granite, marble, and basalt have been more than doubled to permit an annual output of three million metric tons.[18]

Table 6

1937 OUTPUT OF COAL AND OTHER MINERAL PRODUCTS
WITHIN POLISH PREWAR AND POSTWAR BOUNDARIES
(THOUSANDS OF METRIC TONS)

Product	*Prewar Boundaries*	*Postwar Boundaries*	*Percentage Increase (+) or Decrease (−)*
Pit coal	36,200	64,650[a]	+78.6
Coke	2,124	5,353	+152.0
Brown coal	18	7,611	+41,200.0
Iron ore	792	865	+7.9
Crude oil	501	141	−71.9
Salt	603	537	−10.9
Potash	522	nil	−100.0
Zinc and lead ore	492	1,214	+146.8

Source: United Nations Relief and Rehabilitation Administration, *Operational Analysis Papers, No. 35*, p. 6.
 [a] Output of coal in postwar boundaries reached a peak of over 90 million tons in 1943.

Poland's installed electric power generating capacity was about doubled upon acquisition of the German provinces,[19] and by 1946

[17] U.S. Dept. of Commerce, *op. cit.*, p. 4.
[18] Central Board of Planning, *op. cit.*, pp. 15–16.
[19] Estimated from *Mały rocznik statystyczny—1938*, p. 116; and Statistisches Amt, *Statistisches Jahrbuch für das Deutsches Reich, 1937*, p. 172.

the new territories were supplying about 28 percent of the total Polish electric power output in spite of the recency of Polish occupation and the war's devastation.[20] Poland's other gains include very important elements of heavy and light engineering industry, electrical engineering industry, cement works, lime kilns, ceramic plants, glass industry, and nickel and copper mines. It is clear that the industrial capacity of the western territories is a very important factor in the realization of the planned production goals of the postwar Polish economy.

Transport and Communication

Railways. As might be expected from the high level of development in the new western territories in comparison with the areas ceded to the USSR, Poland realized very important gains in the quality and density of the transport and communications network by the changes in boundaries. According to Polish official figures, Poland lost 6,121 kilometers of railway lines in the east and gained 11,654 in the west. The corresponding change in densities was from 34 kilometers of railway line per 1,000 square kilometers in the ceded eastern provinces to 111 kilometers of line per 1,000 square kilometers in the acquired western territories.[21] Qualitatively, the rail system acquired from the Germans ranked much above the ceded lines in the east, but this fact was modified by the extensive destruction by war and the great losses in equipment and rolling stock.

Highways, inland waterways, and seaports. According to Polish sources, the number of hard-surfaced roads in postwar Poland has increased over prewar by the acquisition of 41,139 kilometers in the west against the loss of only 8,000 kilometers in the east. The change resulted in raising the density of roads per 1,000 square kilometers in the whole country from 16 to 31 kilometers.[22] The highway network of the new western lands represents about 44 percent of Poland's postwar total. The area ceded to the USSR possessed a system of poorly developed rivers and canals, which was adapted primarily to small vessels, barges, and log rafts. On the other hand, the Oder river system which Poland acquired from Germany was

[20] Polish Ministry of Foreign Affairs, *op. cit.,* p. Ea 42.
[21] *Ibid.,* p. Kb 2.
[22] *Ibid.,* p. Kb 10.

a well-developed artery which in 1935 carried almost nine million tons of commodities.[23] In the same year, the entire Polish internal waterway system carried only slightly more than seven hundred thousand tons.[24] The Oder is particularly important for the movement of bulk commodities such as coal, cement, and iron ore between the Baltic Sea and industrial Silesia.

Poland's gains included the major ports of Stettin and Danzig, and several lesser ones along the Baltic Sea and the Bay of Danzig. The acquisition of Stettin is particularly important for coal traffic and import of iron ore and other materials for the Silesian industries. Poland's coastline on the Baltic has increased from 140 kilometers in 1938 to 581 after World War II,[25] thus permitting an expansion of coastal shipping and fishing. The acquisition of the Oder river system and the Baltic ports provided a position of great potential importance for transit trade.

Agriculture and Forestry

Utilization of land. As shown in Table 7, the principal changes in land utilization caused by the shift in boundaries were the more than proportionate reductions in orchards and gardens, meadows, and pastures, and an increase in the ratio of arable land to the total area. The forest area was reduced in about the same proportion as the over-all area. In general, the areas ceded to the USSR were tilled with relatively primitive methods, small capital intensity, and little use of artificial fertilizers. Large estates, checkerboard peasant holdings, common lands, and a tangle of easements characterized the system of land tenure. The areas Poland acquired in the west also featured large estates, but the peasant holdings were integrated, and the agriculture of this area utilized more advanced methods and a higher level of capital intensity.

Table 8 compares prewar yields of the principal grains, potatoes, and sugar beets in Poland with the yields in the eastern provinces ceded in whole or in part to the Soviet Union, and in the eastern provinces of Germany which later came in whole or in part under

---

[23] *Ibid.*, p. Ea 50.

[24] *Mały rocznik statystyczny—1939,* p. 202. The figure does not include live animals and timber rafts.

[25] *Statistical Yearbook of Poland—1948,* p. 16. The Hel Peninsula accounts for 71 kilometers.

Table 7

PREWAR LAND USE IN AREAS WITHIN POLISH PREWAR AND POSTWAR BOUNDARIES

	TOTAL AREA	FARM LAND					FORESTS	OTHER
		Total	Arable Land	Orchards and Gardens	Meadows	Pastures		
A. IN THOUSANDS OF HECTARES								
Prewar boundaries	37,897	25,589	18,557	552	3,804	2,676	8,322	3,986
Ceded to USSR	17,240	10,990	6,966	314	2,255	1,455	4,107	2,143
Postwar boundaries	30,745	20,864	16,479	346	2,410	1,630	6,909	2,972
New Territory	10,088	6,265	4,887	108	861	409	2,694	1,129
Old Territory	20,657	14,599	11,592	238	1,549	1,221	4,215	1,843
B. IN PERCENTAGES OF TOTAL AREA								
Prewar boundaries	100.0	67.5	49.0	1.5	10.0	7.0	22.0	10.5
Postwar boundaries	100.0	67.8	53.6	1.1	7.8	5.3	22.5	9.7

Sources: *Mały rocznik statystyczny—1939*, p. 72; *Statistical Yearbook of Poland—1948*, p. 44. Note: The data refer to 1931 for the old territories of Poland and to 1938 for the new areas.

Polish administration. The 1934–38 average annual per hectare yield for Poland in prewar boundaries was slightly higher than that of the ceded eastern provinces in nearly all instances. In comparison with the provinces ceded to the USSR, the German areas under Polish administration averaged a yield about twice as great in wheat, barley, and oats, and approximately one and one-half times as great in rye, potatoes, and sugar beets.

Table 9 gives a comparison of average prewar production of principal grains, potatoes, and sugar beets within prewar and postwar Polish boundaries. The smaller area included in the postwar bounda-

Table 8

COMPARATIVE PREWAR YIELDS PER HECTARE FOR SELECTED CROPS
IN POLAND'S OLD AND NEW TERRITORIES
(YIELDS IN CENTNERS)

Region	Rye	Wheat	Barley	Oats	Potatoes	Sugar Beets
All Poland[a]	11.2	11.9	11.8	11.4	121.0	216.0
Eastern Provinces[b]	10.2	10.0	9.7	9.7	112.0	174.0
Białystok	9.5	9.0	9.1	8.7	114	158
Wilno	7.9	7.5	7.4	7.7	99	. . . .[c]
Nowogródek	10.2	9.5	9.6	9.8	114	. . . .
Polesie	10.2	9.2	8.2	9.0	112	. . . .
Wołyn	11.4	12.1	12.3	11.8	107	182
Lwów	10.0	10.4	9.8	9.7	110	189
Stanisławów	11.1	10.9	10.1	10.2	114	174
Tarnopol	11.3	11.4	10.8	11.0	124	166
Eastern Provinces of Germany[a,b]	15.2	20.0	20.5	17.7	161.8	294.1
Grenzmark Posen-West Prussia	13.2	18.6	19.6	15.9	153.8	256.8
East Prussia	16.0	17.7	19.1	17.5	154.7	310.5
Brandenburg	14.3	21.3	20.1	16.5	161.7	298.3
Pommern	16.1	23.0	21.8	19.4	167.2	290.0
Lower Silesia	15.0	19.5	20.8	17.1	161.0	286.4
Upper Silesia	16.6	20.1	21.4	19.8	172.4	322.5

Sources: *Mały rocznik statystyczny—1939*, pp. 78–79; and *Statistisches Jahrbuch für das Deutsches Reich, 1934–37*, Sec. III, Table 18.

[a] The data are the annual averages for 1934–38 for Polish regions and 1935–37 for German.

[b] Unweighted arithmetic averages of the provinces listed.

[c] . . . . = none reported.

ries had in fact a larger agricultural production in all the crops listed. However, in taking over the former German farms, the Poles faced initial disadvantages in the extensive wartime destruction of buildings, equipment, livestock, and draft power, as well as in new techniques to master in order to attain the prewar output in the new area. Nevertheless, with a much reduced population the per capita production outlook in postwar Poland is far more favorable than in prewar.

Table 9

1934–38 AVERAGE ANNUAL PRODUCTION OF MAJOR CROPS WITHIN
POLAND'S PREWAR AND POSTWAR BOUNDARIES
(MILLIONS OF METRIC TONS)

Area	*Bread Grain*[a]	*Coarse Grain*[a]	*Potatoes*	*Sugar Beets*
Prewar boundaries[b]	8.53	3.97	35.01	2.8
Postwar boundaries[c]	8.82	4.46	38.01	5.4[d]

[a] Bread grain includes rye and wheat; coarse grain includes barley and oats.
[b] *Mały rocznik statystyczny—1939*, pp. 78–79.
[c] United Nations, Economic Commission for Europe, *Economic Survey of Europe in 1949*, p. 17.
[d] Estimated from 1934–36 averages as given in footnote (b) above and *Statistisches Jahrbuch für das Deutsches Reich, 1934–36*, Sec. III, Table 18.

War Damage to the Polish Economy

Poland was the first country to be overrun in World War II and among the last to emerge from the theater of hostilities. The war wrought widespread destruction to the national wealth, but very likely not as great damage as the Polish official estimates would indicate. These estimates apparently were intended to serve as a basis for reparations and economic assistance or to magnify the subsequent performance of the economy. Thus a statement in the text of the law for the Six-Year Plan asserted that the losses from war and requisitions led to a 33 percent reduction in the national wealth.[26] Another Polish estimate placed the capital losses in industry for the period 1939–45 at 11.5 billion U.S. dollars, or equivalent to about 11.5 percent of the entire national property.[27]

[26] *Dziennik Ustaw*, 1950, No. 37, Item 344, Sec. 1, Par. 2. This presumably includes the losses in the new territories, but the base for the percentage is unstated.
[27] Polish Ministry of Foreign Affairs, *op cit.*, p. Ia 1.

Still another statement of the Polish government placed the material losses in the old territories of Poland within present boundaries at 18.2 billion U.S. dollars, of which 5.7 billion was allocated to industry and 3.5 billion to transport and communications.[28] The same source equated these losses to some 50 percent of the prewar capital value. It added that over 20 percent of the prewar industrial facilities in the new western territories were destroyed or removed.

War damage to the communications system was particularly great. It was estimated that main railway lines were damaged to the extent of 40 percent, secondary lines 30 percent, and stationary equipment 70 percent.[29] Thirty percent of the small railway bridges and 70 percent of the large ones were reported destroyed, and the lines were practically denuded of rolling stock.[30]

War losses in agriculture were particularly great in livestock. The Office of War Reparations of the Polish government reported these tentatively as follows: (1) horses—2,776,000, or 75 percent of prewar numbers; (2) cattle—8,541,000, or 60 percent of prewar; and (3) pigs—6,434,000, or 80 percent of prewar.[31] Approximately 467,000 farm buildings within the new boundaries were estimated to have suffered destruction amounting to over 15 percent of their value, or a loss of about 2.5 billion zlotys at 1939 prices.[32]

The Polish Ministry of Reconstruction estimated the losses in urban buildings which were over 10 percent destroyed at about 527 million cubic meters, valued at over 9.5 billion zlotys in 1939, which was equivalent to about 1.8 billion U.S. dollars of that date. Slightly more than half of this value of loss was allocated to the new western territories.[33] Of a total of nine million rooms of urban housing that existed in the present territory of Poland in 1939, about four million were estimated to be damaged more than 10 percent of their value.[34]

---

[28] United Nations Relief and Rehabilitation Administration, *op. cit.*, p. 2.
[29] Polish Ministry of Foreign Affairs, *op. cit.*, p. Kb 2.
[30] *Ibid.*, pp. Kb 2, 9–11.
[31] *Poland of Today*, May, 1946, p. 6. It is not clear whether these figures refer to the prewar livestock population within present or prewar boundaries. In any event, they are not consistent with the data for either case for the year 1938, which is the latest prewar year for which data are available. Cf. *Mały rocznik statystyczny—1939*, p. 91, and *Statistical Yearbook of Poland—1947*, p. 51.
[32] *Statistical Yearbook of Poland—1948*, p. 30.
[33] *Ibid.*, p. 30.
[34] Polish Ministry of Foreign Affairs, *op. cit.*, p. Fa 16.

These statements of loss are presented to give a more complete description of Poland's economic potential at the outset of planning in the postwar period. The losses probably are overstated. They afford, however, some indication of the magnitude of losses incurred. On balance, it seems clear that Poland in her postwar boundaries possessed a much more favorable opportunity for economic development than in prewar in practically all the major sectors of production.

III

Evolution of the Postwar Polish Government

SINCE economic planning requires various measures of influence or control, whether direct or indirect, over the national economy, its character usually depends on the aims and ideology of the central political authority in the state. Any analysis of the situation attained up to the present and any forecast of future developments must therefore take account of the political framework. It is the political factor that determines the extent and character of state intervention in the basic functions of the economy. What is to be produced, the allocation of factors to production, the distribution of the product into shares for investment, consumption, and other uses, and the associated problem of rate of economic development—all these problems reflect a high degree of centralized decision making in postwar Poland. To some extent the active participation of the government in these basic economic questions was a legacy from the prewar period, but to a much larger extent it followed from Soviet influence over the postwar Polish government.

Rise of the Post-World War II Government

Effect of liberation from the east. The character of Polish postwar economic organization and development was profoundly influenced by the course of political events during and after World War II. The war originated on Polish territory, and in the course of its first month Poland's army was defeated and its territory partitioned between Germany and the USSR. Eventually many Polish political leaders found their way to England and established a government-in-exile that rallied an important war effort by the Poles abroad. The Polish government at London was officially recognized in the West as the legal Polish government. If Poland had been liberated from the west, undoubtedly its subsequent political and economic development would have differed greatly from that which actually occurred, for then it would have remained under strong Western influence and probably would have developed on modified capitalist lines with a large state-owned sector. Poland, however, was liberated from the east. The Soviet military forces in Poland, eastern Germany, and other countries in eastern Europe sealed off these areas from direct access to countries outside the Soviet sphere and provided support for Moscow-oriented governments. Moreover, the territorial arrangements, whereby the German provinces east of the Oder and Neisse rivers, Danzig, and part of East Prussia were placed under Polish administration, obliged Poland to look to the USSR for help in the event of revisionist aims by Germany.

Diplomatic relations between the USSR and the Polish government at London were established in July, 1941, following the German attack on Russia. The subsequent period of military collaboration between the two governments came to a sudden halt in mid-1942, when Russia ordered the prompt evacuation of the newly organized Polish forces from the USSR to the Middle East. Relations between the two governments reached an impasse over the refusal of the Poles to agree to Russia's demands for changes in Poland's eastern boundary and for certain changes in the Polish government. In April, 1943, the USSR broke off diplomatic relations, thus making it impossible for the Polish government at London to take over the administration of subsequently liberated areas of Poland.

Rise of the Lublin Polish government. Meanwhile the Soviet-sponsored Union of Polish Patriots was beginning to exercise some of the functions of a government, including the formation of a Polish army to fight alongside the Soviet army. Thus, circumstances were created, whereby, in addition to support by the Soviet army, the Union of Polish Patriots had its own instrument of state power to offset the military support of the underground organizations within Poland for the government-in-exile at London.

The Communist Party within German-occupied Poland took the initiative in the formation of a Soviet-type government. In December, 1943, twenty-two delegates of various Polish organizations representing primarily leftist groups met in a conference that designated itself the National Council of Poland, and assumed leadership of local councils that were coming into existence in various parts of Poland.[1] The newly formed National Council of Poland is reported to have met again in January, 1944, and to have decided upon the Soviet-recommended boundaries for Poland. In March, 1944, a delegation of the council set out for the Soviet Union and two months later reached an understanding with Stalin. The Union of Polish Patriots organized in the USSR subordinated itself to the National Council of Poland, and the latter in July, 1944, created the Polish Committee of National Liberation, which, under Soviet auspices, established itself at Lublin and became the effective government of Poland in the areas liberated by the Soviet army. The Lublin committee organized itself into departments which later matured into ministries. It issued decrees having the force of law and foreshadowed many elements of economic policy which were later formalized into law.[2]

The National Council of Poland was dominated by its small presidium under the chairmanship of Bolesław Bierut, a member of the Communist Polish Workers' Party. At the opening of the sixth session of the National Council, this presidium consisted of only five persons and was controlled by the Communist-Socialist alliance, which continued to dominate the political scene until eventually the Socialist junior partner was engorged in a merger that resulted in a new essentially communist party. At this session, December, 1944–January, 1945, the National Council enlarged itself by admitting representatives of various groups approved by the presidium,[3] and it transformed the Polish Committee of National Liberation into the Temporary Government of Poland.

Provisions of the Yalta Conference. One of the chief problems faced at the Yalta Conference in February, 1945, was the solution of the Polish question.[4] The Soviet government, on January 5, 1945, had recognized its protégé springing from the Polish Committee of National Liberation, while the United States and Britain still recog-

---

[1] Rzeczpospolita Polska, Krajowa Rada Narodowa (Republic of Poland, The National Council), *Sprawozdanie stenograficzne z posiedzeń krajowej rady narodowej w dn. 31 grudnia 1944 r. oraz 2 i 3 stycznia 1945 r.* (Stenographic Report of Sessions of the National Council, December 31, 1944, and January 2–3, 1945), pp. 10–12.

[2] *Ibid.*, pp. 13, 59–60, 78.

[3] *Ibid.*, pp. 14–15.

[4] Cf. Stanisław Mikołajczyk, *The Rape of Poland*, pp. 106–20.

nized the Polish government at London. The Big Three finally agreed that the Curzon line should be Poland's eastern frontier and that Poland should receive substantial accessions of territory in the north and west, but that final delimitation of the western frontier should await the Peace Conference. The Yalta Powers further agreed that the Lublin Provisional Government functioning in Poland should be reorganized on a broader democratic basis with the inclusion of democratic leaders from Poland and from Poles abroad. The resulting new government should then be called the Polish Provisional Government of National Unity, and it would be obliged to hold free and unfettered elections as soon as possible.[5] The Yalta Agreement finally provided that Molotov, Averell Harriman, and A. Clark Kerr, representing the Soviet Union, the United States, and Britain, respectively, should constitute a commission to oversee the prescribed reorganization of the Lublin government.

Four months after the Yalta Conference, and only after many disagreements over the composition of the new Polish government, the problem was settled very largely on the basis of the Soviet position. The Lublin Poles gained two thirds of the ministerial posts, while the London Poles received only three, the rest being distributed to Polish leaders not represented by these two groups.[6] The United States and Great Britain recognized the new provisional government and at the same time withdrew recognition from the London Poles.

Up to the eve of the elections for the Sejm or Parliament, required by the Yalta Agreement, the Polish Cabinet consisted of twenty-one ministries, distributed among the various parties as follows: Communists—six seats in the cabinet; Socialists—five departmental ministries and one minister without portfolio; the pro-government Peasant Party and the Polish Peasant Party led by Stanisław Mikołajczyk, former premier of the London Poles' government—three ministries each; and the Democratic Party—two cabinet posts. The Minister of Defense, though nominally a nonparty man, was a dependable supporter of the Communists.[7] The Communist Polish Workers' Party maintained an exceptionally strong position in the government through its control of the strategically important ministries of National Defense, Public Security, Food,

[5] Edward R. Stettinius, Jr., *Roosevelt and the Russians: The Yalta Conference,* pp. 346–47.

[6] Mikołajczyk, *op. cit.,* pp. 131–32; Jan Ciechanowski, *Defeat in Victory,* p. 400.

[7] *Times* (London), January 13, 1947.

and Industry. In particular, the Ministry of Public Security, which controlled the state police, limited the political activity and the press of the Polish Peasant Party opposition, and assured victory for the Communist-Socialist coalition in the elections for the Sejm on January 19, 1947.[8]

In these elections, the government bloc led by the Communist and Socialist parties obtained 327 seats, while the chief opposition party, the Polish Peasant Party, received only 24. Twenty-one seats were scattered among a few minor parties. The peasant opposition was broken, and its leader, Mikołajczyk, fled from Poland in October, 1947. At the Potsdam Conference, August, 1945, Marshal Stalin offered a pre-election estimate of the future course of events. He is stated to have remarked concerning elections in eastern Europe: "A freely elected government in any of these countries would be anti-Soviet, and that we cannot allow." [9]

Further consolidation of Communist hegemony over the state. In its drive for exclusive control over the state, the Communist Workers' Party set for itself the task of achieving a merger of the Socialist and Workers' parties into a single party based on Marxist-Leninist principles and gaining control of the peasant parties by means of new leadership. After the elections of January, 1947, Communist pressure upon the Socialist Party for organic fusion was intensified. Władysław Gomułka-Wiesław, at that time the secretary-general of the Workers' Party, announced in a speech on May Day, 1947, that preliminary preparations for a merger were under way. He argued that the single class of workers should be represented by a single party, and he urged that the differences separating the parties be made clear and removed to facilitate union. The Socialists' rebuttal charged that the Communists were using the Ministry of Industry as a political instrument through control over jobs in the state enterprises so as to enlarge their membership at the expense of the Socialists. By resolution of their party's Central Committee, the Socialists indicated that further consolidation of the workers' parties demanded an equalization of influence over political life and an increasing loyalty toward law and the state.[10] They were beginning to feel more keenly the effects of Communist control over the

[8] Arthur Bliss Lane, *I Saw Poland Betrayed*, pp. 276–302, 320–27.

[9] Stettinius, *op. cit.*, p. 310, citing Philip E. Mosely, *Face to Face with Russia*, "Headline Series," No. 70, p. 23.

[10] New York *Times*, May 12, 1947.

Ministry of Public Security, which had extensive powers to maintain order and security by administrative decision rather than by ordinary legal procedure.

The Socialists were reluctant to give up their independent existence. They regarded their party as an independent equal of the Communist Workers' Party and considered the mutual trust of the two parties as the basis of the united-front government.[11] This stand was reaffirmed in the December, 1947, congress of the Polish Socialist Party despite increased Communist pressure for fusion.[12] At this congress, Julian Hochfeld, a member of the party's Central Executive Committee and a former editor of the Socialist newspaper *Robotnik,* elaborated a set of conditions for merger of the two parties which specified that:

1. Socialist revolution throughout Europe must first be achieved in order to avoid Poland's participation in an exclusive geographical bloc.
2. International understanding must be achieved so that peace will be assured.
3. Internal social reform must be completed to the point where the average Pole's standard of living equals the average in the most advanced capitalist countries.[13]

This would have placed unity in the distant future, but even in the remote time when a one-class society should exist, the Socialists contended that competing political groups were necessary to promote efficiency in government. In addition, for the present, the Socialists urged a restraint of police terror to insure the maximum degree of personal rights and political freedom consistent with revolutionary needs, and an effective parliamentary system permitting a loyal opposition and full debate, rather than discussion limited to compliments.[14] The Communist reply to Hochfeld's propositions asserted that the unity of the parties should not depend on events outside of Poland; that building of a planned socialized economy could not safeguard citizens' rights generally, but only the rights of the "people's masses"; that the personal rights and political freedom of the former exploiter classes must be limited to

[11] *Przegląd Socjalistyczny* (Socialist Review), September, 1946, pp. 3–4.
[12] *Christian Science Monitor,* January 24, 1948.
[13] *Economist* (London), January 31, 1948.
[14] *Ibid.*

permit the expansion of the socialized economy; and that in his emphasis on parliamentary and legal procedures Hochfeld failed to appreciate the sharpness of the class struggle indispensable for the realization of socialism.[15]

Perhaps the basic difference separating the parties concerned their conceptions of the goal of political and social development. The majority of the Socialist Party's leadership apparently regarded Poland's revolution as being largely completed. They envisioned an economy of three sectors—private capitalist, cooperative, and state-owned—as being a "golden mean" between the model afforded by the Soviet Union and that of the leading capitalist countries of the world. The Polish state of "people's democracy" was regarded by them as a final step of political development, a peculiarly Polish synthesis of reformist social democracy and revolutionary socialism.[16] The Communists opposed this view categorically. They saw no possibility of harmonious coexistence of the private and socialized sectors but rather the ultimate complete socialization of the economy. They emphasized that the state of "people's democracy" must be strengthened, not decentralized, and they denied the need of guarantees for the liquidation of dictatorial means of exercising state power which were regarded as indispensable in the transition period.[17]

Under strong Communist attack, the Socialist leaders abandoned the position regarding unity that they had assumed at the December party congress. The chief proponent of the unity theses, Julian Hochfeld, was dropped from the party's politburo, and in March, 1948, this bureau announced its decision in favor of the merger of the two parties.[18] Premier Cyrankiewicz gave as reasons for the announced merger: (1) that Western socialists had ceased opposing the reactionary forces, and (2) that they had a different attitude toward the German problem than that of socialists in Poland and Czechoslovakia, who had experienced the bitterness of German rule.[19] The real reason, however, is found in the presence of Russian

---

[15] Roman Werfel, "O wyjaśnienie zasadniczych zagadnień" (About the Elucidation of Fundamental Problems), *Nowe Drogi* (New Ways), January, 1948, pp. 132–34.

[16] Oskar Lange, "Od lewicy socjalistycznej do Marksizmu-Leninizmu" (From the Socialist Left to Marxism-Leninism), *Robotnik* (The Worker), September 29, 1948.

[17] Werfel, *op. cit.*, pp. 133–37.

[18] New York *Times,* January 13, 1948; March 19, 1948.

[19] *Christian Science Monitor,* April 24, 1948.

power in eastern Europe.[20] According to Kertesz, the Soviet Union ordered the Communist parties in these states to accomplish a merger of the Communist and Socialist parties by the end of 1948.[21]

Between March, 1948, when the Socialists announced their readiness to merge with the Communist Party, and December, 1948, when the merger was formally consummated, both parties made an effort to arrive at a common ideology.[22] Moreover, this period was devoted to purging the membership of both parties of those elements which did not accept the principles of Marxism-Leninism as the basis for the United Party.[23]

During 1948 the character of the Communist Polish Workers' Party changed under the impact of the Soviet-Yugoslav dispute over the jurisdiction of the Communist Information Bureau and the proper relationship between a Communist party of a country of "people's democracy" and that of the Soviet Union. The Communist Party of the Soviet Union accused the Communist Party of Yugoslavia of an incorrect line on the main questions of home and foreign policy and expected that, in consequence of the senior role of the Soviet party with respect to a Communist party in a country of "people's democracy," the Yugoslav party should admit the propriety of the accusations and correct the specified shortcomings. If the Yugoslav party had behaved accordingly, it would have been acknowledged no right to self-determination, except subject to approval by a higher authority. Failing to bend the Yugoslav party to its wishes, the Communist Party of the Soviet Union referred the matter to the Communist Information Bureau, which was composed of the parties in question, plus those of Poland, Czechoslovakia, Hungary, Rumania, Bulgaria, France, and Italy. The Cominform duly adjudged the Soviet position as entirely correct and placed the blame upon nationalist elements in the leadership of the Yugoslav party. It issued a call for the membership of the latter to disavow their errant leadership and to select

[20] It had been apparent, for example, in the summer of 1947, that the Polish government did not possess independent authority, for under Moscow's direction it had to recant its initial acceptance of the invitation to the Marshall Plan deliberations in Paris.

[21] Stephen Kertesz, "The Method of Soviet Penetration in Eastern Europe," in Waldemar Gurian (ed.), *The Soviet Union*, p. 98.

[22] Oskar Lange, "Wspólna partia—wspólna ideologia" (A Mutual Party—A Mutual Ideology), *Nowe Drogi*, May-June, 1948, pp. 16–20.

[23] New York *Times*, September 23, 1949.

new leaders who would adhere to the party line as interpreted by the Communist Party of the Soviet Union and the Cominform.[24] As a result of this dispute, the remaining junior parties in the Cominform proceeded to purge themselves of "rightist-nationalist" elements.

In Poland this rectification of the party line resulted in the removal of Władysław Gomułka from his post as secretary-general of the Polish Workers' Party. Bolesław Bierut, his successor, accused Gomułka of "rightist-nationalist" deviation in connection with the Soviet-Yugoslav dispute and in certain matters of domestic economic policy. He charged Gomułka with departure from basic class struggle as the means for attaining revolutionary ends, with stressing the independence of the Polish workers' movement without connecting it with the whole pattern of class war of the proletariat, and with failure to understand fully the ideological assumptions of Marxism-Leninism which always guided the Communist Party of the Soviet Union.[25] Bierut further accused Gomułka of desiring to accept some rightist-Socialist conceptions into the ideology of the new Polish United Workers' Party, whereas, Bierut insisted, this party must be a highly disciplined party brought up strictly on the proved basis of Marxism-Leninism. No other ideological conceptions could be admitted, the old cadres of the Socialist Party notwithstanding.[26] Gomułka admitted "his errors" in an elaborate self-criticism. He asserted that his chief failure was the lack of understanding of the essential ideological content of the relationship between countries of "people's democracy" and the USSR and of the leading role of the Communist Party of the Soviet Union "in the struggle against imperialism." He attributed his erroneous stand to nationalist and social-democratic conceptions in his system of thought, and he pledged himself to liquidate these by all means possible.[27]

In the discussions at the plenum of the Central Committee of the Workers' Party dealing with the Gomułka deviation, the leader-

---

[24] *The Soviet-Yugoslav Dispute* (London: Royal Institute of International Affairs, 1948).

[25] Bolesław Bierut, "O odchyleniu prawicowym i nacjonalistowym w kierownictwie partii i o sposobach jego przezwyciężenia" (Concerning Rightist and Nationalist Deviation in the Leadership of the Party and Methods of Overcoming It), *Nowe Drogi*, September-October, 1948, pp. 17, 24.

[26] *Ibid.*, p. 25.

[27] *Nowe Drogi*, September-October, 1948, pp. 43, 144.

ship of the party clearly indicated that it had drawn the correct conclusion from the Soviet-Yugoslav dispute, and that the entire party, as well as the Polish United Workers' Party to arise from the Socialist-Communist merger, would be thoroughly schooled regarding the proper attitude it should take toward the Communist Party of the Soviet Union.[28] Since membership in the United Workers' Party was to be initially two-thirds Communist and one-third Socialist,[29] it appears clear that the new party's leadership would adhere to the party line as established by the Communist Party of the Soviet Union.

The new Polish United Workers' Party controls the government of Poland, but it permits the existence of other parties subservient to it, apparently to facilitate its control over the population. After the flight of Stanisław Mikołajczyk, the new leadership of the Polish Peasant Party acquired an ideology acceptable to the government, and, in November, 1949, the party was merged with the government-sponsored Peasant Party into the United Peasants' Party. The ideological basis of the new organization stressed the worker-peasant alliance, friendship with the USSR, class war against the wealthier peasants, and a program calling for socialization of agriculture by means of production cooperatives.[30] In 1950 the other two remaining parties—the Democratic Party and the Labor Party—despite their opposing traditions, were integrated into a single organization under the Democratic Party label. While ostensibly representing the petit bourgeoisie, the new party in fact is a tool of the government. Its program calls for the socialization of handicrafts and retail trade by means of cooperatives.[31]

The Communist drive for consolidation of political power in postwar Poland is essentially completed. The new United Workers' Party, governed by its Marxist-Leninist-Stalinist ideology, enjoys exclusive power in the formulation of social and economic policy. The formal machinery of government is merely an instrument of control to insure the execution of the policy of the United Workers' Party.

[28] Bierut, *op. cit.*, pp. 24, 33–39. The ideological declaration of the Polish United Workers' Party stressed, among other points, that the merger of the parties was based "on the experience of the party of Lenin and Stalin" and "on an understanding of the historic role of the USSR." (*Nowe Drogi*, January-February, 1949, p. 20).

[29] New York *Times*, August 23, 1948.

[30] *Poland of Today*, November, 1949, pp. 15–16; *ibid.*, January, 1950, pp. 16–17.

[31] National Committee for a Free Europe, *Poland in the Year 1951, Part I*, pp. 22–25.

The Formal Machinery of Government

The highest organs of the central government. Officially Poland is a state of "people's democracy," an intermediate point on the road leading from capitalism to socialism. Progressive changes in the organization of the postwar government were directed toward strengthening the central authorities so as to enable them to carry out dictatorial functions designed to eradicate capitalist elements, expand the socialized sector, and set up and operate a centrally planned socialized economy. The piecemeal changes in the postwar years were finally brought together in the new Polish constitution of July 22, 1952, which defined the role of the state, its social and economic objectives, the rights and duties of citizens, and the chief organs of the public authority.[32] Changes in the constitution can be readily effected since they require only a two-thirds majority in the Sejm, with at least one half of the full number of representatives being present.

The highest organs of the state are (1) the Sejm, or legislature, (2) the State Council, which exercises both executive and legislative functions, (3) the Government proper, consisting of the Council of Ministers, which carries on the state administration, and (4) the Supreme Court and the Procurator General in the administration of justice. As the highest formal authority of the state, the Sejm passes laws and controls the activity of other organs of the state authority. It enacts the long-term national economic plans and the annual state budget.[33] After the elimination of the Polish Peasant Party opposition and the subsequent absorption of the Socialist Party into the Communist-controlled Polish United Workers' Party, the Sejm performs a somewhat ornamental function giving the appearance of democratic processes, whereas the effective decisions are made by the Workers' Party leaders.

The Sejm is elected for a four-year period by direct popular vote. At its first session it selects fifteen of its members to comprise the State Council, which functions until reconstituted by the next Sejm.

---

[32] *Dziennik Ustaw,* 1952, No. 33, Item 232. The description of the central authorities which immediately follows is based on this source.

[33] Before the approval of the 1952 contitution the Sejm also enacted the annual national economic plans. The latter are now finally approved by the Council of Ministers.

Among other duties, the State Council orders elections for the Sejm, summons the latter to its sessions, issues decrees having the immediate force of law when the Sejm is not in session but subject to its confirmation at the next session, represents Poland in certain diplomatic functions, and supervises the local people's councils. Members of the Council of Ministers, the chief executive and administrative organ of the state, are appointed and can be recalled by the Sejm, or when the latter is not in session, by the State Council subject to subsequent confirmation by the Sejm. Duties of the Council of Ministers include the coordination of the activities of the individual ministries and their subordinate agencies, preparation of drafts of the state budget and long-term national economic plans for submission to the Sejm, approval of annual economic plans, supervision over the execution of the national economic plans and the state budget, and direction of the work of the presidiums of local people's councils.

Although courts have charge of the administration of justice, they have no right to investigate the validity of laws and decrees which were properly published. In many instances fines and other penalties under the laws and decrees may be levied by administrative officials without reference to the courts. The Procurator General carries out the functions of a public prosecutor and may act independently of local authorities.

The local government and its relation to the central government. In the postwar period up to March 20, 1950, a dual system of authority existed on the provincial and lower levels of government: (1) administrative officers representing the central government and (2) a network of local people's, or national, councils with executive organs of their own. The national councils were organized in pyramidal manner. The village or municipal council was subordinated to the county council, the latter in turn to the provincial council, and this, finally, to the National Council of Poland, which was the topmost body. Up to the election of the Sejm in January, 1947, the National Council of Poland performed the functions of the supreme legislative body. Following the elections, the National Council of Poland was dissolved and its supervisory functions over the lower level councils were taken over by the State Council.

By the law of March 20, 1950, the system of local government was reorganized to eliminate the centrally appointed provincial, county, and municipal officers.[34] The new law defined the regional people's councils as the local organs of the unified state authority. There are fourteen provincial[35] councils in Poland and two city councils of equal rank, namely, those of Warsaw and Łódź. Below these come county councils and those of other incorporated cities and the boroughs of Warsaw and Łódź. The lowest level consists of people's councils of unincorporated towns and rural townships. The councils are elected by the people in accord with the provisions of a special law prescribing election procedure, size of councils, and length of term of office. The scope of economic activity of the local councils on their respective terrains includes:

1. Direction of economic, social, and cultural activity
2. Election and recall of a presidium of the people's council, appointment of committees of the council, and supervision over the work of these bodies
3. Enactment, within the framework of the national economic plan, of regional economic plans and supervision over their execution
4. Enactment, within the framework of the unified state budget, of local budgets and control over their fulfillment
5. Determination of local taxes and fees within the framework of the council's legal authority
6. Performance of social supervision over the activities of offices, enterprises, establishments, and institutions in their localities.

The local councils and their executive organs operate within the limits of regulations prescribed by the State Council, the Council of Ministers, and the State Commission of Economic Planning. In addition, each people's council and its principal executive organ, the presidium, are directly subordinated to the council and the presidium of the next higher level of the hierarchy. This subordination even extends to corresponding departments of the presidiums of various levels, thus establishing a chain of authority from the Council of Ministers and the separate ministries through the provincial and county presidiums to those of the lowest level. The State Council can set aside any enactments or resolutions of lower

[34] *Dziennik Ustaw,* 1950, No. 14, Item 130. The following account is based on the text of this law. The 1952 constitution confirms the provisions of the 1950 law.
[35] The Polish term *województwo* is translated as "province."

people's councils that are contrary to law or incompatible with state policy, and the same authority extends to other people's councils and their presidiums with respect to their subordinate councils. The Council of Ministers can suspend execution of the enactments of provincial councils and their presidiums and submit the question to the State Council for decision. The entire system of government and public administration, therefore, was designed to facilitate implementation of centrally established policies.

Role of the Polish United Workers' Party. The above picture of the formal government organization in Poland does not reveal the principal center of decision making, which resides in the Polish United Workers' Party. The party regards itself as the advance guard, organizer, and leader of the workers' class and the Polish nation in the construction of socialism. Under the party's control the Polish state of "people's democracy" carries out "the basic functions of the dictatorship of the proletariat, which consist of the liquidation of capitalist elements and the organization of a socialist economy." The formal machinery of government is merely an instrument for carrying out the decisions of the party. Members of the party occupy the most important posts in the government and in the principal social organizations and thus insure conformity of state action with the party's policy.[36] Since this party operates on Marxist-Leninist principles and stresses "democratic centralism," the policy-making power over public activity is further concentrated into the hands of the leaders at the highest level of the party hierarchy. The party's statute requires monolithic adherence of all members to the party's decisions. There can be no place in the party for views contrary to Marxism-Leninism.[37] Deviations from the party line are dealt with summarily, and purges of party ranks insure ideological uniformity.[38] Strongly centralized control over the instruments of state power facilitates the enforcement of party decisions, but the party does not hesitate to retreat temporarily or delay a drive for a final goal in the interest of safeguarding its control over the country.

[36] "Deklaracja ideowa PZPR" (Ideological Declaration of the Polish United Workers' Party), *Nowe Drogi,* January-February, 1949, pp. 12, 19. Cf. Eduard Táborský, "Government in the 'People's Democracies,' " *Annals of the American Academy of Political and Social Science,* September, 1950, p. 59.

[37] "Deklaracja ideowa PZPR," *Nowe Drogi,* January-February, 1949, p. 20.

[38] *Poland of Today,* January, 1950, p. 15.

Poland's postwar economic policy, controls over economic activity, and planning mechanism reflect the origin and subsequent development of the central political authority. The postwar government arose under Soviet auspices and continued to look to the USSR for guidance in its social and economic policy. In the early postwar years the Communist Polish Workers' Party shared power with the Polish Socialist Party, but by the end of 1948 the latter vanished in a merger with the dominant Workers' Party. By 1950 the other remaining political parties were captured and revamped to become tools of the new Polish United Workers' Party in the reshaping of Polish society along Soviet lines. The highly centralized government which arose from this political background was declaredly a tool for effecting the "dictatorship of the proletariat." As will be seen in succeeding chapters, expanding state controls over economic activity and more highly centralized planning accompanied the growing political hegemony of the Workers' Party.

IV

The Extension of State Control

EFFECTIVE economic planning requires some means of influencing the allocation of factors of production, the blending of these into an assortment of goods and services, and the distribution of the latter among the various needs of consumption and investment. Without significant means of exercising such influence, the concept of planning is an empty one. The influence may be indirect, as through propaganda and education aimed at securing voluntary cooperation in the attainment of planned goals; it may be less indirect, as in the application of the tools of public finance; or finally, it may consist of some form of direct state control over the country's population, resources, and capital. The Polish context supplies examples of each of these types of influence. Increasingly, however, the state has extended its direct controls in keeping with the Communist ideology that the state's apparatus of compulsion must first be expanded in order to attain the higher level of socialism.[1]

The orderliness of the progressive extensions of state control over the economy was not so apparent at the time the measures were taken, but in retrospect these actions represent a relentless, purposeful sequence designed to establish Soviet-type economic planning in Poland. As Poland was liberated, the Soviet-sponsored government took over large- and medium-scale industry and communications, and in February, 1946, it legalized the acquisition by formal nationalization. Land reform was decreed in September, 1944, and progressively put into effect following the retreat of the German armies. Thus the state came into immediate possession of the "commanding heights" in industry, and at the same time it employed the familiar weapon of class war to eliminate the opposition of the large landowners while temporarily appeasing the land hunger of the peasants. In the land reform, however, the government laid the basis

[1] Roman Werfel, "O wyjaśnienie zasadniczych zagadnień" (About the Elucidation of Fundamental Problems), *Nowe Drogi*, January, 1948, pp. 134–37.

for further structural changes in agriculture leading to socialization by retaining a substantial share of the arable land for state farms and for support of collective farms to be formed at a later date, and by making the new peasant farms uneconomically small.

During the period of the Three-Year Plan, 1947–49, the economic measures of the government reflected the progressive establishment of complete Communist hegemony in the political sphere. This period witnessed the limitation of private business enterprises through licensing, taxation, and government regulation; a massive assault against private trade leading eventually to its almost complete extinction in the succeeding long-term plan; the extension of state control over urban housing; and the introduction of assorted government controls over real estate, industrial equipment, raw materials and semimanufactures, and basic consumer goods. The autonomy of the cooperative sector bowed to the requirement of centralized planning and control, and concomitantly the handicraftsmen were regimented into state-controlled guilds and chambers for the sake of harmony with central planning. Socialized financial institutions dominated banking as early as 1947, and since that time the services of finance were remodeled into tools of discipline implementing socialist planning.

The Polish population as a source of labor and as consumer of a portion of the national product was recognized early as a factor that should be harnessed to the achievement of the government's plans. Universal obligation to work was decreed in October, 1945, and men and women of working age were required to register and be subject to assignment by state employment offices for periods of service not exceeding two years. During 1948 planned economy was extended to medicine, dentistry, and other professions, obligating qualified practitioners to serve in state establishments upon assignment by government agencies. In succeeding years veterinaries, pharmacists, engineers, technicians, and other specialists were placed at the disposal of the central authorities to meet the exigencies of economic planning. In February, 1949, youth was subjected to obligatory vocational training and work assignments. The educational system was transformed to supply the skills required in the national economic plans. As consumers, the population on the one hand found its income reduced by taxation and compulsory saving, and on the other it found its purchases circumscribed by rationing.

The restraints, controls, and regulations imposed on the factors of production, on private entrepreneurs, and on consumers during the Three-Year Plan in general were refined in subsequent years. A number of measures to insure "socialist labor discipline" were introduced to combat absenteeism, tardiness, and labor turnover. A very significant beginning was made in the collectivization of agriculture, and obligatory deliveries at nominal prices were imposed on a broad basis on peasant producers. The government continued to play its theme of class war, inciting the poorer peasants against their more fortunate neighbors with the hope of collectivizing production. Taxation, compulsory deliveries, and state aid were established under discriminatory schedules in order to weaken the more successful peasant producers on one hand and to induce the poorer peasants to join producer "cooperatives" on the other.

The momentum was continued up to the death of Stalin in 1953, but by the end of that year a tactical slowdown was ordered, without forsaking, however, the gains in state control already realized. Under the objectives announced for 1954–55, the consumer should fare somewhat better than in the past, less pressure would be put on peasants to form collective farms, and compulsory deliveries would be stabilized at the 1953 levels. Progressive socialization of agriculture under discriminatory state tax, credit, and procurement policies remained the avowed aim of the government. There was no retreat from socialization; instead, further gains would be made less coercively.

Industry and Communications

Nationalization. The ideological inclination of the postwar Polish governments strongly indicated socialization of large- and medium-sized industrial enterprises. The Polish economy between the two World Wars had already featured a large state-owned sector in industry, particularly in undertakings that failed to attract private capital. Moreover the course of events during the German occupation and subsequent liberation, in many cases, rendered extension of state ownership or operation of industrial enterprises almost inescapable. In western Poland, which was annexed to Germany, the occupation authorities confiscated nearly all Polish factories and workshops. Although the economy in the so-called General Government, comprising the portion of Poland not annexed by the Soviet Union or Germany, was somewhat different, nearly all industrial plants were partially or totally submitted to German private or state administration.[2] The evacuation of factories during military operations, as well as direct damages caused by war, contributed to the disorganization of the economy. As Poland was liberated, the government mobilized industry to provide for military and civilian needs without awaiting the untangling of ownership titles. Finally, on January 3, 1946, the government formally nationalized the basic branches of industry and communications and large enterprises in other sectors.[3]

The nationalization law asserted that state ownership was necessary to permit planned reconstruction of the national economy, to assure the country economic sovereignty, and to raise the level of general welfare.[4] In subsequent extensions of state ownership or control the same reasons appeared with great regularity, but with stronger emphasis on the needs of effective planning. By the provisions of the nationalization law, the state, without compensation, assumed ownership of all enterprises in industry, mining, communications, banking, insurance, and trade which belonged to: (1) the German Reich and the former Free City of Danzig, (2) their citizens with the exception of those of Polish nationality or others persecuted by the Germans, (3) legal persons under German law or that of Danzig, (4) firms controlled by citizens of Germany or Danzig or by the governments of these areas, and (5) persons who fled to the enemy. In addition the state nationalized the following with compensation:[5]

A. Mining and industrial enterprises in the following branches of the national economy:

    1. Mines and mining grants subject to mining law

    2. The petroleum and natural gas industry together with wells, refineries, gas works, other processing plants, and pipelines, and the synthetic fuel industry

    3. Enterprises producing, transforming, transmitting, or dis-

---

[2] Central Board of Planning, *Some Facts Concerning the Polish Economy*, p. 29.
[3] *Dziennik Ustaw*, 1946, No. 3, Item 17.
[4] *Ibid.*, p. 21. The account that follows is based on the text of the nationalization law.
[5] The compensation was to be established by special commissions and was to consist of bonds, or in exceptional cases, cash.

tributing electrical energy for profit or supplying it to public centers of communication

4. Enterprises producing, processing, transmitting, or distributing gas for industrial or home use
5. Waterworks covering more than the terrain of one municipality
6. Foundries of iron and nonferrous metals
7. Enterprises in the armament, aviation, and explosives industries
8. Coke works
9. Sugar works and refineries of sugar
10. Industrial distilleries, refineries of spirits, and spirits factories
11. Breweries with a productive capacity in excess of 15,000 hectoliters annually
12. Yeast factories
13. Flour mills with a capacity above 15 tons of grain per day
14. Vegetable oil works with a capacity above 500 tons annually and all refineries of edible fats
15. Cold storages
16. Large- and medium-scale textile industry
17. Printing industry

B. Industrial enterprises not listed under A, provided that they were able to employ more than fifty production workers per shift. However, the law excluded enterprises in the construction industry, regardless of capacity for employing workers. It permitted the Council of Ministers to raise the fifty worker per shift lower limit in industries that were little mechanized, or of a pioneer or seasonal character, or which produced articles not widely used.

C. Enterprises in communications (railroads, electric railways, airlines) and telecommunications.

Any enterprises listed in A, B, or C above which belonged, in whole or in part, to local governments or cooperatives were exempted from nationalization to the extent of such ownership. The law permitted the Council of Ministers to exempt particular enterprises or categories of enterprises from nationalization as well as to extend state ownership to nonlisted categories such as banks, warehouses, storage and loading facilities, especially in ports or along railroads or waterways. Monopolies in important branches of the economy which were in existence on the date that the nationalization law went into effect could also be nationalized by the government under the provisions of this law. The establishment of new enterprises in the branches of the economy included in A and C above thereafter would require a concession from the appropriate minister in agreement with the chairman of the Central Board of Planning. The law authorized the state to operate the nationalized enterprises on its own account or to transfer them to local governments or cooperatives. The enterprises in A, numbers 9–15, were designated for assignment either to local government or to cooperatives upon decision of the Council of Ministers. The industrial enterprises which were based exclusively or primarily on local raw materials and which served chiefly local needs, or which were integrally connected with the economic functions performed exclusively or chiefly by cooperatives, were to be transferred to cooperatives or unions of cooperatives.

The private sector. The scope of the private sector in industry and trade was defined in a companion measure also enacted on January 3, 1946. This law provided that industrial and trading enterprises not included in the stipulations of the nationalization law comprised inviolate private ownership. Everyone had the right to establish a new industrial or commercial enterprise subject to fulfillment of legal requirements. Whoever established a new industrial or commercial enterprise could demand a statement from an appropriate state official confirming that the new enterprise did not belong to categories subject to nationalization or requiring a concession under the nationalization law of January 3, 1946. The newly organized enterprises would not be subject to nationalization even if they were capable of employing more than fifty production workers per shift. The law provided further that the Council of Ministers could make the conduct of certain categories of enterprises subject to gaining a concession. Finally, the state assured owners of enterprises under the provisions of this law the freedom of development of the enterprises and support of their economic activity within the framework of the state economic plan.[6]

The two laws described above laid the basis for a mixed economy

[6] *Dziennik Ustaw,* 1946, No. 3, Item 18.

similar to that of the Soviet Union during the mid-twenties. The private sector in industry and trade at best had a narrow field for development, and this, moreover, could be narrowed by the instrumentality of concession permits or the exigencies of planning. The squeeze was not long delayed. On October 17, 1946, the Council of Ministers ordered that concessions be obtained before setting up new enterprises in the branches of industry and communications that had been taken over into state ownership earlier in the year.[7] Private enterprise in the nonnationalized branches of the economy was also increasingly subjected to the requirement of concessions,[8] as envisioned in the basic law defining the limits of the private sector in industry and trade.

In October, 1947, the government decreed the compulsory registration of all persons engaged in the conduct of industry and certain professional activities. In connection with the registration, the state levied a fee ranging from 10 percent to 30 percent of the turnover achieved in the supply of professional services and from 6 to 22 percent of turnovers in the supply of materials or a combination of materials and services, the base of the levy being the month of June, 1947, or an acceptable substitute. The fee increased progressively with the size of the turnover.[9] Inasmuch as the socialized enterprises, including cooperatives, were exempted from the fee, it appears that the government sought to discriminate against the private sector.

Perhaps the most decisive step in the subordination of private industry to state control was the introduction of compulsory membership of private enterprises in state-directed associations. This action resulted in the formation of nineteen country-wide associations by 1950 and permitted the state to direct private industry toward the attainment of goals set for the national economy.[10]

The increasingly disadvantageous circumstances which the private sector in industry faced in the postwar period were reflected in the decline of the share of total industrial production originating in this sector. In 1946 the share of the capitalist sector, excluding handicrafts, amounted to slightly less than 9 percent of the gross value of

---

[7] *Ibid.*, No. 63, Item 347.

[8] *Ibid.*, No. 43, Item 250.

[9] *Ibid.*, 1947, No. 66, Item 403; No. 71, Item 443.

[10] Janina Fihelowa, "Drogi rozwojowe drobnej wytwórczości w mieście" (Paths of Development of Small-Scale Production in Cities), *Życie Gospodarcze* (Economic Life), February 1–15, 1950, p. 115.

industrial output,[11] by 1950 it had fallen to 5 percent,[12] and in 1953 it declined further to less than 1 percent.[13] The rapid decline exceeded the anticipations of the planners. Only by 1955, under the provisions of the Six-Year Plan, was the share of private enterprise in the output of industry and handicrafts expected to decline to about 1 percent.[14]

Control over materials and real estate. In order to implement the centrally established economic plans, the Polish government decreed that the economic authorities could issue regulations governing the general economy of raw materials, semimanufactures, final products, machines, technical equipment, animals, and farm and forest products.[15] These regulations could control the production, processing, turnover, distribution, storage, purchase, sale, collection, possession, sorting, marking, transport, and consumption of the specified articles. The intent of the decree was that the general economy of articles having basic significance for the national economy should take place in the framework of national economic plans on the basis of central material balances and central machine balances.[16] The chairman of the State Commission of Economic Planning establishes the list of articles to be balanced centrally, and he also establishes the list of articles to be distributed centrally and performs the central allocation. Regulations governing the economy of the specified articles are issued by the chairman of the planning commission in instances affecting several ministries or the private sector and also in the case of centrally balanced articles. In other cases the ministry directly concerned with the articles issues the regulations. To the extent that the regulations do not otherwise provide, an article allocated for a given use cannot be used for other purposes, sold, or given away free of charge without the permission of the regulating authority. Penal provisions under this decree include fines or arrest up to one year, or both, for failure to register the possession of the regulated

---

[11] Hilary Minc, *Osiągnięcia i plany gospodarcze* (Economic Plans and Attainments), p. 10.

[12] Fihelowa, *op. cit.,* p. 115.

[13] Polish Embassy, Washington, *Press Release,* March 22, 1954, p. 6.

[14] Oskar Lange, "Polskie gospodarstwo narodowe w drugim roku planu 6-letniego" (The Polish National Economy in the Second Year of the Six-Year Plan), *Ekonomista* (The Economist), Second Quarter, 1951, p. 9.

[15] *Dziennik Ustaw,* 1952, No. 44, Item 301. The 1952 decree supersedes similar but less comprehensive measures passed in 1947–50.

[16] These balances provide a reconciliation of planned uses against planned supplies.

articles, and more severe penalties for destruction of such articles. The decree does not apply to the compulsory deliveries from agriculture, which are covered by other measures.

In the early postwar years such regulatory measures applied chiefly to grain, grain products, meats, fats, and scrap metals,[17] but in later years, with increasing comprehensiveness of centralized planning, the regulations have become important for implementing the goals of production. In 1950, private owners of industrial equipment were required to register the possession of such equipment with the state authorities, and idle equipment could be taken over by the socialized sector for compensation.[18] The use of electric and heat energy was subjected to special regulation by the decree of January 28, 1953. Among other provisions, this decree authorized the Minister of Energy, in understanding with the chairman of the state planning commission, to establish norms of use of energy per unit of output, regulate use of energy during peak hours, and establish specifications for energy-using equipment.[19]

Piecemeal socialization of real property essential for the realization of national economic plans was permitted by a decree of the Council of Ministers on April 26, 1949. According to the provisions of this decree, the following agencies enjoy the right of acquisition, disposal, and transfer of real property in the interest of fulfillment of national economic plans: (1) state offices and state-owned and state-administered enterprises, (2) local governments, (3) organizations of economic self-government, and (4) cooperatives. The Chairman of the State Commission of Economic Planning decides whether the property transfer is essential and grants the necessary permission.[20] In cases where the owner of the real property fails to agree to release the property for the consideration offered him, the property may be expropriated by administrative decision.

Cooperatives. Cooperatives in industry, as well as in trade, enjoyed a considerable measure of autonomy within the framework of national economic planning until 1948. It seems clear that the Polish Socialist Party, which until that year had exercised an important voice in the government and controlled the Central Board of Plan-

[17] See *Dziennik Ustaw,* 1949, No. 46, Item 341; No. 56, Item 444; and 1948, No. 27, Items 184, 185, 188.
[18] *Ibid.,* 1950, No. 31, Item 285; 1951, No. 19, Item 155.
[19] *Ibid.,* 1953, No. 9, Item 26.
[20] *Ibid.,* 1949, No. 27, Item 197, Section III; 1952, No. 4, Item 31.

ning, regarded the economy of three sectors—state, cooperative, and private—as a desirable end product of the economic revolution in Poland. Moreover, the Socialists appeared to favor the application of fewer direct controls over the nonstate sectors of the economy than the Communists advocated. This attitude appeared in the theses propounded by Julian Hochfeld at the Wrocław Congress of the Polish Socialist Party in December, 1947, and Oskar Lange asserted in September, 1948, that he and the majority of the party leaders in varying degrees shared this view, even though they may not have set it down in writing.[21] However, in an elaborate self-criticism, Lange acknowledged his "errors" and assumed a new attitude, that of Marxism-Leninism.[22] The consequences of the conversion of the Socialist Party leadership and its decision in favor of merger of the Socialist and Communist parties on the basis of the communist ideology manifested themselves in structural changes in the cooperative movement, as well as in other parts of the national economy.

Under the provisions of the laws concerning cooperatives enacted May 21, 1948, the cooperative sector was firmly subordinated to the Council of Ministers. The Minister of Industry and Trade was empowered to establish hybrid state-cooperative enterprises and state-cooperative central boards to operate directly under his supervision.[23] Henceforth the cooperatives were to function as part and parcel of the nationalized economy, with their production defined by the over-all economic plan and subject to its discipline. The new ideology of the cooperative movement defined a twofold role for cooperatives. In the first place, the cooperatives, as instruments of class war, collaborate with nationalized enterprises in crowding out large-scale capitalist elements both in the city and in the village. Secondly, as a form of socialist economy, the cooperatives are considered the most efficient means for socialization of small-scale business and for its eventual transformation into large-scale economic units with modern techniques and operating methods.[24]

In view of the controls which the state exercises over the private and cooperative elements in the national economy, the significance

---

[21] Oskar Lange, "Od lewicy socjalistycnej do Marksizmu-Leninizmu" (From the Socialist Left to Marxism-Leninism), *Robotnik*, September 29, 1948.

[22] *Ibid.*

[23] *Dziennik Ustaw*, 1948, No. 30, Items 199, 200, and 201.

[24] Oskar Lange, "Cooperatives in Poland," *Poland of Today*, November, 1949, p. 18.

of these labels diminishes. The relative unimportance, moreover, of private and cooperative industry can be gauged from the size of employment in these sectors as compared with employment in state industry. While the latter employed about 1,400,000 workers in March, 1949, the cooperative sector engaged 98,000 at the same time, and the private industrial enterprises accounted for about 74,000.[25] Since that time, private industry has shrunk to insignificant proportions, and the industrial cooperatives have been more firmly tied to the state-owned enterprises under central planning.

Agriculture

Land reform. The land reform decree of September 6, 1944, issued by the Polish Committee of National Liberation, and subsequent decrees applying to the German lands placed under Polish administration officially envisioned an agricultural structure based on "strong, sound, and productively capable" privately owned farms.[26] These measures provided for the nationalization of estates in excess of one hundred hectares in total area as well as the properties of Germans and certain other categories of persons regardless of size of holdings. The land and properties thereon thus obtained, plus lands already owned by the state, were to be distributed under the land reform. Its principal aims were to create new farms for landless peasants, augment the size of dwarfish farms, set aside suitable lands for the use of the state in connection with agricultural education and experimental purposes, provide orchard and garden plots for urban dwellers, and create a land reserve for expansion of cities and various other purposes.

The execution of the land reform was such that in 1949 the government owned about 90 percent of the country's forest lands and about 10 percent of the total agricultural land, thus permitting direct control over these areas.[27] The reform permitted the state to appease temporarily the land hunger of the poorer peasants. It appears, however, that the resulting structure of land ownership did not create circumstances for healthy, individual peasant agriculture. Nearly two thirds of the peasant farms in 1949 were less than ten

[25] *Rocznik statystyczny—1949* (Statistical Yearbook—1949), p. 38.
[26] *Dziennik Ustaw*, 1945, No. 3, Item 13, Par. 1.
[27] *Rocznik statystyczny—1949*, pp. 53, 67.

hectares in area, while about 8 percent of the total peasant acreage was in farms of twenty hectares or more in area.[28] This circumstance permits the state to press "class war" in the villages, with the aim of eliminating the influence of the richer peasants and simultaneously organizing the poorer peasants into production cooperatives under state control. If the policy of the Polish government indeed were directed toward an agriculture of efficient family-sized farms, the land reform would have assured larger farm units. The official ideology proclaims, however, that capitalist agriculture is incompatible with socialized industry and that the two cannot coexist in equilibrium for fear of regeneration of capitalist enterprise in the nonagricultural sector.

Government controls in agriculture. The state has practically complete control over production and distribution of artificial fertilizers, tractors, and larger types of agricultural machines, and it has not failed to apply a "class" policy in supplying these important items to agriculture. Tractors are distributed only to state farms and state-owned machine centers. Rental of traction power and equipment from these centers operates on a discriminatory basis, which aims to eliminate the wealthier peasantry as a class and simultaneously to transform the others into collective farmers. The same policy is apparent in the supply of artificial fertilizers, credits from state institutions, and taxation.[29] Parcels included in producer cooperatives or joint tillage associations received a preferential reduction of the land tax amounting to 30 to 50 percent during 1949 and 1950.[30]

In order to force individual peasants to farm their land "fully and properly," the government decreed on February 9, 1953, that the presidiums of the local people's councils should watch over the utilization of farm land and initiate corrective action where they deem it necessary.[31] Individual farmers who are unable to meet the requirement of complete and proper utilization of land are obliged to report the facts in the case to the presidium of their local people's council. This body may decide whether to assist the peasant by means of credit, technical aid, and allocation of draft power and equipment from neighboring farms, or to transfer the parcel in

[28] *Ibid.*, p. 53.

[29] Minc, *op. cit.*, p. 13. See also *Nowe Drogi*, July-August, 1948, p. 139.

[30] *Dziennik Ustaw*, 1949, No. 16, Item 101; and No. 54, Item 425; 1950, No. 43, Item 392; and No. 48, Item 438.

[31] *Ibid.*, 1953, No. 11, Item 40, p. 774.

question to the use of collective farms or to the poorer peasants who will undertake to farm the land. Such transfers are made for a period of three years, at the end of which time a given parcel can be returned to the former possessor if the presidium of the local council concludes that he can then utilize it fully. Failure of a peasant to report his inability to exploit his land adequately is punishable by corrective labor up to one month, or a fine; and failure to utilize land fully and properly is subject to punishment by corrective labor up to three months, or a fine. This decree appears to provide a legal basis for expropriating land from the wealthier peasants in favor of the collective farms or poorer peasants, and at the same time it may be intended to coerce the peasantry to produce a greater output in the absence of adequate market incentives.

With the rapid socialization of wholesale and retail trade during 1948 and 1949 the state acquired another instrument of control over agriculture. By the end of 1949 the collection of grain and meat was to be entirely taken over by the socialized sector.[32] Compulsory deliveries, which were eliminated by 1946, were gradually reintroduced on a broad basis. The tax on land may be demanded in kind,[33] and, in addition, by the decree of July 23, 1951, and a series of laws and decrees in 1952–53, farmers were required to deliver quotas of grain, potatoes, meat, milk, or other produce to state agencies according to norms based on the area of the farm, its fertility, location, and other factors.[34] Typically the quotas per unit of area for producer cooperative farms, or collectives, were set lower than for individual farmers as an incentive for collectivization. In addition to less direct controls exercised through taxes, tax relief, and barter for the products of the socialized industry, various direct measures of the government ordered the use of the peasants' draft power and equipment for up to fourteen days per year in the reconstruction of neighboring farms and villages,[35] and forbade the slaughter of livestock suitable for breeding purposes even for the peasants' home use.[36] Thus it appears that the extent of state control

[32] *Ibid.*, 1950, No. 37, Item 344, p. 428.
[33] *Ibid.*, 1950, No. 27, Item 250.
[34] *Ibid.*, 1951, No. 39, Item 297; 1952: No. 8, Item 46; No. 22, Item 142; No. 32, Item 214; No. 37, Item 225.
[35] *Ibid.*, 1947, No. 59, Item 320; 1948, No. 58, Item 461. In 1952 this requirement was extended to the end of 1954 (*ibid.*, 1952, No. 1, Item 7).
[36] *Ibid.*, 1946, No. 2, Item 12; 1950, No. 18, Item 152.

over the agricultural sector, though not as great as in industry, is nevertheless very substantial.

This control appears destined for further extension since one of the aims of the Six-Year Plan, 1950–55, is to create conditions for taking over an important part of the peasant farms into producer cooperatives, or collective farms. The law for the plan set no numerical goal for this endeavor,[37] perhaps through fear of a peasant reaction similar to that which occurred in the Soviet Union during the collectivization drive under the First Five-Year Plan. The Soviet peasants, in fear of forced collectivization, slaughtered their livestock in such proportions that the loss was not fully recovered until the eve of World War II. The Polish United Workers' Party, apparently profiting from the Soviet experience, adopted a cautious policy with respect to the peasantry. The agricultural production cooperatives were to be formed by the peasants on their own volition. These cooperatives were begun on a modest scale in 1949 and were expected to cover no more than 1 percent of peasant production in that year.[38] In fact, only 120 farm cooperatives were established by the end of the Three-Year Plan in 1949.[39] However, the tempo was accelerated in 1950 and by the end of 1953 about 8,000 cooperatives were in existence, covering 1.4 million hectares of land in agricultural uses,[40] or about 7 percent of total farm land. State farms and the cooperatives together accounted for about 20 percent of total farm land at the end of 1953.[41]

Internal and Foreign Trade

The state extended its control over private trade since 1945 through three methods: (1) direct extension of state network of wholesale and retail stores, (2) liquidation of the autonomy of the cooperative distributive network, and (3) subordination of private trading enterprises to state policy. The issue of the role of the three sectors in domestic trade was one of the first to reveal basic differences between the policies of the Communist Polish Workers'

[37] *Ibid.*, 1950, No. 37, Item 344, p. 440.
[38] *Nowe Drogi*, September-October, 1948, p. 204.
[39] *Poland of Today*, April, 1950, p. 5.
[40] *Nowe Drogi*, October, 1953, p. 67.
[41] *Nowe Rolnictwo* (New Agriculture), April, 1954, p. 7; *Nowe Drogi*, January, 1954, p. 65, and April, 1954, p. 16.

Party and the Polish Socialist Party. Events early in 1947 brought these differences to public attention. The liquidation of UNRRA aid at that time found the Polish government unprepared to deal with a sharp inflation in prices of basic consumer goods, especially food. In local party conferences in May, 1947, the spokesmen of the parties advanced proposals for halting the inflation. Hilary Minc, Minister of Industry and Trade and member of the Workers' Party politburo, blamed the private traders and cooperatives for the rise in prices. He proposed: (1) creation of a government agency for the purchase of basic agricultural products with the right to compel various state, cooperative, and private enterprises to sell their goods, (2) rigorous price control backed up by inspection bureaus to insure price conformity and prevent tax evasion, and (3) establishment of state-owned department stores.[42] The Socialist spokesman, Stanisław Szwalbe, declared that apart from abuses of speculation, the basic difficulty consisted of a domestic grain shortage which could be remedied only by imports. He defended the cooperatives, asserting that they were performing their tasks properly, and argued against the creation of the state agencies proposed by Minc, proposing instead an extension of the cooperative organizations to fulfill the same objectives. The two parties were agreed on price control supported by strong enforcement agencies.[43]

The so-called battle for trade initiated in May, 1947, was fought largely with the prescription proposed by Minc. The autonomy of the cooperative sector was overcome in 1948 by way of a structural reorganization of the cooperative organization which transformed it into a reliable tool of state policy and an instrument of direct planning under the supervision of the Council of Ministers.[44] By the end of 1949 the socialized sector in wholesale trade controlled practically all wholesale turnovers, whereas in 1946 it controlled 80 percent.[45] In retail trade the change was even more pronounced. The share of the socialized sector grew from 22 percent of retail turnovers in 1946 to 55 percent at the end of 1949,[46] and by the end of 1951 it exceeded 93 percent. This expansion continued through 1953 by

---

[42] *Poland of Today,* July, 1947, p. 15.
[43] *Ibid.*
[44] Cf. *supra,* p. 58.
[45] *Dziennik Ustaw,* 1950, No. 39, Item 344, p. 428. The socialized sector includes both state and cooperative enterprises.
[46] *Ibid.*

extension of the network of cooperative retail outlets and the establishment of state-owned stores.[47]

As a parallel to this expansion of the socialist sector, there took place not only the concomitant shrinkage of the share of private trade, but also a profound change in its character. By the provisions of a law enacted on June 2, 1947, the conduct of a trading enterprise or the professional performance of trading activity required prior permission from the proper industrial authorities.[48] To gain a permit, the applicant should show the necessary professional qualifications, certify compliance with all tax provisions, and abide by merchants' ethics, but, in any event, the final decision rested with the Ministry of Industry and Trade. It might refuse a permit in cases where the applicant's activity did not fit into the framework of a plan for the distributive network as elaborated by the ministry. The Minister of Industry and Trade was authorized to issue regulations for particular branches, territories, and categories of trading enterprises, specifying the standards to which the equipment of trading enterprises must conform, and he might revoke the permits of such enterprises which failed to abide by the regulations.[49] The law and the orders based on it aimed to establish firm state control over domestic private trade and to eliminate any undesirable or superfluous distributive outlets from the point of view of the Ministry of Industry and Trade.

Coincidentally with the introduction of the requirement of permits to conduct private trade, a series of price control measures appeared in the form of laws, decrees, and executive orders. The basic price control law of June 2, 1947, established control over wholesale and retail margins for certain categories of goods and services and set maximum prices for others. It required display of prices and sale of goods to all comers to the amount of normal usage at the posted prices. Records of certain categories of transactions were required, and sales slips were to be issued on demand. The Minister of Industry and Trade established the maximum retail and wholesale prices on basic necessities, using for this purpose the established margins and an average of farm market prices reported at periodic intervals.

[47] Communiques of the State Commission of Economic Planning, *Gospodarka Planowa* (Planned Economy), February, 1952, p. 8; March, 1954, p. 6.
[48] *Dziennik Ustaw*, 1947, No. 43, Item 220.
[49] *Ibid.*, No. 57, Item 311.

He likewise established the maximum prices on goods produced by private handicraft and industry and the socialist sector.[50]

The organs for enforcement of price control include authorities of the general administration, treasury authorities, courts, and the agencies of the Special Commission for Combating Waste and Economic Sabotage, as well as an array of social commissions for price control set up by local people's councils from among representatives of labor unions, the Peasants' Mutual Aid Association, economic self-governments, cooperatives, and social organizations. All of the foregoing control organizations possessed the right to enter trading enterprises, verify inventories and records, and require full explanations of the transactions completed. Violation of price control regulations were subject to fine up to five million zloty or sentence up to five years in prison, or both.[51]

The Special Commission for Combating Waste and Economic Sabotage received special emphasis in the task of enforcement of price control regulations. This commission, created by the National Council of Poland, consisted of eight members selected, one each, from candidates presented by the Prime Minister, the Ministers of Justice, Defense, Public Security, and Public Administration, the Director of the Bureau of Control connected with the Presidium of the National Council of Poland, the Central Commission of Trade Unions, and the Peasants' Mutual Aid Association. Since nearly all of these agencies were dominated by the coalition of the Socialist and Workers' parties, and later by the Polish United Workers' Party, the actions taken by the Special Commission could be expected to conform to the ideology of the coalition, and later, to the Communist ideology. The Special Commission and its immediate subordinate organs were authorized to investigate and sentence transgressors of price regulations to a maximum of two years in a labor camp without resort to courts.[52] In 1947 the Special Commission dealt with about 74,000 cases, and in 1949 it made over 350,000 checks and initiated over 46,000 charges for trial.[53]

[50] *Ibid.*, No. 43, Item 218; No. 61, Item 346; No. 67, Item 418; 1948, No. 23, Item 157.
[51] *Ibid.*, 1947, No. 43, Item 218.
[52] *Ibid.*, 1945, No. 53, Item 302; 1946, No. 23, Item 149; and 1947, No. 43, Item 218.
[53] Stefan Rosada and Jozef Gwozdz, *Forced Labor and Confinement without Trial in Poland*, p. 27, citing *Państwo i Prawo* (State and Law), December, 1950, p. 82, and *Political and Economic Yearbook for 1948* (Polish), pp. 417 ff.

Within the shrinking portion of retail trade in private ownership, aside from price controls, the merchants were subjected to the discipline of the socialist wholesale organizations and the government procurement agencies for agricultural products. For example, by the end of 1949, the socialized sector was assigned a complete monopoly in the collection of grain and meat.[54] Moreover, in areas where scarcities do not prevail, the competition of the state and cooperative retail outlets can assure the success of the state's price policy.

Polish foreign trade in the postwar period early became a state monopoly exercised by the Ministry of Foreign Trade and its organs. This direct state control over imports and exports is an important tool in the control of private domestic trade and industry and in economic planning generally.[55]

Other Sectors of the Economy

The preponderance of socialized financial institutions in postwar Poland likewise became practically a complete monopoly at an early date. State institutions dominated the field in 1947, supplying over 80 per cent of the short- and medium-term credit. In the same year, joint-stock banks supplied less than 2 percent of such credit, while cooperative and municipal banks accounted for the rest.[56] State control over the vestige of private banking and over cooperative banks and credit societies, however, is comprehensive, so that in effect all banking and credit institutions serve the needs of planning. In addition to control over saving through taxation and price policy, the state introduced the requirement of compulsory saving by the population by the law of January 30, 1948.[57] This law established a Social Saving Fund into which participants deposited required amounts on a pay-as-you-go basis on a progressive scale according to income.[58]

---

[54] *Dziennik Ustaw,* 1950, No. 37, Item 344, p. 428.

[55] *Wiadomości Narodowego Banku Polskiego* (News of the Polish National Bank), March 15, 1946, p. 18.

[56] *Statistical Yearbook of Poland—1948,* p. 145.

[57] *Dziennik Ustaw,* 1948, No. 10, Item 74.

[58] *Infra,* p. 229. Depositors were permitted to withdraw annually 5 percent of the balance of deposits at the end of the preceding year except in cases of hardship when larger withdrawals were allowed. This law was repealed in part on February 29, 1952 (*Dziennik Ustaw,* 1952, No. 12, Item 72).

The future of handicraft production as envisioned by the United Workers' Party called for its socialization by means of producer co-operatives. As a transitional measure, however, in order to facilitate control by the government, the organization of handicrafts was revised by decree on April 3, 1948. This decree provided that all independent handicraftsmen must belong to guilds and the latter to proper territorial unions of guilds set up by the Minister of Industry and Trade. The unions of guilds must belong to the proper chambers of handicrafts and conform to their orders,[59] and the chambers, in turn, were subordinated to the Union of Handicraft Chambers. The latter must supply the proper minister and the state planning office with all the information concerning handicrafts which is necessary for preparing economic plans and insuring their performance.[60]

Government control over housing expanded greatly in the period after World War II. Although the state, beginning in 1932, had participated directly in new housing construction, this activity amounted to only about 3 to 4 percent of the country's total housing construction.[61] As a result of annexation of the eastern German provinces after World War II and the nationalization of German property on both the old and new territories of Poland, it was estimated that scarcely half of urban real estate remained in private ownership.[62] The state, moreover, assumed control over the use of private housing in many localities where housing was scarce. This sphere of control has grown since its introduction in 1945 as a result of the increasing urban population outstripping new housing under the program for rapid industrialization. Practically all the larger cities and many smaller localities were included in the direct public economy of housing, while other areas were subjected to public control of leasing and rent ceilings.[63] The public housing authorities establish the minimum number of persons per room in the various localities under the public economy of housing and, if the owner or principal lessee fails to fill his space up to the established minimum

---

[59] *Dziennik Ustaw,* 1948, No. 18, Item 130.

[60] *Ibid.,* No. 23, Item 155.

[61] Adam Andrzejewski, "Ku gospodarce planowej na odcinku mieszkaniowym" (Toward Planned Economy on the Housing Sector), *Gospodarka Planowa,* September, 1948, p. 395.

[62] *Ibid.,* p. 396.

[63] *Dziennik Ustaw,* 1946, No. 4, Item 27; 1948, No. 36, Item 259; and subsequent modifications and orders.

from people of certain specified categories, the housing authority may assign the space directly. Moreover, the public authorities may order owners of housing to divide independent housing or apartments in excess of three rooms into two or more independent dwellings.[64]

Private industrial, handicraft, and trading enterprises must accommodate themselves to the plan for location of such establishments as drawn up by public urban administrations and approved by a commission appointed by the prime minister. In effect, this provision permits the state's central administration to relocate private establishments or even to deny them the right of existence by not allocating space to them. Allocation of business housing for the establishment or expansion of activity of an enterprise may be made contingent upon the assurance that there exists the necessary space for workshops and workers' dwellings or subject to the enterprise's obligation to provide the necessary space through reconstruction or repair of damaged buildings or construction of new ones. Existing enterprises may be ordered to construct, reconstruct, or repair a prescribed quantity of housing within a fixed period sufficient for the needs of the enterprise and its workers.[65] In the allocation of business housing, priority is given to state and local government enterprises. Finally, the recipient of a dwelling or business housing under the public housing economy may be removed from such space to a substitute location for the benefit of a new approved tenant who shall bear the cost of transfer of his predecessor.[66]

From September, 1944, to July, 1948, rents on dwellings in old buildings were maintained at the level effective on September 1, 1939, which, in view of the government's prewar housing policy, was at that time below free market levels. However, as a result of the subsequent inflation, these rents became nominal in the postwar period and by no means covered the costs of necessary maintenance of the properties. Many owners, either by choice or inability to administer their buildings in such circumstances, deserted their properties. The public administration took over the deserted housing, but likewise could not prevent extensive decapitalization on the basis of the low rentals. Finally, by a decree of July 28, 1948, the

[64] *Ibid.,* 1946, No. 4, Item 27, Sec. II.
[65] *Ibid.*
[66] *Ibid.*

level of rents was revised upward on a discriminatory class basis, and, at the same time, the area of private disposition over the still meager returns from housing rentals was sharply circumscribed.[67] The decree provided that rentals on the old level should apply unchanged to hired laborers and certain other groups, such as scientists, teachers, artists, and temporarily unemployed workers. Members of labor cooperatives and handicraftsmen employing at most one member of their family and, in some cases, one hired worker were to pay rent for dwelling space at 50 percent of the newly established level. All other categories, and particularly payers of business turnover tax on their own account, were to pay rent at the full new level. This provision, by discouraging private business enterprise, was an important weapon in the state policy for complete socialization of the economy.

Another provision of the same decree established a Fund for the Housing Economy and obliged lessors to make payments into this fund amounting to 35 percent of the rental receipts at the new half-level rates and 55 percent at the full new rates. The fund makes grants for capital repairs of the most depreciated buildings, not necessarily those of the contributors, according to plans drawn up by the administrators of the fund. Buildings of not more than eight dwelling rooms were exempted from payments into the fund.[68] These provisions were designed to effect a transfer from the returns on high-rental, well-kept buildings in favor of low-rental, poorly kept buildings in which the workers and other nominal payers of rent reside. In addition, the decree provided that the lessors must bear the costs of operation and current repair from the rental receipts, and it designated block and building committees, as well as other authorities, to watch over the performance of this obligation. In particular, the landlord must expend at least 15 percent of the rental receipts at the half-level rates and 30 percent at the full level for current maintenance and repair.[69]

For the purpose of administration of the private housing sector, the decree required the formation of compulsory associations of private owners to function under regulations issued by the Ministers of Public Administration, Treasury, and Reconstruction. The

[67] Andrzejewski, *op. cit.,* pp. 397–99.
[68] *Ibid.,* p. 399.
[69] *Dziennik Ustaw,* 1948, No. 36, Item 259, Div. II, Sec. 1.

order which set up the compulsory associations specified that they should cooperate with the proper authorities in the supervision over members of the associations in the matter of administration and exploitation of buildings. If an association fails to conform to the provisions of the law, the district public administration authorities may dissolve the governing body of the association and appoint an administrator to carry out the functions of the association.[70]

In the area of new construction, orders of the Minister of Industry and Trade required building enterprises to obtain permits from the state's industrial authority. Permits are granted only if the builder or enterprise belongs to a state-approved builders' association and agrees to abide by the orders the association issues under the charter which it receives from the Minister of Industry and Trade. The recipient of a permit must make it possible for experts delegated by the Minister of Industry and Trade, or other proper authority, to carry out a check of the activity of the builder independently of other control provisions.[71]

In view of the state's control over the allocation of privately owned housing, the specification of minimum intensity of utilization of dwelling space, the regulations governing the use of rental receipts, and the control over construction activities, it appears that state control over urban dwelling and business housing is practically complete. Outright confiscation of the remaining privately owned urban housing would not afford much greater control, although it might simplify somewhat the administration of the housing sector in the type of centralized economic planning practiced in Poland today.

Labor and the Professions

Labor as a factor in the implementation of economic plans has come under increasingly stringent control in postwar Poland. As early as October 11, 1945, the Council of Ministers of the Polish government decreed the universal obligation of work for men of ages eighteen to fifty-five and women eighteen to forty-five. This obligation was reiterated in a decree issued on January 8, 1946, which specified that the devastations of war and the shift of boundaries of the country demanded hard and fruitful work from all citi-

[70] *Ibid.*, 1949, No. 51, Item 386.
[71] *Ibid.*, No. 24, Item 161.

zens and the speediest settlement of the newly acquired western territories. The state asserted that it would not tolerate avoidance of socially useful work on the part of its citizens. Men and women within the age limits listed above were required to register at employment offices. The decree exempted the following categories: (1) delegates to the Polish National Council, persons on active military duty, and judges and other personnel in the administration of justice; (2) clergy; (3) state and local government officials and workers in state and local government enterprises; (4) professors, lecturers, and scientific personnel of the state and private academic schools; (5) persons belonging to the free professions to the extent that they are registered in the proper professional self-governing chamber or association, or, in the absence of such, have acquired permission from the authorities of the public administration to carry on the profession; (6) persons gaining a livelihood from conducting a farm, orchard, or forest enterprise, and members of their families who are employed on the area of the enterprise; (7) persons who are registered on the basis of other decrees concerning the duty to work.[72] The first, third, and seventh categories include persons who are already at the disposal of the state. Of the remaining ones, the clergy was excluded, no doubt, in order to avoid large-scale church-state friction. The educational personnel would in any case have to be provided for schools, and the fifth category, professional personnel, came under separate regulations by later laws. In effect, therefore, only the peasantry actually engaged in farming operations and members of their families working with them were exempted from registration.

The decree empowered the state employment officers to order registered persons to work in all branches and types of labor in accordance with their qualifications for a period of service not in excess of two years. Certain groups of registered persons were exempted from being ordered to jobs. These included physically disabled persons, pregnant women and those exercising maternal care over at least one child under fourteen years of age, private school teachers and students in middle and higher schools, and owners and workers of industrial, handicraft, and commercial establishments to the extent that the given establishment or type of work is acknowledged as useful for the national or local economy.

[72] *Ibid.*, 1946, No. 3, Item 24.

Persons summoned to work on the basis of this decree are to be permitted to choose the type as well as location of the available employment in one of two localities if the employment is to occur away from the person's residence. The decree further provided that the compensation of a person assigned under it was not to be lower than that of other employees in the same position in the branch of work. Stern sanctions were specified for failure to register or to report for work when ordered. In the latter case the punishment might be as high as five years' imprisonment and loss of certain rights of citizenship.

Planned economy in medicine, dentistry, and other aspects of health service was introduced by law on October 28, 1948. Aside from making provisions for setting up new units or taking over existing institutions into the public health service, this law introduced many controls over practitioners in the fields of medicine, surgery, dentistry, nursing, and pharmacy.[73] They are obliged to work in the public health service a specified number of hours per week, according to norms set up by the Minister of Health. The minister establishes the quota of practitioners for various districts of Poland and sets up a procedure for the transfer of doctors, dentists, and technicians from areas where they are considered in oversupply to districts where additional ones are needed. Failure to comply with the regulations results in forfeiture of the right to follow the profession. The authorizations of the Minister of Health in the allocation of practitioners to various parts of the country were scheduled to expire after three years from the date of announcement of the law.[74] However, he was empowered for a period of five years from the date of entry into force of the law to order doctors to serve for a period not exceeding two years in localities threatened by serious diseases. Apparently it was expected that after the initial reshuffling to even out the supply of trained personnel, the regulations binding graduates of schools to serve up to three years in specified localities could be relied upon to fulfill economic plans for the socialized health service.

In April, 1949, veterinaries were subjected to planning as to den-

[73] *Ibid.*, 1948, No. 55, Item 434, Sections IV and VI.
[74] By the law of July 18, 1950 (*ibid.*, 1950, No. 36, Item 327), the authority of the Minister of Health to order a doctor to work up to two years in a socialized health service establishment located beyond the doctor's residence or place of practice was extended to January 1, 1955.

sity in various parts of the country very much along the pattern set for doctors.[75] Finally, in January, 1951, the state nationalized all private pharmacies and obligated the trained personnel working in these establishments to remain at their jobs for at least one year.[76]

The far-reaching transformations which took place in the field of the professions are typified by the laws passed during 1950 defining the professions of doctor and lawyer. In the field of medicine and health the Minister of Health exercises supreme jurisdiction. A doctor may have a private practice only after serving a specified number of hours per day in the socialized health establishment, unless specially exempted by the Minister of Health.[77] Under the provisions of the law of July 27, 1950, the Minister of Justice is empowered to supervise the new compulsory lawyers' associations, establish the wages lawyers may receive, and specify the total number of lawyers and law applicants for the various regional associations according to a plan drawn up by him. He may overrule decisions of organs of the lawyers' associations, dissolve these bodies if he considers it essential to do so in the public interest, and appoint temporary authorities in their stead.[78]

State control over youth was extended by the law of February 25, 1948, which established obligatory vocational, physical, and military training for youth.[79] Youths of both sexes between the ages of sixteen to twenty-one are required to gain vocational training through study and work assignments under a paramilitary organization called "Service for Poland." The obligatory period of steady work cannot exceed six months for pre-recruitment age youth or the period of basic military service for older youth, and is deductible from the two-year period of work specified in the law of 1946 mentioned above.[80] In addition, youths undergoing training may be required to perform occasional work assignments not exceeding three days per month. The law aimed at organized participation of youth in the planned reconstruction and expansion of the economy.

State employment offices exercise a monopoly in the field of organized labor market information and assistance in conclusion of con-

[75] *Ibid.*, 1949, No. 25, Item 178.
[76] *Ibid.*, 1951, No. 1, Items 1, 2, 3, 4.
[77] *Ibid.*, 1950, No. 50, Item 458.
[78] *Ibid.*, No. 30, Item 275.
[79] *Ibid.*, 1948, No. 12, Item 90.
[80] *Supra,* p. 71.

tracts for labor or vocational training.[81] Intrusion of private employment agencies is forbidden under penalty of arrest or fine, or both.

Under the provisions of a law passed on March 7, 1950, the Polish socialized economy may claim the services of graduates of middle vocational schools and higher educational institutions.[82] The prologue to this law stated:

The growing needs of the socialist economy require that a planned policy be conducted in the sphere of employment of newly qualified cadres, above all of the technical. The People's State—designating enormous sums for the education of youth in vocational schools and higher schools—should direct in a planned manner the inflow of graduates of these schools into socialized establishments of work and assure youth the possibility of immediately joining in the socialist construction.

Graduates of these schools can be ordered to work in the field of their specialization in specified state or local government enterprises or in other socialized establishments for a period not exceeding three years. The chairman of the State Commission of Economic Planning establishes the annual quantitative plan for employment of graduates.

Another law also passed on March 7, 1950, asserted that the needs of the socialist economy demanded that the socialized establishments of work and state and local government institutions be assured qualified cadres continuously connected with them. With the aim of preventing harmful turnover of qualified cadres, "inconsistent with the fundamentals of the planned economy," the law provided that persons possessing qualifications in professions or specializations particularly important for the socialized economy could be required to remain in the socialized establishments of work in their present positions, or in other positions corresponding to their qualifications.[83] The minister in the government having jurisdiction over a particular establishment was authorized to order the relevant personnel to remain at their present employment for a period not exceeding two years under the terms of the current agreement between the employer and the employee. Individual orders did not need to be tendered, since the State Council, on recommendation of the chairman of the State Commission of Economic Planning, could sus-

[81] *Dziennik Ustaw,* 1945, No. 30, Item 182.
[82] *Ibid.,* 1950, No. 10, Item 106.
[83] *Ibid.,* Item 107.

pend for two years the right of entire categories of workers employed in especially important vocations to terminate their contracts for work. Penalties for deserting jobs despite an order to remain ranged up to six months' confinement, or fine up to 250,000 zlotys, or both.

On April 17, 1950, this law was applied to the following groups of workers without regard to the kind of qualifications they possessed:

1. Employees in state offices, establishments, and institutions, and socialized enterprises in industry, communications, and transport, in the following categories:
   a. Engineers, technicians, architects, foremen, veterinaries, geologists, surveyors, and geodesists
   b. Chief and senior bookkeepers and workers of equal rank in financial departments
2. Doctors, assistant surgeons, and other persons possessing sanitation training and employed in the health service
3. Tractor drivers employed in socialized agriculture.[84]

The coverage of this law was extended on September 13, 1950, to include technicians in trade and agriculture; officers, navigators, and mechanics of the Polish Merchant Marine; and operators of sound and cinema equipment and certain art school personnel. The law is so framed that executive orders based upon it can be made to apply to almost any additional type of skill or profession. To combat absenteeism of workers in the socialized sector, a law was passed on April 10, 1950, setting up a schedule of penalties ranging from reproach and warning, through loss of pay for a number of days actually worked, to demotion or reduction of wages up to 25 percent.[85]

To construct, maintain, and guard certain public works, such as the communication network, schools, public buildings, waterworks, parks and playgrounds, and market places, and to implement other public aims such as reforestation, the government, on June 30, 1951, decreed that services of labor, equipment, and materials may be exacted in rural areas and towns. Owners of farms, buildings, and

---

[84] *Ibid.*, No. 18, Item 153. The order requiring specified categories of employees to remain in their present positions until December 31, 1951, was later extended to April 25, 1952 (*ibid.*, 1952, No. 63, pp. 531–32.)

[85] *Ibid.*, No. 20, Item 168.

land not in agricultural use and persons engaged in vocations subject to the turnover tax are obligated under this decree. The extent of the obligation may amount to several days of labor per year.[86]

Poland's array of government controls over the economy expanded enormously in the postwar period. Socialized enterprises became dominant in every major sector of production except agriculture. Even in this field, by the end of 1953, about one fifth of the arable land was either in state farms or peasant collectives, and individual peasant producers faced compulsory deliveries of grain, potatoes, milk, and livestock. The exigencies of centralized planning led also to the extension of direct state control over the population. Legal restraints were imposed on the free choice of employment, and the educational system was reoriented to meet the planned requirements for trained manpower. In addition to these direct controls, the government could exercise indirect control over the allocation of resources to production through its wage and price policies. Through taxation, compulsory saving, and price policy on consumer goods, it could enforce abstention from current consumption in favor of investment. When one adds to these controls the overriding emphasis on industrial expansion in the postwar plans, it is not surprising that impressive industrial growth was in fact realized.

[86] *Ibid.*, 1951, No. 38, Item 284.

V

The Administration of the
Planned Economy

T HE expansion of the role of the state in the Polish postwar economy is reflected in the growth of the apparatus established to effect state control. As production revived, the problems of management became more complex, requiring changes in administrative organization. Equally important, however, was the changing concept of economic planning that accompanied the concentration of political power within the grasp of the new Polish United Workers' Party. The experience of the Soviet Union in the construction of socialism became the prime pattern for the Polish planners. Accordingly, the economic administration was adapted to meet the needs of highly centralized, direct control over production and distribution.

In Polish planning, the economic policies and major goals of activity are first established by the United Workers' Party. It then becomes the task of the central economic agencies of the government to translate these objectives into over-all plans specifying the production goals, giving the distribution of the national product to the various end uses, and identifying the means for carrying the plans into effect. In addition to their planning responsibilities, the central agencies administer the economic program of the government, which entails elaborate coordination of the various economic activities, close supervision over the socialized enterprises, regulation of the private sector of production to ensure its performance of specified obligations, and enforcement of various restraints upon the population to promote the achievement of economic goals. The enterprises at the production level are subordinated to the requirements of centralized planning through their charters and through legal regulations which limit the scope of independent decision making at the local level.

The Central Authorities

The Economic Committee of the Council of Ministers. From 1945 up to September 21, 1950, the Economic Committee of the Council of Ministers directed the national economy. This committee supervised the Central Board of Planning until the latter was abolished on February 10, 1949,[1] at which time a new planning office, the State Commission of Economic Planning, came into being. The chairman of the commission served also as chairman of the Economic Committee of the Council of Ministers. The committee's membership included on a regular basis fourteen economic ministers, the Ministers of National Defense and Public Administration, and two vice-chairmen of the planning commission. Other ministers participated with a full vote in discussions concerning their respective spheres of activity, while the chairman of the Polish National Bank and representatives of the Supreme Control Chamber, the Chancellery of the State Council, the Presidium of the Council of Ministers, the Central Commission of Trade Unions, the Central Union of Cooperatives, and the Peasants' Mutual Aid Association participated with advisory votes.

The committee's sphere of activity included the determination of basic economic policy, approval of economic plans, preparation of economic legislation, and supervision over the performance of plans. It acted as a clearing agency on economic matters for the Council of Ministers.[2] The committee lost legal status on September 21, 1950, and its important policy and coordinating functions were transferred to the Presidium of the Council of Ministers, while lesser matters came under the jurisdiction of the economic planning commission.

The economic ministries. When the Polish Committee of National Liberation began to function as a government on July 21, 1944, it possessed only four economic departments, namely, Agriculture and Agrarian Reform, National Economy and Finance, Labor and Social Welfare, and Transport, Posts, and Telegraphs.[3] Upon the transformation of the Lublin Committee into the Provisional

[1] *Dziennik Ustaw*, 1945, No. 52, Item 298; 1949, No. 7, Item 43.
[2] *Monitor Polski* (The Polish Monitor), May 12, 1949.
[3] Polish Ministry of Foreign Affairs, Press and Information Department, *Information on Poland*, p. Cz 1.

Government of Poland on December 31, 1944, the process of multiplication of ministries was initiated. The Department of National Economy and Finance was succeeded by three ministries—Treasury, Industry, and Food and Trade; and the Transport, Posts, and Telegraphs Department emerged as two new ministries—Transport, and Posts and Telegraphs. The formation of the Government of National Unity on June 28, 1945, gave rise to four new economic ministries, namely, Forestry, Shipping and Foreign Trade, Reconstruction, and Recovered Territories. Except for a consolidation of the administration of industry and domestic and foreign trade into the omnibus Ministry of Industry and Trade on February 7, 1947, and the liquidation of the Ministry of Food,[4] the administrative organization remained relatively stable until 1949.

The concentrated control over industrial production and distribution held by the Communist Ministry of Industry and Trade was an important weapon in the struggle for political supremacy in Poland. It permitted the Workers' Party to exert pressure upon the Socialist Party for merger; and on the economic sector it coincided with the so-called battle for trade in which private trade was largely liquidated or socialized. By 1949, the hegemony of the Communists over the state was assured by the engorgement of the Socialist Party into the new United Workers' Party. Consideration of more efficient forms of administration in which the management of production units would be more directly under ministerial supervision could then be admitted.

The Ministry of Industry and Trade had expanded enormously with the reconstruction of the economy and further extension of state control over the private and cooperative sectors. On February 10, 1949, this ministry was dissolved in favor of six new ones, namely, Mining and Energy, Heavy Industry, Light Industry, Agricultural and Food Industry, Internal Trade, and Foreign Trade.[5] The Ministry of Recovered Territories was dissolved in January, 1949, at the same time that these areas were brought under the general state administration.[6] Also during 1949, the Ministry of Reconstruction was abolished, and a new Ministry of Construction came into being,[7] signifying recovery from the more important

[4] *Ibid.*, pp. Cz 2, 3.
[5] *Dziennik Ustaw*, 1949, No. 7, Item 43.
[6] *Ibid.*, No. 4, Item 22.
[7] *Ibid.*, No. 30, Item 216.

devastations of war and entry into a period of new construction.

The process of multiplication of economic ministries continued into 1953.[8] During 1950 four new ministries were created and two old ones abolished. The Ministry of Construction was replaced by the Ministry of Construction of Cities and Settlements and the Ministry of Industrial Construction. Following the transformation of the local people's councils into the regional organs of the monolithic state authority, the Ministry of Public Administration was abolished, and some of its economic functions were added to those of the newly created Ministry of Communal Economy. Administration of the chemical industry was split off from the Ministry of Heavy Industry and raised to the ministerial level. The elaboration of ministries in 1951 resulted in the replacement of the Ministry of Communications by two new ministries, namely, Railroads, and Highways and Air Transport; the substitution of the new ministries of Agriculture and State Farms for the former single ministry of Agriculture and Agrarian Reform; and the elevation of the Central Office of Small-Scale Production to ministerial rank as the Ministry of Small-Scale Industry and Handicrafts. Continued specialization of economic administration in 1952 led to a three-way split of the Ministry of Heavy Industry, giving rise to the new ministries of Metallurgy, Electric Energy, and Machinery Industry. The new ministries of Meat and Dairy Industry, Wood and Paper Industry, and Building Materials Industry were created by reducing the scope of the old ministries of Internal Trade, Light Industry, Chemical Industry, and Forestry, and by assignment of certain new functions. Toward the end of 1952, the new Ministry of State Control was created to replace the former Supreme Control Chamber in the exercise of auditing and control functions over administrative offices and economic enterprises. Finally the announced changes through December, 1953, were completed by the replacement of the Central Office of Procurements and Contracting by the new Ministry of Procurement, which deals with the collection and processing of certain agricultural products, including the compulsory deliveries and deliveries under contract to the state, milling of grain and sale of grain products, and the collection, processing, and sale of feedstuffs.[9]

By the end of 1953 the four original economic departments of the

[8] *Ibid.*, 1950–53, *passim.*
[9] *Ibid.*, 1953, No. 20, Item 77.

Lublin Committee had proliferated into twenty-six ministries concerned primarily with the administration of the national economy. This expansion, however, does not afford a complete description of the growth of the economic administration. The remaining, primarily noneconomic ministries of the government have certain economic functions, and in addition many central offices and special commissions directly under the Council of Ministers, the State Council, and the State Commission of Economic Planning have been created to deal with special problems in economic administration and planning.

The orders of the Council of Ministers defining the sphere of activity of the new industrial ministries specified the particular industries within the jurisdiction of each new ministry. Thus, for example, the scope of activity of the Ministry of Light Industry as defined in 1949 included matters concerning the following industries: textile, clothing, leather, wood, match, paper, mineral, and printing. For each of these industries, the detailed activity of the ministry included:[10]

1. Economic planning and investment policy
2. Direction of the activity of subordinate state, state-cooperative, and state-administered enterprises
3. Direction and supervision of the industrial activity of central offices of cooperatives, state-cooperative central offices, and co-operatives
4. Supervision over technical arrangements
5. Arbitration in property matters between enterprises and institutions subordinate to the ministry
6. Provision of professional personnel and skilled workers, including cooperation with proper authorities in problems of employment
7. Organizing of scientific research, publication of materials, and supervision of institutions of scientific research.

The definition of the sphere of activity for other industrial ministries followed the outlines of the above example very closely. In cases where jurisdictions of ministries overlapped, the orders of the Council of Ministers specified that understanding of the ministers

[10] *Ibid.,* 1949, No. 23, Item 154. Since 1949, the number of industries under this ministry has been reduced by transfers of certain industries to newly created ministries.

concerned must be attained, or otherwise they specified the order of authority. The authority of the Minister of Internal Trade extended to all matters of domestic trade, both socialized and private, including price matters and supervision of trading enterprises.[11] The Ministry of Foreign Trade had a correspondingly defined area of activity, which included the conduct of negotiations and preparation of agreements in international trade and supervision over their execution. The Ministry of Communal Economy was given jurisdiction over matters of housing, except new construction, and over the construction and maintenance of streets, parks, public utilities, and other communal establishments. Within the sphere of activity of the Ministry of Small-Scale Production and Handicraft were included matters of small-scale industry, supervision of state industry under the local people's councils, supervision and support of handicrafts, supervision of private industry, and planning, coordination, and supervision of the economic activity of labor cooperatives.[12] The content of the administrative authority of the other economic ministries, with the exception of the Ministry of Finance, in large measure may be inferred from their names. In all cases the ministries were given responsibility for economic planning in their respective branches or sectors of the economy and for supervision of enterprises under their authority.

The Ministry of Finance is one of the most important control agencies in the Polish economy. It is directly responsible for comprehensive financial planning, supervision, and audit of the accounts of the various establishments in the socialized sector. Much of the control function of the ministry is performed by its subordinate banking system. On the ministerial level, the sphere of activity as of April, 1950, included:[13]

1. Preparation of the estimates for the state budget and execution of the budget
2. Setting norms for the composition of local budgets
3. Examination of the budgetary estimates of income and expenditures of establishments included in the state budget and supervision of their financial economy
4. Examination of financial plans of socialized enterprises, super-

---

[11] *Ibid.*, No. 10, Item 62.
[12] *Ibid.*, 1951, No. 32, Item 247.
[13] *Ibid.*, 1950, No. 22, Item 188.

vision of their financial economy, and control over the legality and correctness of their expenditures in the area of finances, number and ranks of personnel, wages, and administrative outlays

5. Setting norms for the elaboration and execution of the cash and credit plans[14]
6. Settlement of accounts in the socialized economy
7. Personal and material insurance, pensions and annuities, lottery monopoly, matters of taxation and tax collection, and protection of the customs boundary of the state
8. Supervision over the activity of banks and credit institutions, organizing saving by the population, and emission of state loans
9. Cooperation with the State Commission of Economic Planning in the elaboration of price and wage policies.

In order to fulfill its tasks of audit and financial control over state institutions, socialized enterprises, and social organizations profiting from state financial aid, the Ministry of Finance was authorized to carry through financial inspection; verify the cash on hand; examine valuable papers, promissory notes, bookkeeping entries, and all other documents concerning the financial condition of the unit; demand written explanation and copies of documents; and receive from controlling organs facts turned up in connection with their inspections and review. The ministry was empowered to issue orders necessary for removal of offenses in the sphere of the financial economy and in special circumstances to suspend the financing of institutions violating financial discipline.[15]

The Central Board of Planning. The first state planning body, the Central Board of Planning, was created by decree of the Council of Ministers on November 10, 1945. It functioned under a Socialist chairman and was supervised by the Economic Committee of the Council of Ministers.[16] Early in 1948, this office came under strong Communist criticism in connection with a discussion of the national economic plan for that year. Hilary Minc, at that time the Minister of Industry and Trade, charged the office with an assortment of malpractices, the chief of which were the lack of appreciation of Marxist economic science in the calculation of national income and a

[14] See *infra*, pp. 258, 260.
[15] *Dziennik Ustaw*, 1950, No. 22, Item 188.
[16] *Ibid.*, 1945, No. 52, Item 298.

passive attitude toward execution of the national economic plan. What was needed, Minc asserted, were laws that mobilized the means of fulfillment of plans, not those that demobilized.[17] In consequence of the attack, Czeslaw Bobrowski, the Socialist head of the Central Board of Planning, was transferred to a diplomatic post, and a nominal Socialist took over the planning office.[18] The character of the annual plan was changed to meet some of Minc's objections, and finally on February 10, 1949, the planning office itself was abolished in favor of the new State Commission of Economic Planning headed by Minc.

The new planning commission was given a much wider sphere of activity than the former office. Its functions were stated in broad terms early in 1949 [19] and then were more closely defined by an order of the Council of Ministers on April 22, 1949. The general instructions to direct the entire structure of state economic planning were spelled out in detail:[20]

1. Elaboration of drafts of national economic plans (annual and for periods of many years), investment plans, combined financial plans of the enterprises in the socialized economy, economic plans in the social and cultural spheres, and other detailed plans[21]

2. Assure the full utilization of the potentialities of the economy and prevent disproportion in the development of particular branches

3. Matters of organization, methodology, and technique of economic planning

4. Control and coordination of plans of all divisions of the state administration, plans of the socialized economy, and regional plans to insure harmony

5. Supervision over the execution of national economic plans and other state economic plans; supervision of departmental organizations of control over the execution of economic plans

6. Matters of organization, methodology, techniques, and coordination of reporting the execution of economic plans

[17] H. Minc, "O właściwe metody planowania w Polsce" (Concerning Proper Methods of Planning in Poland), *Nowe Drogi*, March, 1948, p. 37.

[18] New York *Times*, March 13, 1948, and February 5, 1949.

[19] *Dziennik Ustaw*, 1949, No. 7, Item 43.

[20] *Ibid.*, No. 26, Item 190.

[21] See *infra*, pp. 120–29.

7. Preparation of reports on the fulfillment of national economic plans, investment plans, and other state economic plans
8. Elaboration of commodity balances and allocations of raw materials and deficit articles
9. Instruction of departmental planning organs
10. Matters of planned spatial use of the country within the scope defined by separate regulations
11. Matters of statistics; establishing the direction of the activity of the Central Statistical Office and other organs of the statistical service in accord with the needs of economic planning
12. Make certain that programs of scientific research units take account of the needs arising from economic plans.

The coordination aspect of the activity of the planning commission included:[22]

1. Elaboration of the state policy of employment and wages, setting norms of labor and its organization, and establishing proper proportions among the particular branches of the economy in the areas of employment and wages
2. Elaboration of principles of organizational structure, technique of administration, and typical personnel organization by ranks and numbers for enterprises, institutions, and central administrations in the socialized economy
3. Elaboration of principles of state policy with regard to handicrafts, household industry, labor cooperatives, and private industry
4. Supervision over chambers of handicrafts, their unions, and industrial-trade chambers.

With regard to the plan for development of technology, the planning commission's responsibility included matters of control over the execution of the plan for technological advance, elaboration of principles in the area of organization and methods of technical control of production, and matters of patents, trademarks, norms and standards, development of inventions, and rationalization of economic processes.

In the area of finance, the planning commission was directed to work in harmony with the Ministry of Finance. In particular the

[22] *Dziennik Ustaw,* 1949, No. 26, Item 190.

following matters came within the scope of the planning commission:[23]

1. Elaboration of financial plans extending over many years
2. Elaboration of the program of financial objectives of the national economic plan and of the over-all financial limits that arise from these objectives
3. Giving opinions as to the conformity of drafts of financial plans, budget estimates, and other financial aims with the national economic plan
4. Preparation of quarterly and annual balances of money income and expenditures of the population
5. Examining and passing opinion upon departmental proposals in the matter of establishing prices, tariffs, and margins of the distributive apparatus in the socialized economy, and confirming these prices, tariffs, and margins in accord with separate regulations
6. Elaboration of plans of lowering costs of production in the socialized economy and control over the performance of these plans
7. Elaboration, from the point of view of costs and prices, of proposals in the area of financial settlements in the socialized economy and giving opinions of the bases of these settlements.

An examination of the sphere of activity of the State Commission of Economic Planning and the individual economic ministries reveals the close-knit administrative character of Polish postwar economic planning. It is distinguished by the comprehensive coordination of activities by the central authorities and by the provision for intimate control over the production establishments.

The Central Office of Vocational Education. This office was created by the law of February 10, 1949, to supply the basic branches of the national economy with the cadres necessary for meeting the goals set by economic plans and to insure the correct distribution of these cadres among the various branches of the national economy. Up to the time of creation of this new agency, the Ministry of Industry and Trade carried on an extensive vocational training program through schools and courses within its own control, and

[23] *Ibid.,* 1950, No. 22, Item 188.

a much larger program came under the Ministry of Education. The new central office, which was independent of the Ministry of Education, now combined the two programs. Its sphere of activity included the elaboration of plans for training cadres for industry, trade, handicrafts, and other branches of the national economy as designated by the Council of Ministers. The new office supervised the plans of training, facilities, and curricula of agencies possessing their own vocational schools, with the exception of the Ministry of Agriculture, which conducted its own vocational schools below the level of higher education.[24]

Graduates of middle vocational schools and higher institutions were obligated to work for periods up to three years in socialized establishments as directed by the Chairman of the Central Office of Vocational Education or the minister in charge of the schools.[25] By this means, the economic authorities could regulate directly the inflow of trained technical personnel into particular branches of the economy and into particular enterprises. Inflow of trainees into vocational schools and courses was assured by the universal obligation of youth to acquire vocational training.

Intermediate and Lower Levels of Administration

Intermediate administrative levels in the state sector. The organization of state enterprises and intermediate administrative offices has changed over time with a tendency toward uniformity, but even currently there exists a wide diversity of forms of organization of state enterprises. The pattern in industry, which is described below, appears to be followed in most of the other sectors as well.

At the outset of the postwar period, large- and medium-scale state enterprises were grouped into central administration boards by industrial types. Within the Ministry of Industry there were fourteen such boards early in 1947, representing coal mining, metallurgy, textiles, chemicals, and other industries. Other ministries had fewer central boards. Initially, the central administration boards functioned as departments within a ministry, but by resolution of the Economic Committee of the Council of Ministers on October

[24] *Ibid.*, 1949, No. 40, Item 283.
[25] *Ibid.*, 1950, No. 10, Item 106.

22, 1946, the boards became commercialized state enterprises endowed with separate legal and financial status.[26] The state enterprises comprising a central board were grouped into commercialized associations on branch or branch-territorial principles. Typically, therefore, two intermediate levels of administration separated a production enterprise from its supervising ministry. Administration was based on the principle of functional subordination of lower elements to several departments within higher ones, which led to a weakening of the role of managers on lower levels.

A resolution of the Presidium of the Government on December 23, 1950, decommercialized the central administration boards and brought them back into the ministries.[27] Thus one intervening level of administration between a ministry and its subordinate production enterprises was eliminated. At the same time the functions of the central administration boards were redefined and their relationship to departments within ministries placed on a new basis. The departments were no longer expected to operate as executive and supervisory organs over the central boards and the underlying enterprises. Instead, they became advisory units whose tasks included the elaboration of problems in such areas as planning, production techniques, employment, and wages. All executive orders of the minister were to be directed to the central board for fulfillment, thereby strengthening management on this level.

A central board combined all enterprises in the same or related type of activity in the country as a whole or within a smaller area, depending upon the number of enterprises within the branch of activity. The aim was to limit the number of subordinate enterprises within one central board so as to facilitate efficient direction by the board. The central board was financed from the state budget, whereas the underlying associations and enterprises operated on commercial principles, financing their expenditures from their incomes. The central boards, however, continued to perform certain commercial functions in the area of conclusion of planned agreements between branches and in matters of supply and sale.

[26] Polish National Economic Bank, *Quarterly Review*, XV (1947), No. 5, 5. A commercialized establishment finances its expenditures from its income and normally does not depend on support from the state treasury. Such an establishment is said to operate on "commercial principles" or on the basis of "economic calculation" (same as the Russian term *khozraschet*).

[27] *Życie Gospodarcze*, March 1–15, 1951, pp. 262–64. The following account is based on this reference.

The basic tasks of central boards under the new regulation included matters of planning, supervision, coordination, technology of production, accounting and reporting, and control over the execution of plans. The central boards translated the principles of the national economic plan into goals and basic indexes for their subordinate units. They reviewed the correctness of drafts of plans of lower units and combined these for integration into higher departmental plans. In their control function the central boards organized and supervised the accounting, statistical, and operational reporting of their subordinate enterprises. This demanded on-the-spot checking of reports, analysis of fulfillment of plans, a study of causality and interdependence of particular phenomena, and deductions therefrom which would indicate corrective measures.

With regard to production, the central boards were concerned with the introduction of new technology and improved methods, utilization and care of machines and equipment, and direction of the rationalization movement of workers. The control of quality of production and increased diversity of assortment of products received special emphasis among the activities of the central boards. They were closely concerned with employment and wages, including the development of labor competition, raising average productivity, and improving labor discipline. Other tasks of the central boards included supervision over the financial economy of subordinate units, the question of proper financing and crediting, suitable use of working capital so as to insure faster turnover, the campaign for saving and profitability, the planning of investments of subordinate units, and the training of personnel.

The new economic organization below the ministerial level was not uniform, but rather displayed a variety of structural arrangements. Where the number of enterprises on the lowest level was small, the central board administered them directly, but if the number was large, auxiliary intermediate forms such as associations or trusts could be used. Even in the latter case, exceptions could be made to permit some units to come directly under the central administration boards while others in the same branch were subordinated to the intermediate organs. Particularly important enterprises could be directly subordinated to ministers, thus avoiding all intermediate levels of administration.

Initially, state-owned enterprises of local importance were not taken over by central administration boards but functioned instead under local industry managements attached to the provincial level of the public administration under the general supervision of the Ministry of Industry and Trade.[28] Following the reorganization of local government in 1950, the presidiums of local people's councils took over in large measure the direction of purely local economic activity. A resolution of the Presidium of the Government on February 3, 1951, laid the basis for current organization of local industry.[29] This resolution envisioned three groups of enterprises in state-owned local industry, namely, those which were directly subordinated to (1) authorities of local municipalities or townships, (2) provincial authorities, and (3) the Central Office of Small-Scale Production, which later became the Ministry of Small-Scale Production and Handicraft. Industrial establishments whose production was destined primarily for satisfying the needs of the municipality or township in which they were located and service establishments hitherto subordinated to provincial managements of local industry were organized into state enterprises of local industry of the first category. Each enterprise ordinarily encompassed many plants. The management of such an enterprise consisted of a director subordinated to the presidium of the local people's council. The enterprise possessed legal personality and operated on commercial principles.

Industrial establishments, which hitherto were under the provincial managements of local industry, whose production was destined for local consumption in more than one municipality remained organized as enterprises of provincial local industry. Such an enterprise could consist of a single large plant or a combination of several smaller ones. The management consisted of a director subordinated to the provincial administration of local industry, which supplied coordination, supervision, control, and general direction over municipal and provincial local industry. The provincial administrations of local industry functioned as commercialized legal entities headed by directors nominated by the presidiums of the provincial people's councils and confirmed by the Chairman of the Central Office of Small-Scale Production or its successor, the Ministry of Small-Scale

---

[28] Polish National Economic Bank, *op. cit.*, p. 7.

[29] Adam Fonar, "Nowa organizacja państwowego przemysłu terenowego" (New Organization of State-owned Local Industry), *Życie Gospodarcze,* April 16–30, 1951, pp. 460–62.

Production and Handicraft. Economic planning for the first two categories of state-owned local industry was performed jointly by the provincial administrations of local industry and the provincial commissions of economic planning.

Industrial establishments heretofore subordinated to local industry managements which, in view of their production and supply of goods to consumers or industry of the whole country, were not transferred to local governments were administered directly by the Ministry of Small-Scale Production and Handicraft. Such establishments were organized into branch administrations of local industry which entered into the composition of the ministry. The branch administrations performed for their subordinate enterprises very much the same activities that the central boards carried on for large- and medium-scale state industry.

All three categories of state-owned local industry are based on local raw materials and remnants of processed materials from large-scale industry. Though at present not of great importance, local industry, in the view of the Polish planners, is expected to expand greatly through exploitation of unused reserves of machines, equipment, housing, labor force, and other factors.

Management of state enterprises. In the early postwar period state enterprises were organized on the basis of prewar legislation, but by the decree of January 3, 1947, new legal bases were prescribed and remained in effect until near the end of 1950. According to the provisions of the 1947 decree,[30] the minister in charge of a given branch of the economy, in understanding with the Minister of Finance and the Chairman of the Central Board of Planning, could order the creation of state enterprises in industry, mining, trade, and services. The newly created enterprises operated on commercial principles on the basis of financial and economic plans approved by higher levels of the economic administration. The state treasury endowed the enterprises with real property for their use and administration, but not ownership, and with movable property for ownership. An enterprise could acquire real property only for the ownership of the state treasury, whereas it could acquire and dispose of other property for its own account. In any event, the obligation of the state treasury on the account of the state enterprise did not exceed the value of the real property. The appropriate minister

[30] *Dziennik Ustaw*, 1947, No. 8, Item 42.

or a subordinate organ designated by him approved the statement of profit and loss and closing of accounts of the enterprise and in other respects supervised the enterprise directly or by the intermediation of central boards and associations of enterprises. The decree further provided that each enterprise should have a managing board for administration and a board of social supervision as a control and advisory body. The latter was an element of external control functioning under the supervision of the State Council. Members of the board of management were appointed and removable by the supervising ministry or a designated subordinate agency.

On October 26, 1950, the Council of Ministers issued a new decree governing the creation of economic enterprises.[31] The provisions of the new measure in most respects duplicated those of the 1947 decree. In addition, the new decree allowed the presidiums of local people's councils to create state enterprises subject to the agreement of the proper minister. Perhaps the most significant change made by the new legislation was the provision for a single director independently to conduct the enterprise and be responsible for it. The manager was appointed and removable by the appropriate minister or with his concurrence in the case of local industry where the presidiums of local people's councils exercised primary control. Enterprises could be merged or liquidated at the discretion of higher administrative authorities.

The decree further provided that the Council of Ministers would define the principles of internal organization and the system of financing the enterprise and specify the rights and obligations of chief and senior bookkeepers, who are important figures in internal control of the enterprises. Detailed regulations concerning internal organization were to be issued by the Chairman of the State Commission of Economic Planning, while those concerning finances would flow from the Minister of Finance with the understanding of the planning commission. The coverage of the 1950 decree could be extended by order of the Council of Ministers to include enterprises which were exempted under earlier provisions, and likewise the coverage could be reduced in order to exempt certain enterprises currently operating under the provisions of the decree.

In setting up new enterprises, economic authorities were given

[31] *Ibid.*, 1950, No. 49, Item 439.

considerable flexibility as to choice of enterprise types through charter provisions, permissible exemptions from the model organization specified in the October, 1950, decree, and the order of subordination to ministerial authority. The director of an enterprise, however, had limited scope for independent determination of the internal organization of the enterprise and even less discretion concerning what was to be produced and the quantity of output. Both the inputs of factors of production, or norms of their use, and the outputs of final products were planned in considerable measure by the higher authorities with the advice of the management of the enterprise. The chief avenue for initiative at the plant level consisted of devising schemes for cost reduction and increased output within the framework of the plant's economic plan and subject to the capital and organizational limitations imposed from above. In practice, the range of discretion of managers was much greater than the legal provisions suggest since the planning procedures and controls were relatively new and imperfect and managers were forced to improvise when plans went awry.

The cooperative and private sectors. The character of state control over the cooperative and private sectors and some indication of the administrative organization to implement it have already been sketched in Chapter IV. The cooperative movement was thoroughly reorganized during 1948 to render it responsive to centralized planning and control, and in 1949 the movement was integrated into the national economic plan as part of the socialized establishment under direct planning.[32] The subordination of the cooperative sector to the government economic administration was accomplished by the pyramidal structure of cooperative organizations into central boards topped by the Central Cooperative Union. The administration of the union enforces economic discipline over central boards and lower levels of organization and may suspend from duty officials who fail to carry out their obligations. Although appeal may be made in such cases to the Chief Cooperative Council, an organ of the Central Union, its decisions can be set aside by the Council of Ministers, which supervises the activity of the Central Union.[33] The subordination of cooperatives to direct central planning was evidenced by the provisions of the new model charter introduced

[32] *Polish Cooperative News Service,* May, 1950, p. 5.
[33] *Dziennik Ustaw,* 1948, No. 30, Item 199.

in 1949 for urban consumer cooperatives, which stated that the aim of the cooperative was to operate "within the framework of the state economic plan." [34] The authority of ministers extends directly to the activities of cooperative central boards and the underlying cooperative units.[35] Financial discipline of the cooperative sector closely parallels that of the state enterprises. In both cases, the socialized banking system is responsible for close supervision over the use of working capital and investment funds according to the provisions of the economic plans.[36]

The most important direct administrative control measure in private nonagricultural small-scale production and trade consisted of the formation of compulsory associations of private enterprise for disciplinary and planning purposes. Final supervision over the activities of such associations rests with the appropriate ministry. Economic discipline is enforced through the socialized financial system and the state-controlled supply of raw materials and finished products made possible by the predominant role of socialized industry and complete state control over wholesale trade.[37]

Administrative Procedures and Supervision in the Socialized Sector

In a perfectly competitive economy and to some extent in the decentralized, so-called competitive socialist model, prices acting as parameters effect the coordination of economic activity. In the Polish postwar economy, however, the basic decisions concerning what is to be produced and the allocation of factors of production and distribution were largely made by the central planning authority. The government can issue orders in the form of national economic plans or as enabling measures and set penalties for noncompliance, but the fact of transgression must be determined or prevented. Therefore, the economic planning practiced in Poland required an elaborate control mechanism.

[34] Marian Niczman, "Nowy Statut wzorcowy" (New Model Charter), *Społem* (Together), April 20, 1949, p. 3.

[35] Cf. *Dziennik Ustaw*, 1949, No. 10, Item 62.

[36] Tadeusz Gibuła, "Uporządkowanie gospodarki finansowej w spółdzielniach" (Setting in Order the Financial Economy in Cooperatives), *Społem*, April 5, 1949, pp. 10–11.

[37] Cf. *Życie Gospodarcze*, September 16–30, 1949, p. 773.

The highest level of state control.[38] The legal provisions concerning the execution of state audit and other control over the socialized economy in the postwar period underwent a series of modifications culminating in the repeal of earlier laws and regulations and the abolition of the Supreme Control Chamber by the law of November 22, 1952. This law redefined the scope, aims, and procedures of state control and established the Ministry of State Control to carry out the new directives.[39] According to the provisions of this law, the scope of state control includes: (1) ministries and other leading organs of the state administration as well as their subordinate offices, (2) state-owned and state-administered enterprises, establishments, and institutions, (3) cooperative organizations and enterprises, and (4) organizations and institutions benefiting from state aid or carrying out activities delegated to them by the state. Tasks of the new ministry include control over the productive, financial, organizational, and administrative activities of the controlled units; observation of the timeliness and of the method of execution of the state budget and reporting thereon to the government; watching over the safeguarding of public property and the observance of legality, honesty, efficiency, and conformity with economic plans and official policy in all the activities of the controlled units; and coordination of state control activities with the control exercised by the financial institutions and other agencies.

Three stages of control were envisioned in the law: (1) control of intended activities, (2) control of current activities, and (3) a check of the completed activities, but the first is carried out only in special instances designated by separate resolutions of the government. The Ministry of State Control carries out its tasks both on a planned basis and by occasional checks either from its own initiative or upon request of the government. In order to carry out its duties, the representatives of the ministry were authorized to examine the account books and all relevant documents of the controlled units, to require all kinds of explanations and information, and to participate in conferences of the ministers of the government and those of subordinate bodies and enterprises. Where violations of regulations or state policy are determined, the ministry can confiscate documents, report the incidents to the supervisory body over the

[38] "Control" as used here means audit, review, or verification of activities.
[39] *Dziennik Ustaw,* 1952, No. 47, Item 316.

unit at fault, and require corrective action to be undertaken within a specified period. Criminal cases are referred to the public prosecutor with recommendations for action. For lesser violations of financial and economic regulations the Ministry of State Control was empowered under administrative procedure to penalize derelict employees of the controlled units to the extent of requiring indemnity for the damage done, but not in excess of three times the average salary received by the individual over the preceding three months. In addition, with the approval of the Chairman of the Council of Ministers, other penalties may be imposed ranging from warning and censure to removal from position of employment.

Internal control. The chief elements of control over the economic establishments within a given ministry were set forth in a resolution of the Council of Ministers of April 26, 1948.[40] Three levels of control were provided, namely, in (1) ministries, (2) central boards and independent offices, and (3) subordinate offices and enterprises. The scope of internal control includes the organization, administration, and operation of the given units with respect to legality, veracity, correctness, and compliance with plans. Each control level conducts planned control over the immediately subordinate administrative level and occasionally of lower levels in case of need. On each level, the inspection or control element is subordinated to the administrative head of that level, but must be independent of the administration of lower levels which it supervises. Three phases of control were envisioned, namely, of intended, current, and completed activities. The control organs cannot issue orders to the controlled unit, except in urgent matters, and are authorized only to make suggestions or recommendations to the director of the controlled unit as to measures necessary to correct the observed shortcomings. Matters involving sabotage or malpractice, however, must be directly reported to the public authorities for the prosecution of violations, and the administrative superior of the unit at fault must be informed. The organs of internal control collaborate with external control agencies. The local people's councils may not interfere directly on their own account in effecting control over enterprises on their terrain and may only suggest that such control be carried through by the internal control agencies. The latter, for their part, are obliged to invite representatives of the local people's

[40] *Monitor Polski,* June 1, 1948.

council to participate in the inspections, whether these be undertaken at the behest of the council or from internal initiative.

The banking system. The banking system has long been regarded as a powerful regulator of economic activity. In postwar Poland this role has been changed with the autonomy of banks being completely subordinated to the economic policy of the state contained in the national economic plans. In this process, the avowed model for the new structure was the Soviet banking system.[41] The aim was to transform the banking system into a country-wide accounting apparatus performing settlements for transactions in production and distribution and enforcing financial discipline according to the economic plan.

The evolution of the postwar banking system reflects the centralization of political authority in the Polish United Workers' Party. During the period of relative stability of the three-sectored economy—private, cooperative, and state—each sector possessed its own banks. These banks, however, were under close state control. The Polish National Bank functioned as the central bank and the principal short-term credit institution. One of its main duties was to finance the nationalized sector. The National Economic Bank was the central state institution for medium- and long-term credits and the principal financial agency implementing the state investment plan. The state Agricultural Bank financed the production and sale of agricultural products and investments in agriculture. Accumulation of savings was the primary function of the Postal Savings Bank. The cooperative sector was represented by two banks, which by 1947 had merged into the Bank of the Cooperative Economy, serving the needs of short-term and investment credit for cooperatives and meeting the needs of credit cooperatives. Two joint-stock banks, the Commercial Bank in Warsaw and the Bank of Cooperative Societies, whose stock in major part was owned by the state, served the needs of private enterprises in the field of short-term credit and long-term investment credit within limits of the state investment plan. Two institutions, the Municipal Bank in Warsaw and the Municipal Credit Bank in Poznań, serviced the financial needs of local governments and served as financial centers for the Municipal Savings Banks. These banks accumulated

[41] Jan Kizler, "Reforma bankowa" (Banking Reform), *Życie Gospodarcze*, April 1–15, 1951, pp. 399–401.

local funds and financed handicrafts, small-scale industry and trade, and other elements of small-scale production not served by the other institutions mentioned above. A system of credit cooperatives financed the needs of their members and acted as agents of the Bank of the Cooperative Economy and other central credit institutions.[42]

The major banking reform introduced by the decree of October 25, 1948, specified more carefully the control functions of the banking system in the planned economy. The state sector of banking was strengthened by the addition of new banks and by liquidation of cooperative, communal, and private institutions and transfer of their activities to the state banks. Additional measures to reconstruct the Polish banking system on the Soviet model culminated in a revised decree concerning the banking reform issued on June 4, 1951.[43] This decree subordinated the banking system to the supervision of the Minister of Finance. Three categories of banks acquired the exclusive right to carry on banking activities in Poland, namely, the state banks, banks in the form of joint stock companies, and village credit cooperatives.

The state banks possess legal personality and operate on commercial principles, using their earnings to cover their expenditures. The highest level of the banking organization is occupied by the Polish National Bank, which was charged with regulation of the circulation of currency and credit and conducting financial settlements in domestic and foreign turnovers. Its detailed tasks include:

1. Preparation of cash and credit plans for the national economy, the plan of foreign exchange, and other financial plans requested by the Minister of Finance[44]
2. Execution of plans in its own competence and control over the execution of plans by other banks and economic units
3. Financing the national economy within the framework of the credit plan directly by granting turnover credits to economic units and indirectly through credits to other banks
4. Control over the economy of units it finances and of other units designated by the Minister of Finance

[42] Polish Ministry of Foreign Affairs, *op. cit.,* pp. Hd 3–4.
[43] *Dziennik Ustaw,* 1948, No. 52, Item 412; 1951, No. 36, Item 279.
[44] Credit planning relates primarily to the provision of credits for working capital for socialized enterprises. Concerning cash and credit planning, see *infra,* pp. 257, 260.

5. Service of the state budget, which includes both central and local budgets, and cooperation in control over budget execution

6. Organization and execution of settlements between enterprises, institutions, and organizations; watching over the observance of the principles of sound financial management

7. Watching over the realization and expansion of noncash turnovers

8. Making of foreign settlements and financing of foreign trade.

The state Investment Bank's task is: (1) financing of investments with the exception of those investments which belong to the sphere of competence of other banks; (2) control over the execution of investments financed by the bank to see that they conform to plans; and (3) financing and financial control of enterprises that carry out the investment work in the sphere financed by the bank. The state Agricultural Bank supplies both turnover and investment credit and supervises the financial economy of agriculture. Like the Investment Bank, it was charged with the control functions specified in (2) and (3) above. The state Municipal Bank finances and controls current operations in the area of communal economy as defined by the Minister of Finance. It finances investments and capital repairs in this area and exercises control over this activity in the sense of (2) and (3) above. The state General Savings Bank functions as the central saving institution accumulating individual savings and carries out activities connected with money transfers by means of checks. Each state bank is headed by a director who independently manages the activity of the bank and is responsible therefor, thus putting an end to the collegiate boards of management under the 1948 version of this decree.

Only two joint-stock banks with greatly restricted areas of activity were permitted to continue to exist, namely, the Commercial Bank in Warsaw, which may operate only in foreign transactions as delimited by the Minister of Finance, and the Bank of the Polish Welfare Fund, which may carry on banking within an area to be defined by the Minister of Finance. Credit cooperatives serve the needs of farmers within limits of one or a few townships and act as auxiliary organs of the state Agricultural Bank. The latter functions as the financial, organizational, and auditing superior of the rural credit cooperatives.

Under the provisions of the 1951 reform of the banking system the Minister of Finance was authorized to liquidate particular banks in keeping with the needs of the economy and to transfer their functions to the remaining banks. This authority was used in the liquidation of the Communal Bank on January 1, 1952.[45] Its activities were taken over by the National Bank of Poland insofar as they related to the financing and control of the current operations and capital repairs in the communal economy and by the Investment Bank in all other areas.

The banking system has been constructed with a view toward establishing rigorous financial discipline in the execution of the national economic plans. Ideally, the financial organization of the Polish planned economy envisions each economic enterprise being monitored by a bank to which it is obliged to turn for working capital and investment funds. The bank is expected to grant the credits according to the financial plan of the enterprise and to maintain a current watch over the use of credits to see that they are not diverted to uses other than those specified in the plan. To facilitate control by banks, the law of July 1, 1949, extended the obligation of participating in noncash turnovers to all enterprises and establishments in the socialized sector, persons of public law, banks, insurance institutions, independent funds, and enterprises, establishments, and persons that engage in professional activity and are obliged to keep commercial books or simplified accounts under the law specifying tax procedure.[46] In practice, the effectiveness of control exercised by the banking system has been far from the ideal set forth in laws.[47]

State arbitration commissions. Prior to the decree of August 5, 1949, establishing the state system of economic arbitration, there existed arbitration commissions attached to the Ministry of Industry and Trade. The state system is based on the experience of the latter and that of the Soviet Union.[48] It established a system of

---

[45] *Monitor Polski,* 1952, No. A-18, Item 222, p. 277.
[46] *Dziennik Ustaw,* 1949, No. 41, Item 294.
[47] See *infra,* p. 259.
[48] Eugeniusz Jabloński, "Polskie prawo arbitrażowe" (Polish Arbitration Law), *Przegląd Ustawodawstwa Gospodarczego* (Review of Economic Legislation), July-August, 1949, pp. 157–59.

arbitration commissions whose function is to resolve disputes between units in the state-owned sector of the economy. A separate system was envisioned for cooperative organizations. The arbitration commissions which handle disputes within a given ministry are distinct from those dealing with disagreements between enterprises belonging to different ministries. An appeal procedure is provided terminating finally with the appropriate minister or the chairman of the state planning commission, respectively, for the two cases. The commissions may act upon complaint of aggrieved parties, at the request of the state planning commission, or from their own initiative. In the last case they may anticipate frictions and attempt to settle the trouble before it starts.

A particularly important segment of activity of the state arbitration commission consists of mediation in the matter of conclusion of planned agreements for the supply of goods and services and the settling of disputes arising from the performance of these agreements. The law of April 19, 1950, which introduced the requirement of planned agreements, drew heavily on the current Soviet practice in this field.[49] The purpose of the law was to develop a coordinated system of supply and procurement which would assure discipline in the performance of economic plans, make more efficient the cooperation of economic units in planned tasks, and establish a basis for calculating costs of production. The obligation of concluding planned agreements for supply of goods and services extends to nearly all of the socialized sector including the hybrid state-cooperative organizations and the cooperative central boards. The law provided for three types of agreements: (1) general, (2) detailed, and (3) direct. The general agreements are concluded between higher level economic units and specify the contract partners of detailed agreements from among their subordinate enterprises. In the absence of general agreements or in the event that they do not cover an enterprise's entire output or requirements, the lower level economic units must contract directly for the sale or purchase of goods and services. The agreements must be highly specific as to

---

[49] *Dziennik Ustaw*, 1950, No. 21, Item 180. Cf. J. Baranow, "Umowa gospodarcza jako środek wykonania planów państwowych" (The Economic Agreement as a Means of Executing State Plans), *Życie Gospodarcze*, January 1–15, 1950, pp. 21–26. The coverage of the 1950 law was extended to additional units in the economy on May 15, 1953, by order of the State Commission of Economic Planning. *Dziennik Ustaw*, 1953, No. 28, Item 109.

kinds and qualities of goods and services, dates of delivery, prices, and other considerations. A party may seek compensation for losses suffered due to improper performance of the contract provisions. The state arbitration commissions may be called upon to settle precontract differences as well as to decide in cases of claims of nonperformance of agreements.

Other control agencies. Among other control agencies, perhaps the most important are the organs of the local people's councils, the Polish United Workers' Party, and the factory labor councils. Provisions were made to safeguard the management of an enterprise from direct intervention by these organizations, but they may appeal to higher authorities with their grievances. The factory labor council functions as the representative of the employees in discussions with the management in such matters as supervision of work conditions, hiring and firing, and collective bargaining. The decree of February 6, 1945, establishing the councils, further defined their activity to include (1) maintenance of labor discipline, (2) propaganda to increase quantity and quality of output, and (3) social control over production in accordance with instructions from the organs of the State Council.[50] The independent encroachment of the council into management is inadmissible. Disputes between labor and management must be submitted to arbitration boards whose decisions are final. In an endeavor to lower real costs of production, representatives of the factory council, outstanding workmen, technical personnel, and party leaders may meet with the management in production conferences. It appears, however, that such meetings have tended to become time consuming formalities grudgingly attended by the management and without substantial economic results.[51]

The activities of the Special Commission for Combating Waste and Economic Sabotage and other agencies in connection with the administration of price control regulations have been mentioned in Chapter IV.[52] The Special Commission was also charged with investigation and prosecution of violations of legal regulations which threaten the economic life of the country, and especially theft of public property, corruption, bribery, and speculation. In addition

---

[50] *Dziennik Ustaw,* 1945, No. 8, Item 36.

[51] Jan Grzedzielski, "Usprawnienie organizowania narad wytwórczych" (Making Efficient the Organizing of Production Conferences), *Życie Gospodarcze,* March 16–31, 1951, pp. 352–53.

[52] *Supra,* p. 65.

the Commission was authorized to enforce economic discipline over the compulsory associations of private industry, which because of their charters are obliged to observe the obligations arising from the national economic plan as interpreted by the Minister of Industry and Trade.[53]

As part of the reform of the Polish system of justice, the law of July 20, 1950, endowed the office of public prosecutor with supervision over the activity of units of the national economy as regards legality. The prosecutor was charged with watching over the execution of the decree concerning socialist discipline of labor, and he also took over the functions formerly carried out by the Special Commission.[54]

Having largely eliminated capitalist forms of economic organization through socialization of business enterprise, and having introduced centralized economic planning, the Polish government found it necessary to develop an administrative organization and schemes of control to manage the new system and police its efforts in the absence of the automatic coordination effected by prices. For this purpose the Soviet model was liberally copied. The resulting administrative mechanism represents a set of channels radiating from the decision-making center in the Council of Ministers through the ministries and central administrations representing branches of the economy down to the basic production enterprises. Coordination is effected largely by planning, by the requirement of planned agreements for interindustry flows of goods and services, and by the financial supervision by the banking system. To police the operation the state depends on internal supervision by the elements in the chains of command, on a system of incentives for exemplary performance, and on various control elements which cut across the lines of command.

In 1953, after several years of experience, the administrative and control machinery still failed to come up to the desires of the planners. Official criticism indicated that plans were not carried out uniformly; poor interplant cooperation led to breakdowns of delivery schedules and derangement of production; too much attention was being directed to large-scale key enterprises to the neglect of

[53] *Ustawodawstwo Gospodarcze* (Economic Legislation), January, 1949, p. 18.
[54] *Ibid.*, September, 1950, pp. 232–34.

smaller secondary enterprises; and in an attempt to meet immediate production goals, the plans for technological advance were slighted. Notwithstanding the overfulfillment of plans for numbers of employed workers, an excessive amount of overtime was worked. The enterprises near Warsaw received a great deal of attention, but those farther afield received not enough supervision and control.[55] Despite all these difficulties, the planning system developed in Poland made it possible for the government to achieve a rapid rate of growth in a few high priority branches of the economy. This expansion, however, was at the cost of alternative growth in other directions.

[55] *Gospodarka Planowa,* June, 1953, pp. 2–7.

VI

Postwar Economic Plans: Evolution, Over-all Aims, and Performance

Evolution of Postwar Economic Planning

UNDER the Communist ideology which came into full authority in Poland during 1948, the primary aim of the state's economic policy is the transformation of the existing society via "people's democracy" into socialism. In this transition the government exercises dictatorial functions aimed at the control and elimination of capitalist elements and the expansion of the socialized sector to include the entire economy. Producer cooperatives, aided and directed by the state, are the chosen means for converting small-scale production into socialist enterprises. In keeping with the "Leninist-Stalinist science of the state," the government applies the "class struggle," setting up opposing factions in the society, in order to achieve its objectives.[1] The Polish United Workers' Party, which has assigned to itself the role of "advance guard, organizer and leader of the workers class and the Polish nation," endeavors, among other aims, to strengthen the authority of the state, to extirpate all forms of nationalism, and to educate the people in the spirit of socialism as exhibited in the ideology of Marxism-Leninism.[2] Some of the principal aspects of the expansion of state control over the economy have been discussed in Chapters III–V. The present chapter examines the development of Polish postwar economic planning and the results thus far achieved.

In the early postwar years the chief concern of national economic planning in Poland was the restoration of the war damaged economy and the raising of living standards. Later, however, with the growing

[1] "Deklaracja ideowa PZPR" (Ideological Declaration of the Polish United Workers' Party), *Nowe Drogi*, January-February, 1949, p. 124.
[2] *Ibid.*, pp. 15–17.

hegemony of the Communists over the state, primary emphasis was placed upon the expansion of the productive capacity of the country, especially in heavy industry and machine building as the basis for the forced industrialization of the country.[3] Poland, in view of the Polish United Workers' Party, is a constituent part of a monolithic bloc headed by the USSR,[4] and therefore Poland's rising industrial production must be regarded as an increment to the military potential of the Soviet bloc. The original ambitious goals for expansion of production during 1950–55 were set far higher for industry than for agriculture, and at the outset of the period these goals were revised sharply upward. In practice the high priority accorded to expansion of heavy industry was further accentuated at the cost of alternative growth of consumer goods industry and agriculture. By the end of 1953 the Polish government recognized the imbalance between economic sectors that its priorities had induced. For the two remaining years of its long-term plan, 1954–55, the government announced measures to aid the stagnant agricultural sector and to increase the output of consumer goods, and thus to redeem at least in part its pledge to raise the people's scale of living. At the same time the new policy called for continued growth of heavy industry with special attention to its raw material and energy basis.

Partial planning in 1945–46. Although nationalization of large- and medium-scale industry, communications, banking, and other important elements in the national economy did not occur formally until early in 1946, the state in fact came into possession of the key positions in the national economy immediately upon liberation from German occupation. In view of the conditions of destruction and disorganization, the postwar Polish government, although committed to economic planning as an objective, did not find it possible to make a coordinated planning effort until the beginning of 1947. At the outset, the state directed its efforts to the immediate necessities, which were met by improvisation. Nonuniform war devastations caused many bottlenecks in production within plants and industries and between sectors of the economy. The planning authorities, moreover, were inexperienced and did not possess a reliable inventory of the factors of production, established foreign trade rela-

---

[3] Hilary Minc, *Osiągnięcia i plany gospodarcze* (Economic Plans and Achievements), p. 88.

[4] *Ibid.*, p. 87.

tions, or suitable domestic reserves. Primary attention, therefore, was directed toward a rapid restoration of production by overcoming these key obstructions.

A second preparatory approach to economic planning consisted of planning of discrete fields of state industry. The first of such plans was put into effect for the coal industry in April, 1945, and by the fourth quarter of that year planning was extended to other industries under the control of the Ministry of Industry. Such plans at first covered only matters of production and employment, but later included technical questions and supply of materials. By the second half of 1946, these plans encompassed cost and financial planning. Similar sectoral plans concurrently came into effect in communications, reconstruction, and other areas of the national economy, but the totality of these plans did not represent a fully coordinated effort.[5]

A third approach to economic planning during 1945–46 consisted of a partial systematization of national policy with respect to prices, wages, investments, and rationing and allocation of raw materials and articles in short supply. This effort, like the sectoral planning in industry and communications, did not take adequate account of intersectoral relationships. Until April, 1946, the Polish government operated on quarterly budgets, but the remaining three quarters of that year were treated as a unit in the state budget and in the investment plan for the national economy. At the same time the degree of coordination among sectoral plans was increasing, and by the end of 1946, plans were being drafted for the national economy as a whole.[6]

The period of economic reconstruction: 1947–49. The partial planning efforts described above proceeded from an assumption of stability of national income, or at most its variation depending upon factors internal to the discrete area of planning. In contrast to these earlier efforts, economic plans from 1947 to the present time proceed from the assumption of an expanding national income and accordingly shape the plans of the several constituent parts of the economy to the rising level of the total output. This dynamic approach was made possible in the Polish context by the comprehen-

[5] Polish Ministry of Foreign Affairs, Press and Information Department, *Information on Poland*, pp. Hx 2–3.
[6] Czesław Bobrowski, "Kolejny etap" (The Next Stage), *Przegląd Socjalistyczny* (Socialist Review), September 1, 1946, pp. 16–18.

siveness of the planning effort itself and by the prior institutional changes, especially nationalization of important components of the economy, which made it possible for the state not only to designate certain sums for investment but also to control in large measure the allocation of investment funds to particular activities.

At the outset of the Three-Year Plan in 1947, the leaders of the Socialist-Communist coalition regarded the economy of three sectors—state, cooperative, and private—as a stable structure. Hilary Minc, the Minister of Industry and chief Communist spokesman on economic matters, declared on September 21, 1946, that the form, sphere, method, and effects of planning were to be different for each of these sectors. He envisioned central planning and control for the state sector. The cooperative sector, however, was to rule itself autonomously without any question of applying the forms of planning used in the state sector. Instead, the cooperative organizations were to draft their own economic plans on the basis of the economic policy of the national economic plan, and these plans were to be harmonized with the plan for the state sector. As concerns the private sector, comprising peasant farms, handicrafts, various shops, and factories, Minc declared that state influence would be restricted to policies of prices, market regulation, investments, taxation, and finance, without any question of planning in the sense applied to the state or the cooperative sectors. He concluded that the positions occupied by the two socialized sectors were sufficiently important to influence the private sector in the desired directions and thus permit construction of a plan for the entire economy.[7]

Eugeniusz Szyr, a leading Communist economic spokesman, declared in July, 1946, that the state was making a definitive distribution of industry among the three sectors so as to still for all time existing doubts as to the government's intention with regard to private initiative. He asserted that the continuing emphasis on private initiative was based on appreciation of its need in the type of economic model being created in Poland, which was regarded as a synthesis of the pattern of planned economy in the Soviet Union and the positive aspects of the economy of the Western democracies.[8]

---

[7] Polish Ministry of Foreign Affairs, *op. cit.*, p. Hx 2. The cooperatives in Poland are regarded as a second form of socialized economy, the first or higher form being the state-owned enterprises.

[8] *Życie Gospodarcze*, July 15, 1946, pp. 454–55.

Again, in January, 1947, speaking of the limited, definitive nationalization, Szyr emphasized:

The Government of National Unity purposely limited the scope of nationalization of industry, maintaining the right of ownership for millions of small-scale producers, for thousands of smaller capitalist enterprises, for tens of thousands of private trading enterprises.

This was not a temporary concession of a political nature, nor likewise something in the nature of a *peredyshka*,[9] of which the handicraftsmen, industrialists, merchants, and a part of the peasants, misled by enemy propaganda, were so apprehensive. No one even thought of trying collectivization of peasant property, just as no one thought about expropriation of other small private property.[10]

Socialist spokesmen were even more firmly, and apparently more sincerely, in favor of a balanced mixed economy. Oskar Lange in 1946 insisted that the fields of peasant farming, handicraft, and small- and medium-scale industry should remain the terrain of private initiative. He specified that in order to assure a lasting basis for the development of democratic forms of social existence, the Polish economic structure must, among other things, prevent the concentration of economic power either in the hands of private capitalists and landed gentry or in the hands of the state bureaucracy. He was especially fearful of the latter and urged that all centers of economic management should be (1) strictly separated from the administrative-political apparatus of the state as, for example, independent courts are separated from the executive authority, and (2) organized on the basis of democratic self-government and democratic control from below. In particular, democratic control over the socialized part of the economy should be strengthened by the existence of an independent workers' movement, cooperatives, and suitable organizations representing the economic interests of the peasants.[11] Tadeusz Dietrich, the Socialist successor after Czesław Bobrowski to the chairmanship of the Central Board of Planning, likewise concluded that the revolution in Poland should not be widened, but rather stabilized on the basis of several autonomous sectors whose results should be combined into the over-all economic plan. The autonomous play of the sectors should be directed with the aid of

[9] Russian word meaning "breathing spell."

[10] Eugeniusz Szyr, "Inicjatywa prywatna w planie trzyletnim" (Private Initiative in the Three-Year Plan), *Nowe Drogi*, January, 1947, pp. 95–96.

[11] Oskar Lange, "Gospodarcze podstawy demokracji w Polsce" (Economic Bases of Democracy in Poland), *Przegląd Socjalistyczny*, March, 1947, p. 10.

state intervention within limits envisioned in the national economic plan.[12]

Communist dissatisfaction with the autonomy of the private and cooperative sectors appeared early in 1947. Hilary Minc, in discussing the future prospects of state industry, declared that private and cooperative trade were acting against the interests of socialist industry by gaining speculative profits on goods produced in the state sector. In his view, the economy of three sectors began to appear as a temporary expedient on the road to thoroughgoing socialist economic organization, although at this time Minc still did not speak for forthright nationalization of domestic private trade and small-scale industry. The short-range goal was to transform the private capitalism in industry and trade into a species of "state capitalism," wherein ownership would remain private, but the state of "people's democracy" would so regulate and control the private enterprises that they would find it impossible to retain through trading any of the Marxist "surplus product" created in the state-owned sector. Minc held that such an arrangement would give state industry a more completely socialist character. Unless this action were taken, he asserted that state industry would retrogress first to a "state capitalist" type allied with private industry and subsequently to private capitalism. He defined a cooperative not as a type of social structure but rather as an association of small producers which could either operate in connection with the state sector and under state control or serve as a means for dodging state control. He urged the former alternative but made it clear that at best cooperatives even under state control as a form of socialist organization were inferior to state ownership. To make cooperatives the dominant form of socialist property would be a step in the direction of retrogression to capitalism. On the basis of his analysis, Minc concluded that the struggle for completion of the construction of an economic system of "people's democracy" was a sharp and difficult class war.[13]

Although the Socialists tried valiantly to stem the tide toward centralization of economic power, their opposition was futile, and in the course of the ensuing year their party was forced into submission. Some of their leaders, including Oskar Lange and Józef

---

[12] Tadeusz Dietrich, "Gospodarka weilosektorowa" (The Many-sectored Economy), *Przegląd Socjalistyczny*, January, 1947, p. 13.

[13] Hilary Minc, "Charakter i tendencje rozwojowe naszego przemysłu" (Character and Developmental Tendencies of Our Industry), *Nowe Drogi*, May, 1947, pp. 40–44.

Cyrankiewicz, the prime minister, hastened to adopt the Communist ideology and via elaborate self-criticisms to disavow their former beliefs. Indeed, they vied with their erstwhile adversaries in sketching the perspectives of future development toward socialist organization on the Soviet model. The final numbers of the Socialist Party's journal are devoted to self-criticism of the party's former stand for division of economic power among three autonomous sectors and for stability of lines of demarcation between them.[14] Thereafter policy declarations and related discussions are found primarily in the publications of the new Polish United Workers' Party, and they all speak with practically the same voice. An opposition press does not exist in Poland today.

The shape of future economic policy and planning was forecast by Szyr in June, 1948.[15] It called for the most rapid and efficient expansion of socialist elements of the national economy; broadening of the scope of socialized—state, local government, and cooperative —industry; limitation of private capitalist elements and their conversion to elements of "state capitalism"; and gradual inclusion of small-scale peasant and handicraft economy within the framework of the planned economy by means of cooperative forms of organization of sale, supply, and production and by the system of contracting between the state sector and the cooperatives.

The economy of the autonomous sectors quickly yielded to the measures of expanded state control. Although Minc had denied that the state contemplated liquidation or administrative limitation of elements of market capitalism, the private capitalist sector in trade has almost completely disappeared under the rigid controls imposed by the government and the competition of state and cooperative enterprises. Direct planning under the control of the economic ministries was extended in 1949 to cover the economy of cooperatives and local governments, while the activity of private industry, handicrafts, and private construction enterprises in considerable measure was tied to the national economic plan by means of the supply of materials from the directly state-controlled sector.[16] The

---

[14] *Przegląd Socjalistyczny,* October-December, 1948, pp. 63–64.

[15] Eugeniusz Szyr, "Węzłowe zagadnienia naszej polityki gospodarczej" (Key Problems of Our Economic Policy), *Nowe Drogi,* May-June, 1948, p. 82.

[16] Jan Sokołowski, "Rozszerzenie zasięgu planowania w planie roku 1949" (Broadening the Scope of Planning in the 1949 Plan), *Gospodarka Planowa,* September, 1948, pp. 389–93.

hitherto autonomous plans of cooperatives and local government became parts of the departmental plans of relevant ministries and subject to the same planning procedure as state enterprises, although with their own planning organs below the ministerial level.

During 1948 the Central Board of Planning was sharply criticized with regard to its theory and methodology of planning. Czesław Bobrowski, the Socialist chairman of the planning office, envisioned an ideal planned economy as one that could operate without reserves of productive factors under the condition of rapid, efficient decision making by the economic authorities and the assurance that the population would understand these decisions and carry them into effect. He conceded, however, that mistakes in the early stages of planning should be expected in view of the extensive destruction from war and the lack of planning experience. The Polish planned development, in his choice, would avoid both the heroic road of the most far-reaching sacrifices for the future and the "middle class" route seeking only immediate comfort. It would strive, instead, to reconcile care for the person with care for the machine, not forsaking tasks of creating bases for future development and not forgetting realization of real benefits for the population during the course of the plan. Accordingly, the Three-Year Plan would compromise between the aims of reconstruction and transformation of the economy and at the same time have for its chief goal the raising of the standard of living of the population above the prewar level. Bobrowski judged that the reserve of heroism of the present generation had already been strongly exhausted during the war and occupation, but this did not mean that the easy way out should be taken.[17]

The Communists attacked the so-called primacy of consumption in the economic plan. Pointing to the scheme of coordination of plans employed by the Central Board of Planning, in which the leading place was taken by the plan for the national income followed on successive subordinate levels by (1) the plan of consumption and investment, (2) the plan of supply of goods and services, and (3) the plan of agricultural and industrial production, Hilary Minc charged that this revealed the influence of marginal utility or consumer preference theories and certainly was contrary to the

---

[17] Czesław Bobrowski, "Ekonomika i polityka w planie odbudowy" (Economics and Politics in the Plan of Reconstruction), *Przegląd Socjalistyczny*, October, 1946, pp. 8–9.

Marxist theory which emphasized production as the basic economic fact. The real plan of production must become the basis of planning, and the plan of national income must flow as a derivative. Minc accused the Central Board of Planning of combining directly and indirectly planned magnitudes with others that were only predicted, thus giving the whole structure of planning the imprint of the bourgeois theory of business cycles. Planning requires more than goals; it demands assignment of means for fulfilling the plan. The Socialist planners in the Central Board of Planning, according to Minc, by confusing prognosis with planning, had failed to prepare drafts of plans that would mobilize means of execution of the plan.[18]

Eugeniusz Szyr elaborated upon Minc's attack, calling for a massive ideological offensive that would breed new cadres for economic planning thoroughly imbued with Marxist theory. He reiterated Minc's charge of the use of an incorrect, non-Marxist definition of the national income in the Central Board of Planning, which followed the bourgeois practice of counting certain services as productive.[19] Szyr asserted that the theory of primacy of consumption over production and investment was being used to retard the industrialization of the country under the cry of injustice to man, and thus it was contrary to harmonious planned development of productive forces as a means of transition toward socialism. He ridiculed the criticisms directed against overfulfillment of plans and the conception of a plan as an almost perfect work of mathematicians which must be executed exactly 100 percent. The latter would forestall all struggle for exceeding the plan. No plan, he asserted, could foresee all the possibilities hiding in the mobilization of the masses and in their initiative and enthusiasm. These elements appear only during the course of execution of the plan. The long-term plan is only a first approximation, while the full calculation of elements of the plan is to take place only in the course of the struggle to fulfill and exceed the plan. Szyr maintained further that a plan should be a battle assignment and must operate with certain

[18] Hilary Minc, "O właściwe metody planowania w Polsce" (Concerning Proper Planning Methods in Poland), *Nowe Drogi*, March, 1948, pp. 34–36.

[19] See *ibid.*, pp. 28–33. Minc decried, among other things, the practice followed by the Central Board of Planning of counting all of the income originating in trade, personal services, and the services of the public administration as part of the national income. Such practice, in his view, lessened the importance of socialized industry as a source of national income.

variable magnitudes and certain reserves, and these not only the hidden ones, which appear during the course of realization of the plan, but also those established at the start as insurance against unforeseen difficulties. He castigated all "false, harmful, and inimical views," however they might be masked, which reduce to the common denominator of unwillingness to see a growing role of the state in the planned economy. Szyr concluded that the struggle for the planned economy is a class struggle waged on the political, economic, and ideological fronts, a struggle which is simultaneously a fight for Marxist theory and practice of planning.[20]

The Communist criticism of the Central Board of Planning was primarily a restatement of the Communist position with respect to the character of economic planning in Poland. Whereas the Socialists and their representatives in the planning office regarded Poland's revolution as largely completed and favored relatively decentralized planning with substantial autonomy for the private and cooperative sectors and a modest rate of investment with more immediate benefits for the consumers, the Communists had in mind the Soviet model of centralized planning with far-reaching state control over practically all aspects of economic activity and a high rate of investment in productive capacity. A planning office that would serve adequately under one model clearly would be inappropriate for the other. The issue was decided on the basis of political supremacy.

Early in 1949 the Central Board of Planning was abolished in favor of the new State Commission of Economic Planning headed by Hilary Minc as chairman and Eugeniusz Szyr as vice-chairman. Thereafter the development of the Polish planned economy proceeded by forthright reference to the experience of the Soviet Union for guidance. The prime sources of authority for the resolution of problems of economic policy and planning became the works of Marx, Lenin, and Stalin, with sharply increasing prominence being given to the Stalinist approach to socialist construction.

Following the Soviet-Yugoslav dispute and the Cominform decision defining the position that a junior Communist Party should take with regard to the Communist Party of the Soviet Union, the Polish United Workers' Party proceeded to rectify its line on matters of agricultural policy in the light of the Cominform communi-

[20] Eugeniusz Szyr, "Węzłowe zagadnienia naszej polityki gospodarczej" (Key Problems of Our Economic Policy), *Nowe Drogi*, May-June, 1948, pp. 84–86.

que. The Cominform prescription was accepted in full: elimination of the kulak class is possible only on the basis of mass collectivization of agriculture, and the liquidation of the kulaks is an organic component of collectivization.[21] The successful collectivization of agriculture requires long-continued preparatory work by the party, a strengthening of the worker-peasant alliance under the direction of the working class, and expansion of socialist industry to provide machines for collective tillage. Hilary Minc interpreted the decision for the Polish context.[22] If in the building of socialism in Poland a 100 percent increase in industrial output is set as a goal, then the concomitant necessary growth of towns and labor force will require food and other resources which must come from agriculture. An increase of 40 to 50 percent in agricultural output is called for in a short time, and, Minc continued, individual farms cannot meet the requirement. Collectivization is to be accomplished by means of cooperatives, first of supply and sale, and, as soon as tractors and farm tools become sufficiently available, by producer cooperatives organized on a voluntary basis. At the same time the wealthier peasants should be persecuted by class war which entails denying them the right to participate in the direction of municipal and cooperative affairs, a differentially higher tax burden to be enforced by social control of the poorer peasants, obligation to pay "decent" wages to hired help, obligation to participate in helping poorer neighbors with equipment at state-set charges, and a discriminatory policy with respect to the use of equipment from state and municipal machine centers.

The consequences of elimination of the kulaks for collectivization are clear. It removes practically all hope for a peasant's economic betterment through individual endeavor, for to mature into a kulak is to invite elimination. At the same time the initial inducements of tax reductions and other state aids to collective farms place the individual peasant on his small acreage at a disadvange. The hope of the Polish planners is that the peasants will recognize this situation and join in organizing collective farms as quickly as the state provides the necessary equipment. Collectivization of agricul-

[21] "Resolution of the Cominform on the Situation in the Communist Party of Yugoslavia," *Nowe Drogi*, July-August, 1948, p. 17.

[22] *Nowe Drogi*, July-August, 1948, pp. 138–39. The goals for industrial and agricultural output mentioned by Minc in this reference were revised upward in the Six-Year Plan as approved by the Sejm in 1950.

ture not only would place this sector of the economy at the disposition of the state for direct planning, which means that the state could direct what crops to plant and claim its share for urban consumption and export through direct compulsory levies according to acreage and through payment in kind for services of the agricultural machine centers, but also would release peasants for employment in the expanding socialized industry. Initially, however, in order not to discourage peasants from joining collective farms, the official Communist policy declared that the relations between the collective and the state were to be purely market connections.[23]

Basically, the Three-Year Plan remained a plan of reconstruction throughout its course, but, in the field of economic policy for the future, the Polish planned economy showed a quickening drift toward Soviet-type economic organization, policy, and control. With the aim of achieving a full mobilization of reserves of productive forces, the state on one hand sought to perfect its direct control over factors of production, and, on the other, it began to devote greater attention to incentives to raise the quantity and quality of output. Campaigns were set in motion to organize labor competition in production, inculcate socialist labor discipline, and reduce costs of production by means of rationalization and invention on the part of workers. In its final year, the Three-Year Plan was concerned to a large extent with new investments that would give a head start to the "construction of the bases of socialism" in the Six-Year Plan that followed.

The Six-Year Plan. Preparatory work on the long-term plan to follow upon the conclusion of the Three-Year Plan in 1949 was undertaken as early as 1948. At the December, 1948, Unity Congress of the Socialist and Workers' parties, Hilary Minc presented a set of guiding principles for the "preparation of a six-year plan for the expansion and transformation of the Polish economy." In explaining the choice of a six-year period, Minc asserted that the term should be long enough for major investments to come into fruition but yet not so long as to depart from a realistic basis for planning. He added significantly that the choice was influenced by the need to establish uniformity in terminal dates for the long-term plans in the Soviet sphere. Discussing the tempos of expansion of industry, Minc declared that the rates of increase of production realized in the

[23] *Nowe Drogi*, September-October, 1948, pp. 178, 204.

Three-Year Plan could not be matched in the new plan since reconstruction was easier to accomplish than new construction, but he regarded the 11–12 percent annual increase in industrial production as extremely high and requiring a great effort.[24]

A year and a half later the 1948 guiding principles emerged much changed and amplified in the final version enacted as law after having passed through an intermediate version in May, 1949. Pointing to the big changes that were made, Minc explained that the experience gained by the planners and the economy since 1948 justified far higher targets than originally set. He belabored the "very harmful tendency" which held that the fast tempos achieved in industrial production during reconstruction could not be continued in a succeeding period. Minc observed that since 1948 the Polish planners had appropriated the bolshevik methods of planning which proved successful in Russia. He introduced the final version of the Six-Year Plan as a maximal variant based on the most complete exploitation of production capacity, the fullest utilization of technological progress, and the complete mobilization of production reserves in the economy.[25]

Some of the principal changes in the targets of the Six-Year Plan from the guiding principles of December, 1948, to the version finally enacted into law on July 21, 1950, are shown below:[26]

	1955 GOALS AS GIVEN BY:	
	1948	1950
Item and Units	*"Principles"*	*"Law"*
National income (1949 = 100)	170–180	212
Gross investment (1949 = 100)	230–250	350
Gross output of socialized industry (1949 = 100)	185–195	258
Gross output of agriculture (1949 = 100)	135–145	150
Raw steel (million metric tons)	3.8	4.6
Crude petroleum (thousand metric tons)	170	394
Hard coal (million metric tons)	90–95	100
Electric energy (billion kwh)	17.5–18.0	19.3
Tractors (agricultural) (thousands)	10–12	11

[24] Hilary Minc, *Osiągnięcia i plany gospodarcze,* pp. 62–66.
[25] Hilary Minc, "Sześcioletni plan rozwoju gospodarczego" (The Six-Year Plan of Economic Development), *Nowe Drogi,* July-August, 1950, pp. 9–11.
[26] The data for the 1948 version are taken from Hilary Minc, *Osiągnięcia i plany gospodarcze,* pp. 90–108; and for the law, from *Dziennik Ustaw,* 1950, No. 37. Goals under the May, 1949, version stand roughly midway between the initial and the final draft.

The long-term plan formally approved as a law on July 21, 1950, aimed at extensive development of productive forces and a transformation of society toward the goal of socialism. During 1950–51, further institutional change and operational adaptation according to the Soviet model strengthened the role of the state in direct economic planning. Specific measures were introduced to adapt the population to the needs of the planned economy.[27] These included direct controls for limited periods of time over specialized personnel, graduates of vocational schools and higher institutions, members of certain professions, and youth. A comprehensive reform of the educational system adapted the curricula to the needs of the economy and, among other things, provided a prominent place for the study of dialectical materialism. The ideology of Marxism-Leninism was being widely disseminated through all avenues of communication in order to educate new cadres loyal to the regime and implementing its aims.

Since the final formulation of the Six-Year Plan, some of the targets of this plan for the years 1951–53 have been superseded by higher goals in the annual plans, particularly in industry, with a view toward fulfilling the Six-Year Plan in less than six years. For example, the target for gross output of socialized industry in the 1952 national economic plan was set 16.8 percent higher than the level established for that year in the Six-Year Plan.[28] In discussing the new tasks for 1952, Bronisław Minc referred to the threatening international situation as a cause for strengthening the Soviet sphere. In addition to higher tempos for heavy industry and especially machine building, he enjoined the necessity for expanding the output of raw materials—iron ore, copper, and basic chemical raw materials—in preparation for economic warfare.[29]

During the latter part of 1953, following the earlier example set by the USSR and several of the Soviet East European satellites, the Polish United Workers' Party revised its economic policy for 1954–55 to give greater attention than heretofore to the lagging agricultural sector and to increase the output of consumer goods so as to realize at least in part the Six-Year Plan goals for raising the level of consumption. The earlier overriding emphasis on the machinery

---

[27] See *supra*, pp. 70–76.
[28] *Gospodarka Planowa*, March, 1952, p. 3.
[29] Bronisław Minc, "Zmiany w metodologii planowania na r 1952" (Changes in Methodology of Planning for 1952), *Gospodarka Planowa*, July, 1951, pp. 7–8.

and equipment industries was diminished somewhat, added emphasis was put on expansion of the raw material and energy base supporting industry, and investment plans were reoriented to implement the new objectives. By these means the party hoped to redress some of the imbalance between sectors of the economy that its earlier priorities had produced and to gain popular support for its programs. These proposals were subsequently implemented by government measures adopted in December, 1953, and the first half of 1954.

The keynote of the postwar planning effort was full mobilization of productive factors under direct state control to be accomplished by class war against the remaining vestiges of larger elements of private capitalism and by transformation of petty capitalist elements of small-scale production, namely, handicrafts, small-scale peasant agriculture, and household production, into socialist elements by means of state-controlled cooperative organizations. State industry, by concentrating on the output of means of production, primarily sources of energy, metals, and their derivatives such as machines and structural materials, was scheduled to provide the material basis for the transformation of underdeveloped Poland into a modern industrial nation. The relationship between agriculture and industry was to be mutually reinforcing, with industry providing the tools for higher productivity for itself and for collective organization of agriculture on one hand, and with controlled agriculture on the other simultaneously supplying the growing industrial centers with food, raw materials, additions to the labor force made possible by collectivization, and machines and materials financed by export of agricultural products. The developmental effort was to be based primarily upon internal sources of expansion supplemented by foreign trade with the non-Soviet world and by coordinated planning within the Soviet sphere. The Soviet Union was hailed as the main bulwark of support in the construction of the new society by its grant of investment credits and supply of raw materials, machines, technology, and planning experience. Such, in brief, was the character of Polish economic planning as viewed by the Polish planners and implemented by legal enactments and official policy.

That the functioning of the Polish planned economy did not uniformly measure up to the expectations of the economic authorities was apparent in the numerous criticisms and self-criticisms that appeared in the controlled press. The official policy as defined by the Central Committee of the United Workers' Party was not challenged, but its application, especially on lower levels, was the subject of much critical review. Hilary Minc, in summarizing the discussions of the fifth plenum of the Central Committee devoted to an examination of the Six-Year Plan, stated that there was much use of high-sounding phrases with respect to raising labor productivity and lowering costs of production but not enough concrete analyses of difficulties and specific methods of overcoming them.[30] Party members were relying upon legislation to correct breaches of labor discipline and were not making a suitable political effort at the plant level to help the laws work their cure. Minc asserted further that the party comrades were so charmed by the talk of new techniques of production and labor-saving machines that they were discounting the effect long before it had even begun to appear. In many production enterprises the principle of one-man control was being violated by the intrusion of party workers into the affairs of management. Quoting Lenin and Stalin on this matter, Minc called upon party and trade union representatives to observe the new management principle.

Plans and Performance

The drafting of economic plans. Polish planning methodology passed through several stages of evolution, becoming more elaborate at each stage. The content of the economic plans and the methodology employed in the more recent postwar years are illustrated by the outline and instructions for 1952.[31] According to this outline, the plan would consist of (1) a detailed national economic plan, which was not to be published, and (2) a published law concerning the plan and giving its principal objectives. The detailed plan would consist of the following sections:

1. A summary statement
2. A program of production for (a) industry, (b) agriculture and forestry, and (c) communications and transportation

[30] *Nowe Drogi,* July-August, 1950, pp. 216–20.

[31] Bronisław Minc, "Zmiany w metodologii planowania na r 1952" (Changes in Methodology of Planning for 1952), *Gospodarka Planowa,* July, 1951, pp. 7–16. The account which follows is based on this source.

3. A program for development of technology
4. A program of investment and construction
5. A program for consumption, including internal trade, social and cultural services, and communal services and housing
6. A plan of employment and wages
7. A plan of the costs of production
8. A financial program
9. The balance sheet for the national economy
10. Provincial cross sections of the plan
11. A balance of income and expenditure of the socialized economy
12. Norms of use of the more important materials and fuel
13. Material balances and the plan of material-technical supply
14. The plan for foreign trade.

The summary statement includes the basic indexes of the plan showing the growth of gross production, its sources and distribution, and the growth of socialist forms in the economy. Several changes were introduced in 1952 in the planning of industrial production. In the first place, according to the instructions, industrial production not only was considered from the point of view of gross output, including the unfinished products, but also was refined to show commodity production, that is, that part of total output which is actually sold outside the enterprise. This change permitted the planners to relate the plan of industrial production to the plan for trade and to other elements of the over-all plan. Second, the planning of industrial production in terms of current prices was scheduled to find much wider application than heretofore. Output was to be valued both at current prices and in terms of "fixed" or "unchanged" prices. Valuations in terms of current prices would permit comparison of the value of output with its cost of production, and would facilitate relating the plan of industrial production to the plan for trade, to the plan for costs of production, and to the plan for accumulation, or saving. Third, the 1952 plan was to be based on a more up-to-date calculation of production capacity including the increments to capacity appearing in 1951 and 1952. Fourth, the plan was to have a separate section dealing with the introduction of new products which heretofore were included in the over-all plan of production according to quantity. Fifth, the instructions for the 1952 plan introduced a plan of cooperation on direct deliveries for heavy industry, specifying suppliers and purchasers of semimanufactures, parts, and subassemblies, and giving quantities and terms of delivery. Sixth, the plan for capital repairs was to be organically related to the plan of production so that the latter could be based on a better knowledge of dates and duration of major repairs of machinery and other equipment. The national economic plan was to include a list of the most important installations scheduled for major repairs and to provide for supervision over this work. A final major change in planning industrial production in 1952 was the inclusion of an expanded number of technical-economic indexes or coefficients which were linked to and provided a basis for the program of production. These indexes include:[32] (1) coefficients showing the degree of electrification, mechanization, and technical equipment of production, and a grading of equipment to show the share of the most modern elements in the total pool of equipment in production enterprises; (2) indexes of exploitation of productive capacity, such as the output of coal per month per coal-digging machine; (3) norms of use of fuel, electric energy, raw materials, and semimanufactures, as, for example, the amounts of iron ore and coke per ton of pig iron or the amount of coal used per kilowatt hour of electricity generated; (4) indexes of hours of labor consumed per unit output of the more important products; and (5) indexes of quality of output, such as the share of sorted and washed coal in the total output of coal.

In planning the production of agriculture for 1952, the revised methodology called for more detailed breakdowns of gross output showing the unfinished production, the amounts designated for sale outside the producing enterprises, and the sources of production, including individual farms, state farms, producer cooperatives, and state and cooperative machine centers. The method of balances showing requirements against availability was scheduled for wider application in such matters as draft power, seeds, and fertilizers. Similar refinements were projected for forestry operations. Planning of communications and transportation was expected to show wider application of technical planning, and the plan of loadings was to be based on shippers' announcements.

[32] Bronisław Minc, "Program produkcji narodowego planu gospodarczego" (Program of Production of the National Economic Plan), *Gospodarka Planowa,* February, 1952, pp. 23–24.

The program for the development of technology included plans for the introduction of new processes, development of substitutes for materials in scarce supply, mechanization of heavily labor-consuming operations, development of prototypes of new products, expansion of serial production, elaboration of designs for standards and norms, and scientific research and experimentation. The program was to be prepared according to the branches of the economy, giving dates of introduction of new developments and specifying the responsible organizational units.

According to the official instructions, the investment plan for 1952 would place strong emphasis on putting investments into immediate production, and in this connection the plan would include a comprehensive list of projects with binding dates for their completion. Construction and installation work was to be given not only in value units but also in physical terms, such as cubic meters of housing and kilometers of various types of roads. The instructions envisioned wider application of technical-economic norms in construction projects.

Modifications in planning the program of consumption in 1952 were directed toward more refined calculation of regional requirements based on data concerning income and expenditures of the population and aimed at balancing purchasing power against the mass of goods and services available for the market. In the sphere of planned employment and wages, the official instructions provided a new sixfold classification of industrial employees, distinguishing workers, engineering and technical employees, administrative personnel, apprentices, guards, and maintenance personnel, whereas the former classification provided for only two loosely defined groups, namely, production workers and other employees. Labor productivity was to be calculated in value terms per industrial employee and per worker, and indexes of labor productivity in natural units were slated for wider application. The plan of production costs aimed at a reduction of personnel and material costs of production by way of increased skill of workers, more rational organization of production, and improved technology. Specific cost reduction targets were to be set for many of the more important products indicating the planned unit costs and percentage of cost reduction over the previous year.

The financial program for 1952 as the balance of the complete income and expenditure of the financial system included, besides the basic items of the state budget, the credit plan, the budget of the Central Council of Trade Unions, the budget of the State Establishment of Mutual Insurance, and the basic items of the plan for the socialized enterprises. The financial program was related to the balance of income and expenditure of the socialized economy.

One of the most fundamental parts of the Polish economic plan is the balance sheet of the national economy, a statement which reflects the processes of production and the basic proportions of the plan. In 1952 this balance was scheduled to become more comprehensive than in the previous year and to include: (1) a balance of the gross output of all divisions of material production with a breakdown into producer goods and consumer goods, and giving the sources of the product by economic sectors, namely, state-owned enterprises, cooperatives, private small-scale production, and larger capitalist enterprises; (2) a balance showing the connection between industry and agriculture and indicating the supplies of fixed and working capital from industry to agriculture and the agricultural raw materials furnished to industry; (3) a statement of the national income showing origin by divisions of production and by economic sectors as in (1) above; allocation of the national income to individual consumption, collective consumption, and saving, and giving net investment in fixed capital, increase in working capital, and reserves; and distribution of the national income by social classes; (4) a balance of the means of production showing in value terms the requirements for these means and their coverage; (5) a balance of consumer goods giving the total supplies and total requirements, with a division between cities and the countryside; (6) a balance of the total money incomes and expenditures of the population with a quarterly breakdown by provinces; (7) a balance of fixed capital showing changes in total capital and giving a distribution by divisions of the economy; and (8) a balance of the supply of labor.

The programs of production are related to the material balances by means of the norms of use of the more important materials and energy, and the plan of material-technical supply translates the material balances into an operational plan. The plan for foreign trade completes the system by accounting for the external connections of the economy.

Typically, the first step in drafting the economic plan consisted of formulation of the basic outlines of the plan by the Council of Ministers on the basis of general instructions from the Central Committee of the Polish United Workers' Party. The state planning commission translated these basic outlines into goals for the economic ministries and transmitted them with instructions and forms to the appropriate ministries for further elaboration. Before the 1952 plan, the departmental plans continued their journey down the administrative levels gathering greater detail until they reached the production enterprises, at which point the journey was reversed. At each stage counterproposals could be considered for adjustment. The detailed plans of the lower levels served as the basis of the summary plans at higher levels and eventually for the over-all national economic plan. Any change in the latter would require changes on lower levels and sometimes even complete revision.[33]

Polish experience in drafting the national economic plan has not been satisfactory from the point of view of the planners themselves. Because of the cumbrous ladder-like scheme of dependence of economic units upon the contributions of antecedent units, any significant adjustment in the goals of production or consumption would require a manifold reworking of plans on lower levels. Although the instructions for drafting the 1952 plan aimed at the elimination of the numerous trips up and down the ladder of economic administration by having the production enterprises submit only the necessary technical-economic data to enable the ministries to prepare the departmental plans on the basis of a skeleton outline submitted by the planning commission, with the detailed elaboration of operational plans by enterprises to come after the approval of the national economic plan, in practice this intention was poorly realized. Criticism of the experience in drafting the plan for 1953 indicated that the central administrations in the ministries produced large volumes of technical calculations but did not give enough attention to key problems. The practice developed that each change resulting from analysis of a draft on higher levels led to recalculation of plans in the enterprises, eventuating in more than a dozen versions of the draft of the plan, each elaborated anew in all the planning units. As a result, the situation was adjudged worse than in the preceding

[33] Bronisław Pilawski, "Plan techniczno-przemysłowo-finansowy na rok 1952" (The Technical-Industrial-Financial Plan for 1952), *Życie Gospodarcze*, January 14, 1952, pp. 67–69.

year.[34] Typically, the Sejm has approved the national economic plan only toward the end of the first quarter or the beginning of the second quarter of the year for which the plan applies.

In discussing the instructions of the Presidium of the Government for the preparation of the 1954 plan, the journal of the state planning commission pointed out that by 1952 the Polish planners had mastered the Soviet *methodology* of planning and did not need to introduce any further substantial changes. On the other hand, the Polish *procedures* in drafting the economic plans still differed in many respects from the current Soviet practice and could profit from a closer approximation to the Soviet model.[35] These instructions required that the state planning commission present to the Presidium of the Government by mid-July an outline of the plan for the coming year, specifying only the key problems, chief goals, and the rates of development of the various parts of the national economy. On the basis of the outline approved by the Presidium, the ministries, including the central administrations, would elaborate departmental plans for all the relevant sections of the national plan, thus relieving lower levels from making drafts of the plan. These subordinate levels, however, were expected to contribute proposals embodying norms of use of the more important raw materials, semimanufactures, labor, and equipment; unit cost calculations for the more important products; and a variety of technical and economic data and suggested goals of activity. The ministries would prepare their drafts using these materials as well as their own collections of data.

The directive emphasized that preparatory work on the 1954 plan should begin in May, 1953, in the enterprises and ministries without awaiting the government-approved skeleton draft of the plan. In their preparatory work the enterprises should base themselves on the Six-Year Plan goals for the given year, the orders they would have already received for the next year, and other relevant information. Mechanical calculation of requirements with an eye toward easy fulfillment of goals was discouraged. Such practices in the past led to total requirements for labor, machines, and materials far beyond the capacity of the economy to supply them and entailed fre-

---

[34] Roman Zaleski, "Uwagi o sposobie opracowania narodowego planu . . ." (Observations about the Manner of Preparing the National Plan . . .) *Gospodarka Planowa*, April, 1953, p. 7.

[35] *Ibid.; Gospodarka Planowa*, June, 1953, p. 54.

quent revisions of drafts of plans. Ministries were expected to begin work on their draft plans on the basis of the Six-Year Plan assumptions, tentative agreements with sales organizations and collaborating ministries, and special directives of the government. Final formulation of the drafts proposed by ministries would proceed by taking account of the data and proposals submitted by central administrations and leading enterprises from below and the draft outline of the plan from above. Ministries were expected to submit their proposals to the planning commission by mid-September.

At the same time that the ministries prepared their plans, the state planning commission would prepare its independent draft of the over-all plan basing itself on data available in the commission, reports of plan fulfillment in the current year, proposals submitted by central administrations and leading plants, and field inquiries. Although the planning commission and the ministries would draft independently, contacts between them were to be maintained.[36] Differences between the drafts of the commission and the ministries were to be examined in the commission with the participation of the ministries. The drafting instructions provided that the draft of the over-all national economic plan submitted by the commission to the Presidium of the Government should contain an annex giving the drafts submitted by ministries and the presidiums of the provincial people's councils as regards local economic activity, together with an explanation and justification of the differences by the unreconciled parties. These differences were then to be settled by the Presidium of the Government.[37] Formulation of detailed operational plans by enterprises would take place after the government approved the over-all economic plan. The instructions for drafting the 1954 plan aimed at the completion of the plan before the beginning of the year. At all levels of the economic administration, the drafters of plans were enjoined to keep in mind the most probable outcome of economic activity in the current year and the goals of investment for the following year.

Postwar plans for the development of the various sectors of the economy were expected to take account of all the interconnections between branches of production and to conform to the real possibilities of growth. Tempos set for particular branches were

---

[36] Zaleski, *op. cit.*, p. 9.
[37] *Ibid.*, p. 9; *Gospodarka Planowa*, June, 1953, p. 57.

guided by the goals set by the party and the government.[38] The demands of the economy for the more important producer goods were established on the basis of the planned outputs of goods and services by the application of norms of use of the various inputs into production. Requirements for labor were similarly established by the use of input coefficients.

The production plans for enterprises in general set goals in physical units and specified the full assortment and quality. In the plans of higher levels, however, the goals of production in physical units were given only for the more important articles or for commodity groups. At the highest level, the national economic plan took account of production in kind of all deficit articles[39] having economy-wide significance and especially of the production of heavy industry. The program of production in natural units served as the basis for the elaboration of material balances for the basic commodities and for establishing proper proportions for production in the various branches of the economy.

In the light of numerous failures of enterprises to fulfill the goals of assortment in production in 1951, the plans for the succeeding years provided for closer supervision over flows of semimanufactures and components of final products between enterprises. In heavy industry in particular, the 1952 plan specified the suppliers and consignees, the quantity to be shipped, and the terms of delivery.

In its final form, the national plan consisted of a set of balanced estimates which sought to reconcile production with the demands of consumption and investment, taking account of foreign trade and domestic reserves. In practice the performance of the economy was by no means as closely integrated as the planning methodology would suggest. Uneven fulfillment of production goals has been common, and the lack of synchronization of purchasing power and the supply of consumer goods at the existing prices led to persistent inflation in the postwar period which the government tried to meet by rationing and price control up to 1949 and again in 1951, by monetary reform in 1950, and by drastic revision of prices and wages coupled with the abolition of rationing in 1953.

[38] Bronisław Minc, "Program produkcji narodowego planu gospodarczego" (The Program of Production of the National Economic Plan), *Gospodarka Planowa*, February, 1952, pp. 14–29. The description of planning methodology which follows is based on this source.

[39] Articles in short supply.

The national economic plans were prepared for periods of several years and also for annual periods, the latter specifying the scope and manner of carrying out the long-term plan within the given year. The provisions of the long-term plan which related to the first year of the period usually were regarded as the national economic plan for that year. The tasks set for a given year in the long-term plan, however, could be modified during the period of the plan. Failure to publish detailed economic plans and the details of the methodology used in the construction of aggregative measures of performance contributes to the difficulty of analyzing Polish planning.

The role of consumers' preferences in deciding what is to be produced. Polish economic plans show an awareness of the interdependence of the various sectors of the economy, and, more particularly, of the complementarity of production in the different branches of activity. This awareness followed from the recognition of the existence of input-output relationships and the fact that if the output of a few key products is established, a chain of supply and demand relations must follow. Some of the difficulties associated with the planning of production and distribution in Poland arose from the two possible sources of decision making regarding the volume and assortment of production, namely, consumers' preferences and the planners' preferences.

Oskar Lange described models of a socialist economy wherein either source of decision making could be the determining factor, but in which the implementation of the preferences occurred via the price-setting activity of the planning authority. In these models the consumers have freedom of choice of occupation and in consumption, the prices are accepted as given without any attempt on the part of the consumers or the managers in the socialized industries to modify them, and the managers of enterprises and industries faithfully follow rules which require that the factors of production be blended in such fashion that the average cost be minimized under the effective schedule of prices, and the scale of output be set at the level where the marginal cost equals the price. The role of the planning authority consists of (1) setting the prices by trial and error so that demand is equilibrated to supply, and (2) determining the rate of investment by means of the retention of profits from the operation of socialized industry and the distribution of this accumulated capital through appropriate manipulation of the interest rate. In the model wherein the consumers' preferences are decisive, the only arbitrary factor on the part of the planning authority is the regulation of the rate of collective accumulation and investment. In the case where the planners' scales of preferences are decisive, the distribution of consumer goods in the presence of consumers' freedom of choice in spending their incomes would require two price systems, one to govern production under the planners' preferences, and the other to insure the distribution of the available consumer goods. In each system the planning authority would adjust the prices to insure equilibrium of supply and demand. A third alternative would rule out freedom of choice of occupation and in consumption, the allocation of labor taking place by assignment and the distribution of consumer goods by rationing, but this would be successful only where the standard of living was so low as to make welcome any increase whatever in the rations.[40]

The Polish planning experience shows the application of some of the elements described above as well as others in the formulation of production decisions. Extensive rationing of essential consumer goods was continued after World War II until the end of 1948. Such rationing was never universal, but amounted primarily to a subsidy to certain groups of the nonagricultural population depending on the wages earned in the nationalized sector, the physical intensity of the work, and other factors. In effect, the rationing scheme established a two-price system for consumer goods. In one market the price was determined by the operation of supply and demand, and in the other the price was set at an artificially low level for purchases of limited quantities of goods by the ration card holder, who could make additional purchases to the limit of his income on the free market. The deficit incurred by the state on the ration account was covered by its profits from its sales in the free market at prices which exceeded the costs of production.[41] In the free market the preferences of consumers influenced the production decisions, especially in the private sector, but had little effect upon the government's decisions. Within the rationed goods' market with artificially low prices there was no problem in disposing of the necessities of

[40] Oskar Lange and Fred M. Taylor, *On the Economic Theory of Socialism,* pp. 72–96.

[41] United Nations Relief and Rehabilitation Administration, *Operational Analysis Papers, No. 44, Finance in Poland,* pp. 5–7.

life which were made available to card holders. The period was one of great scarcity, and production was directed first of all toward essential commodities without close regard for matching costs against prices. During this period and continuing up to the present time, the choice of occupation was not completely free since the state in certain instances exercised the right to assign workers for limited periods of time to certain jobs and to particular geographic areas.[42]

As political power became more and more consolidated in the hands of the Communist Workers' Party, the preferences of consumers in guiding the production of industry steadily gave way before the preferences of the planning authority, which were guided by the desires of the party. In planning the program of production, the Polish methodology separates producer goods from consumer goods. The needs of the former are established in the framework of proportions set for the development of different branches, taking account of the economic interconnections between particular sectors and aiming at the "fastest possible" expansion of production. The planned output of consumer goods is geared to the planned growth of purchasing power of the population. In establishing the production of particular articles of consumption, the methodology specifies that account should be taken of "rational" norms of consumption and changes in the structure of demand.[43]

In view of the high rate of gross investment financed by various forms of taxation and public saving, and in particular by the application of varying rates of turnover tax on the sale of consumer goods, the role of consumers' preferences in deciding the magnitude of output of particular goods was diminished. The application of a turnover tax in varying levels in effect divorces the stimuli arising from consumers' preferences from the attention of producers who, to the extent that their production programs are not specified in detail as to quantity and assortment, are guided by planned prices reflecting current costs[44] or by fixed planning prices of an earlier period. The system of fixed prices used in Poland for planning production consisted of the 1937 prices with various adjustments.[45] The disadvan-

[42] Cf. *supra,* pp. 70–75.
[43] Bronisław Minc, "Program produkcji narodowego planu gospodarczego" (The Program of Production of the National Economic Plan), *Gospodarka Planowa,* February, 1952, p. 15.
[44] *Infra,* p. 242.
[45] *Infra,* p. 136.

tage in the use of these prices is that they fail to reflect the current structure of costs. From the point of view of indexes in fixed prices, enterprises have an opportunity to concentrate upon the output of products which with relatively small current cost outlays show relatively large values in fixed prices, thus violating the production plan as regards assortment.[46] By 1951, however, the advantages of using current prices in planning were more fully recognized, and these prices were slated for wider application in the 1952 plan.

The attempt to predict the demand for particular consumer goods at the state-set retail prices and on this basis to specify the quantity and assortment for industry met with uneven success both in large-scale industry and in small-scale local industry, which was expected to be more sensitive to shifts in demand. The failure to produce a proper assortment of goods in small-scale state enterprises and co-operatives was shown by the growing residue of unsold goods or unseasonal ones. In state industry, if the status on January 1, 1950, be taken as 100, then the index of unsold goods for January 1, 1951, and March 31, 1951, stood at 159 and 221, respectively. For cooperative industry, the index for January 1 and May 31, 1951, increased respectively from 100 to 157.[47]

Similarly, an article in a leading economic journal reported that in 1951, light industry widely failed to meet its plans for variety in assortment, especially of goods destined for sale in rural areas.[48] For example, the goals of assortment in 1951 in cotton textiles were met only about 96 percent, in knitted wear in some months barely 80 percent, and in stockings even as low as 73 percent. Since these are average figures, and in practice the assortment for the village was the most slighted, it appears that nonurban preferences were not adequately met. The same source complained that in many establishments the execution of the plan as regards assortment took last place while the main effort to fulfill the plan quantitatively

[46] Bronisław Minc, "Program produkcji narodowego planu gospodarczego" (The Program of Production of the National Economic Plan), *Gospodarka Planowa*, February, 1952, p. 20. The managers of enterprises are under special pressure to fulfill plans quantitatively, and production goals were set in fixed prices.

[47] Adam Żebrowski, Minister of Small-Scale Industry and Handicraft, "Uwagi o planowaniu terenowym w drobnym przemyśle" (Remarks on Local Planning in Small-Scale Industry), *Gospodarka Planowa*, August, 1951, p. 7.

[48] Grzegorz Złotnicki, "Przestawienie asortymentowe w premyśle dla zaspokojenia potrzeb wsi" (Shifts in Assortment in Industry for Satisfying the Needs of the Village), *Życie Gospodarcze*, January 26, 1952, pp. 120–22.

overshadowed considerations of quality and assortment. Frequently the plans of assortment were established carelessly and without sufficient regard for the demands of the distributive apparatus, which often failed to receive what it had ordered.

Recognition of the poor connection between demand in the countryside and the supply which should be forthcoming to meet it brought forth a resolution by the Presidium of the Government on December 1, 1951, directed toward improvement of the distribution of goods and at the same time ordering a correction in the plan of supply from industry with the possibility of widening the assortment of goods produced for the village.[49] The resolution obligated the textile industry to orient its production toward an appropriate assortment for the village with a broad range of colors, designs, and qualities demanded in particular regions of the country, and similarly it directed the Ministry of Small-Scale Production and Handicraft to designate in the various provinces of the country particular plants which would produce goods for the village needs. The implementation of the government's order, however, met with obstacles. In the two months that elapsed since the order was issued, both the Ministry of Light Industry and the Ministry of Small-Scale Industry and Handicraft waited without results for precise orders for the village market. Meanwhile, the cooperative distributive network, which handles nearly all of the retail trade in the village, was busy preparing analyses of local demand in an effort to derive a pool of goods required by the village, an effort which should have been made long ago, according to the article. The blame for the lack of adequate knowledge of the structure of the village market in part was placed on the Institute of Trade and Collective Feeding, which had devoted all its efforts toward analysis of economic phenomena in the cities and only expected to begin similar analyses for the village market in 1952. This shortcoming hindered the cooperative distributive network and made it necessary for this network to carry through a new analysis, which, the article further complained, failed to take account of the specific regional requirements and the diversity of needs and purchasing power in various areas, but proceeded instead on the basis of population statistics and the previous year's experience. In the meantime the production establishments proceeded with approved monthly and, in some cases, quarterly plans

[49] *Ibid.*, p. 121.

which failed to take account of the shifts in demand, and which the plants were loathe to change in view of the completed arrangements for production.

Criticism of the poor adjustment of consumer goods production to the preferences of consumers continued into 1953 and 1954. Poor quality of goods, their limited assortment, crude finish, bad packing, and failure to meet consumers' tastes are reiterated in these complaints.[50] One writer indicated that a single person, an official of the clothing central at Łódź, decided what models of ready-to-wear clothing should be produced,[51] apparently without consultation with trading outlets concerning the quality, sizes, and assortment of production. The result, he stated, was a shortage of desirable merchandise on the market and at the same time an overloading of warehouses with unpopular items. Local small-scale enterprises were rebuked for their failure to cater to local demands. During the first nine months of 1953 such enterprises under the supervision of provincial people's councils carried out their plans for assortment of production only 51 percent, and cooperative production enterprises achieved only 44 percent of their assortment plans.[52] These enterprises in many cases allegedly preferred to manufacture producer goods in support of large-scale socialized industry rather than cater to local consumers.

Production of consumer goods in Poland, however, could not proceed wholly in disregard of consumers' preferences simply because the consumer could refuse to buy. The necessary corrections in assortment did not take place through the automaticity of the price mechanism influencing the immediate producers' decisions, but administratively through a more precise specification of the assortment which would be likely to meet with the consumers' favor. The planned assortment had to be enforced administratively since the price system which the producers faced inclined them to modify the prescribed assortment in order to fulfill or overfulfill their production plans in value terms. In view of the continuing complaints, it appears that the enforcement of planned assortment of consumer goods production was ineffective.

Polish economic information. The increasing effectiveness of the

---

[50] Polish Embassy, Washington, *Press Release,* March 22, 1954, pp. 22–23.

[51] Władysław Matwin in *Nowe Drogi,* November, 1953, p. 146.

[52] *Życie Gospodarcze,* November 15, 1953, p. 1175.

control of the Communist Workers' Party over the affairs of the Polish state is reflected in the tightening of control over economic information. A decree of October 26, 1949, concerning state and official secrets, is designed to prevent unauthorized disclosure of information about the magnitude and character of production, direction and localization of investment, technical methods of production, price policy, public finance measures, import and export, and other areas of economic activity.[53] The decree established penalties ranging up to ten years' imprisonment to insure compliance with its provisions. While the amount of information that continued to be published was substantial, several important statistical series were discontinued or modified so as to reveal less detailed information. New series have been introduced and the content of certain indexes changed, making earlier years of a given series not strictly comparable with the most recent years. In many cases, goals and results of economic plans are stated purely in relative terms; absolute figures, however, are available for many basic items of output.

In view of the continuing socialization of remaining elements of private enterprise, the output of the socialized sector was increased thereby without a corresponding change in the national product. Similarly, certain items of agricultural, handicraft, and household production which initially had not entered into official statistics were later replaced by factory-processed items which entered the official series. In view of the shift of population to socialized non-agricultural pursuits and the increasing employment of women in industry under the postwar plans, the official index of production of consumer goods probably was substantially inflated without a corresponding real increase in national output.

Polish postwar official indexes of production usually refer to gross output. The gross output of a production unit, however, takes no account of inputs from other units, and therefore the total gross output of a sector of the economy, defined as the sum of gross outputs of production units, is affected by changes in the organization of enterprises, merger tending to lower the total and atomization and specialization to increase it. In order to deal with this problem the Polish planning authorities introduced the concept of typical semi-manufactures, which are included in the gross value of production

---

[53] *Przegląd Ustawodawsta Gospodarczego* (Review of Economic Legislation), December, 1949, pp. 241–43.

independently of whether they are consumed internally in an enterprise or are sold. Bronisław Minc stated that the number of typical semimanufactures to be included in gross output according to the instructions for 1952 was to be smaller than in earlier years and, in addition, only certain enterprises where the typical semimanufactures are specially significant would be allowed to include them in gross production.[54] By implication it would appear that the indexes of gross output in previous years had been inflated on this score. The production indexes and national income figures presented below must also be considered with the additional caution related to the shift in boundaries and the resulting change in production potential.[55]

As a consequence of the patterning of the Polish economic planning and reporting on the Soviet model, the criticisms of Soviet statistics are increasingly applicable to the official Polish data. Whereas the Soviet indexes up to 1951 relied on 1926–27 prices, the Polish series similarly used 1937 prices. In that year relative prices were disadvantageous to the agricultural sector, and their application in post-World War II years tends to magnify the output of industry relative to agriculture. Moreover, as in the Soviet experience under the First and Second Five-Year Plans, Polish industry in the postwar period entered upon large-scale production of many articles formerly produced in small quantities or not at all, and the valuation of such output at the "unchanging" or "fixed" prices of an earlier period very likely could give an upward bias to the gross value of industrial production. The so-called fixed prices used in computing Polish indexes of output appear in fact to have been quite variable before March, 1949. According to Stanisław Róg, these prices were to be based on the effective prices of 1937, but their application in industry possessed a series of shortcomings.[56] First of all, these prices were not uniformly prepared by the various central administrations of industry. In some cases, a series of articles of the same kind and same quality produced by enterprises under different central administrations were valued at different prices. The

---

[54] Bronisław Minc, "Program produkcji narodowego planu gospodarczego" (Program of Production of the National Economic Plan), *Gospodarka Planowa*, February, 1952, p. 18.

[55] See *supra*, Chapter II.

[56] Stanisław Róg, "Ceny niezmienne" (Fixed Prices), *Życie Gospodarcze*, July 1–31, 1949, pp. 565–66.

source stated further that for certain articles the fixed prices were set too high, as, for example, for coal and metallurgical products. Moreover, in many cases the "fixed" prices were changed even during the course of a year. Finally on March 15, 1949, the Economic Committee of the Council of Ministers directed the State Commission of Economic Planning to prepare a catalogue of fixed prices on the basis of certain principles set forth in the order. These provided that the fixed prices to be prepared should be based on the fixed prices used in industry in 1948, the latter being based on average prices of 1937 realized by producers at wholesale, f.o.b. the factory, not including excises. On the basis of this instruction, uniform fixed prices were set for about 450 items. Certain corrections were introduced which lowered the price of coal and metallurgical products. The catalogue was regarded as incomplete, however, and supplements were expected to be added shortly afterward in order to cover articles so far not included and to correct certain items. Prices on articles hitherto not produced were to be computed on the basis of calculated costs of the group of articles most closely related in a technological sense.

The effect of 1937 prices upon the composition of Polish national income is shown in the official calculation for 1947. According to 1937 price weights, the shares of industry and agriculture in the national income for 1947 amounted to 43.7 and 23.3 percent, respectively, whereas 1947 price weights for the same year placed the shares at 35.3 and 37.7 percent, respectively, for industry and agriculture.[57] With industry expanding at a much faster rate than agriculture under the postwar plans, the use of 1937 prices would tend to show a faster rate of increase of the national product than would the more recent prices. Although the "fixed prices" used after 1949 reportedly "correct" the 1937 prices,[58] it appears that industry is still being favored by the selected prices. In the annual plans for the years 1950 through 1952, the contribution of industry to the national product was set at 44.0, 49.4, and 53.0 percent, consecutively.[59] A part of this represents the more rapid growth of indus-

[57] *Rocznik statystyczny—1949* (Statistical Yearbook—1949), p. 27.

[58] *Ibid.* "The correction is based on smoothing out the level of industrial prices through lowering the prices of articles of cartelized industry and on adjusting the agricultural prices to the level of industrial prices. Moreover, the fixed prices do not include excises."

[59] *Dziennik Ustaw,* 1950, No. 21, p. 232; 1951, No. 18, p. 178; and *Gospodarka Planowa,* March, 1952, p. 6.

try compared to other sectors, but a considerable part appears to be due to the use of relative prices more favorable to industry than, for example, the 1947 prices.[60]

Economic development under postwar plans. In comparison with Poland's development from 1913 to 1939, the results achieved after World War II are impressive in industry, but much less so in other sectors of the economy, especially agriculture. Up to 1939 Poland had not progressed very far beyond the level of production achieved in 1913, although important steps were taken toward unifying the country economically and lifting it from its relatively underdeveloped status. However, the absolute production of many basic industrial products in 1938 was still below the 1913 level, despite an increase of about 20 percent in industrial output from 1928 to 1938.[61] The economy failed to solve the pressing problems of surplus agrarian population and cyclical urban unemployment, and World War II intervened before the ambitious state plan for industrialization could get well under way. The rapid development after World War II must be viewed in the light of the physical changes induced by the war and the institutional changes culminating in national economic planning. Under the first factor, Poland's population, shrunken by about one third, was displaced westward into a richer environment, wherein, by reattaining the prewar level of production in present boundaries, the population could greatly increase its national product per capita. Secondly, the complex of institutional changes resulted in the emergence of a dictatorial government dedicated to rapid economic development and armed with tools to insure compliance with its decisions.

The official national income figures shown in Table 10 were computed according to a Marxist definition which excludes services not directly connected with material production. Since the output of these services very probably increased at a much lower rate than production in other sectors, their inclusion would tend to depress

[60] If the 1947 sector contributions to national income at 1947 prices be advanced to 1949, using the indexes of expansion of value added by sectors computed at 1937 prices, then in 1949 the contribution of agriculture is still slightly greater than that of industry. Using 1947 sector weights based on 1937 prices, however, would show industry accounting for about 45 percent of the national income, or nearly twice the share of agriculture. (See *Rocznik statystyczny—1949,* p. 27, for the estimated indexes.)

[61] *Supra,* p. 11. The 1913 production of coal, crude petroleum, lead, zinc, pig iron, and steel was above the 1938 level (*Mały rocznik statystyczny—1939* [Little Statistical Yearbook—1939], pp. 128–29).

the rate of growth of national product.[62] Moreover, the "fixed prices" used in official national income calculations magnify the contribution of Poland's rapidly expanding industry and diminish the contribution of stagnant agriculture. Until more is known about the prices and methodology used in the official computations, the Polish indexes must be regarded with reserve.

The Polish official indexes of national income cannot be directly used for international comparisons; however, they permit certain inferences concerning the growth of the Polish economy. Table 10 shows that the annual rate of growth of the economy was very rapid through 1950 but that it declined sharply thereafter. The rapid expansion in the early postwar period can be attributed in large measure to the added industrial capacity afforded by the territories acquired from Germany, to the high efficiency of capital investment in increasing production during the period of reconstruction, to the rapid expansion of urban employment made possible by the reserves of unemployed labor, and to the high rate of saving enforced by the government to support its investment program. The rate of growth of national income achieved in the period 1950–53 failed to come up to the expectations of the Six-Year Plan.[63] In view of the rapid exhaustion of labor reserves and the revised economic policies promising greater benefits to consumers and a reduced share of the national income to investment, the annual rate of growth may be expected to decline further in 1954–55. Indeed, the increases of industrial and agricultural output for 1955 over the 1953 level, 23 percent and 10 percent, respectively, as given in the revised plans adopted at the end of 1953, imply that the Six-Year Plan target for national income will not be reached by a considerable margin. An increase on the order of 30 percent would be necessary to reach the target, but the two major sectors contributing to national income have much lower goals.

The composition of the Polish national product changed from the preponderance of agriculture in prewar output to that of industry in postwar. In 1938, according to an estimate in prices of that year,

---

[62] For example, a United Nations estimate for 1948 taking account of these services showed Polish national income about 6 percent below 1938 instead of 6 percent above as in Table 10. The UN estimate was based on 1938 prices which probably were close to the adjusted 1937 prices used in the Polish official figure. (Economic Commission for Europe, *Economic Survey of Europe in 1948*, p. 235.)

[63] *Nowe Drogi*, October, 1953, p. 28.

Table 10

POLISH NATIONAL INCOME, OFFICIAL ESTIMATES

Unit	1938[a]	1947	1948	1949	1950	1951	1952	1953	1955[b]
Billion zlotys[c]	15.4	13.4	16.3	19.2	23.2	25.9	28.5	31.3	40.7
1938 = 100	100	87	106	125	151	168	185	203	264

Sources: See Appendix A. The Polish definition of national income excludes services not directly connected with material production.

  [a] Prewar boundaries.

  [b] Six-Year Plan goal.

  [c] 1938–49 in fixed prices; for remaining years see notes in Appendix A.

agriculture accounted for about 55 percent of the total output of the two sectors.[64] However, in 1947, on the basis of 1937 prices, industry represented about 65 percent of the combined output, although at 1947 prices the two sectors were about equal.[65] The 1951 economic plan scheduled the following percentage division of national income to be realized in the course of the year: industry and handicraft—49.4; agriculture and forestry—29.3; construction—5.8; communications and transport—4.5; and other—11.0.[66] The prices were not specified, but appear to be the "fixed prices" based on prices of 1937. The role of the handicrafts in the national income is relatively unimportant, amounting to 4 to 6 percent in 1947 in prewar and postwar prices, respectively,[67] and a smaller share thereafter.

The share of the socialized sector in the national income grew from 56 percent in 1947 to 76 percent in 1953.[68] This increase represents partly a growth in the output of the socialized sector and partly the socialization of additional elements of the economy, especially internal trade. Within the socialized sector in 1947, the activities of the central state authorities, local governments, and cooperatives accounted for 88.5, 3.8, and 7.7 percent of the sector's output, respectively.[69] After the reorganization of the cooperative movement

[64] Centralny Urząd Planowania (Central Board of Planning), *Narodowy plan gospodarczy* (National Economic Plan), p. 119.

[65] *Rocznik statystyczny—1949*, p. 27. The slight change in relative prices from 1937 to 1938 does not destroy the significance of the comparison.

[66] *Dziennik Ustaw*, 1951, No. 18, Item 146, Art. 104.

[67] Główny Urząd Statystyczny (Central Statistical Office), *Dochód narodowy polski—1947* (Polish National Income—1947), p. 16.

[68] *Ibid.*, p. 18, for 1947; *Gospodarka Planowa*, March, 1954, p. 6, for 1953. The prices apparently are 1937 prices for 1947, and unspecified "comparable prices" for 1953. The socialized sector includes cooperatives.

[69] Główny Urząd Statystyczny, *Dochód narodowy polski—1947*, p. 18.

in 1948 and the extension of centralized control over the local governments' economy in 1949, the divisions within the socialized sector became much less significant.

Table 11

INVESTMENT AS A PERCENTAGE OF POLISH NATIONAL INCOME, SELECTED YEARS, 1938–55

	1938	1947	1949	1950	1951	1952	1953	1954	1955
Percent (1)	12.7	19.0	21.8	22.7[a]	25.0[a]				28.0[a]
(2)				27.2	28.1	26.9	25.1	21.2[b]	19.8[b]

Sources: 1947 taken from Kazimierz Secomski, *Podstawowe Zadania Planu Sześcioletniego* (Basic Tasks of the Six-Year Plan), p. 55. Data for other years in line (1) are taken from *Życie Gospodarcze*, February 1–15, 1951, p. 134. Figures in line (2) were given by Bolesław Bierut, *Nowe Drogi*, October, 1953, p. 28. The prices though not specified are apparently "fixed prices."
  [a] Six-Year Plan goals.
  [b] Revised goals announced in October, 1953.

Polish postwar economic development depended primarily on domestic saving, enforced chiefly by tools of public finance and expended through state investment plans. As may be seen from Table 11, the share of national income allocated under the Six-Year Plan to total investment, including increments to fixed capital, working capital, and various reserves and stockpiles, was expected to increase from about 22 percent in 1949 to 28 percent in 1955. In the performance of the plan, however, the actual allocation to investment was raised to about 27 percent of the national income in 1950, and 28 percent in 1951, and then it declined to 25 percent by 1953. As part of the revised economic policy established in October, 1953, investment in 1954–55 was expected to remain at the same absolute level as in 1953, but as a percentage share of the national income it was expected to decline to 19.8 percent by 1955.[70]

Since the earlier postwar state investment plans were primarily concerned with reconstruction, which involved principally capital repairs, and the later plans gave increasing emphasis to growth of fixed capital, the outlays for successive years are not fully comparable. They do, however, all the more strongly indicate the great increase in productive capacity envisioned in the Six-Year Plan. The

[70] The national income definition used by the Polish sources for this table excludes certain services not directly connected with production, and therefore the percentage share of investment is higher than it would be under a more inclusive definition of national income.

role of new investment in the state investment plans grew steadily, as shown in the following percentage shares in the planned total outlays: 1946—7.0; 1947—16.0; 1948—34.5.[71] In 1950 a large part of the capital repairs in the socialized sector were transferred from the investment plan to a new plan for capital repairs, and in 1951 this process was to be completed.[72] At the same time, the scope of planned investments was broadened so that their share in the total investment in Poland grew from about 59 percent in 1947 to about 81 percent in 1949, with a further increase to about 93 percent set for 1955.[73] Under the Six-Year Plan approximately 77 percent of total investment was designated for productive purposes and the remainder for housing, social services, and other uses not directly connected with production.[74] In 1953 about 70 percent of total in-

Table 12

PERCENTAGE ALLOCATION OF GRANTS AND CREDITS
UNDER POSTWAR INVESTMENT PLANS

	1946	1947	1949	1950	1953	1950–55[a]
1. Industry, handicrafts, and mining	29.1	35.4	38.5	38.8	52.4	⎰ 45.4
2. Building enterprises	....[b]	....[b]	3.0	3.3	3.2	⎱
3. Agriculture and forestry[c]	15.6	15.9	10.5	10.1	9.0	11.9
4. Transport and communications	40.8	27.5	18.1	15.7	13.5	14.9
5. Trade[d]	1.2	2.2	5.7	5.1	2.9	4.2
6. Social and cultural works[e]	5.0	6.4	7.4	8.3	4.3	8.8
7. Housing	4.3	8.5	⎰ 11.0	10.8	10.5	⎰ 11.5
8. Communal economy	1.2	1.1	⎱		3.4	⎱
9. Other	2.9	3.0	5.8	7.9	0.8	3.3
10. Total	100.0	100.0	100.0	100.0	100.0	100.0

Sources: 1946–48 data are taken from *Życie Gospodarcze*, March 1–15, 1950, p. 213; 1949–50 data taken from *Życie Gospodarcze*, February 1–15, 1951, p. 136; 1953 data taken from *Inwestycje i Budownictwo*, February, 1953, p. 5; 1950–55 average data taken from *Dziennik Ustaw*, 1950, No. 37, Item 344, p. 438.

[a] Goals of the Six-Year Plan for the whole period.

[b] Up to 1949 these were included in item 8.

[c] Including fishing through 1948; unspecified thereafter.

[d] The growing share of trade reflects the rapid socialization of additional elements after 1947.

[e] Beginning with 1949, social investments which formerly were included in items 1, 3, 4, and 5 appear thereafter in item 6.

[71] *Gospodarka Planowa*, January 5, 1948, p. 5.
[72] *Życie Gospodarcze*, March 1–15, 1950, p. 210.
[73] Kazimierz Secomski, *Podstawowe zadania planu sześcioletniego*, p. 58.
[74] *Ibid.*

vestment was designated for increments to fixed capital and 30 percent for working capital and various reserves.[75]

The changing structure of the national economy reflecting the rising importance of industry was implemented by allocations under postwar state investment plans. These allocations came from three sources:[76] (1) investment grants or endowments from the state budget, which were not to be repaid and were noninterest bearing, (2) interest bearing, repayable bank credit, and (3) the investor's own sources. From 1946 through 1948, bank credit accounted for more than half of the total planned investment funds, but thereafter grants became the chief source.[77]

Table 12 shows the high priority given to transport and communications in the state investment plans in the immediate postwar years when the reconstruction of the facilities damaged by war was essential to the general revival of production. The share of total planned investment allocated to industry rose sharply during the first four years of the Six-Year Plan, from about 39 percent in 1950 to nearly 54 percent in 1952.[78] At the same time the shares allocated to agriculture and trade fell substantially below the average levels planned for the six-year period.

The distribution of planned investment shown in Table 12 does not reveal the priorities established within the industrial sector. In 1949 about 75 percent of planned industrial investment outlays were concentrated upon producer goods industry, and by 1955, under the provisions of the Six-Year Plan, this share was expected to rise to over 76 percent of the expanded share for industry.[79] This initial high priority was revised upward in the annual plans through 1953. For example, the investment plan for 1953 allocated 52.4 percent of total planned investment to industry,[80] and in practice 46.7 per-

---

[75] Bronisław Minc, "W sprawie nowego rozstawienia sił w gospodarce Polski ludowej" (Concerning the New Distribution of Forces in People's Poland), *Nowe Drogi*, November, 1953, pp. 86–87.

[76] The state banks supervise the use of planned investment funds.

[77] *Życie Gospodarcze*, February 1–15, 1951, p. 138. In the 1951 plan, grants accounted for about 95 percent of the total planned investment fund.

[78] *Inwestycje i Budownictwo* (Investments and Construction), February, 1953, p. 5.

[79] *Nowe Drogi*, July-August, 1950, p. 32. The question of criteria for determining the allocation of investments received much attention from Polish economists, but admittedly the problem was not solved satisfactorily either in theory or in practice. See, for example, the remarks by Bronisław Minc, *Ekonomista*, First and Second Quarters, 1950, pp. 11 ff.

[80] *Inwestycje i Budownictwo*, February, 1953, p. 5.

cent of the total,[81] or about 89 percent of the planned total industrial outlays, went to producer goods industry. Investment in consumer goods concomitantly received a smaller share than originally
provided in the Six-Year Plan, and the share of the total planned
outlays for agriculture declined from approximately 12 percent
established in the Six-Year Plan to about 8 to 9 percent in the 1952–
53 annual plans. The failure to achieve the Six-Year Plan goals for
increases in the scale of living and in real wages can be traced in
part at least to these investment decisions.

By the end of 1953, following the lead of the USSR, Poland modified its economic policies to slacken somewhat the rate of growth
of heavy industry, to expand the domestic raw material base for industry, to provide added resources to the stagnant agricultural sector, and to increase the output of consumer goods. The proposed
new goals included maintenance of capital investment outlays for
1954–55 on the same absolute level as in 1953; reduction of the
share of producer goods industry in total planned investment from
46.7 percent in 1953 to 40.4 percent in 1955, implying a 14 percent
reduction in outlays; and redistribution of investment among other
sectors.[82] Outlays for agriculture within the framework of both the
investment and credit plans[83] in 1955 would increase 80 to 100 percent over 1953; outlays for basic consumer goods industry would
increase about 25 percent; for communal services 30 to 35 percent;
and for social and cultural facilities about 35 percent.[84] By these
measures the government proposed to redeem at least in part its Six-
Year Plan goal to raise the scale of living of the population.

The occupational structure of Poland's population changed very
significantly from the prewar predominance of agricultural pursuits
to that of nonagricultural employment in the postwar period. According to the census of 1931, nearly 61 percent of the population
obtained its livelihood from agriculture and 39 percent from other
occupations.[85] There is no reason to believe that this distribution
changed in any important degree by 1939. According to the census

---

[81] *Nowe Drogi,* October, 1953, p. 30.

[82] *Ibid.*

[83] In October, 1953, it was proposed to increase state investment in agriculture in
1955 about 45 percent over 1953. The credit plan presumably would facilitate investment by collective farms and individual peasants.

[84] Polish Embassy, Washington, *Press Release,* March 22, 1954, p. 30.

[85] *Mały rocznik statystyczny—1939,* p. 33.

of December, 1950, the percentage of population depending on agriculture for livelihood was slightly less than 46 percent of the total, while the nonagricultural population amounted to about 54 percent.[86] However, the absolute number of persons depending for livelihood on nonagricultural pursuits remained practically unchanged, as may be readily seen by applying the percentages given above to the prewar and postwar populations, amounting to approximately 35 and 25 millions, respectively. In the same period the agricultural population declined almost one half.

In the four years 1950–53, nonagricultural employment reportedly increased about 1.5 million, while the total increase of population in the employable age groups amounted to about 650 thousand.[87] Total nonagricultural employment in 1953 was about 5.5 million.[88] Thus the realized average annual rate of increase of nonagricultural employment in the period 1950–53 amounted to about 8 percent. Accretions to this labor force were drawn principally from the rural population, young people entering the working age, and women. By the end of 1953, it was recognized that the agricultural population in certain localities had become inadequate to utilize fully the available land on an intensive basis.[89] The contemplated increase in nonagricultural employment under the revised economic policy for 1954–55 was about 3 percent per year,[90] to be drawn from youth entering working age and from women at present outside the labor force. The stagnation of Poland's agriculture at a time when industry was expanding rapidly can in part be understood in terms of these shifts in employment. The labor force in agriculture declined both in quality and in quantity.

The growth in industrial employment was impressive, rising from 913 thousand in 1938 to 1800 thousand in 1950,[91] while the total population declined by almost a third in the same period. By the end of 1953, employment in socialist industry reached about 2.5

[86] *Życie Gospodarcze,* May 1–15, 1951, p. 494. It is estimated that the urban population increased from less than one third of the total in the prewar period to around two fifths in 1950.

[87] Polish Embassy, *Press Release,* March 22, 1954, p. 30, reporting Hilary Minc's report to the Polish United Workers' Party's Second Congress, March 10–17, 1954.

[88] *Nowe Drogi,* October, 1953, p. 46.

[89] Bronisław Minc, "W sprawie nowego rozstawienia sił w gospodarce Polski ludowej" (Concerning the New Distribution of Forces in the Economy of People's Poland), *Nowe Drogi,* November, 1953, p. 83.

[90] Polish Embassy, *Press Release,* March 22, 1954, pp. 30–31.

[91] *Życie Gospodarcze,* May 1–15, 1951, p. 495.

million persons,[92] and under the provisions of the Six-Year Plan it should reach close to 2.8 million in 1955, or over a million more than at the end of the Three-Year Plan in 1949.[93] This expansion could not take place in any important degree at the expense of private industrial employment, for the latter had already been reduced to insignificant proportions by the end of 1948.[94]

Employment in the socialist sector excluding agriculture, but including services as well as industry, had risen to about 3.6 million persons by the end of 1949, and under the Six-Year Plan it was scheduled to reach 5.7 million by 1955, an increase of 2.1 million, or about 60 percent.[95] In the period 1950–53, an increase of about 1.8 million was reported realized.[96] The share of women in this sector was planned to increase from 29.1 percent in 1949 to 33.5 percent in 1955.[97] A part of the increased employment in the socialized sector excluding agriculture clearly occurred through socialization of additional elements of small-scale production and services. The extent of such proposed change in designation without real change in total employment was not specified in the published national economic plans, but it could affect a very substantial number of employees and proprietors. Handicrafts alone in 1948 employed 384 thousand persons, predominantly in private establishments,[98] and by the end of 1949 there still existed remnants of private industry and trade and other services. The goal for the socialization of handicrafts by means of producer cooperatives was unofficially placed at 80 percent of the total employment in this sector by the end of 1955.[99]

The rapid rates of development of industry shown in Table 13 reflect Polish emphasis on industrialization. During 1950–53 industry forged ahead of its Six-Year Plan schedule while agriculture seriously lagged behind. Production of consumer goods in socialist industry reportedly increased 99 percent over the 1949 level, and

[92] *Gospodarka Planowa*, February, 1952, p. 8; February, 1953, p. 5; and March, 1954, p. 6, reported 2.2 million in 1951 and a 6 percent increase per year in 1952–53.

[93] *Nowe Drogi*, July-August, 1950, pp. 54–55. Socialist industry consists of state-owned and cooperative enterprises and currently accounts for the overwhelming share of total industrial employment.

[94] *Supra*, p. 59.

[95] *Nowe Drogi*, July-August, 1950, p. 40.

[96] *Ibid.*, November, 1953, p. 83.

[97] *Ibid.*, July-August, 1950, p. 40.

[98] *Rocznik statystyczny—1949*, p. 42.

[99] *Życie Gospodarcze*, November 16–30, 1950, p. 1167.

Table 13

POLISH ECONOMIC DEVELOPMENT UNDER POSTWAR PLANS, SELECTED YEARS, 1947–55[a]

| Item and Unit | 1937 = 100, PREWAR AREA | | | | 1949 = 100 |
	1947	1949	1953	1955 Goal Six-Yr. Plan	1955 Goal Six-Yr. Plan
1. National income index[b]	87	125	203	264	212
2. All industry, index of gross value of production, "fixed prices"	106	177	386	400	226
3. Large- and medium-scale state industry, index of gross value of production, "fixed prices"[c]	102	177		418	236
(i) Producer goods		207		525	254
(ii) Consumer goods		146		309	211
4. Agriculture, index of gross value of production[d]	59	86	94	129	150
5. Railway freight, index of ton-kilometers carried[e]	95	146		271	186
6. Population, index	70[f]	71	78	. . .[g]	. . .

[a] Based on official reports. For sources and derivation, see Appendix A.
[b] 1938 = 100, except last column. For remarks on prices, see Appendix A notes for Table 10. The Polish official definition of national income excludes services not directly related to material production.
[c] Large- and medium-scale state industry accounted for 80 to 90 percent of total industrial production, with the share rising in the later years.   [f] 1946.
[d] See Appendix A for a note on prices.   [e] 1938 = 100, except last column.   [g] . . . = not available.

output of producer goods increased 136 percent.[100] An important part of consumer goods production was exported so that consumption did not keep pace with production.

Late in 1953, following the lead of the USSR and several of its satellites in eastern Europe, Poland revised its economic policy for 1954–55 in an attempt to eliminate some of the disproportions between sectors of the economy resulting from the prior overemphasis on heavy industry and relative neglect of agriculture and light industry. Although the Six-Year Plan had promised a 50 to 60 percent increase in the scale of living of the population, and a 40 percent increase in real wages in the socialized sector, official reports indicated that in the four years 1950–53, real income of the population had risen only about 15 to 20 percent and real wages had increased only imperceptibly.[101] The contents of the official real wage and scale of living indexes were not specified, and the widespread official criticisms of the failure to better the consumers' lot suggest that the official measures exaggerate the change in consumption.

The new goals for 1954–55 envision a 23 percent increase in gross industrial production in 1955 over the 1953 level, with the output of producer and consumer goods expanding at the same rate; a 10 percent increase in agricultural output in the same period; and a 15 to 20 percent increase in the real wages of industrial workers and in the incomes of working farmers.[102] If these goals are achieved, the Six-Year Plan for over-all industrial production will be overfulfilled, but agricultural output will fall far short of the original goal, and real wages will have risen only about half as far as promised in the Six-Year Plan.

If one assumes a uniform rate of increase of planned output during the Six-Year Plan, the percentage increases in Polish industry during the first five years of this period would exceed the goals set for Soviet industry in the Third Five-Year Plan but would be lower than the officially reported achievements in the Second Five-Year Plan. Table 14 shows that Soviet emphasis on a higher rate of expansion for heavy industry in comparison with consumer goods production was closely paralleled in the Polish experience. In agricul-

[100] Polish Embassy, *Press Release*, March 22, 1954, pp. 6, 22. Socialist industry includes large- and medium-scale state enterprises, industry under the control of local people's councils, and industrial production cooperatives.

[101] *Ibid.*, p. 11.

[102] *Ibid.*, pp. 11, 26.

Table 14

POLISH PLANNED DEVELOPMENT IN INDUSTRY AND AGRICULTURE UNDER THE
SIX-YEAR PLAN COMPARED WITH SOVIET RESULTS AND GOALS

PERCENTAGE INCREASE

	SOVIET UNION		POLAND
Item	*Realized 1933–37*	*Planned 1938–42*	*Planned 1950–54*
All industries, gross output	121	88	97
(i) Heavy industries, gross output	139	103	117[a]
(ii) Consumer goods industries, gross output	100	69	86[a]
Agriculture, gross output	54	52	40
(i) Plant production	54	36	32
(ii) Animal production	54	94	54

Sources: The Polish data is calculated from Table 13 by applying the average annual rate of increase to the first five years of the Six-Year Plan. The figures for Soviet industries are taken from: Abram Bergson, "The Fourth Five Year Plan: Heavy Versus Consumers' Goods Industries," *Political Science Quarterly*, June, 1947, p. 205; and for Soviet agriculture, from Naum Jasny, *The Socialized Agriculture of the USSR*, p. 775.

[a] A component of large- and medium-scale state-owned industry for which the planned increase in total output for the five years was 105 percent.

ture, the realized Russian tempos were the same for plant and animal production, whereas the Polish goal for increase of animal production was significantly higher. The increases shown in this table must be qualified by the character of both the Soviet and Polish official statistics. The former values output in terms of 1926–27 ruble prices which are regarded by Western students as imparting an important upward bias due to inflated values attached to new commodities introduced after 1926–27.[103] Polish valuations in terms of "fixed prices" based on 1937 prices likewise must be regarded with reserve.

Fulfillment of economic plans. The Polish postwar economic plans aimed at a rapid rate of development in all branches of the economy, but with particular emphasis upon heavy industry as affording the basis for equipping the other branches. In keeping with the Communist view that the plans should be ambitious and

[103] See Abram Bergson (ed.), *Soviet Economic Growth;* and Naum Jasny, *The Socialized Agriculture of the USSR,* for appraisals of Soviet official indexes of industrial and agricultural production.

overfulfillment regarded as more desirable than precise execution of the plans, the Polish plans were very similar to their Soviet precept. Nevertheless, the Polish planners did not hesitate to lower some of the targets established at the outset of the Three-Year Plan for the later years of this period. For this reason, the reported fulfillment of the national economic plan in a given year stated in percentages of the goals set but without specific statement of absolute goals or performance must be regarded with caution. Certain absolute indicators of Polish economic development, however, are available, and some of these will be presented in the following chapters.

The communique of the State Commission of Economic Planning reporting the execution of the Three-Year Plan referred to the targets set at the outset of the period.[104] According to this source, the Three-Year Plan was carried out two months ahead of schedule, and the performance of particular industrial ministries in this period, stated in percentage of fulfillment of production goals at 1937 prices, is given in Table 15.

Table 15

FULFILLMENT OF THE THREE-YEAR PLAN BY MINISTRIES

Ministry	Percent of Fulfillment of the Three-Year Plan
Mining and energy	99
Heavy industry	101
Light industry	97
Agricultural and food industry	108
Forestry	118
Shipping	99

The harvests in agriculture for a number of crops exceeded the Three-Year Plan goals in percentage terms as follows: wheat—8; rye—22; potatoes—12; sugar beets—11; fiber plants—56; and oil plants—27. Similarly, the livestock numbers at the end of the period exceeded the goals by 3 percent for horses and 22 percent for cattle, while the results for pigs reached only 68 percent of the original goal [105] although surpassing the quota under the 1949 annual plan.

By the end of October, 1949, the transportation of passengers and

[104] *Życie Gospodarcze*, December 1–15, 1949, pp. 1012–13. The data on the Three-Year Plan mentioned below are from this source.
[105] *Infra*, Table 36, p. 216, and *Dziennik Ustaw*, 1947, No. 53, p. 859.

commodities on standard gauge railways attained 114 and 102 percent of the Three-Year Plan's goals, respectively, and the State Automotive Communications network exceeded goals in passenger and commodity traffic by about 20 percent.

In comparison with the goals set for the national income, the performance of the economy in the later postwar years failed to come up to expectations. Expressed as the annual percentage of increase over the immediately preceding year, these goals for 1950 through 1952, consecutively, were 15.2, 18.9, and 17.0, whereas the corresponding officially reported increases were 21.0, 12.0, and 10.0.[106] In 1953 the national income was below the Six-Year Plan target for that year, and the new production goals for 1954–55 imply that the Six-Year Plan national income goal for 1955 has been abandoned.

The annual official communiques announcing the fulfillment of the yearly plans since 1949 emphasized the rapid expansion of gross output of socialized industry. Since the annual targets for 1951–52 were raised over the levels set originally in the Six-Year Plan as approved in 1950, the performance since 1950 was officially estimated to hasten the realization of the industrial production goal of the plan by approximately 14 months.[107] The officially reported annual gains in gross output over the previous years are shown in Table 16.[108] Under the revised economic policy adopted in March, 1954, gross output of socialist industry in 1954–55 would increase about 11 to 12 percent per year,[109] a significantly lower rate than realized in the four preceding years.

Typically, the official communiques presented an extended list of products for which the performance with respect to the planned goal or with regard to the level of output of the preceding year was impressive, and less conspicuously they mentioned a smaller list of products for which the output failed to come up to the targets. Among the products which have failed to reach the established goals under the annual plans in two or more years since the beginning of the Six-Year Plan were pig iron, locomotives, machine tools, bricks

[106] The national income goals for 1950 and 1951 are taken from *Dziennik Ustaw,* 1950, No. 21, p. 232; 1951, No. 18, p. 178. The 1952 goal is taken from *Gospodarka Planowa,* March, 1952, p. 6. Fulfillments are taken from Table 10, *supra,* p. 140.

[107] *Gospodarka Planowa,* February, 1953, p. 6.

[108] See *supra,* pp. 135–36, for comment on Polish indexes of gross output.

[109] Polish Embassy, *Press Release,* March 22, 1954, p. 26.

Table 16

EXPANSION OF GROSS OUTPUT OF SOCIALIST INDUSTRY, 1949–53
(IN PERCENT OF INCREASE OVER THE PRECEDING YEAR
UNLESS OTHERWISE INDICATED)

Year	Six-Year Plan Goals	Realized
1950	22.0	30.8
1951	20.7	24.4
1952	16.1	20.0
1953	. . .[a]	17.5
1953 over 1949	97.1	128.6

Source: Polish official indexes from *Gospodarka Planowa*, February, 1953, p. 6; March, 1954, p. 2; and Polish Embassy, Washington, *Press Release*, March 22, 1954, p. 6.

[a] . . . = not available.

and cement, sulfuric acid, and calcined soda.[110] The relatively slow expansion of output of such basic products as coal, iron ore, zinc, and industrial crops from agriculture caused expressions of concern by the planning commission. In particular the shortage of scrap iron and the inadequate output of pig iron were regarded as serious bottlenecks in the economy. Against the background of raw material shortages, problems of supply of semimanufactures and equipment between branches of industry became serious, leading to irregular production rhythm. Labor shortages became more apparent with each successive year. The annual rate of increase in employment in the socialized sector of industry declined sharply, dropping from about 16 percent in 1950 to about 6 percent in 1952 and 1953.[111] Labor turnover was regarded officially as excessively high and recruitment as improperly organized. In an endeavor to meet production goals some ministries resorted to excessive use of overtime and exceeded their planned wage funds.[112]

According to official reports, Poland's agriculture successfully fulfilled its goal of gross output in 1950 but lagged badly behind industry and failed to reach its targets in 1951–53. Unfavorable weather conditions, migration of farm labor to urban areas, inade-

[110] Official communiques published in *Życie Gospodarcze*, February 1–15, 1951, and *Gospodarka Planowa*, February, 1952, 1953. Unless otherwise indicated, the data on plan fulfillments given below are based on these sources.

[111] *Gospodarka Planowa*, February, 1953, p. 5; March, 1954, p. 6; and *Życie Gospodarcze*, February 1–15, 1951, p. 181.

[112] *Gospodarka Planowa*, February, 1953, pp. 11–12.

quate investment, and the government's pressure for socialization of agriculture adversely affected production. Gross agricultural output in 1953 was officially reported only 10 percent above 1949,[113] and the goal for 1955 under the revised policy adopted in 1953 is an increase of about 10 percent over the 1953 level.[114] The 50 percent increase by 1955 over 1949 scheduled by the Six-Year Plan has thus been abandoned as impractical. The failure of agriculture to provide the required supplies for the market is reflected in the imposition of compulsory deliveries on farmers in 1951–52.

Both freight and passenger transport by railroads in 1953 were reported ahead of the goals set by the Six-Year Plan,[115] although the targets set in annual plans for 1951 and 1952 were not reached. Freight carried by the State Motor Transport Service continued to show large annual gains since 1949: almost a fourfold increase in 1950, about 66 percent in 1951, 17 percent in 1952, and 45 percent in 1953. Inland water freight transport similarly showed large annual increases: 5 percent in 1950, 23 percent in 1951, 48 percent in 1952, and 63 percent in 1953.[116] It is not clear whether these percentages refer to tons carried or ton-kilometers, but they probably relate to the former. Freight carried by ocean shipping also showed large annual gains: 33 percent in 1950, 45 percent in 1951, and 12 percent in 1952.[117] Both inland water transport and highway shipping remained relatively minor freight carriers in comparison with the railroads.

During the period 1946–53, centralized economic planning in Poland was greatly strengthened by expansion of direct state control over economic activity. Because of the comprehensiveness of this control it was possible to concentrate the country's resources on the industrial sector and to achieve impressive gains in industrial production. These gains, however, were offset by the poor performance in agriculture and by the failure to reach goals for increases in real wages and in the scale of living of the population. When Polish eco-

[113] Polish Embassy, *Press Release,* March 22, 1954, p. 8.
[114] *Nowe Drogi,* October, 1953, p. 70.
[115] Polish Embassy, *Press Release,* March 22, 1954, p. 28.
[116] Annual reports of plan fulfillment: *Życie Gospodarcze,* February 1–15, 1951, p. 180; *Gospodarka Planowa,* February, 1952, p. 7; *ibid.,* February, 1953, p. 4; *ibid.,* March, 1954, p. 5.
[117] *Ibid.*

nomic policies for 1954–55 were revised to overcome in part at least the stagnation in agriculture and to increase the output of consumer goods, the planned rate of expansion of industrial production was sharply cut back from the reported increases for earlier years. To some extent this planned slowing down was a reflection of the declining share of investment in the national product for 1954–55, but to a greater extent it reflects the end of a period of easy gains beginning from a low postwar base made possible by the mobilization of underemployed labor and capital and by the application of a backlog of technological progress achieved in more advanced areas of the world.

VII

Postwar Planning in Industry

POLISH industry has been accorded a favored status over other sectors of the economy in the allocation of investment resources and in the assignment of particularly rapid rates of development. This emphasis stems from the conviction of the planners that industry must be expanded more rapidly than other sectors in order to provide the capital goods necessary for expansion of production in general, to augment the military strength of the country in particular, and to provide a more numerous proletariat as a stronger support for the exercise of political power by the presently dominant Polish United Workers' Party.[1] In selecting the assortment of industries and determining their respective rates of development, the planners were guided by the further requirement that Poland should seek economic independence with respect to capitalist countries and at the same time increase the degree of economic collaboration within the Soviet sphere.[2]

Basic Policy Decisions Concerning Industrialization

Priorities in the development of industry. The current Polish planning effort applies the so-called socialist law of industrialization which Bronisław Minc interpreted as follows:[3]

1. The development of industry must precede the development of other branches of the economy.
2. The development of industry must apply to socialist industry, and not industry in general.

[1] Bronisław Minc, "Zmiany w metodologii planowania" (Changes in the Methodology of Planning), *Gospodarka Planowa*, August, 1951, p. 7.
[2] Hilary Minc, "Sześcioletni plan rozwoju gospodarczego" (The Six-Year Plan of Economic Development), *Nowe Drogi*, July-August, 1950, pp. 38–39.
[3] Bronisław Minc, "Zmiany w metodologii planowania," *Gospodarka Planowa*, August, 1951, p. 16.

3. The development of the producer goods industry must outstrip the growth of the consumer goods industry.
4. The machine building industry must expand more rapidly than the producer goods industry of which it is a part in order to afford a basis for the development and technical reconstruction alike of heavy and light industry, agriculture, and communications.

In deciding that the development of industry must be more rapid than that of all other branches of the economy, the Polish policy makers emphasized that industry is the key element in the general economic advance since it facilitates an increase in the per capita output of the country, provides for military and economic defense, and affords a basis for building socialism. In view of the ideological inclination of the dominant political party, it is difficult to see how any other policy could have been adopted. The nationalization of large- and medium-scale industry in January, 1946, had placed the key industries within the compass of direct planning, and the ever more closely regulated private sector has shown a progressive shrinkage. In 1947 the private sector accounted for about 17 percent of the gross value of the output of industry and handicrafts;[4] by 1949 it had declined to 11 percent; and by the end of 1955 it was expected to amount to about 1 percent, most of which would consist of small-scale handicraft production.[5] It is interesting to observe the corresponding growth of socialized small-scale production projected for the period of the Six-Year Plan. The gross value of the output of the private industry sector, including handicrafts, was expected to fall from 2.1 billion zlotys in 1949 to 0.4 billion in 1955 as measured in fixed prices, or a decline of about 80 percent. In the same period, the gross value of the output of socialized small-scale industry, which includes cooperative industry, was planned to increase from 1.5 billion to 7.3 billion zlotys, an increase of 384 percent.[6] An appraisal of the planned expansion of small-scale pro-

[4] *Dziennik Ustaw*, 1947, No. 53, Item 285, pp. 862, 864. The values shown for the public, cooperative, and private sectors were combined, and the share of the private sector was derived therefrom.

[5] Hilary Minc, "Sześcioletni plan rozwoju gospodarczego" (The Six-Year Plan of Economic Development), *Nowe Drogi*, July-August, 1950, p. 35.

[6] The decline of the gross value of the output of private industry and handicraft is calculated by applying the percentage shares given in the text above to the totals of gross value of output of all industry and handicraft. These totals are obtained as follows: The Six-Year Plan, *Dziennik Ustaw*, 1950, No. 37, p. 430, gives the 1955 goal

duction, taking account of the absolute decline in the private sector of industry and handicraft, would show an expected net gain in the whole field of small-scale production, including the socialist and private sectors, of about 215 percent. In view of the shrinkage of the private sector to insignificant proportions by the end of 1953 [7] and its planned almost complete extinction by 1955, it is clear that the second part of the policy prescription for Polish industrialization was effected.

The further implementation of this prescription is shown in Table 13.[8] The index of gross value of output of industry exceeds the corresponding indexes for agriculture and transportation, and the index for producer goods exceeds all the others. During the Three-Year Plan the output of the machine building industry expanded greatly over the prewar level within the prewar boundaries. The volume of production of machine tools for metal- and woodworking in 1949 was reported nearly six times the prewar output, and the output of agricultural machines and implements was 74 percent greater than prewar.[9] Under the Six-Year Plan, the 1955 output goal for the machine building industry was 364 percent of the 1949 output, one of the highest targets in the plan. In keeping with the goal of socializing and mechanizing agriculture, the output of tractors and farm implements in 1955 was scheduled at four times the 1949 level, and for transportation equipment, the corresponding goal was an increase of 171 percent. As a consequence of the expansion of the machine building industries, their share in the gross value of the output of large- and medium-scale industry increased from 7 percent in 1937 to about 10 percent in 1949, and was planned to reach 14 percent in 1955.[10] The output of the socialized construction or building enterprises, which carry out investment projects, shows correspondingly high planned rates of increase during the Six-Year Plan. Over-all, the production of the socialized

of output of the socialist sector in industry at 43.8 billion zlotys in fixed prices, or 158 percent more than in 1949. Since the socialist sector represents 89 and 99 percent of the total production in 1949 and 1955, respectively, the total production of all industry and handicraft is derived immediately. The rise in value of output of socialized small-scale production is given in the text of the Six-Year Plan, p. 430, as cited in this footnote. For a note on the fixed prices, see *supra*, p. 136.

[7] *Supra*, p. 55.
[8] *Supra*, p. 147.
[9] *Dziennik Ustaw*, 1950, No. 37, Item 344, p. 428.
[10] *Nowe Drogi*, July-August, 1950, pp. 13–14.

construction industry during the six years was planned to increase by 280 percent. Given the autarkic policy followed by Poland, the faster tempos planned for the capital goods industries were justified since these industries had not only to meet the demand for replacement and maintenance but also to provide for substantial additions to capacity in all the branches of production. In order to provide the resources necessary for increasing the productive capacity of the economy, the Polish plans designated a large and increasing percentage share of the growing national product for investment and a declining percentage share for consumption, which could nevertheless result in absolute increases.

Under the revised economic policy adopted at the end of 1953, however, total investment in 1954–55 was scheduled to remain at the same absolute level as in 1953. With national income increasing, this would entail a fall in the percentage share of income allocated to investment.[11] At the same time the average annual increase in gross industrial production was reduced from 17.5 percent reported for 1953 to 10–11 percent planned for 1954–55, with producer and consumer goods expanding at the same rate. This rate of growth would assure overfulfillment of the Six-Year Plan goal for producer goods.[12]

Table 17

PLANNED DEVELOPMENT OF SELECTED BRANCHES OF THE POLISH ECONOMY
IN THE SIX-YEAR PLAN

Sector of the Economy	1955 Output (1949 = 100)	Average Annual Percent Increase in Output, 1950–55[a]
1. Agriculture	150	7.0
2. All industry	226	14.6
3. Large- and medium-scale state industry	236	15.4
(i) Consumer goods	211	13.3
(ii) Producer goods	254	16.8
4. Machine building industry	364	24.3
5. Railway freight, ton-km	186	10.9

Sources: Table 13 above, and *Nowe Drogi*, July-August, 1950, p. 13.
  [a] The annual rates of increase are obtained from the indexes for 1955, assuming a constant annual rate.

[11] *Supra,* p. 141.
[12] Polish Embassy, Washington, *Press Release,* March 22, 1954, p. 26.

For the purpose of comparing the planned rates of development of production in the chief branches of the Polish economy during the Six-Year Plan, Table 17 presents indexes for the final year with respect to the status at the beginning of the period and also computed annual average increases over the six years. The planned rates of expansion for machine building and producer goods were highest, and according to official reports they were achieved through 1953. On the other hand, the relatively low rate set for agriculture was poorly supported by state investment priorities and was underfulfilled by a wide margin. Despite the rapid gains in output of producer goods, Poland found it necessary to import large quantities of machinery and capital equipment to implement the plans for industrialization.[13]

In addition to increasing production by new investment and increased employment, the Polish planners placed great emphasis upon increasing output by means of increased skills and greater effort on the part of production workers, better plant layout and other rationalization measures, and more intensive utilization of production equipment. Clearly, the gains arising from these actions would help to augment the new production made possible by additions to capacity.

Location of industry. Polish policy for the planned location of industry followed Soviet precepts.[14] Its goals included the general aims of industrialization mentioned at the beginning of this chapter and in particular the aim that planned location should promote rapid economic development by providing for the specialization of regions within the country and the "fullest" development of each region.[15] According to the official policy, the specialization of a region was to be based upon exploitation of natural resources, even of some of the less valuable, such as peat and poor ores, which might not be profitably exploited in a capitalist economy,[16] and upon the existing productive skills of the population. On the other hand,

[13] *Infra,* p. 276.

[14] Professor Mikołaj Niekrasow, "Zasady lokalizacji socjalistycznego przemysłu" (Principles of Location of Socialist Industry, *Życie Gospodarcze,* November 1–15, 1951, p. 1156.

[15] Cf. Stanisław Berezowski, "Regionalizacja gospodarcza w Polsce ludowej" (Economic Regionalization in People's Poland), *Życie Gospodarcze,* December 1–15, 1951, p. 1270.

[16] The Polish scheme of industrial pricing provided subsidies for certain branches of the economy and for particular enterprises in otherwise profitable branches. See *infra,* pp. 243–46.

the full development of an economic region should assure complete exploitation of the local reserves of labor and give the fullest possible coverage of the consumption needs of the region from its own production. Such regional autarky was expected to reduce excessively long hauls and increase the ability of the country to defend itself.[17]

An economic region in Polish planning is regarded as an area containing a mutually interconnected system of many kinds of production, combining both industry and agriculture. Services, including transportation, are regarded only as the extension of the production process, and not as a directly important factor in the determination of economic regions. The Three-Year Plan, for purposes of planning the reconstruction of the economy, divided the country into the central area and the so-called recovered territories, in order to place special emphasis on the more extensive needs of reconstruction and settlement in the latter. The plan did not envision any important shift in the location of economic activity; however, the Six-Year Plan which followed sought a more uniform distribution of productive activity. Efforts were directed toward establishing areas with a large measure of economic self-sufficiency which should serve both as territorial units for the planning of economic development and as political subdivisions for administrative purposes. The pre-existing province was accepted as the basic territorial unit, and in order to bring the administrative units into coincidence with the concept of economic regions, some provinces were split and boundaries of others were shifted. This was regarded only as the beginning of a continuing process of adapting the administrative areas to the changing territorial requirements of economic regions. The resulting provinces correspond to the oblasts of the European part of the USSR, whose experience on this score furnished the pattern followed in eastern Europe.[18]

Defense considerations appeared to enter the decision to further the deglomeration of the old industrial districts, particularly Łódź and Silesia, by relieving such areas of dispensable functions.[19] The development of areas of relative economic self-sufficiency was expected to lessen the demand upon the transportation network which

[17] Berezowski, *op. cit.*, p. 1270.
[18] *Ibid.*, pp. 1268–69.
[19] Bolesław Malisz, "Aktywizacja terenow nieuprzemysłowionych" (Activization of Non-industrialized Areas), *Życie Gospodarcze*, December 1–15, 1951, p. 1274.

might become a bottleneck during a war, but for a country as small as Poland it is not likely that defense industries themselves could escape destruction in modern total war unless placed underground. Insistence upon a large measure of regional self-sufficiency would mean a loss of efficiency that more thoroughgoing specialization could bring.

Polish locational planning recognizes the costs associated with the production and distribution of goods and services. Both of these activities involve transport costs which tend to orient productive activity toward the sources of raw materials or the centers of consumption of products. The direct processing costs of production are affected by the costs of various blends of factors of production which in part are a function of the environment of the given activity. The so-called Stalinist-Leninist principles of location of industry emphasized the creation of industrial complexes in the economic regions of the country so as to take advantage of external economies, and particularly a saving of transport costs insofar as the selected complex of industries provides for complementary relations.[20] Moreover, the development of new industrial complexes was regarded as automatically creating markets at the location of the activity, since the latter attracts workers whose spendable income represents demand for some of the products created.[21] An example of the consideration given to the selection of an industrial site is found in the construction of the metallurgical combine, Nowa Huta, near Kraków. In describing the location of this major investment under the Six-Year Plan, the chief director of the new combine referred to the comparison of several alternative locations in different parts of the country, not only from the technical point of view relative to the kind of terrain, quantity of industrial water available, and similar factors, but also equally from the economic point of view relative to transport costs of raw materials from their sources and of the combine's products to their users. He asserted that exacting calculations proved that the chosen location was the most favorable.[22] The presence of a reservoir of manpower in the vicinity and

[20] Niekrasow, *op. cit.*, p. 1156.

[21] Bolesław Malisz, "Rozmieszczenie sił wytwórczych w planie 6–letnim" (Location of Productive Forces in the Six-Year Plan), *Gospodarka Planowa*, October, 1950, p. 508.

[22] Jan Aniola, "Rola Nowej Huty w postępie technicznym hutnictwa" (Role of Nowa Huta in the Technological Progress of Metallurgy), *Gospodarka Planowa*, July, 1951, p. 26.

of the social, cultural, and communal establishments of nearby Kraków which were expected to be used by the workers of Nowa Huta were further important elements in the selection of the construction site.[23]

In giving effect to its locational policy, the Polish government has at its disposal a wide assortment of tools,[24] which is to be expected under a dictatorship in a socialized economy. Not only is the state the owner of nearly all of the fixed capital in industry, but it also controls in a very close manner the nonnationalized sector of business activity and can regulate its locational choice through the control of land use. The mobility of labor is subject to state control through positive powers permitting the state to assign certain categories of its population to work in designated activities at particular locations and through various restraints designed to keep employees at their places of work once these are chosen. Moreover, the state through its direct control over major investments not only can benefit from the external economies associated with a properly chosen combination of activities for a given location, but also can modify the transportation network through new construction. All these direct controls are additional to the indirect methods, such as taxes, subsidies, tariffs, research and information services, price control, and aids to communication, which are used less frequently with the extension of direct planning and the contraction of the private sector.

Although the Polish discussion of the planned location of industry emphasized the creation of relatively self-sufficient economic regions and a more even distribution of industry over the country, the Three-Year Plan did not change the pre-existing distribution in any significant degree, and the Six-Year Plan set modest goals in this sphere. It recognized the limitations imposed by the capital requirements, the supply of materials, and the possibilities of expanding the skilled and unskilled labor force in selected localities. Moreover, the expansion of existing establishments was regarded as a less expensive way of increasing production than through new construction.[25] Three groups of compact industrial districts based on local

[23] Stanisław Zralek, "Z doświadczeń budownictwa Nowej Huty" (From the Experience of Building Nowa Huta), *Życie Gospodarcze,* January 1, 1952, p. 21.

[24] *Supra,* Chapter IV.

[25] Bolesław Malisz, "Rozmieszczenie sił wytwórczych w planie 6-letnim" (Location of Productive Forces in the Six-Year Plan), *Gospodarka Planowa,* October, 1950, p. 509.

raw materials and reserves of labor were recognized in the Six-Year Plan: (1) the old industrial districts which were already relatively highly invested and in which a further agglomeration of industries and services would create complications in production and worsen living conditions, (2) industrial centers whose expansion was regarded as necessary for the full exploitation of their raw material possibilities and the existing investment, and (3) districts and centers whose industrialization would be initiated during the Six-Year Plan.[26]

The first of these groups consisted of Upper and Lower Silesia and the district around Łódź. The province of Katowice[27] in the Upper Silesian industrial basin was scheduled to decline in relative importance as measured by industrial employment from 32 percent of the total in 1949 to about 26 percent in 1955, but nevertheless it would still remain Poland's chief industrial area. Its further development would continue on already established lines, namely, the extraction of coal, ferrous metallurgy, the chemical industry, and other industries directly related to the raw material base of the area. New industrial establishments not organically connected with the established lines would be located outside the limits of the coal basin in furtherance of the principle of deglomeration of congested areas. A similar development based on exploitation of mineral wealth was planned for the Subsudetan district with a concurrent avoidance of excessive investments not directly connected with the raw material base at Wałbrzych (formerly Waldenburg) and Dzierzoniów (formerly Reichbach). Poland's largest textile center, Łódź, under the Six-Year Plan would have its assorment of industries enriched in order to offset its current one-sided specialization. New textile plants, especially those requiring considerable quantities of water, would be located outside of the city of Łódź in view of the shortage of water. As a result of the relative de-emphasis in the planned expansion of group (1), its share in the country's total industrial employment should decline from 65.8 percent in 1949 to 54.3 percent in 1955.

The second group included, among others, the Kraków, Częstochowa, and Opole (formerly Oppeln) districts, in which

[26] *Ibid.*, p. 510. The discussion which follows is based on this source, pp. 510–12.
[27] Renamed Stalinogród following Stalin's death (*Dziennik Ustaw*, 1953, No. 13, Item 51).

chiefly metallurgy, metal goods, and chemical production would
be expanded. These require coal and therefore preferably should
be near, although not necessarily directly connected with, the coal
basin. The Kraków district would take second place after Upper
Silesia in the magnitude of investment during the Six-Year Plan.
Its industry would be expanded in a belt along the Vistula river
from the coal basin west of the city of Kraków to Tarnów and the
upper Dunajec river. The major investment of the Six-Year Plan
would be the development at Nowa Huta, near Kraków, which
would include a metallurgical combine and a series of secondary
industries. In the heavily populated rural eastern part of the district
there was planned a dam on the Dunajec river and also the development of industry which required clear water and which would
afford employment for the excess agrarian population in this area.
The expansion of the industrial district around Częstochowa would
be based on the significant growth of the existing metallurgical and
metal goods industries which reflect the low grade iron ore deposits
in this area and the adjacent coal fields of Silesia. Other districts in
the second group included the industrial region along the upper
Oder river at Opole, which was scheduled to construct plants for
the manufacture of chemicals and metal products based on the
resources of neighboring Upper Silesia, and cement works based
on local raw materials; the city of Warsaw and its environs, for
which the plan specified precision manufacturing and other industries which could utilize the special skills found in large cities;
the industrial port districts centering at Stettin, Danzig, and Gdynia,
which would concentrate on the development of shipbuilding, shipping, and deep sea fishing along with the expansion of other existing industries; the industrial clusters at Wrocław (Breslau), Poznań,
Zielona Góra (Grunberg), Bydgoszcz, Torun, and Inowrocław; and
the old Polish industrial district in Kielce province, which would
expand the extraction of iron ore and quartzites, and exploit the
deposits of limestone, marble, and gypsum.

The third group consisted of districts within which the development of industries would only be initiated during the Six-Year
Plan. These included the area around Konin and Kłodawa, where
a future industrial district would be based on local deposits of
lignite and potassium salts. The eastern part of Poland, thus far
almost completely unindustrialized, would develop industry based

on agricultural raw materials, food processing, metal products, textiles, wood products, and other light manufacturing which should help relieve the population pressure in the rural districts. The southern part of the Rzeszów province would expand the extraction of petroleum.

Despite the attempt to spread industry widely throughout the country, there would still remain large unindustrialized areas in the northern and eastern parts of Poland. The industrial complexes planned for the third group above represented typical first steps in industrialization, namely, food processing, preparation of textile fibers and wood products, and other activities which provide for the elementary human needs. In view of the concentration of most of the significant mineral resources, particularly coal, iron ore, petroleum, ores of nonferrous metals, and various salts in the southern part of the country, and especially in Silesia, these areas are likely to retain their lead in industrial development. Transport cost economies may facilitate the gain of the backward areas in the products destined for local consumption which gain in weight, bulk, or perishability during processing. Indeed, this type of industry is urged for all areas of the country uniformly, but due to a later beginning the backward areas can show a relative gain. Table 18 shows that the least industrialized provinces, namely, Białystok, Lublin, Olsztyn, Koszalin, and Szczecin ranked among the highest in the planned rates of increase in value of gross industrial production, but their total planned employment for 1955 is small in relation to the more highly developed regions.

During the first four years of the Six-Year Plan, a substantial redistribution of industrial employment had occurred in Poland. In 1949 about 37 percent of total industrial employment was outside the three most highly industrialized provinces—Łódź (city and province), Stalingród (formerly Katowice), and Wrocław (formerly Breslau); but by 1953 this share had risen to about 50 percent.[28]

Investment, employment, and technology. The emphasis placed in Polish economic plans upon the development of industry producing means of production is exemplified by the distribution of planned industrial investment among particular branches of in-

---

[28] Mieczysław Lesz, "Zmienia się oblicze kraju" (The Face of the Country Is Changing), *Nowe Drogi*, September, 1953, p. 42.

Table 18

REGIONAL INDUSTRIAL DEVELOPMENT UNDER THE SIX-YEAR PLAN

Region	1955 Gross Value of Production of Socialized Industry as a Percentage of 1949	1955 Level of Industrial Employment in Thousands
Warsaw City	450	100
Warsaw Province less Warsaw	350	100
Łódź City	180	250
Łódź Province less Łódź	250	150
Other Provinces:		
Kielce	300	100
Lublin	500	60
Białystok	550	40
Olsztyn[a]	400	30
Gdańsk[a]	260	90
Wrocław[a]	220	300
Opole[a]	300	120
Stalinogród[b]	200	650
Kraków	300	230
Bydgoszcz	250	100
Koszalin[a]	300	27
Szczecin[a]	300	46
Zielona Góra[a]	350	70
Poznań	250	140
Rzeszów	350	75

Source: Approximate goals set in the Six-Year Plan, *Dziennik Ustaw*, 1950, No. 37, Item 344, pp. 446–50.

[a] The Polish names of the indicated localities have the following German correspondents: Olsztyn—Allenstein, Gdańsk—Danzig, Wrocław—Breslau, Opole—Oppeln, Koszalin—Koslin, Szczecin—Stettin, Zielona Góra—Grunberg.

[b] Formerly Katowice.

dustry. Table 19 shows this distribution of the so-called limited investment funds, which accounted for approximately 85 and 95 percent of the total investment covered by the investment plans in 1948 and 1949, respectively.[29] Since the state investment plans cover practically all but the insignificant part of industrial investment belonging to the private sector, their influence upon the character of the developing Polish industry is decisive. Table 19 illustrates the importance of the coal, metallurgical, energy, chemical, and

[29] Kazimierz Secomski, "Plan inwestycyjny na rok 1951" (The Investment Plan for 1951), *Życie Gospodarcze*, February 1–15, 1951, p. 138. The limited funds cover all sources except the investor's own funds.

metal products industries, which claimed nearly two thirds of the planned total for industry in 1948–49. The official policy declared that approximately three fourths of all industrial investment during the Six-Year Plan must be allotted to the development of the production of the means of production.[30] In the early years of the Six-Year Plan this ratio was revised upward. Industry as a whole in 1952 claimed about 54 percent of total state investment outlays. In the 1953 plan it was scheduled to receive about 52 percent,[31] and producer goods industry alone reportedly received about 47 percent of the actual total.[32]

Table 19

PERCENTAGE DISTRIBUTION OF PLANNED INDUSTRIAL INVESTMENT
FROM LIMITED FUNDS, 1948–49

Industry	1948	1949
Coal	20.4	17.0
Metallurgical	13.4	16.9
Energy	11.1	10.5
Chemical	10.3	10.2
Metal products and machinery	9.7	9.5
Textile and clothing	8.0	8.6
Others	27.1	27.3
Total	100.0	100.0

Source: Kazimierz Secomski, "Plan inwestycyjny na rok 1949" (The Investment Plan for 1949), *Życie Gospodarcze*, February 16–28, 1949, p. 148.

Under the revised policy advanced in October, 1953, total annual investment in 1954–55 would remain at the same absolute level as in 1953, and the share of producer goods industry in state investment would decline to about 40 percent. At the same time, investment in agriculture, consumer goods industry, housing, and social-cultural construction would rise substantially over the 1953 level.[33] Despite the over-all decline in investment in producer goods industry proposed for 1954–55, Polish spokesmen stressed that the capital goods industry was still in the process of expansion and that this expansion would continue beyond the present Six-Year

[30] Hilary Minc, "Sześcioletni plan rozwoju gospodarczego" (The Six-Year Plan of Economic Development) *Nowe Drogi*, July-August, 1950, p. 32.
[31] Kazimierz Secomski, "Plan inwestycyjny na rok 1953" (The Investment Plan for 1953), *Inwestycje i Budownictwo* (Investment and Construction), February, 1953, p. 5.
[32] *Nowe Drogi*, October, 1953, p. 30.
[33] *Ibid.*

Plan.[34] Particular emphasis was directed toward expansion of Poland's raw material base, especially of the production of iron ore, coal, zinc and lead ore concentrates, and sulfur.

The allocation of investment funds within given branches of industry permits a choice between numerous small-scale projects and fewer large-scale ones. The Polish plans favor the latter alternative even to the extent of revising earlier plans to eliminate projected small-scale constructions and using the funds thus freed to hasten the realization of large-scale investments.[35] This choice is illustrated in the construction of the metallurgical combine Nowa Huta, which upon completion is expected to produce as much steel as all the metallurgical establishments in prewar Poland combined.[36] Even in the industrialization of such an undeveloped area as Białystok province in eastern Poland, the planned textile combines were each expected to employ several thousand workers,[37] and large- and medium-scale industries would account for about three fourths of the expected total 1955 industrial employment in this province.[38] Since the Polish planners are aware of the excessive transport costs which might be involved in concentration of production in, say, a single large plant for a given product, and they have, moreover, the advice of specialists who had knowledge of the disadvantageous aspects of gigantomania from Soviet experience, it does not appear likely that Polish concentration of investment in large-scale projects will be carried to uneconomic extremes.

The relative importance of the various industries shown in Table 20 is expected to change under the official investment policy which gives priority to the producer goods industries. The chemical industry, metallurgy and fabrication of metals, and the production of basic industrial raw materials were scheduled for especially rapid expansion during the Six-Year Plan. Tables 21–25, showing the achieved and planned output of leading industrial products, give an indication of their relative rates of expansion.

The Polish assortment of industries appears adequate for an inte-

[34] *Ibid.;* see also Polish Embassy, *Press Release,* March 22, 1954, p. 25.

[35] Kazimierz Secomski, "Plan inwestycyjny na rok 1951" (The Investment Plan for 1951), *Życie Gospodarcze,* February 1–15, 1951, p. 135.

[36] Marian Sikora, "Wielkie budowle socjalizma" (Great Constructions of Socialism), *Życie Gospodarcze,* December 16–31, 1951, p. 1320.

[37] Anna Szyszkowska, "Województwo Białostockie w planie 6-letnim" (The Białystok Wojewodship in the Six-Year Plan), *Gospodarka Planowa,* March, 1951, p. 37.

[38] *Ibid.,* pp. 37–38.

Table 20

EMPLOYMENT IN POLISH INDUSTRY, MARCH, 1949

Industry	Number of Employees	Percentage of Total
Total, all branches	1,609,444	100.0
Mining	246,906	15.3
Mineral	102,457	6.4
Metallurgical	96,223	6.0
Metal	242,812	15.1
Electrotechnical	36,216	2.3
Precision and optical	7,091	0.4
Chemical	98,233	6.1
Textile	316,374	19.7
Paper	36,706	2.3
Printing	23,324	1.4
Leather	11,671	0.7
Wood	89,313	5.5
Musical instruments	380	0.02
Agricultural processing and food	149,693	9.3
Clothing	75,742	4.7
Refrigeration	538	0.03
Electric power plants	51,441	3.2
Waterworks	9,436	0.6

Source: *Rocznik statystyczny—1949*, pp. 38–39.

grated industrial development. Indeed, in the period 1950–53 the Polish planners apparently had attempted to provide production facilities for an excessively broad assortment of industrial products. Hilary Minc, a leading economic spokesman, asserted that many decisions to start new types of production failed to take account of the possibilities for economic cooperation among the countries in the Soviet sphere, and that in the future these countries would achieve a higher degree of coordination of planning taking account of their mutual needs and thereby realizing lower costs through specialization.[39]

The tempos of economic development set in the Six-Year Plan assumed the application of advanced technologies and skills, and the development of new processes through scientific research.[40] In actual practice in Polish industry, the old, relatively obsolete proc-

[39] Polish Embassy, *Press Release,* March 22, 1954, p. 27.
[40] Hilary Minc, "Sześcioletni plan rozwoju gospodarczego" (The Six-Year Plan of Economic Development), *Nowe Drogi,* July-August, 1950, pp. 43–46.

esses continued in use along with newer ones and with the construction of projects embodying the latest technical advances in a given
branch of industry. This is illustrated by Polish metallurgy, which
is backward with respect to that of highly industrialized countries,
but which is undergoing modernization of the old plants along with
the construction of new metallurgical combines which are expected
to embody the most recent technological advances, far-reaching
mechanization and automatization of processes, and complete lab-
oratory control of production through use of precision instruments
and self-recording apparatus.[41]

The requirements of Polish industry for technicians and managers are regarded as an essential part of the economic plans. The
educational system has been modified to this end, and youth is being trained for specific assignment to the various branches of the
economy. This permits an economy in the training of specialists
but involves the sacrifice of possible broader training which would
insure greater flexibility in the use of the trainees and a better
understanding on the part of the latter of their role in the industry
and the economy at large. This narrow specialization, which in
part is dictated by the immediacy of the demand for services, facilitates the reduction of labor turnover, one of the chief concerns of
the managers of industry.

The Development of Selected Branches of Industry

Fuels and energy. Table 21 shows the achieved and planned development of the fuel and energy industries. Although the rate of
expansion of output of the coal industry is lower than that of petroleum or electric power, coal will remain the outstanding source of
energy in Poland for many years to come. It was estimated that in
1949 Poland consumed the equivalent of 38.6 million tons of coal
in the form of coal, coke, and lignite, not counting the use of these
fuels for generating electricity, while all electric power plants supplied the equivalent of only 5.0 million tons of coal,[42] and about
95 percent of this energy came from thermal plants using mostly

---

[41] Jan Aniola, *op. cit.*, p. 26.
[42] United Nations, Economic Commission for Europe, *Economic Survey of Europe in
1949*, p. 12. Unless otherwise specified, the unit of weight is the metric ton.

coal and lignite.[43] The energy derived from petroleum is relatively insignificant compared to coal in view of the small Polish consumption of petroleum products, but this source is very important for internal combustion engines and for various lubricants. The use of wood as a fuel declined progressively from the prewar level. In 1938, approximately 6 million cubic meters of wood were utilized as fuel,[44] whereas in 1947, the state forests, which comprised about 85 percent of the total forested area, produced only 2.6 million cubic meters of wood fuel, and this declined to about 2.0 million cubic meters by 1949.[45] Thus, wood as fuel is a relatively unimportant source of energy in postwar Poland.

Table 21

POLISH PRODUCTION OF FUELS AND ENERGY, 1913–55

(MILLION METRIC TONS UNLESS OTHERWISE INDICATED)

					ELECTRIC ENERGY	
Year	COAL	LIGNITE	COKE	CRUDE OIL (*thousand tons*)	*Installed Capacity* (*thousand kw*)	*Production* (*billion kwh*)
1913[a]	41.0	0.2		1,100	831[b]	1.8[b]
1938[a]	38.1	1.1	2.3	510	1,692	4.0
1947	59.1	4.8	4.5	128	2,284	6.6
1948	70.3	5.1	5.1	150	2,460	7.5
1949	74.1	4.6	5.8	170	2,786	8.0
1950	77.8	4.9	6.0	180	2,970	9.0
1951	81.7	5.1[c]	6.3	194	....[d]	10.6
1952	84.5	5.3[c]	7.3	231	....	12.0
1953	88.7	9.3	10.6	....	....	13.6
1955[e]	100.0	8.4	9.9	394	5,406	19.3

Sources: See Appendix B.

[a] The 1913 and 1938 data refer to the boundaries before World War II. Coal production for the postwar area in 1943 reached a peak of 91.4 million tons (Central Planning Board, *Some Facts Concerning the Polish Economy*, p. 84).

[b] The data refer to 1925.

[c] The 1951 figure is the planned output; the 1952 figure is computed on the assumption that the 1951 output coincided with the planned goal.

[d] .... = not available.

[e] Planned.

[43] United Nations, Economic Commission for Europe, *Economic Survey of Europe in 1950*, p. 170.

[44] *Mały rocznik statystyczny—1939*, p. 89.

[45] *Rocznik statystyczny—1949*, p. 68.

Poland possesses two important coal basins, one in Upper Silesia and the other in Lower Silesia. The first of these contains estimated reserves on the order of 70 billion tons,[46] while the other may contain about 4 billion tons, making the total reserves equivalent to approximately 74 billion tons.[47] The Upper Silesian basin, though possessing small reserves of coking coal, contains chiefly coal suitable for energy and chemical transformation. The former German areas in the vicinity of Gleiwitz and Waldenburg, now called Gliwice and Wałbrzych, respectively, provide postwar Poland with most of its coking coal for metallurgical purposes.[48] Reserves of lignite estimated at 18 billion tons[49] are scattered through central and western Poland and were expected to provide the energy for thermal electric power plants and heating. Peat deposits in eastern Poland and in other parts of the country are to be similarly exploited during the Six-Year Plan.[50]

The average depth of the Polish coal seams, about 325 meters, and the average thickness of the seams, about 3.5 meters, make them, respectively, the shallowest and thickest seams of any major European coal producer, excluding the USSR. Output per man-shift in Polish mines accordingly ranked among the highest in Europe.[51] Under the Three-Year Plan, Poland sought to reconstruct its coal mines after the devastation of World War II, and by the end of 1948 production within postwar boundaries had reattained its 1938 level.[52] The Six-Year Plan called for a 35 percent increase in output of hard coal in 1955 as compared to 1949, a gain of about 26 million tons, over half of which was to come from 11 new mines and 36 new levels in the old mines. At the same time the output per man-shift was expected to rise from 1,232 kilograms in 1949 to 1,700 kilograms in 1955, an increase of about 38 percent.[53] The Six-Year Plan

[46] Andrzej Bolewski, "Zagadnienie węgli koksujących w Polsce" (The Problem of Coking Coals in Poland), *Hutnik* (The Metallurgist), January, 1950, p. 1.

[47] *Przegląd Techniczny* (Technical Review), January-February, 1949, p. 23.

[48] Bolewski, *op. cit.*, p. 1.

[49] *Przegląd Techniczny*, January-February, 1949, p. 23.

[50] Hilary Minc, "Sześcioletni plan rozwoju gospodarczego" (The Six-Year Plan of Economic Development), *Nowe Drogi*, July-August, 1950, p. 15.

[51] United Nations, Economic Commission for Europe, *Economic Survey of Europe in 1951*, pp. 157, 162.

[52] United Nations, Economic Commission for Europe, *Economic Survey of Europe in 1950*, p. 62.

[53] *Dziennik Ustaw*, 1950, No. 37, p. 432.

assumed that the over-all increase in output of hard coal would be accomplished without an increase in employment by raising the output per man-shift through increased skill, rationalization, and extensive new investment which over the six-year period would be five times as great as the investment in the industry during the Three-Year Plan.[54] In practice, however, the goals of labor productivity were difficult to realize and the coal industry found it necessary to resort to excessive overtime work.[55]

The Polish petroleum industry lost about two thirds of its productive capacity in the areas ceded to the USSR after World War II, or about 350,000 tons of crude oil production out of a total 1938 production of 510,000 tons.[56] Only by the end of 1949 had the remaining producing areas within Poland reattained their 1938 level of output. In 1938 Poland consumed about 400 thousand tons of petroleum products. The postwar requirements, in view of the plans for industrialization and for mechanization of agriculture, would be much greater. For example, the Six-Year Plan called for a 1955 agricultural park of 80,700 tractors in terms of 15 horsepower units,[57] which in itself is nearly double the total number of tractors and all other motor vehicles in Poland in 1938.[58] The Polish consumption of petroleum products in 1948 amounted to 19 kilograms per capita, or a total of about 450 thousand tons. In this total the share of petroleum for illumination was about 8 percent, whereas in the prewar total it was about 28 percent. The territorial displacement of Poland to the east provided electric energy as a substitute for kerosene, but at the same time it increased the power demands for petroleum products.

At the time of the formulation of the first draft of the Six-Year Plan, the total requirements for petroleum products in 1955, under an assumption of an 85 to 95 percent increase in industrial production and a 35 to 45 percent increase in agricultural output, were estimated at about two and one-half to three times the 1948 con-

[54] Tadeusz Lipski, "Węgiel decydującym czynnikiem . . ." (Coal the Decisive Factor . . .), *Życie Gospodarcze,* March 16–31, 1950, pp. 264–65.

[55] *Gospodarka Planowa,* March, 1953, p. 19.

[56] Józef Mokrzyński, "Aktualne problemy przemysłu naftowego" (Current Problems of the Petroleum Industry), *Życie Gospodarcze,* September 16–30, 1947, p. 728.

[57] *Dziennik Ustaw,* 1950, No. 37, p. 441. "Park" as used here refers to the total number of items of the indicated capital equipment.

[58] Mokrzyński, *op. cit.,* p. 728.

sumption.[59] In view of the subsequently raised targets for industrial and agricultural production to 126 percent and 50 percent increase, respectively, for 1955 over 1949, the requirements for petroleum products would be raised to about four or five times the 1948 consumption. The planned production of 394 thousand tons of crude petroleum for 1955 would need to be supplemented by production of synthetic liquid fuels and petroleum substitutes and by imports.

Only modest increases in output—about 10 to 20 thousand tons annually—were realized from 1947 to 1950. In 1951 production fell short of the goal by 14 percent, and in 1952 the planned 35 percent increase proved too ambitious, only 19 percent being achieved. The official report on 1953 fulfillment makes no mention of crude petroleum, probably because of poor performance in that product.

Since the current production covers only about 25 to 30 percent of the domestic needs,[60] it provides a strong incentive for exploratory drillings to locate new reserves outside the limits of the present producing areas along the Carpathian mountains in the southeastern part of Poland. All of Poland is considered as a geologically possible area for oil deposits, but only the south-central and southeastern regions have proved reserves, which in 1947 were estimated at 2.7 million tons.[61]

The production of benzol from the distillation of coal and absolute alcohol from potatoes and sugar beets in 1948 covered jointly about 10 percent of the liquid fuel requirements, so that taking account of domestic production of petroleum products which met about 30 percent of the needs, the remaining 60 percent had to be met by imports.[62] Although the Six-Year Plan envisioned the establishment of a network of stations for dispensing compressed natural gas for the use of automotive vehicles, the initiation of production of synthetic liquid fuels from coal,[63] and expanded production of benzol and alcohol, the major part of the deficit of petroleum products still would be met from imports. Poland apparently planned

[59] Dr. M. Korolewicz, "Problematyka paliw płynnych w planie sześcioletnim" (The Liquid Fuel Problem in the Six-Year Plan), *Gospodarka Planowa*, February, 1949, pp. 92–93.

[60] Tadeusz Trawiński, "Bilans przemyslu naftowego za rok 1948" (The Balance Sheet of the Petroleum Industry for 1948), *Życie Gospodarcze*, January 15–31, 1949, p. 67.

[61] *Nafta* (Petroleum), November, 1947, p. 336.

[62] Korolewicz, *op. cit.*, pp. 93–94.

[63] *Dziennik Ustaw*, 1950, No. 37, p. 435.

to import a substantial part of her petroleum requirements in the form of crude oil since the planned domestic refining capacity for 1955 was 530 thousand tons of crude petroleum,[64] whereas planned domestic crude petroleum output for the same year was only 394 thousand tons. In keeping with the goal of economic independence from capitalist countries, Poland expected to import a great part of her requirement for crude petroleum, refined products, and capital equipment for natural and synthetic production from the Soviet Union and the east European countries within the Soviet sphere, while at the same time seeking highly specialized petroleum products and equipment from the non-Soviet areas. Czechoslovakia, which already possessed an important synthetic liquid fuel industry and a large engineering capacity, was considered a likely possibility for supplying refinery equipment and cooperating in the production of synthetic fuels.[65]

The production of electricity in Poland is part of the over-all problem of the supply of energy for an industrializing country. To some extent the various types of energy may be substituted for one another and in some cases their production is complementary. This is the case with coal and electric energy in Poland. The planned development of such energy would be based primarily on large power plants operated by coal, especially by abundant coal dust directly on the terrain of the coal basin.[66] Hydroelectric plants would be built only as appendages to the construction of water works and regulation of streams required by the national economic plans.[67] The Silesian coal basins, therefore, would be the main centers of the electric power industry, although the deposits of lignite at Konin in central Poland and lignite and peat in other regions would provide local sources of electric energy under the provisions for new investment in the Six-Year Plan.

Large-scale industry and communications during the course of the Three-Year Plan, 1947–49, consumed over 80 percent of the electric energy produced, while small-scale industry consumed less than 3 percent, and household consumption claimed about 10 per-

[64] *Ibid.*
[65] Korolewicz, *op. cit.*, p. 97.
[66] Hilary Minc, "Sześcioletni plan rozwoju gospodarczego" (The Six-Year Plan of Economic Development), *Nowe Drogi*, July-August, 1950, p. 15.
[67] Joseph Domanus, "Production of Electricity in Poland," *Poland of Today*, December, 1946, p. 4.

cent.[68] In view of the planned 126 percent increase in industrial production from 1949 to 1955 and the expected growth of other uses of power, the projected 130 percent expansion of electric energy production does not seem excessive.

Metallurgy. Iron and steel are at present among the most important basic materials for industrial progress, and the Polish decision to expand the existing industry would appear justified by the abundant deposits of coal, one of the chief ingredients in the making of ferrous metals. Poland's acquisition of the former German Silesian areas strongly augmented the reserves of coking coal on the old Polish territory, but the problem of improving the quality of Polish coke is a pressing one.[69] Polish iron ore reserves, estimated at 58.6 million tons probable, and a further 175 million rated as possible, are located mostly in central Poland in the vicinity of Częstochowa and to the southeast of Radom. Their metal content is low, averaging from 30 to 40 percent.[70] The gain in deposits from the territorial shift after World War II was estimated at less than 1 percent.

The production of iron ores from domestic sources filled about 33 percent of Polish requirements in 1939 and only 15 percent in 1949, and this proportion was expected to reach 30 percent by 1955 according to the Six-Year Plan.[71] Imports of iron ore were obtained chiefly from Sweden and the Soviet Union in exchange primarily for Polish coal. Most of the ferrous alloys likewise were imported,[72] but Polish production of these was expected to increase during the Six-Year Plan.

The development of Polish production of iron ore, pig iron, and steel is shown in Table 22. During the Three-Year Plan, emphasis was placed on reconstruction of the existing metallurgical establishments, and by the end of 1948, the 1938 level of output of crude steel within the postwar boundaries was reached, and the output

[68] L. Dziewicki and J. Wagner, "Elektro-energetyka w walce o pokrycie zapotrzebowania na energie w 1948 r" (Electric Energy in the Struggle to Meet Energy Requirements in 1948), *Życie Gospodarcze,* February 1–15, 1949, p. 114.

[69] Ignacy Borejdo, "Hutnictwo w planie 6-letnim" (Metallurgy in the Six-Year Plan), *Hutnik* (The Metallurgist), September-October, 1950, p. 281.

[70] Roman Krajewski, "Przegląd polskich złóż rudnych z uwagi na ich znaczenie gospodarcze" (Review of Polish Ore Deposits with Regard to Their Economic Significance), *Hutnik,* July-August, 1947, p. 348.

[71] *Dziennik Ustaw,* 1950, No. 37, p. 432.

[72] *Wiadomości Hutnicze* (Metallurgical News), July-August, 1948, p. 23.

within prewar boundaries was exceeded by about 50 percent.[73] The Six-Year Plan set a goal of 100 percent increase in steel output to be achieved by expansion and modernization of existing foundries in order to bring their production up to 3.8 million tons of steel and by the construction of new, completely modern metallurgical combines whose output in 1955 should equal 0.8 million tons. In 1949 the major part of steel production was concentrated in the Katowice (now Stalinogród) province, but the projected new plants near Kraków, Warsaw, Częstochowa, and Gliwice should effect a relative decentralization of the industry in the direction of bringing production closer to the centers of consumption while yet not re-

Table 22

POLISH PRODUCTION OF IRON ORE, PIG IRON, STEEL, AND ZINC, 1913–55

(MILLION METRIC TONS UNLESS OTHERWISE INDICATED)

Year	Iron Ore (Fe content)	Pig Iron	Crude Steel	Crude Zinc (thousand tons)
1913	0.2	1.1	1.7	192.0
1938	0.3	0.9	1.4	108.0
1947	0.2	0.9	1.6	74.0
1948	0.2	1.1	2.0	97.7
1949	0.2	1.2	2.3	107.4
1950	0.3	1.4	2.5	112.8
1951	0.3	1.5	2.8	117.3
1952	0.3[b]	1.7	3.2	124.3
1953	0.5[c]	2.2	3.6	138.0
1955[a]	1.0	3.5	4.6	197.6

Sources: See Appendix B. The 1913 and 1938 data refer to the boundaries before World War II.

[a] Plan.   [b] About 0.35.   [c] About 0.45.

moving it far from the sources of basic raw materials.[74] Crude steel production in the period 1950–53 increased steadily, and the 1955 goal appears feasible. Production of iron ore and pig iron, however, developed more slowly toward the 1955 goals, and Polish officials urged that all possible efforts be made to develop new ore mines to help support the projected steel output.

With the exception of zinc and lead, Poland's production of non-

[73] United Nations, Economic Commission for Europe, *Economic Survey of Europe in 1950*, p. 63.

[74] Borejdo, *op. cit.*, p. 279.

ferrous metals is relatively unimportant.[75] Zinc and lead ores occur in the region near Kielce in central Poland, the Upper Silesia-Kraków area, and Lower Silesia. Prewar Poland exported zinc but found it necessary to import lead. The production of the latter reached 18 thousand tons in 1937 in prewar boundaries,[76] but had fallen to 11.3 thousand tons in 1947 in the postwar area.[77] Since lead and zinc ores occur in compounds with sulfur, the production of these metals yields sulfur and sulfuric acid as valuable by-products. Poland continued to import lead and zinc ore concentrates up to 1953, but thereafter aimed at gradual reduction and eventual cessation of such imports as exploitation of domestic low grade ores increased.[78]

The Six-Year Plan aimed at the expansion of mining of copper-bearing ores to 3.2 million tons in 1955 and the initiation of production of aluminum and magnesium. The production of electrolytic copper was expected to reach 25 thousand tons annually by 1955, which should satisfy an important part of domestic requirements. Electrolytic zinc should account for 54 percent of the entire zinc output in 1955 as against 17 percent in 1949.[79] In the absence of annual goals and production statistics for the nonferrous metals, except zinc, it is difficult to judge the progress being made in this area. Since zinc and lead occur in combination, however, the output of the latter may be expected to rise roughly in proportion to that of the former. If the aims of autarky were pushed to the disregard of profitability of operations, the low grade copper deposits in Lower Silesia could give an annual production of about 20 thousand tons of metal.[80] In the postwar period great emphasis was placed on the collection of all kinds of scrap metals. State enterprises have been designated as monopolies for all transactions in such metals, and all holders of metal scrap were obliged under the penalty of law to safeguard the scrap in their possession and to surrender it upon demand to the monopoly at state-set prices.[81]

Chemicals. The Polish chemical industry was relatively well de-

---

[75] Krajewski, *op. cit.,* p. 348.
[76] *Mały rocznik statystyczny—1939,* p. 150.
[77] *Gospodarka Planowa,* January, 1949, p. 50.
[78] Polish Embassy, *Press Release,* March 22, 1954, p. 26.
[79] *Dziennik Ustaw,* 1950, No. 37, p. 433.
[80] Krajewski, *op. cit.,* p. 349.
[81] *Dziennik Ustaw,* 1948, No. 27, Items 184, 185, 188.

veloped before World War II, producing a wide assortment of basic chemicals including caustic soda, calcium carbide, and sulfuric acid, as well as coal derivatives, soap, explosives, rubber goods, synthetic fibers, and fertilizers. The presence of large deposits of basic raw materials, particularly coal, salt, gypsum, and lime, favored the development of the industry and in large measure determined its specialization.

Table 23 indicates the achieved and projected rates of development in over-all output of the industry and of some of its principal products. The chemical industry was scheduled for an especially rapid expansion during the course of the Six-Year Plan, its goal for 1955 being approximately three and one-half times the 1949 output, while the goal for Polish industry as a whole was an increase of 126 percent. It is difficult to evaluate the progress being made, however, due to the discontinuities in the output statistics.[82] In 1953, gross

Table 23

PRODUCTION OF THE POLISH CHEMICAL INDUSTRY, 1938–55

(THOUSAND METRIC TONS UNLESS OTHERWISE INDICATED)

Item	*1938*	*1948*	*1949*	*1950*	*1955 (Plan)*
Gross output index	100	. . . .[a]	172	. . . .	602
Sulfuric acid	189	218	275	283	540
Caustic soda	30	48	56	65	162
Calcium carbide	64	162	162	173	. . . .
Fertilizers:					
Superphosphate (P₂O₅)	36	45	52	. . . .	250
Nitrogen (N)	51	54	65	. . . .	231[b]
Potassium (K₂O)	108	0	0	. . . .	16
Dyes, tons	2,000	3,100	3,700	4,300	7,900
Automobile tires, tons	1,260	2,505	3,128	4,394	. . . .

Sources: See Appendix B. The 1938 data refer to prewar boundaries. In postwar boundaries, the 1938 production was (thousand tons): Sulfuric acid, 310; calcium carbide, 100 (United Nations, *Economic Survey of Europe in 1950*, p. 175).

  [a] . . . . = not available.

  [b] Goal changed to 180 thousand tons in March, 1954 (Polish Embassy, Washington, *Press Release*, March 22, 1954, p. 21). Other goals were also scheduled for revision (*Życie Gospodarcze*, December 1953, p. 1267).

[82] For example, the United Nations Economic Commission for Europe presented an index of gross output of the chemical industry based on the output of eight products, which indicated a fourfold expansion of the industry in 1949 as compared to 1937, whereas Polish sources indicated less than a twofold expansion for the period 1938 to 1949. (*Economic Survey of Europe in 1950*, p. 167.)

chemical production was reported to be nearly two and one-half times the 1949 level.[83] The chemical industry claimed 13 percent of all industrial investment scheduled in the Six-Year Plan,[84] and the share of the industry in the gross output of large- and medium-scale industry was expected to rise from 8.8 percent in 1949 to 13.7 percent in 1955.[85]

During the Three-Year Plan, the emphasis in the field of chemical production, as in all other branches of industry, was placed on reconstruction of facilities that were damaged by war. The Six-Year Plan, however, sought to expand the production of selected items previously produced and to introduce new products or new technology for old ones. The over-all output of rubber goods, for example, was expected to increase 180 percent according to the initial goals set for the industry, and the output of traction rubber was scheduled for a more than fourfold increase.[86] The annual production of sulfuric acid was scheduled to be doubled in this period by the addition of two new factories, one in Lower Silesia operating on anhydrites of that region, and one in the Kielce district of south-central Poland operating on gypsum. Over one third of the total production of sulfuric acid in 1955 was expected to come from domestic raw materials.[87] Output of this basic chemical, however, lagged behind schedule. Production in 1950 failed to reach more than 85 percent of the planned output, increasing only 3 percent above 1949, and the official silence with regard to the 1951 achievement suggests similar failure to reach the goal. In 1952 a 25 percent increase was reported over the previous year, but a 39 percent gain was planned. Output in 1953 was only 7 percent above 1952.[88] In view of these repeated failures, achievement of the Six-Year Plan goal is unlikely.

The chemical industry in the former German territories placed under Polish administration accounted for about one third of the

---

[83] *Nowe Drogi*, October, 1953, p. 43.

[84] Bronisław Taban, "Powstaje nowa socjalistyczna i pokojowa chemia" (A New Socialist and Peacetime Chemistry Is Rising), *Życie Gospodarcze*, August 1–15, 1951, p. 851.

[85] *Życie Gospodarcze*, June 16–30, 1951, p. 730.

[86] *Przemysł Chemiczny* (The Chemical Industry), April, 1949, p. 219. These goals very probably have been revised upward in the draft of the Six-Year Plan which was approved by the Sejm in July, 1950.

[87] *Dziennik Ustaw*, 1950, No. 37, p. 435.

[88] *Życie Gospodarcze*, February 1–15, 1951, p. 179. *Gospodarka Planowa*, March, 1952, p. 3; February, 1953, p. 2.

total number of plants in the postwar Polish industry; however, about one fourth of the acquired plants required complete reconstruction from the damages incurred during the war, while the rest were less severely damaged.[89] The coke-chemical, artificial fertilizer, inorganic chemical, soap, glycerine, and explosives plants in this area were especially significant additions to the Polish production capacity.

New branches of production to be initiated during the Six-Year Plan included synthetic liquid fuels, textile fibers, fatty acids, synthetic rubber, phenol, cellulose acetate, and various pharmaceuticals. New plants were planned for various regions of Poland, but in view of the raw material orientation of production, the mineral basins of Silesia and southern Poland claimed the major share of the new investment. The production of artificial fertilizers in prewar Poland provided a firm foundation for expansion in postwar years, but the loss of the principal deposits of potassium salts in the areas ceded to the Soviet Union would be only partially remedied by the proposed development of the deposits at Kłodawa in central Poland. Exploitation of these deposits was planned to begin in 1955.[90]

In the chemical industry as well as in other branches of the economy, Polish publications extolled the aid of the Soviet Union given in the form of capital equipment on credit, technological processes, services of experts, training for Polish specialists in the USSR, advice concerning the direction of development of the industry and correction of its deficiencies, and recommendations for increasing the productivity of labor.[91] The extent of net Soviet assistance to the Polish economy, however, is difficult to appraise.[92]

The machinery-metal products industry. The more recent Polish use of the term "metal industry" is nearly synonymous with machine building or engineering production, although in some instances it includes metallurgy. Prewar production of the metal products industries included railway locomotives and rolling stock, machine tools, internal combustion engines, boiler plants, agricultural machines, sheet metal products, and miscellaneous other

[89] *Życie Gospodarcze,* January 31, 1947, p. 85.
[90] Polish Embassy, *Press Release,* March 22, 1954, p. 22.
[91] Rajmund Moskwa, "Przemysł chemiczny na tle wykonania pierwszego roku planu 6-letniego" (The Chemical Industry on the Background of Fulfillment of the First Year of the Six-Year Plan), *Życie Gospodarrcze,* December 1–15, 1950, p. 1222. Cf. *Przegląd Techniczny,* October, 1951, pp. 425–28.
[92] See *infra,* pp. 279, 285.

items. At the outset of planning in 1946, the nationalized sector comprised about 46 percent of the entire metal products industry, not including handicrafts, as measured by the value of production in 1937–38, and about 40 percent if handicrafts are included.[93] In view of the subsequent squeezing out of the private sector and the progressive socialization of handicrafts by means of cooperative associations, Polish figures depicting the growth of the socialist metal products industry must be interpreted with caution. A part of this growth is clearly an extension of the definition without a concurrent increase in the national output, and a part similarly represents replacement of small-scale production by the output of larger establishments.[94] The metal products industry in the new Polish western territories before World War II was about half as large as the Polish industry within the prewar boundaries at that time, but because of the ravages of war, extensive reconstruction was necessary to restore production. Even as early as 1947 this area produced 70 percent of the total Polish output of freight cars, 30 percent of steel cables, 55 percent of precision equipment, and 48 percent of the machinery production.[95]

Both the Three-Year Plan and the Six-Year Plan placed great emphasis on the expansion of output of the metal products. Although the industry suffered greatly from the war, the level of production within the old boundaries reportedly was exceeded by November, 1946.[96] Compared to the 1937 production in the prewar area as 100, the index of engineering production in 1947, 1948, and 1949 was, respectively, 130, 193, and 240.[97] The industry's planned 264 percent increase in output from 1949 to 1955 was one of the highest goals set in the plan.[98] In 1953 its output was reported more than 150 percent greater than in 1949.[99] The value of the gross output of the machine building industry rose from 7 percent of the gross

[93] Ignacy Brach, "Przemysł metalowy w planie trzechletnim" (The Metal Industry in the Three-Year Plan), *Życie Gospodarcze*, June 27, 1946, p. 374.

[94] Cf. *supra*, p. 156.

[95] Mieczysław Lesz, "Przemysł metalowy osiągnął przedwojenny poziom wytwórczości" (The Metal Industry Has Attained the Prewar Level of Production), *Życie Gospodarcze*, January 15, 1947, p. 27.

[96] *Ibid.*, p. 25.

[97] United Nations, Economic Commission for Europe, *Economic Survey of Europe in 1950*, p. 47.

[98] *Życie Gospodarcze*, May 1–15, 1951, pp. 541–42.

[99] *Nowe Drogi*, October, 1953, p. 43.

value of the total output of large- and medium-scale industry in 1937 to 10 percent in 1949, and if the Six-Year Plan goal is met, this share in 1955 will be 14 percent.

Table 24

OUTPUT OF TRACTORS, MACHINE TOOLS, AND AGRICULTURAL IMPLEMENTS IN POLAND, 1937–55[a]

Year	Agricultural Tractors (thousands)	Metalworking and Woodworking Machine Tools (thousand metric tons)	Agricultural Machines and Implements (thousand metric tons)
1937[b]	0	2.04	21.2
1947	0.3[c]	4.61	36.4
1948	1.2	7.23	40.2
1949	2.3	9.83	38.0
1950	3.7	12.54	39.6
1951	3.8	17.70	50.3
1955	11.0	70.80	. . .[d]

[a] See Appendix B for sources. The 1937 figures refer to production within prewar boundaries.

[b] Industrial output in 1937 was lower than in 1938 when a considerable revival of production occurred. Detailed production data for 1938 were not available for the categories in this table.

[c] Planned. [d] . . . = not available.

Table 24 shows the development of output of a few products of the machine building industry from 1937 to 1951 and the Six-Year Plan goals for 1955.[100] The rising output of machine tools is especially significant for the industrialization of the country, while the provision of specially designed tractors and farming equipment is intended to facilitate the collectivization of agriculture.[101] Polish design of machinery for agriculture takes account of the relatively poor servicing the equipment will likely receive and therefore wide tolerances and rugged design are favored. Shortly after World War II, German, Czech, and Italian machines served as models for the Polish engineers and designers, but increasingly thereafter, Soviet technical documentation, production practices, and technical advice

[100] The 1953 output of tractors, types not specified, was reported as 6,700 units, with the comparable 1949 figure given as 2,513 units. Production of metalworking machine tools rose from 9,438 tons in 1949 to 20,300 tons in 1953 (*Nowe Drogi*, October, 1953, p. 43).

[101] Kazimierz Raczyński, "Przemysł maszyn rolniczych . . ." (The Agricultural Machinery Industry . . .), *Życie Gospodarcze*, April 16–30, 1951, p. 460.

have come into prominence.[102] The postwar assortment of the machine building industry was steadily broadened in keeping with defense aims as well as with the needs of the expanding economy. New products to be introduced during the Six-Year Plan included complex machine tools, steam turbines, large-capacity high pressure boilers, mining machinery of various types, production equipment for the chemical industry, agricultural combines, road building machines, cranes, marine engines and pumps, electric locomotives and other communications equipment, ball bearings, optical and precision equipment, electric motors, generators, steel cable, and many other items.[103]

Consumer goods industries. Under the Three-Year Plan, per capita consumption was to be raised above the prewar level, especially in the articles that are widely consumed, namely, food, textiles, clothing, shoes, and household goods. The Six-Year Plan aimed to raise the standard of living from 50 to 60 percent, but a considerable part of this planned increase represented such intangibles as cultural activities, science, education, physical training, health protection, and other social services.[104] Although official reports indicated that the 1953 over-all output of manufactured consumer goods was 99 percent above the 1949 level, the requirements of the population were met poorly.[105] A great volume of self-criticism was directed against the crude finish and bad quality of the goods, their limited assortment, bad packing, and the failure to consider consumer tastes.[106] Production figures, moreover, cannot alone be considered a measure of the welfare of the population since considerable quantities of Polish consumer goods manufactures are exported. Official statements claimed that with increased employment the average real income per capita of the population depending on non-agricultural employment rose about 15 percent in the four years 1951–53,[107] but that the real individual wage "increased only imperceptibly—by about 5 percent." [108]

[102] Zygmunt Keh, "Przemysł budowy maszyn ciężkich w drugim roku planu 6-letniego" (Heavy Machine Building Industry in the Second Year of the Six-Year Plan), *Życie Gospodarcze*, November 1–15, 1951, p. 1168.
[103] *Dziennik Ustaw*, 1950, No. 37, pp. 433–34.
[104] *Ibid.*, p. 443.
[105] Polish Embassy, *Press Release*, March 22, 1954, p. 22.
[106] *Ibid.* See also *Nowe Drogi*, October, 1953, pp. 24–26.
[107] *Nowe Drogi*, October, 1953, p. 29.
[108] Polish Embassy, *Press Release*, March 22, 1954, p. 11.

The range of industrial consumer goods produced in Poland is restricted primarily to the physical and conventional necessities of life, principally processed foods and beverages, textiles and wearing apparel, furniture, bicycles, radio receivers, soap, tobacco products,

Table 25

POLAND'S INDUSTRIAL PRODUCTION OF SELECTED CONSUMER GOODS

Year	Bicycles (thousands)	Leather Shoes (million pairs)	Cotton Fabrics (million meters)	Wool Fabrics (million meters)
1937	39	1.5	399	40
1947	79	2.7	257	32
1948	75	4.9	344	42
1949	91	7.3	403	48
1950	99	7.9	431	54
1951	109	11.2	461	59
1952	. . . [a]	12.2	470	61
1953	. . .	12.9	498	67
1955[b]	. . .	22.2	608	75

Sources: See Appendix B. The 1937 production relates to prewar boundaries. Handicraft production not included.
  [a] . . . = not available.   [b] Six-Year Plan goals.

and the more basic household equipment. Heavy metal consumer durables such as passenger automobiles and washing machines are produced in negligible quantities. Table 25 shows the output of some of the more important manufactured consumer goods. In 1953 the production of cotton fabrics, silk, and other consumer goods failed to reach Six-Year Plan goals. New goals for 1954–55 under the revised economic policy adopted in October, 1953, envision a 12 percent increase in the production of cotton fabrics and 11 percent for wool.[109] If these goals are achieved, the 1955 output will be about equal to the Six-Year Plan goal for wool and about 8 percent below for cotton fabrics.

The territorial distribution of production of light industry and the processed food industry is more uniform than heavy industry, and the Polish plans tend to make it even more uniform. The raw materials required are either widely dispersed geographically, or their transport costs to the centers of fabrication or processing are relatively small compared to the processing costs. Moreover, the

[109] *Nowe Drogi,* October, 1953, pp. 45, 49.

saving on cost of delivery of finished products to consumers on the whole seems to favor local fabrication.

Polish postwar industrial development reflects the priorities established by the national economic plans. Private industrial enterprise almost completely disappeared under the government's confiscatory and discriminatory policies, while socialized industry, especially heavy industry, expanded rapidly, favored by an exceptionally high rate of investment, by price subsidies, and by direct allocation of materials, equipment, and labor. Production of coal, electric power, basic metals, metal products and machinery, and chemicals showed particularly important growth. At the same time the output of crude petroleum, sulfuric acid, iron ore, and certain items of machinery failed to come up to expectations. Consumer goods production expanded more slowly than heavy industry, and the output of handicrafts and independent artisans was adversely affected by the emphasis on socialized industry. During 1950–53 the allocation of new investment brought about a territorial redistribution of industry resulting in the relative decline in importance of the older industrial provinces. The revised economic policies for 1954–55 aim to correct some of the disproportions that the earlier overemphasis on heavy industry had produced. Under the new goals, the output of producer and consumer goods would expand at the same rate, which would be considerably lower than the over-all gains reported in 1950–53.

VIII

Planning and Performance in Agriculture

THERE are two aspects to the problem faced by Polish planning in agriculture: (1) the maladjustments arising from prior historical development, and (2) the consequences of the reform and developmental policies applied by the postwar government. Before World War II the surplus agrarian population could not be profitably employed on farms at the existing level of technology and at the prevailing demand for agricultural products. Associated with this, there were many feudal survivals such as the checkerboard pattern of ownership of farms, common fields, and various usufructs that impeded the development of integrated farms and higher output per unit of land. The character of agriculture varied from highly developed intensive farming in western Poland to extensive farming in the eastern part of the country, and the market orientation diminished correspondingly from west to east. The larger farms everywhere were primarily market-oriented, while the smaller units tended toward self-sufficiency. Over the interwar years the regional variation in intensity of cultivation was leveled somewhat, and although primary emphasis continued to be placed on plant production, animal husbandry was becoming increasingly more popular. State intervention in agriculture was chiefly concerned with policies relating to land reform, prices, and trade. Toward the end of the interwar period, the problem of the surplus agrarian population was being approached in the framework of planning for industrialization.

As may be seen in Chapter II, World War II and the subsequent shifts in boundaries and populations reduced Poland's area about one fifth and its population about one third, so that the density of population per unit of area declined about 15 percent. At the same time the ratio of arable land to total land increased about 5 percent, and as measured by prewar yields per unit area in the leading crops, the newly acquired lands were from one and one-half to two times as productive as the ceded areas.[1] Thus by re-attaining the prewar level of production in the areas included in the new boundaries, the total output of Polish agriculture should increase absolutely over prewar, with the output per capita becoming even greater. However, the task of settling the new areas, overcoming the ravages of war, and reaching the prewar level of output has not yet been accomplished.

In the postwar period the Polish government's policy toward agriculture falls roughly into three phases corresponding to the progressive consolidation of Communist control over the state. In the earliest phase, the leftist coalition sought to strengthen its popular support and weaken that of its opposition by means of a radical land reform which eliminated the large private estates and temporarily assuaged the land hunger of the peasants. Having thus destroyed the large estates which were a major source of the marketed agricultural output, the government in the second phase was concerned with developing means of inducing or forcing individual peasant agriculture to provide the necessary supplies for maintaining the urban population and meeting export requirements in connection with an ambitious program of investment for reconstructing and expanding industry. The second phase overlaps with the third, which began toward the end of 1948 when the Communists had liquidated the Socialist Party and proceeded more boldly toward the socialization of remaining elements of private production, including agriculture.

By the end of 1953 the government had recognized the stagnation induced in agriculture by its discriminatory tax policies favoring collectivized farming, by its correspondingly discriminatory schedules of compulsory deliveries of farm products to the state, by the low investment priority it had assigned to agriculture, and by the sustained draft on the agricultural labor force to meet the needs of industrial expansion. The revised economic policies adopted at the end of 1953 aimed at increasing agricultural production within the framework of continuing socialization of farming and generally unchanged schedules of compulsory deliveries.

[1] *Supra*, pp. 29–30.

Postwar Agricultural Policy

Land reform. Although the prewar land reform brought several improvements, including redistribution of land, a substantial consolidation of scattered small plots into unit farms, a liquidation of easements, and significant melioration of lands, in itself it could not solve the problem of the surplus agrarian population. In contrast to the relatively slow-moving reform from 1919 to 1938, the postwar reform moved extremely rapidly and radically. Beginning on September 6, 1944, the reform was practically completed on the old territories of Poland by the end of 1946. The political motivation of the reform appears to have outweighed the considerations of economic efficiency. Certainly, the resulting destruction of the political power of the estate owners and the partial appeasement of the land hunger of the peasantry contributed to the retention of power by the government.

According to the land reform decree of September 6, 1944, and its subsequent modifications, the agrarian structure in Poland was to be based on private farms which were to be "strong, sound, productively capable units." However, the area allotted to newly created units normally could not exceed 5 hectares of medium quality land, which seems too small to measure up to the need for economic efficiency enunciated in the decree.[2] The arguments currently being offered in support of the government's drive for collectivization of agriculture reenforce this conclusion.

Data showing the distribution of farms according to size in 1931 and 1949 and the share of the various classes in the total area in 1921 and 1949 are shown in Table 26.[3] Under the land reform from 1919 to 1938, the parcellation of about 2.7 million hectares from the large estates and augmentation of smaller units by about another 0.6 million hectares obtained by a liquidation of usufructs effected a total transfer of about 13 percent of the total agricultural land in favor of the smaller holdings. The downward leveling after World War II was not quite as drastic as Table 26 would indicate, since

[2] *Dziennik Ustaw*, 1945, No. 3, Item 13. The small farms reduce their limited scope for efficiency through specialization by practicing a policy of self-sufficiency which distributes their small areas among many uses. The poverty of the small farms coupled with their policy of self-sufficiency leads to overcapitalization in some directions, e.g., draft power, and capital shortage in other lines.

[3] More recent prewar data were not available.

Table 26

DISTRIBUTION OF PRIVATELY OWNED FARM LANDS IN POLAND

SIZE OF UNIT IN HECTARES	NUMBER OF UNITS (THOUSANDS)		PERCENTAGE OF TOTAL AREA OF THE HOLDINGS	
	1931	*1949*	*1921*	*1949*
0– 1.99	747.1	962.1	⎧	5.9
2– 4.99	1136.1	1084.0	⎨ 25.1	21.2
5– 9.99	728.7	906.3	⎩	38.3
10–14.99	190.9	⎫ 347.4	⎰ 37.9	⎫ 26.9
15–19.99	⎱ 118.2	⎭	⎱	⎭
20–49.99		38.9	⎰ 37.0	6.3
50 and over	14.7	3.3	⎱	1.4
Unknown	260.3			
Total	3196.0	3342.0	100.0	100.0

Sources: Data for 1921 and 1931 from *Mały rocznik statystyczny—1939*, pp. 68–69. Data for 1949 from *Rocznik statystyczny—1949*, p. 53.

the state retained in its own possession about 10 percent of the total agricultural land. According to the results reached by January 1, 1949, from a total area of 4409 thousand hectares on the old territories of Poland which were taken over by the state after World War II, 1320 thousand hectares consisting of forests, waters, and roads were exempted from parcellation; 1099 thousand hectares were set aside for state farms, producers cooperative farms, and various public uses; and 1990 thousand hectares were distributed in small parcels.[4]

In the territories Poland acquired from Germany, the agrarian reform proceeded on the basis of the decree of September 6, 1946, which took over all landed property not in the possession of physical persons on that date. Among other provisions, the decree set limits of 7 to 15 hectares for the farms to arise from parcellation, depending on the climate, terrain, soil, and type of farming. However, livestock farms could be as large as 20 hectares, and existing farms smaller than 7 hectares could be allotted without being supplemented. Gardening- and orchard-type farms could not exceed 5 hectares, while plots assigned to settlers engaged in fishing and forestry should not exceed 3 hectares.[5] From the total area taken

[4] *Rocznik statystyczny—1949*, p. 54.
[5] *Dziennik Ustaw*, 1946, No. 49, Item 279.

over by the decree, amounting to 9438 thousand hectares, 2272 thousand hectares consisting of forests, waters, and roads were exempted from parcellation; a further 459 thousand hectares belonging to autochthones were similarly exempted; 2702 thousand hectares were designated for state farms, producer cooperative farms, and various public purposes; and 4005 thousand hectares were distributed among persons authorized to benefit from the reform.[6]

Problem of the marketable surplus. With the exception of the land retained for state farms, the large farms which had been the principal source of a marketable surplus of agricultural products had vanished. As a result, the government faced the problem of extracting a suitable part of the peasant agricultural output to feed the urban population, supply raw materials for industry, and provide for exports. This problem was made more difficult by the government's high priority on investment in heavy industry, requiring on the one hand a relatively low priority on investment in agriculture and consumer goods industries and, on the other, a reduced share of the national product for personal consumption. Moreover, the peasants' traditional self-sufficiency was opposed to the government's attempt to extract a surplus from agriculture through relatively high prices on goods supplied by the socialized sector. The Polish planners sought, therefore, to devise suitable controls over agriculture in order to make it serve the planners' requirements for a high rate of saving to help finance industrialization.

The government approached the problem by policies relating to production and distribution of the harvest. The policies concerning distribution aimed at controlling the share consumed on the farms in the interest of a larger share for the state to allocate to nonagricultural uses. For this purpose, the state at various times employed (1) the device of compulsory deliveries of farm products, (2) manipulation of prices of farm products and of goods coming from the socialized sector, (3) monopoly in the procurement of agricultural commodities for resale, (4) taxation in kind and in money, (5) compulsory saving, (6) contracting in advance for the production of plant and animal products, and (7) attempts to change the institutional structure of agriculture from privately owned individual farms which possess considerable freedom of

[6] *Rocznik statystyczny—1949,* p. 58.

choice in deciding what to produce and how much of the harvest to sell, to socialized large-scale agriculture wherein these decisions will conform to the requirements of the planners. The subjection of agriculture to the kind of discipline prevailing in the nationalized sector of the economy, in the view of the planners, continues to be the chief remaining objective in the path to comprehensive socialized planning.

In the period immediately following liberation, the Polish government exacted compulsory deliveries of agricultural products from the peasants in order to meet the minimum urban requirements, but this system was abolished in 1946, permitting the peasant to produce what he wished and sell or not according to his reaction to the prices offered him. With the introduction of the Three-Year Plan in 1947, attention was turned toward means of tying the agricultural sector into the framework of national economic planning. At first it was thought that the state through its monopoly in foreign trade and expanding control over domestic trade could adequately control the distribution of farm products, and by appropriate manipulation of prices even influence the direction of agricultural production.[7] The prices offered, however, would need to be sufficiently high to attract the peasant's surplus which he might alternatively consume himself.

It was along this line of reasoning that the state expanded its network of socialized trading establishments and at the same time restricted, regulated, and squeezed out private trade. By the end of 1949 the bulk purchase of grain and meat from producers was taken over completely by the socialized establishments, which include the state agencies and the cooperative distributive network. The government's price policy for agricultural products aimed at setting more attractive prices for oilseeds, fibers, tobacco, sugar beets, potatoes, pigs, and milk.[8]

In June, 1947, the Council of Ministers was authorized by law, at its discretion, to collect the land tax in agricultural products instead of money over the whole territory of Poland or parts thereof, and for all farms or only certain categories.[9] This authorization was applied on July 9, 1947, over the whole of Poland, with farms having

---

[7] Mirosław Orłowski, "Problem rolnictwa" (The Problem of Agriculture), *Życie Gospodarcze*, August 30, 1946, pp. 564–65.

[8] *Polish National Economic Plan*, p. 26.

[9] *Dziennik Ustaw*, 1947, No. 43, p. 642.

harvests less than the equivalent of 40 quintals of rye being wholly exempt from payments in kind, those in the bracket from 40 to 60 quintals being required to pay one half of the land tax in kind, and those producing more than 60 quintals obliged to pay the entire tax in kind. Rye was the designated means of payment, but certain substitutions were permitted.[10] In the following years the tax laws substantially repeated the 1947 provisions for collecting the land tax in kind, and at the same time the discipline over collection of grain from farmers by the socialized trading establishments was progressively tightened, proceeding from partial state control in this area in 1947 to 85 percent of the grain purchased from farmers in 1948 and finally complete monopoly by the state and cooperative agencies in 1949.[11] Table 27 shows the growth of state grain purchases and collections and the shares in the total represented by various means of collection.

Table 27

GRAIN COLLECTIONS BY THE SOCIALIZED AGENCIES, 1946–49

(THOUSAND METRIC TONS)

Type of collection	1946	1947	1948	1949[a]
Organized purchase	95	621	1,310	2,100
Compulsory deliveries[b]	230			
Land tax in kind[c]		400	450	530
Total	325	1,021	1,760	2,630

Source: Witold Rościszewski, "Gospodarka zbożowa" (The Grain Economy), *Życie Gospodarcze*, September 16–30, 1949, p. 743.

[a] The 1949 figures represent planned goals.
[b] Compulsory deliveries were abolished in 1946.
[c] Land tax in kind became effective in 1947.

By 1951 it had appeared that the state monopoly in grain purchase and the accompanying price policy was not reaching the goals set by the plans. Apparently the peasant had found means of circumventing the official channels for grain sales and, perhaps, in view of the remedy introduced, was exercising his right not to sell and, instead, consuming the withheld grain on the farm. By decree of July 23, 1951, the state introduced the requirement of compulsory sale of grain by farmers at state-set prices in quantities correspond-

[10] *Ibid.*, No. 55, pp. 905–6.
[11] Witold Rościszewski, "Gospodarka zbożowa" (The Grain Economy), *Życie Gospodarcze*, September 16–30, 1949, p. 742.

ing to norms based on the location, quality, and quantity of land included in a farm.[12] This decree was replaced by the law of July 10, 1952, which appears to establish compulsory deliveries of grain as a permanent feature of state control over agriculture.[13] According to the law, the Council of Ministers prepares the state plan for obligatory deliveries for each economic year, July 16 of the current year to July 15 of the following year. Within this plan, quotas are set for the various regions of the country, these quotas in turn are distributed to localities within regions, and finally allotments are fixed for the farms in the given localities. Nondelivery of the obligatory quota is punishable by administrative action, with fines ranging up to 3,000 zlotys or arrest for a number of days. Willful evasion of the required deliveries or incitement of others to avoid such deliveries is subject to punishment by imprisonment up to three years.

In order to implement the assignment of quotas to farms, the government provides schedules for converting the farm areas in various locations and of differing qualities into uniform "accounting hectares." The delivery quota for a given locality is parceled out to the farms in the area in such a way that the levy per hectare increases directly with the size of the farm. Several schedules are provided for this purpose. In the most steeply progressive schedule under the 1951 decree, the smallest farms were obliged to deliver 0.7 units of grain per hectare, whereas the largest farms, 25 hectares and over, computed their deliveries at the rate of 11.3 units of grain per hectare.[14] By discriminating against the larger private farms, the government's policy could be expected to meet readier acceptance by the small owners, and by discouraging the growth of small farms into large ones while at the same time allowing special reductions in compulsory deliveries to collective farms, this policy was expected to facilitate the socialization of agriculture.

The developments leading to the imposition of compulsory deliveries of grain were paralleled by similar developments for meat, milk, and potatoes. Although the government had attained legal mastery of the meat distributive network by 1950, this control apparently was not sufficiently effective. In mid-1951, due primarily

[12] *Dziennik Ustaw*, 1951, No. 39, Item 297.
[13] *Ibid.*, 1952, No. 32, Item 214.
[14] *Ibid.*, 1951, No. 39, Item 299.

to the failure of the potato crop, but allegedly as well to speculation and sabotage by the kulaks, the state failed to reach its goal in the planned purchase of livestock and meat products. Bojarski refers to widespread failure to live up to contracts for delivery of animals to the state procurement organizations, resort to secret slaughter and illegal trade, and propaganda to inspire no production of livestock at all.[15] A series of measures designed to buttress the system of contracting with private producers failed to remedy the situation, and finally by a law passed on February 15, 1952, obligatory deliveries of meat were imposed on the peasants.[16] These deliveries were incumbent upon individual private farms, garden plots of collective farms, producer cooperatives and other forms of collective agriculture, and state farms. Compulsory quotas were levied on the basis of amount of land in agricultural use. Required deliveries from peasant families belonging to producer cooperative farms were based on the average area per family in the cooperative and ranged from 50 to 70 percent of the corresponding levy on private individual farms. In addition, the established quota for peasant families in such cooperatives was further reduced by 50 percent in the first year of operation of the collective and by 25 percent in the second year.[17]

Compulsory delivery of potatoes was decreed on October 8, 1951, and reenacted apparently in a more permanent version on August 28, 1952.[18] On April 24, 1952, compulsory delivery of milk was decreed.[19] The provisions of these decrees and the special exemptions and reduced rates applicable to cooperative farms were comparable to the legal requirements governing the delivery of meat. Penal provisions corresponded to those in the law on grain.

In December, 1953, as part of its new policy toward agriculture, the government revised its schedules of compulsory deliveries of animal products, in part to encourage livestock production, and in part to adjust to past performance. In general the 1953 norms of deliveries were kept unchanged, but some relief was given owners of very small farms and to the various forms of collective, or co-

[15] Pawel Bojarski, "Gospodarka mięsna na nowym etapie rozwoju" (The Meat Economy on a New Stage of Development), *Życie Gospodarcze*, April 21, 1952, p. 459.

[16] *Dziennik Ustaw*, 1952, No. 8, Item 46.

[17] *Ibid.*, No. 15, Item 91.

[18] *Ibid.*, 1951, No. 52, Item 368; 1952, No. 37, Item 255.

[19] *Ibid.*, 1952, No. 22, Items 142, 144.

operative, farms. Broader exemptions were established for families holding up to two hectares of farm land, quotas were reduced on certain classes of poor land, a wider range of substitutes for the specified deliveries was permitted, and certain exemptions were allowed where peasants raised breeding stock and where they contracted to supply animals to the state.[20] Basically the major concession to the peasants regarding all compulsory deliveries was negative, amounting to a promise that in 1954–55 the delivery norms would not be increased, thus permitting the peasants to sell their surplus in excess of obligatory deliveries at more attractive prices.[21]

Contracting and regionalization of agricultural production. Contracting for plant and livestock production is an important element in the postwar production and trade policies since, thus far, only about 20 percent of the land in agricultural use is socialized. The basic aim of contracting is to assure the necessary supply of agricultural products for industry, food, and export. Since the state exercises a monopoly in foreign trade and controls internal prices, it can use the contracting scheme to develop production of agricultural commodities formerly imported, provided the soil and climatic conditions are suitable. Adequate price policy might be expected to do this alone and even influence the magnitude of production regionally by regional differentiation of the prices offered. However, contracting affords a preview of the outcome of price policy and thus offers a firmer basis for planning.

The Polish policy of planned regionalization of agricultural production in theory takes account of (1) the soil and climatic conditions and the existing pattern of crops, (2) local availability of labor, draft power, and production equipment, (3) transport and communications conditions, (4) the location of consumers and of industries processing various crops, (5) the possibility of complementary crops in a scheme of rotation, (6) the incidence of disease and pests, (7) the specialization of farmers, and (8) the results of previous years of contracting in the various regions. The construction of the plan for contracting applies the method of balanced estimates, which relates the quantities of various commodities desired for direct consumption or as industrial raw materials to the necessary labor, draft

[20] *Ibid.*, 1953, No. 50, Items 244–45, 248–51.
[21] *Nowe Rolnictwo*, April, 1954, p. 8.

power, fertilizer, land, and other requirements of production, while at the same time taking account of the obligatory sales imposed on producers by the state. Consideration of transport costs figures prominently in the location of such crops as potatoes for alcohol distilleries, while an awareness of external economies in production suggests grouping certain industrial crops, such as tobacco and hops, in regions so as to take advantage of joint facilities for tillage and drying and more economical supply of planters with necessities and the services of agrotechnicians.[22] It is difficult to appraise the application of theory to practice; however, the Six-Year Plan discussions indicate that location of industry and agriculture is considered from the point of view of both transport and processing costs.

As may be seen from Table 28, the assortment in state contracting developed from four commodities in 1945 to sixty in 1951, of which fifty-five were plant products and five animal. Although the area encompassed by contracted crops increased about twelvefold, in 1951 it accounted for only 8.6 percent of the total arable land. The 1951 plan for contracting covered nearly all of the pig production destined for the market and an important part of the output of calves and turkeys. In the 1952 plan, contracting was expected to cover about 14 percent of the area of spring planting.[23] With the introduction of obligatory sales of the leading farm products, the significance of contracting diminished, but it remains an important tool of policy for the development of production of special and industrial crops. In order to obtain the desired production of these, the state uses prices, allows special premiums for promptness of delivery and for superior quality, permits the substitution of contracted articles for obligatory deliveries, extends credits for purchase of seeds and fertilizer, and gives the seller priority in the purchase of certain scarce processed agricultural products and industrial commodities. Among the more important crops whose contracted area was expected to increase in 1952 were sugar beets, oil crops, fibers, and potatoes. State contracting of livestock was scheduled to increase sharply in 1954 concomitantly with various exemptions from compulsory deliveries that were granted to owners of small farms.[24]

[22] Władysław Kozak, "Wytyczne polityki kontraktowania produkcji roslinnej w 1952 roku" (Principles of the Policy of Contracting Plant Production in 1952), *Życie Gospodarcze*, February 9, 1952, pp. 174–75.

[23] *Ibid.*, p. 174.

[24] *Nowe Rolnictwo*, December, 1953, pp. 15–18.

Table 28

CONTRACTING FOR AGRICULTURAL PRODUCE, 1945–51

Year	Number of Items Contracted, Including Plant Crops and Livestock	Index of Area Contracted
1945	4	100
1947	10	250
1949	21	443
1950	46	800
1951	60	1,185

Source: Władysław Kozak, "Wytyczne polityki kontraktowania produkcji roslinnej w 1952 roku" (Principles of the Policy of Contracting Plant Production in 1952), *Życie Gospodarcze*, February 9, 1952, p. 174.

Socialization of agriculture. In keeping with the ideology of the Polish United Workers' Party, which asserts after Lenin that even small-scale private agriculture serves as a breeding ground for the regeneration of capitalism, the official plans aim at the transformation of individual private farming into large-scale socialized agriculture. Moreover, socialization was expected to make possible increased output per man and per unit area in agriculture and thus provide a source of labor for industrial expansion. With some reduction of the labor force, the output per worker could be expected to increase somewhat, but large-scale mechanized farms, contrary to Polish expectations, do not automatically produce larger yields per unit of area. Although mechanization may contribute to larger yields by more timely operations, other factors, especially improved seeds, better techniques, and more extensive use of fertilizers are more important.

Two varieties of socialist agriculture are already in existence in Poland, namely, state-owned and state-operated farms, and collectives, or so-called producer cooperative farms. The share of socialized agriculture in the total area in agricultural use for the postwar years increased from about 8 percent in 1947,[25] nearly all in state farms, to about 20 percent in 1953, of which about 12.8 percent was in state farms and the remainder in producer cooperative farms.[26]

Agricultural planning in Poland is applied in its most direct form to the state farms. These operate under the direction of the Cen-

[25] *Ekonomista* (The Economist), Second Quarter, 1951, p. 9.
[26] *Nowe Rolnictwo*, April, 1954, p. 7; *Nowe Drogi*, January, 1954, p. 65, and April, 1954, p. 16.

tral Administration of State Farms, which in April, 1949, consolidated the administration of state agricultural enterprises and later became the Ministry of State Farms. The aims of the state sector in agriculture as enunciated by Hilary Minc in August, 1948, include:

1. Serve as a socialist basis in agriculture and contribute an important part of the food supply for the population, including about 15 to 20 percent of the grain and 7 to 10 percent of the meat supply
2. Assist peasant agriculture by supplying improved plant varieties and animal breeding stock, assist neighboring small farms with the available agricultural equipment, and participate in educating the village in agricultural science
3. Serve the individual peasant farms as a model of large-scale, modern, socialist, mechanized farming, and thus be the decisive stimulus in transferring the small and medium peasants to collective farming.[27]

These aims remain essentially unchanged up to the present time. In furthering the goal of increasing the marketed share of production of state farms, the wage system was changed on April 1, 1950, to eliminate allowances in kind in favor of cash payment, although retaining such services as housing for workers, shelter and fodder for the workers' livestock, a patch for gardening, and fuel.[28] The state farms are regarded as the highest form of socialist agriculture, and accordingly they receive priority in the supply of equipment, fertilizers, and trained personnel. Performance of the state farms, however, was much below the planners' expectations. Although the state farms in 1953 occupied about 12.8 percent of the land in agricultural uses, they accounted for only 9.2 percent of gross agricultural production.[29] The relatively small proportion of total area in state farms gives the state correspondingly limited perspective in the direct planning of production, and therefore it is devoting increasing

[27] Hilary Minc, "O bieżących zadaniach partii w zakresie polityki gospodarczej i społecznej wsi" (About the Current Tasks of the Party in the Sphere of Social and Economic Policy of the Village), *Nowe Drogi*, September-October, 1948, pp. 179–80.
[28] Ignacy Binstein, "PGR ośrodkami wyższej formy gospodarowania na roli" (The State Farms as Centers of Superior Forms of Farm Economy), *Życie Gospodarcze*, September 1–15, 1950, p. 900.
[29] *Nowe Rolnictwo*, April, 1954, p. 7.

attention to the other form of socialized agriculture, the collective farms, or producer cooperative farms as they are called in Poland.

The state's interest in furthering the collectivization of agriculture in part is based on the belief that the collective farms are more productive per unit area and per worker than individual small private farms and in part on the desire to plan the output of agriculture more directly and control the distribution of the harvests more effectively than has been found possible with private farms. The control of the state over producer cooperative farms follows from (1) the hierarchical subordination of cooperatives,[30] (2) the character of the model charters which regulate the activity of the new units, (3) the dependence of the collective farms upon the state machine centers for draft power and special machinery, and (4) the over-all requirements of taxation and obligatory deliveries. A few large units operating under charters granted by the state and serviced by the state-owned tractor and machine stations are likely to be more amenable to state control than numerous small peasant farms with a traditionally independent outlook. In order to facilitate the transformation of peasant agriculture to the collective pattern, the Polish government has been applying various subtle forms of compulsion. The announced intention is a "voluntary" transformation to the collective economy as the peasants become aware of its superiority. Spokesmen of the United Workers' Party, however, acknowledged cases of "violation of the voluntary principle" in what appears to be outright coercion.[31]

For state policy purposes, the peasantry has been classified into three groups principally according to ownership of land: (1) owners of parcels up to 5 hectares, comprising about 60 percent of the total number of farms, are usually identified as the poor or small peasants; (2) owners of 5 to 15 hectares, comprising about 30 percent of the farms, are generally considered medium peasants; and (3) holders of farms larger than 15 hectares, about 10 percent of the total number, are commonly called the village rich.[32] The aim of the Polish United Workers' Party and of the government is to set up opposing factions in the village—the poor and medium peasants against the so-called

[30] See *supra,* p. 58.

[31] *Nowe Drogi,* May-June, 1951, p. 53; October, 1953, p. 69.

[32] Roman Zambrowski, "Aktualne zadania partii na wsi" (The Party's Current Tasks in the Village), *Nowe Drogi,* March-April, 1949, p. 99.

rich or kulaks. In order to further this alignment, the state pursued a discriminatory policy against the "rich" by (1) denying them special aid and privileges in the purchase of fertilizers and the services of the state-owned machine centers which are extended to the poor and medium peasants, (2) excluding them from participation in cooperative societies and organs of local government,[33] and (3) discriminating against them in the levy of taxes, contributions to compulsory savings, and obligatory deliveries of farm products.

At the same time the state has offered a variety of incentives for forming collective farms, including a specially low rate of taxation, provision of special credits for investment, priority in the purchase of fertilizers and services of state machine centers, and land from the state's reserve for this purpose. The response of the peasantry, however, was predominently unenthusiastic. Indeed, the imposition of obligatory deliveries of farm products may be regarded as a temporary substitute for collectivization. Up to April, 1949, only 40 producer cooperatives were registered, 31 in the new territories of Poland and 9 on land taken over from large estates in the old territories.[34] At the end of 1953 over 8,000 producer cooperatives were in existence, including about 200,000 peasant families and over 1.5 million hectares of agricultural land,[35] or more than 7 percent of the total Polish farm area. In 1953 alone, over 3,000 cooperatives were organized, and this rate is envisioned for 1954–55.[36] This is a relatively slow process compared to Russian experience.

Four state-approved types of cooperative farms were introduced in postwar Poland. Proceeding from the least socialized to the most highly collectivized, these are: (1) Land Tillage Associations, (2) Agricultural Cooperative Associations, (3) Agricultural Production Cooperatives, and (4) Agricultural Cooperative Collectives. As of June 1, 1952, they represented, respectively, the following percentages of the total number—8, 7, 22, and 63 percent.[37] All types possess certain common features:

1. A certain minimum of collective labor by the members is required.

---

[33] *Ibid.*, p. 83.
[34] *Ibid.*, p. 88.
[35] *Nowe Drogi*, January, 1954, p. 65.
[36] *Nowe Rolnictwo*, April, 1954, p. 5.
[37] Instytut Ekonomiki Rolnej (Institute of Agricultural Economics), *Wieś w liczbach* (The Village in Figures) (2d ed.), p. 131.

2. Kulaks are excluded and use of hired labor by the cooperative is prohibited with certain exceptions.
3. Members do not lose the right of ownership to the land carried into the cooperative. A household garden plot is allowed for the personal possession and use of members.
4. Membership is voluntary.
5. In principle, the cooperative elects its own administration from among its members, and the general assembly is the highest authority.
6. All producer cooperatives are members of a central union of agricultural cooperatives which instructs and watches over the members.[38]

In the Land Tillage Associations, all the means of production brought into the association not only belong to the member but also remain in his individual possession. These means of production—particularly draft power, machines, and arable land—are pooled only for certain periods of the year. In the other forms the farm land is continuously pooled, but each member of the cooperative is permitted a garden plot from 0.3 to 1.0 hectare in size on which he can keep two cows, their calves, pigs, and chickens. The first type shares only expenses, not earnings; the second and third distribute the collective income according to the capital contributed by the members and their labor;[39] and the fourth distributes income purely on the basis of the amount and kind of labor performed by the individual members without consideration of capital contributions at the outset. In the event of resigning from a producer cooperative, the member receives from the cooperative the capital input he made in kind or in equal value of grain and a parcel of land on the boundary of the cooperative farm of the same value as that originally contributed by the member.[40]

The state fosters the formation of the more highly collectivized

[38] Anatol Brzoza, "Statuty spółzielni produkcyjnych" (Statutes of Producer Cooperatives), *Nowe Drogi*, May-June, 1949, p. 42.

[39] In one of these types the members retain in their individual possession their livestock and equipment, but they are obliged to lend such livestock and equipment to the cooperative at rates computed at "equipment-days" which enter into the calculation of members' shares in the cooperative's earnings. (*Życie Gospodarcze*, February 1–15, 1951, p. 184.)

[40] Michał Sadulski, "Doświadczenia przebudowy rolnictwa" (Experience in the Transformation of Agriculture), *Życie Gospodarcze*, May 1–15, 1950, p. 443.

cooperatives by assigning to their use certain lands without charge, while retaining title to and recovering the assigned areas in the event of dissolution of the cooperative. Members of the fourth type are completely free from paying off their indebtedness to the state arising from their acquisition of land under the land reform and settlement programs. The Land Tillage Associations have benefited from a 30 percent reduction of the land tax and the same reduction on quotas for compulsory saving, while the other types received similar preferential tax reductions and were completely exempted from obligatory saving.[41] It is clear, therefore, that the state, while encouraging the formation of all types of collective farms, offered special inducements to the more highly collectivized types which resemble the Soviet collective farm most closely.

The Polish cooperative farms have been officially criticized for their inadequate development of livestock production, improper work organization, and their lack of enthusiasm for enlarging their membership.[42] State plans for 1954–55 included the formation of more cooperatives in the lagging central and eastern provinces, enlarged membership per cooperative, preferential treatment for the cooperatives in the use of state services and investment credits, educational aid to build up cadres for the cooperatives, closer collaboration between the cooperatives and the state machine centers, and preferential schedules of compulsory deliveries to foster the development of cooperatives and the production of crops most desired by the government.[43] Despite some lesser benefits promised to private agriculture, the current government policy favoring collectivization undoubtedly creates uncertainty concerning the future in the minds of individual peasants and thus adversely affects the growth of production.

Machine and tractor stations. Polish policy regards the rising network of state and community machinery stations primarily as a means of transforming small-scale individual farming into large-scale collectivized agriculture. With respect to the cooperative farms, the state machinery stations fulfill a twofold role, firstly, technical and mechanical assistance, and secondly, political, organizational, and economic guidance. The centers provide professional assistance in

[41] Brzoza, *op. cit.,* p. 46.
[42] *Nowe Drogi,* October, 1953, p. 84.
[43] *Nowe Rolnictwo,* April, 1954, p. 20–25.

the formulation of financial and production plans.[44] Much of this, however, remains in the blueprint stage. In March, 1951, the state machine centers were criticized for their passive mechanical aid to the cooperative farms and for the neglect of agrotechnical advice and political work in converting additional individual farmers to collective farming. In order to remedy this shortcoming, political departments were added to the machine centers to carry on propaganda in favor of further collectivization and to guide the existing cooperative farms to greater emphasis on livestock production and other state aims.[45] By the end of 1953, the state machine centers were still being criticized for their inadequate support of cooperative farms in such matters as fulfilling work contracts on time, introducing new agricultural methods, and carrying on political work to socialize agriculture.[46]

The representatives of the local people's councils and the state machine centers are expected to oversee the annual closing of accounts in order to prevent the cooperative farm from invading its seed and fodder funds in favor of a larger distribution of income in kind among the members and in order to prevent deferring the repayment of credits for the same reason. By his daily contact with the collective farm, the state machine center representative is expected to observe to what extent the cooperative carries out its agreements for agronomic work, whether members show up for work in requisite numbers, and whether the women take advantage of preschools for their children in order to work in the fields.[47]

The state machine centers may conclude contracts for servicing noncollectivized peasant farms, but only on the condition that groups of owners sign contracts for raising the same crop, thus taking a first step in the direction of collective work. In addition to the state machine centers, there exists an extensive network of community machine centers[48] which serve private individual farms. In

---

[44] Wojciech Szmidt, "Państwowe ośrodki maszynowe" (State Machine Centers), *Życie Gospodarcze,* March 1–15, 1951, pp. 290–92.

[45] *Ibid.,* p. 292.

[46] Bolesław Bierut, "Zadania partii . . ." (Tasks of the Party . . .), *Nowe Drogi,* October, 1953, p. 17.

[47] Henryk Grzelak, "Zamknięcia roczne w spółdzielniach produkcyjnych" (Annual Closing of Accounts in Producer Cooperatives), *Życie Gospodarcze,* January 28, 1952, pp. 118–19.

[48] Initially these were organized as cooperative machine centers connected with the distributive outlets of the Peasants' Mutual Aid Association.

May, 1952, the Presidium of the Polish Government placed the state and community machine centers under a single management, with the community machine centers subordinated to the state centers. A single one of the latter typically services an entire county.[49]

In contrast to the state machine centers, which are relatively few in number and possess from 10 to 40 tractors each,[50] the community centers are far more numerous but possess less equipment and little or no draft power.[51] Official policy prescribes that the richer peasant should stand last in the order of priority for use of the equipment of the community machinery centers in the furtherance of the "principle of class struggle" and to promote the collectivization of agriculture. As late as October, 1953, the community machine centers were criticized by Polish spokesmen for alleged failure to pursue a sufficiently discriminatory policy toward the richer peasants in the rental of equipment, for inadequate stocks of equipment, and for failure to keep machinery in repair. As many as one half of the threshing machines and one fifth of the binders and reapers in the village centers were idle for lack of spare parts or because of the bad quality of repairs.[52]

The number of state machine centers increased from an initial 30 organized in 1949 [53] to 401 on December 31, 1953. The number of tractors in the 401 centers existing at the end of 1953 amounted to 16,635 units in 15 horsepower equivalents.[54] An additional 28,737 tractors were on state farms,[55] and an insignificant number were held by the community machine centers and private individual farms. By separating the ownership and control of tractors and the larger items of equipment from the direct users on individual and collective farms and applying discriminatory rates on the services of the machine stations, the government furthered its campaign for collectivizing agriculture. With respect to the collectivized farms of the future, which may be both horseless and tractorless, this policy will serve as a strong means of influencing the production and distribution of

[49] *Nowe Drogi*, November, 1953, pp. 95, 100.
[50] *Życie Gospodarcze*, January 1, 1952, p. 15.
[51] *Nowe Drogi*, October, 1953, p. 18. The Polish revised policy for agriculture adopted in October, 1953, called for adding draft power to the community centers, so that they could better assist the peasants who were not adequately equipped.
[52] *Ibid.*, October, 1953, p. 18; November, 1953, pp. 95–97.
[53] Szmidt, *op. cit.*, p. 292.
[54] *Gospodarka Planowa*, March, 1954, pp. 5, 12.
[55] *Nowe Rolnictwo*, April, 1954, p. 7.

harvests. The fees charged in kind for plowing and other services may then become an important means for meeting urban require- ments for agricultural products. The adverse effects of such a policy on incentives for producers, however, may offset the apparent ad- vantages of centralized control over production.

Development of Agricultural Production

Postwar production problems. Polish postwar agriculture found itself in a greatly changed environment as a result of the structural changes brought about by the land reform, the socialization of in- dustry, the shift of frontiers, and the devastation of war. Conse- quently, its primary tasks consisted of adjustment to the new insti- tutional setup, settlement of the new territories, rehabilitation from the damages of war, and, finally, the expansion of production to higher levels.

As a consequence of World War II and the subsequent shift in frontiers, nearly one third of the population had to change domi- ciles, about one fifth of the capital invested in buildings on farms was reported destroyed, and, perhaps most seriously, there were severe losses of livestock which reduced the numbers of horses roughly by one half, sheep and cattle by two thirds, and pigs by about four fifths.[56] In the transitional period after the war there was a serious lack of many kinds of production equipment and supplies, especially draft power, natural and artificial fertilizers, farm imple- ments, seeds, and insecticides. In the first year after the war only about one half of the arable land was tilled, and except for the assistance of the United Nations Relief and Rehabilitation Adminis- tration, great numbers of the population would have perished. UNRRA's gift of nearly 76 million dollars worth of equipment and supplies for the rehabilitation of Polish agriculture, including about 8 thousand tractors, 145 thousand horses, and 20 thousand cattle,[57] was an important factor in the recovery of production in 1946–47. The problem of eliminating fallows had not been fully resolved even as late as 1953, when about 400 thousand hectares still re- mained to be put under cultivation.[58]

[56] Central Board of Planning, *Some Facts Concerning the Polish Economy,* p. 60.
[57] United Nations Relief and Rehabilitation Administration, *Impact of UNRRA on the Polish Economy, Operational Analysis Papers, No. 45,* pp. 21, 24.
[58] *Nowe Rolnictwo,* April, 1954, p. 4.

Recognizing that restoration of agricultural production to the prewar level and subsequently raising it to new higher levels in an expanding economy required the restoration and expansion of fixed and working capital, the postwar economic plans set high targets for the output of tractors, farm machinery, fertilizers, and other supplies for agriculture. Nevertheless, over-all agricultural investment had a much lower priority than industrial investment, and in the course of the Six-Year Plan this priority was further reduced to the disadvantage of agriculture. Faced by the continued stagnation of agriculture, the United Workers' Party and the government in the fall of 1953 revised the state's economic policy for 1954–55, giving higher investment priorities to agriculture.[59] Table 29 shows the relative displacement of horses by tractors expected by 1955, but assuming that one tractor is equivalent to twelve horses, Polish agriculture by the end of the Six-Year Plan would still derive about 75

Table 29

DRAFT POWER IN POLISH AGRICULTURE, 1938–55

(HORSES, MID-YEAR; TRACTORS, END OF YEAR)

Year	Horses (thousands)	Tractors (thousands 15 hp. equivalents)
1938[a]	3,916	1.5
1947	2,016	14.2
1948	2,297	14.4
1949	2,538	15.5
1950	2,800	22.8
1951	2,884	31.8
1952	. . . .[b]	39.2
1953	2,720	45.4
1955[c]	3,000	80.7

Sources: Horses: 1938 data from *Mały rocznik statystyczny—1939*, p. 91; 1947–48 from *Rocznik statystyczny—1949*, p. 72; 1949–50 from *Dziennik Ustaw*, 1950, No. 21, p. 229, and 1951, No. 18, p. 173; 1951 from *Gospodarka Planowa*, February, 1952, p. 6; 1953 from *Nowe Rolnictwo*, March, 1954, p. 25; 1955 from *Dziennik Ustaw*, 1950, No. 37, p. 441. Tractors: 1938 and 1948–49 from United Nations, Economic Commission for Europe, *Economic Survey of Europe in 1950*, p. 184; 1947 from *Survey* for 1949, p. 293; 1950–52 from *Ekonomista*, Third Quarter, 1953, p. 29; 1953, *supra*, p. 205, adding the tractors in machine centers and on state farms; 1955 from *Dziennik Ustaw*, 1950, No. 37, p. 441. Privately owned tractors are excluded from the above series after 1949. In 1951 there were about 500 such tractors in existence—old ones and not subject to renovation or replacement (*Ekonomista*, Third Quarter, 1953, p. 29).

[a] Prewar area.　　[b] . . . . = not available.　　[c] Six-Year Plan goal.

[59] *Supra*, p. 144.

percent of its draft power from horses as against nearly 100 percent in 1938 and 93 percent in 1949. The expansion of inventory of farm equipment may be expected to consist primarily of replacement of the obsolescent horse-drawn equipment and the expansion of the park of tractor-drawn implements.

Table 30

ELECTRIFICATION OF POLISH AGRICULTURE, 1945–55

End of Year	Number of Electrified Villages	Thousands of Farms Receiving Electricity	Percentage of Total Number of Farms Electrified
1945	3,778	70	2.2
1946	7,548	200	6.0
1947	9,072	285	9.0
1948	10,290	320	10.3
1949	11,500	356	11.0–12.0
1950	12,500	....[a]	....
1951	12,863	....	....
1952	13,213	....	....
1953	13,615	....	....
1955 plan	20,400	1,780	55.0–60.0

Sources: (1) 1945–48 data from *Rocznik statystyczny—1949*, p. 72; (2) 1950 from *Życie Gospodarcze*, February 1–15, 1951, p. 180; the 1949 figures for farms were obtained by adjusting the planned goals downward in proportion to the number of villages actually electrified in 1949 as given in source (2) to the goals for electrification of villages in 1949 as given in source (1); (3) 1951–53 from *Gospodarka Planowa*, February, 1952, p. 6, February, 1953, p. 4, and March, 1954, p. 4; (4) 1955 from *Dziennik Ustaw*, 1950, No. 37, p. 441, by applying the planned increases to the 1949 base. The Six-Year Plan calls for a fivefold increase over 1949 in the number of electrified farms. The percentage of total in 1955 is obtained by multiplying by five the range given for 1949.

    [a] .... = not available.

Under the postwar plans the Polish villages are being gradually electrified, as may be seen from Table 30. The plans intend to supply these villages with electric motors and other equipment, particularly items for collective use. On the average, each electrified farm consumed about 244 kilowatt hours in 1948,[60] which is barely sufficient for lighting purposes alone. The production gains from electrification may be expected to be very modest unless the use of energy per farm is stepped up very substantially over the 1948 level. Relatively slow progress in electrification was achieved by the end of 1953, and the Six-Year Plan goal probably will not be realized.

   [60] *Rocznik statystyczny—1949*, p. 72.

Polish agriculture in the postwar years received increasing quantities of artificial fertilizers, but supplies in 1953 were below the target set for that year in the Six-Year Plan.[61] In the fall of 1953 the revised goal for delivery of synthetic fertilizers to farms in 1955 was set at 35 percent over the 1953 level,[62] which would result in a total tonnage about 10 percent below the Six-Year Plan goal. As may be seen by comparing Tables 23 and 31, Poland expects to continue importing artificial fertilizers even in 1955. The import will consist largely of potassium fertilizers since, according to the Six-Year Plan, domestic industry will be producing only about 16 thousand tons of potassium oxide for fertilizers in 1955, whereas the requirements for agriculture will be on the order of 200 thousand tons of this component.

State action to increase agricultural output includes melioration of farm lands through flood protection and drainage; raising the level of agricultural science and practice through provisions for research, model farms, and vocational education; provision of in-

Table 31

SYNTHETIC FERTILIZERS SUPPLIED TO POLISH AGRICULTURE, 1938–55
(THOUSAND METRIC TONS, PURE COMPONENTS)

For Harvest of the Year	N	P_2O_5	K_2O	Total
1938	29.4	53.0	44.4	126.8
1946	38.7	14.9	35.1	88.7
1947	50.8	41.7	61.9	154.4
1948	63.0	44.2	75.1	182.3
1949	70.8	81.7	109.9	262.4
1950	93.4	102.9	165.9	362.2
1951	. . . .[a]	. . . .	. . . .	373.0
1952	. . . .	. . . .	. . . .	426.5
1953	. . . .	. . . .	. . . .	426.5
1955 Six-Year Plan	201.1	226.3	212.1	640.0

Sources: 1938–49 data from *Rocznik statystyczny—1949*, p. 65; 1950 from *Dziennik Ustaw*, 1951, No. 18, p. 173, for the total, and *Życie Gospodarcze*, February 1–15, 1951, p. 180, for the components (the sum of the components exceeds the total slightly due to rounding of percentages of increase over 1949 in the Polish statistics); 1951 from *Gospodarka Planowa*, February, 1952, p. 6, by applying the reported increase to the 1950 base; 1952–53 from *Gospodarka Planowa*, March, 1954, p. 5; 1955 from *Dziennik Ustaw*, 1950, No. 37, p. 441.

[a] . . . . = not available.

[61] Polish Embassy, Washington, *Press Release*, March 22, 1954, p. 21.
[62] *Nowe Drogi*, October, 1953, p. 74.

creased quantities of high quality seeds and breeding stock from state farms; expansion of veterinary services; and efforts to control plant diseases and pests. During the Three-Year Plan nearly all the flood control and drainage works that had been damaged during the war were restored,[63] and the Six-Year Plan aimed at the renovation of drainage projects on about 190 thousand hectares of arable land and new drainage works on 77 thousand hectares.[64] It is difficult to arrive at a summary measure of the effectiveness of such diverse activities, however, and perhaps the best measure of the over-all effectiveness of planning and other postwar measures in agriculture is found in the trend in output of plant and animal products.

Plans and performance in production. According to Polish indexes, the output of agriculture per capita of the population in 1949 was 18.6 percent above the 1937 level in the prewar boundaries.[65] Although 1937 was a bad year for grain crops, but better than average for sugar beets and potatoes, it would appear that the goal of the Three-Year Plan for a 10 percent increase per capita above the 1936–38 average had been closely approximated. In terms of the gross value of output, the Polish official index, taking 1937 equal to 100 in the prewar area, stood in the postwar years at 59 and 86 for 1947 and 1949, respectively, and under the Six-Year Plan it was scheduled to reach 129 in 1955.[66] United Nations statistics showing the gross value of agricultural output for current consumption, taking the 1934–38 average in postwar boundaries as 100, give the index for the crop years 1947/48, 1948/49, and 1949/50 at 62, 65, and 71, respectively,[67] thus indicating that the prewar production of the present area had been about two-thirds recovered. Viewed in this perspective, the 50 percent increase in agricultural output scheduled under the Six-Year Plan would seem realistic since it could be interpreted as recovery to the prewar level rather than expansion to a new level. Return of fallow land to production facilitated the modest gains from 1947 to 1949, but after 1949 there was much less scope for expansion from this source. The Six-Year Plan

---

[63] *Życie Gospodarcze*, August 1–15, 1951, p. 887.

[64] *Dziennik Ustaw*, 1950, No. 37, p. 441.

[65] *Życie Gospodarcze*, April 7, 1952, p. 389.

[66] *Supra*, p. 147.

[67] United Nations, Economic Commission for Europe, *Economic Survey of Europe in 1950*. The crop year indicated is from July to the following June. Increases in capital, e.g., in the form of larger herds of livestock, are not included.

relied primarily on higher yields per hectare to achieve production goals. The trend in gross agricultural production in the first four years of this plan was uneven, the significant expansion in 1950 being followed by a decline in 1951, stabilization at this level in 1952, and recovery to the 1950 level in 1953. The over-all increase in output was officially reported about 10 percent over 1949,[68] which indicated that the Six-Year Plan for agriculture could not be realized. As part of the revised policy for the two remaining years of the plan, the 1955 goal for gross agricultural production was set 10 percent above the 1953 level,[69] which, if realized, would mean about 20 percent increase over 1949 instead of 50 percent as given in the Six-Year Plan. If the revised goal is achieved, production would still be substantially below the prewar level on the present area.

The Six-Year Plan specified a higher goal for animal products than for plant products, namely, a 68 percent increase as against 39 percent.[70] The plan envisioned a change of emphasis from the less valuable crops, such as rye and potatoes, to the more valuable crops desired for direct consumption and for use as raw materials in industry, particularly wheat, barley, sugar beets, oilseeds, and certain feedstuffs. Quite as important as the over-all growth in plant and animal production were the goals set in the Six-Year Plan for increasing the marketed mass of these products by 88 percent over-all, and 66 and 108 percent, respectively, for plant and animal products.[71] It cannot be presumed that domestic consumption of these products would increase in the same proportion, since, aside from the reserves of grain and other products being created in Poland, an important part of agricultural production finds its way into foreign trade and comes back in the form of investment goods and industrial raw materials.

At the end of 1953 official reports indicated that gross plant production was only about 2 percent above 1949 and animal production about 23 percent higher.[72] The revised plans for 1954–55 anticipate a 10 percent growth in gross agricultural output, with the increase for animal products somewhat higher than for plant products.[73]

[68] *Nowe Rolnictwo*, April, 1954, p. 3.
[69] *Nowe Drogi*, October, 1953, p. 70.
[70] *Dziennik Ustaw*, 1950, No. 37, p. 439.
[71] *Ibid.*
[72] *Nowe Rolnictwo*, April, 1954, p. 3.
[73] *Gospodarka Planowa*, December, 1953, p. 12.

Table 32

SOWN AREA IN POLISH AGRICULTURE, 1934–55

Year	Thousand Hectares
1934–38 annual average[a]	17,629
1947	12,911
1948	14,265
1949	14,804
1950	15,180
1951	15,362
1952	15,504
1955[b]	15,900

Sources: 1934–38 data from *Mały rocznik statystyczny—1939*, p. 77; 1947–49 from *Rocznik statystyczny—1949*, pp. xxi, 62; 1950 from *Życie Gospodarcze*, February 1–15, 1951, p. 197; 1951–52 from *Gospodarka Planowa*, February, 1952, p. 6, and February, 1953, p. 4; 1955 goal from *Dziennik Ustaw*, 1950, No. 37, p. 439.
[a] Prewar boundaries.   [b] Six-Year Plan.

Table 32 shows the sown area in postwar Poland increasing from year to year. This gain occurred almost entirely through the elimination of fallows as the new western territories were settled and through the more complete utilization of state farm areas. The percentage increase in sown area after 1949 is small in comparison with the planned increase in agricultural output by 1955, and therefore increased production was to come chiefly from increased yields per

Table 33

YIELDS OF PRINCIPAL CROPS IN POLISH AGRICULTURE

(METRIC QUINTALS PER HECTARE)

Year	Wheat	Rye	Barley	Oats	Sugar Beets	Potatoes
1909–13[a]	12.4	11.2	11.8	10.2	245	103
1934–38[a]	11.9	11.2	11.8	11.4	216	121
1946	10.2	10.8	11.0	12.0	177	134
1947	8.9	9.3	11.1	11.3	167	134
1948	11.7	12.4	11.7	13.7	189	108
1949	12.3	13.1	12.2	13.1	184	122
1950	12.4	12.7	12.7	12.4	222	140
1955[b]	17.0	15.5	17.0	16.0	240	150

Sources: 1909–13 and 1934–38 annual averages taken from *Mały rocznik statystyczny—1939*, p. 77; 1946–50 from *Nowe Drogi*, May-June, 1951, p. 55; 1955 from *Dziennik Ustaw*, 1950, No. 37, pp. 439–40.
[a] Polish area in 1938 boundaries.   [b] Six-Year Plan.

hectare. At the end of 1953 there were still about 400 thousand hectares of untilled arable land.[74]

Trends in the yields of principal crops per hectare in Polish agriculture have not varied greatly from 1909 to 1950, but the Six-Year Plan envisioned increases from about 20 to 40 percent, as may be seen from Table 33. Heavier applications of fertilizers, better seeds, and a higher level of applied agricultural science were expected to be the principal elements in the proposed gains. While average yields were expected to rise during the Six-Year Plan, this was not to be the case uniformly over the whole country, but rather would represent a gain over prewar in the eastern and central provinces and a loss in the western areas, particularly in the new territories. Table 34 shows the leveling process in the case of wheat yields. This expected development parallels in part the experience after World War I, when the intensively farmed areas of western Poland suffered a decline in yields in competition with the extensive culture of eastern Poland. Under the Six-Year Plan, however, the yields in the eastern part of the country were not expected to remain static as after World War I, but rather to increase very significantly. What the future holds remains to be seen, but up to 1953 progress was very modest. According to the state planning commission's announcement, the yields and harvest in 1951 failed to come up to expectations, being roughly on the same order as in 1950 for the four grains and much lower in the case of potatoes and sugar beets, but no figures were given.[75] In 1952 the total harvest of the four leading grains was about 4 percent higher than in 1951, but in 1953 the grain harvest dropped below the 1952 level although production of sugar beets and potatoes increased substantially.[76] These reports indicate that very little advance, if any, over 1949 has been achieved in yields per hectare. The lowered goal for 1955 gross agricultural production under the 1953 revision of economic plans implies a very substantial reduction in the Six-Year Plan goals for yields per hectare in the principal crops.

Table 35 shows that by 1950 the annual harvest of the principal grains, potatoes, and sugar beets had nearly attained the level of output in prewar boundaries. Since that time agricultural produc-

---

[74] *Nowe Rolnictwo*, April, 1954, p. 4.
[75] *Gospodarka Planowa*, February, 1952, p. 6.
[76] *Ibid.*, February, 1953, p. 4; March, 1954, p. 4.

Table 34

WHEAT YIELDS BY REGIONS, 1934–38, AND THE SIX-YEAR PLAN GOALS FOR 1955
(METRIC QUINTALS PER HECTARE)

Region	1934–38	1955 Goal
Eastern Poland:		
Białystok	9.3	14.0
Lublin	12.4	18.0
Rzeszów	9.9	15.9
Central Poland:		
Olsztyn (Allenstein)	17.3	15.6
Gdańsk (Danzig)	20.4	18.0
Warsaw	11.1	15.8
Bydgoszcz	15.7	18.9
Łódź	13.0	16.5
Kielce	12.7	15.9
Kraków	11.4	15.5
Western Poland:		
Szczecin (Stettin)	22.9	17.0
Zielona Góra (Grunberg)	21.3	17.2
Wrocław (Breslau)	19.6	17.4
Poznań	15.1	16.3
Stalinogród (Katowice)	19.6	18.5

Source: *Gospodarka Planowa*, October, 1950, pp. 505, 513.

tion remained stagnant or declined. Official sources indicate that annual grain harvests in the period 1950–53 increased on the average only 6 percent over 1947–49, while the harvest of buckwheat, millet, and other groats stayed on the same level or rose insignificantly.[77] If one takes account of the harvest data in Table 35, it follows that average annual grain production in 1951–53 was below the 1948 level. The revised goal for 1955 grain production calls for about 600 thousand tons increase over 1952,[78] indicating little or no gain over the period of the Six-Year Plan. Insofar as is known, the figures shown in Table 35 refer to barn crops, rather than biological yields as in the USSR and some other eastern European countries.[79]

According to the Six-Year Plan, the total sown area in 1955 was expected to increase by about 7 percent over 1949, but a redistribu-

[77] *Nowe Drogi*, October, 1953, p. 71.
[78] *Ibid.*, p. 72.
[79] Cf. United Nations, Economic Commission for Europe, *Economic Survey of Europe in 1951*, p. 222.

tion among land uses was planned so as to increase the area planted in wheat by 14 percent, barley 37 percent, sugar beets 25 percent, oil crops 67 percent, and fodder 48 percent. In the same period the area sown to rye would decline about 14 percent.[80] The percentage of sown area allocated to sugar beets, oil plants, and fodder crops increased substantially in the postwar period up to 1952, but grains and potatoes still accounted for about 79 percent of the total, a slight decline from prewar.[81]

Table 35

ANNUAL HARVEST OF LEADING PLANT PRODUCTS

(THOUSAND METRIC TONS)

Year	Wheat	Rye	Barley	Oats	Potatoes	Sugar Beets	Oil Seeds[a]
1909–13[b]	1,678	5,711	1,489	2,814	24,790	4,113	. . .[c]
1934–38[b]	2,064	6,467	1,411	2,558	35,006	2,806	87
1947	986	4,306	930	1,562	30,821	3,493	27
1948	1,620	6,304	862	1,756	26,756	4,228	55
1949	1,772	6,765	1,032	2,314	30,814	4,785	61
1950	1,854	6,503	1,077	2,126	36,802	6,342	66
1955[d]	2,800	6,900	1,960	2,800	39,750	7,800	105

Sources: 1909–13 and 1934–38 annual averages taken from *Mały rocznik statystyczny—1939*, pp. 77–80; 1947–48 from *Rocznik statystyczny—1949*, p. 62; 1949 and 1955 from *Dziennik Ustaw*, 1950, No. 37, p. 439; 1950 from *ibid.*, 1951, No. 18, p. 172; 1950, rye, barley, and oats from *Wiadomości Statystyczne* (Statistical News), February, 1951, p. 7.
   [a] Linseed and hempseed.
   [b] Annual averages over the period indicated for the pre-World War II Polish area.
   [c] . . . = not available.   [d] Six-Year Plan goal.

Polish postwar agricultural policy has fostered the development of animal production by means of price policy, contracting associated with premiums for deliveries in excess of the contracted amounts, priorities given for the purchase of scarce industrial articles in connection with deliveries of livestock to state procurement agencies, tax reductions for raising pigs, honors and decorations for outstanding work in livestock production, and other devices. The postwar recovery of livestock herds shown in Table 36 is impressive, but the official postwar statistics make it appear all the more so by comparing postwar livestock numbers with the 1938 data for the present area instead of the prewar Polish area, as in most of the

[80] *Dziennik Ustaw*, 1950, No. 37, p. 439.
[81] *Gospodarka Planowa*, December, 1953, p. 10.

other official comparisons. The latter area possessed substantially larger numbers of livestock in every category except pigs in 1938.

As part of the revision of agricultural policy in December, 1953, the 1955 goals for livestock numbers were changed from the Six-Year Plan figures shown in Table 36, downward for cattle and upward for pigs and sheep. Since a given number of cattle may be presumed to

Table 36

LIVESTOCK NUMBERS IN POLAND, 1938–55

(THOUSAND HEADS, MID-YEAR)

Year	Horses	Cattle	Pigs	Sheep
1938[a]	3,148	9,924	9,684	1,940
1946	1,730	3,910	2,674	727
1947	2,016	4,746	4,274	983
1948	2,297	5,748	4,626	1,410
1949	2,538	6,365	6,122	1,621
1950	2,800	7,203	8,134	2,198
1951	2,884	7,203	7,320	2,572
1952	....[b]	7,240	7,539	2,906
1953	2,720	7,385	9,730	3,330
1955 Six-Year Plan	3,000	9,500	10,500	3,800
1955 Revised goals	....	8,000	10,750	4,250

Sources: 1938 and 1947–48 data taken from *Rocznik statystyczny—1949*, p. 72; 1946 from *Życie Gospodarcze*, October 16–31, 1949, p. 838; 1949 from *Dziennik Ustaw*, 1950, No. 21, p. 229; 1950 from *ibid.*, 1951, No. 18, p. 173; 1955 Six-Year Plan goal from *ibid.*, 1950, No. 37, p. 440; 1951–52 from *Gospodarka Planowa*, February, 1952, p. 6, and February, 1953, p. 4. The 1952 cattle numbers reported about 2 percent below 1953 in *Gospodarka Planowa*, March, 1954, p. 4; 1953 data and 1955 revised goal from *Nowe Rolnictwo*, March, 1954, p. 25, and December, 1953, pp. 12–13, respectively.

[a] Area within postwar boundaries. Within prewar boundaries the numbers of the livestock in 1938 were as follows, in thousands: horses—3,916; cattle—10,554; pigs—7,525; sheep—3,411 (*Mały rocznik statystyczny—1939*, p. 91).

[b] .... = not available.

be considerably more valuable than the same number of either pigs or sheep, the reduction of the goal for cattle by about 1.5 million head far outweighs the 0.45 million and 0.25 million increases for sheep and pigs, respectively. The 1955 goals for livestock numbers given in the Six-Year Plan did not appear unreasonable in view of the recovery of herds in 1946–49 and of the prewar numbers sustained in the same area. All the more, the revised goals established in 1953 appear attainable since pig and sheep numbers can be increased more rapidly than cattle herds.

Success in achieving the revised goals in agriculture will depend in large measure on the peasants' reaction to the government's policy with respect to compulsory deliveries, collectivization, prices, and investment. If the government can halt the drift of farm youth to urban employment, provide an adequate supply of consumer goods for the village market, and seriously implement its plans for supplying agronomic services, fertilizers, and productive equipment to agriculture, an important part of its goal may be realized. A 10 percent increase in production within two years, however, is an ambitious goal, especially in the light of past experience. Only minor concessions have thus far been made in compulsory deliveries; the discriminatory pressures favoring collectivization remain essentially unchanged; and the projected rate of formation of new collective farms for 1954–55 has not been reduced from the relatively rapid rate achieved in 1953. The planned increases in state agricultural investments apply to low initial levels, and moreover these investments are not likely to have an immediate productive effect. Achievement of the new, lower production goals for 1955, therefore, may prove difficult.

IX

Polish Postwar Financial Planning

IN postwar Poland, both money and financial institutions are tools at the disposal of the state by means of which it seeks (1) to influence the factors of production not directly controlled by it toward the fulfillment of national economic plans, (2) to control the distribution of the national product in such a way that the plans for economic development may be implemented, (3) to supervise the execution of economic plans by the socialized sector, and (4) to enlarge the socialist sector at the expense of the private. By means of wage and price policies, taxation, and other financial measures, the government seeks to direct the decisions of the population in the role of consumers and as suppliers of services of labor, and the decisions of entrepreneurs outside the socialized sector toward the achievement of the goals outlined in economic plans. In practice, however, consumers' choice of quantities to buy at the existing prices, workers' decisions concerning where and how long to work at the wages offered, and the plans of farmers and other independent producers regarding the assortment and quantity of their production and the disposal of their output came into conflict with the objectives of the national economic plans. In the absence of harmony at the state-set prices and wages, the freedom to make these decisions has been restricted by measures which expanded the direct controls exercised by the state. At present, peasant agriculture is subjected to compulsory sales of farm products, and the freedom of choice of occupation and mobility of labor have been restricted. In the period under review there were persistent inflationary pressures, two monetary reforms, and two periods of rationing of consumer goods followed by price and wage revisions and abolition of rationing. The period was characterized by continuing efforts on the part of the government to provide financial incentives for the efficient operation of socialized enterprises and at the same time to devise direct supervision over them in order to insure their compliance with the production objectives detailed in the economic plans. By means of discriminatory taxation, compulsory saving, price policies, and monetary reform, the government has reduced and plans eventually to eliminate the private sector of production which remained after the early measures of nationalization and land reform.

The State Budget

Role and scope of the budget. Under the system of planning followed in Poland, every economic unit encompassed in the national plan must have its activity reflected in an operational financial plan which serves as the basis for supervision by the financial organs of the state. Among the central operational plans, the state budget over the postwar years has become the chief instrument for unifying the functions of accumulation and disbursement of financial resources and for exercising control over the economic activity of the socialized sector. The quarterly plans of the credit system supplement the central budget by providing temporary augmentation of the working capital for units of the national economy and by mobilizing financial reserves not entering the budget system.[1]

The scope of the state budget expanded progressively over the postwar years until by 1950 it included the net results of various equalization funds of the socialized establishment and the surplus and reserves of banks and insurance companies. Compared to earlier state budgets, the 1951 budget and its successors through 1953 were much broader in coverage and were more intimately woven into the fabric of centralized planning. A resolution of the Council of Ministers on April 17, 1950, directed that the 1951 budget be expanded and become more closely related to the national economic plan. The resolution specified that the budgetary system be revised in order to (1) make the state budget the basic financial plan for the accumulation and redistribution of financial resources, (2) relate the basic elements of the state budget to the indexes of the national economic plan, (3) subordinate the financial plans of particular branches of the economy to the state budget, and (4) base the state budget on the principle of democratic centralism and budgetary

[1] Cf. Zbigniew Pirożyńzki, "Podstawowe zasady przebudowy systemu budżetowego" (Basic Principles of the Transformation of the Budget System), *Życie Gospodarcze,* May 16–31, 1950, p. 482.

unity while simultaneously allowing for initiative by local authorities.[2] Thus, beginning in 1951, the state budget became the central financial plan for the planned economy. Democratic centralism in this context meant that the directives from the planning center would effectively reach the local levels through the detailed hierarchical subordination of public authorities from the lowest level to the highest.

On the expenditures side, the 1951 state budget included the financing of the national economy, social-cultural outlays, national defense, public security, the judicial establishment, and the political and economic administration. The financing of state enterprises in the framework of the budget provided for investment, the seasonal-low requirements for working capital, and in exceptional cases also planned losses. Enterprises which performed exclusively the functions of management, coordination, planning, supervision, and research for subordinate enterprises were supported directly by the state budget. Production enterprises were expected to operate as quasi-independent firms, covering their expenditures from the sale of their output and meeting temporary requirements for working capital above their own resources by borrowing from the state banks. The intention of the planners was to set up a system wherein the management of an enterprise would strive to reduce costs and maximize profits while producing the assortment and quantities of goods set forth in state-approved operational plans and selling the output at the planned prices.

The income side of postwar budgets beginning in 1951, and for most of the earlier years as well, consisted of the following:

(1) payments from socialized enterprises under the heading of taxes, profits, excess working capital, and equalization differences arising from various advantageous departures from average cost conditions,

(2) taxes and compulsory savings from the population and private business, and

(3) fees and other income associated with public administration.

Receipts from state loans were considered current income, while the expenditure side of the budget included service of the state debt.

[2] *Ibid.*, p. 483.

In comparison with earlier budgets which had expanded progressively up to 1950 by inclusion of the net balances of equalization funds for state enterprises and local governments, the 1951 state budget incorporated the complete budgets of local governments, social insurance, and various social funds, and was more directly connected with the state enterprises. The incomes and expenditures of equalization accounts for working capital and price differences down to the level of central administrations were brought into the state budget.[3] As a result of its enlarged scope and the expansion of economic activity, in 1951 the budget was about twice as large as in 1950.[4] In 1952, the classifications were further standardized upon the pattern used in the over-all national economic plan, thus permitting closer control over the execution of the plan,[5] and in 1953, the trend established in the preceding years was continued. In view of the continuing changes being made in the scope and methodology of the state budget, the comparison of budgets of the early postwar years with later ones may be misleading. The growth of the state budget in large measure is attributable to its taking over the financing of activities formerly outside its domain without a necessary connotation of over-all increase in economic activity.

The income side of the state budget. Owing to the steadily expanding scope of the national budgets and the changing format of reports, as well as the attenuating supply of information, it is difficult to prepare breakdowns of the total revenues and expenditures into categories that are fully comparable over the postwar years. The budgets for the period through 1950, being similar in composition, although of progressively expanding scope, are shown in summary form in Table 37, while the budgets for 1951–53, being very similar in coverage and planning categories, are shown in Table 38. The first table shows only the central budgets whereas the second includes central and local budgets. The share of local governments in the combined revenues and expenditures of central and local authorities ranges from 12 to 16 percent in the postwar period,

[3] Zbigniew Pirożyński, *System budżetowy Polski ludowej* (The Budget System of People's Poland), p. 119. See *Finanse*, No. 2, 1954, pp. 53–56, and No. 4, 1953, p. 48, for detailed provisions of enterprise settlements with the state budget.

[4] Julian Rataj, "Budżet państwowy na rok 1951" (The State Budget for 1951), *Życie Gospodarcze*, April 16–30, 1951, p. 439.

[5] Kazimierz Rapaczyński, "Budżet pokoju Polski ludowej" (The Budget of Peace of People's Poland), *Gospodarka Planowa*, April, 1952, p. 17.

Table 37

REVENUES AND EXPENDITURES OF THE POLISH CENTRAL BUDGET, 1947–50

(BILLIONS OF CURRENT ZLOTYS)

Item	1947	1948	1949 (Plan)	1950 (Plan)
REVENUES				
Total revenue	223.9	451.2	612.1	848.0
Turnover taxes[a]	102.6	172.4	229.4	291.7
Income tax and other taxes[b]	54.7	90.8	116.8	158.0
Payments from state enterprises	44.2	137.1	125.3	302.9
Special funds[c]		1.0	81.1	68.7
Other revenue	22.4	49.9	59.5	26.7
EXPENDITURES				
Total expenditures	208.9	406.1	612.1	848.0
Financing the national economy	45.2	121.4	277.2	374.7
Social-cultural outlays[d]	39.1	51.9	86.9	125.3
Food subsidies	46.4	98.3	11.4	
Defense	26.3	38.4	56.4	85.7
Public security	17.6	25.4	36.8	44.0
Service of state debt	0.3	1.5	2.0	3.4
Government administration and other	34.0	69.2	141.4	214.9

Sources: Data for 1947–49 taken from *Rocznik Statystyczny—1949*, pp. 150–52; 1950 figures from *Dziennik Ustaw*, 1950, No. 16, pp. 147–69.

  [a] Includes profits of state monopolies.

  [b] Includes wage and salary tax, tax on other incomes, land tax, and minor taxes and fees.

  [c] Surplus of insurance societies and the Social Saving Fund, and incomes from the Land Fund, Local Government Equalization Fund, and other funds.

  [d] Current budget outlays for the Ministries of Education, Culture and Art, Labor and Social Welfare, and Supply, plus pensions and annuities. Outlays for social and cultural aims in other parts of the budget are not included above.

and its inclusion for the years 1947–50 in Table 37 would not seriously alter the distribution of expenditures and revenues shown there. Since public administration and social-cultural activities are more important locally than in the central budget, the shares of these categories in the combined central and local budgets would increase relatively to the other categories of expenditures. On the income side of such combined budgets, property taxes and the miscellaneous group also would gain relatively, especially the latter. The local authorities are highly dependent upon support from the central budget for a very substantial part of their revenues. In the

1953 budget, for example, the local governments received only about one fifth of their revenues from purely local taxes and obtained the remaining four fifths from sharing in the income of the central budget and from grants from the central budget.[6]

Table 38

PLANNED REVENUES AND EXPENDITURES OF THE COMBINED
CENTRAL AND LOCAL GOVERNMENT BUDGETS, 1951–53
(BILLIONS OF CURRENT ZLOTYS)

Item	1951	1952	1953[a]
REVENUES			
Total	55.971	63.788	101.069
Socialized economy	44.564	44.800	76.501
Nonsocialized economy and the population	5.998	7.898	10.053
Loans and deposits	1.234	1.141	.820
Social insurance[b]		7.011	10.361
Miscellaneous	4.175	2.938	3.335
EXPENDITURES			
Total	51.891	62.905	97.018
National economy	21.143	26.560	49.434
Social-cultural activities	16.336	16.228	23.541
Defense	3.750	6.624	10.479
Administration[c]	6.694	7.332	9.838
Service on state debt	.446	.656	.570
Reserves and miscellaneous	3.522	5.505	3.157

Sources: 1951 budget taken from *Dziennik Ustaw*, 1951, No. 18, Item 145, p. 162; 1952 from *Gospodarka Planowa*, April, 1952, p. 17; 1953, *Dziennik Ustaw*, 1953, No. 26, Item 101.
[a] Prices and wages were revised sharply upward at the beginning of 1953.
[b] It is not clear where this item was placed in 1951.
[c] Includes outlays for public security and the execution of justice as well as for the public administration.

In comparing categories in Tables 37 and 38, it is necessary to keep in mind possibly divergent definitions of similarly labeled categories. The budgets for 1951–53 were not available in sufficient detail to permit an examination of the content of the groups of revenues and expenditures shown, or to construct new classifications which might be adaptable for the entire period under review. Under the financial reform at the end of October, 1950, 3 new zlotys became the equivalent of 100 old zlotys for the translation of wages

[6] *Dziennik Ustaw*, 1953, No. 26, Item 101, p. 159.

and prices, and this ratio is used in Table 39 for comparing the post-reform budgets with the earlier ones. It is necessary, however, to keep in mind the expanding scope of postwar budgets, and, more-over, if purchasing power in real terms were considered, the difference in magnitude between the early postwar budgets and the later ones would be further diminished. The big difference between 1952 and 1953 in Table 39 is accounted for largely by the very substantial upward revisions of prices and wages at the beginning of 1953.

Table 39

REVENUES AND EXPENDITURES IN POSTWAR POLISH STATE BUDGETS, 1947–53
(BILLIONS OF CURRENT ZLOTYS)

Year[a]	Revenues	Expenditures
1947	6.72	6.27
1948	13.54	12.18
1949 Plan	18.36	18.36
1950 Plan	25.44	25.44
1951 Plan	55.97	51.89
1952 Plan	63.79	62.91
1953 Plan	101.07	97.02

Sources: Tables 37 and 38 above, converting the pre-1951 budgets by the ratio of 3 new zlotys equal 100 old.
 [a] 1947–50, central budget only; 1951–53, all public authorities.

The role of the socialized economy as a means of extracting surplus purchasing power from the population has become increasingly prominent. In part this is a result of the relative expansion of the socialized sector to the disadvantage of the private and the expansion of economic activity as a whole, and in part a consequence of the greater coverage of the later budgets in comparison with the earlier ones. Table 38 shows that about 70 to 80 percent of the total revenue was to be derived from the socialized economy and only a small part from the private economy and the population directly, but this feature, which was praised as a special attribute of such socialized economies as Poland,[7] does not necessarily mean that the population escapes being taxed. Clearly, sales taxes on products originating in the socialized economy and the profits of state enterprises included in the prices paid by consumers extract surplus purchasing power in the same sense as a tax on incomes. Nonuniform

[7] Kazimierz Rapaczyński, "Budżet pokoju Polski ludowej" (The Budget of Peace of People's Poland), *Gospodarka Planowa*, April, 1952, p. 17.

sales taxes, however, distort cost-price relationships and reduce the effectiveness of the price mechanism as an indicator of the desires of consumers, whereas a direct tax on incomes does not have this disadvantage.

The taxes on turnovers of goods and services accounted for more than one third of the total revenues of the Polish budgets from 1947 to 1950. With the transition to Soviet-type budgets in 1951, the share of these taxes in total revenues presumably increased markedly. Turnover taxes were levied on transactions by both the private and the socialized sectors at rates in 1946–48 ranging from 1 to 10 percent for most categories, but significantly higher on alcoholic beverages, as shown in Table 40. The rate on petroleum products was high relative to coal and presumably indicated a desire to limit the use of the former, which must be imported in large quantities to augment the modest supply from domestic production. Perhaps the

Table 40

TURNOVER TAX RATES ON SELECTED GROUPS OF GOODS AND SERVICES, 1946–48

Item	Rate (Percent of Selling Price)
Products of the state enterprises:	
Petroleum	10
Coal	4
Iron, steel, and nonferrous metals	5
Building materials	4
Electrotechnical goods	5
Fabricated metal products	4
Chemicals	6
Wood products	4
Leather products	6
Textiles	10
Paper products	6
Potato products, yeast, sugar, coffee, edible oils, and food substitutes	4
Wine	10–35
Beer	22
Playing cards	50–75
Lawyer's services	6
Doctor's services	4
Raw materials, semimanufactures, and final goods produced by cooperatives	1.5

Source: *Dziennik Ustaw*, 1946–48, *passim*.

motivation was the same in the case of textiles, which likewise depended upon imported raw materials. The turnover tax on goods proceeding from several branches of state industry was paid as an integrated tax by the central sales offices serving the various branch organizations, and usually it was not levied again on further turnovers of the goods.[8]

By 1953 the turnover tax was applied in two forms, the "object" type in which a specific tax is associated with a given object, and the "difference" type wherein the tax consists of the difference between the selling price of the commodity and the factory price representing the industry's average cost of production plus the planned profit. The latter is the basic type and conforms to the Soviet model.[9]

The direct taxes indicated in Table 37 include income taxes in both the socialized and private sectors, a separate income tax pertaining only to wages and salaries, the land tax, and assorted lesser taxes and fees. The wage and salary tax was levied progressively on earnings at rates ranging in 1948 from 0.75 percent in the lowest taxed category to 23.0 percent in the seventeenth, or highest, category, where the earnings were approximately seven times as great as in the lowest. A 25 percent reduction of the computed tax was allowed for a taxpayer supporting more than two children, 50 percent for more than four, and complete exemption for more than six; but childless married persons and unmarried persons over twenty-five years of age were required to pay from 10 to 20 percent more than the basic tax. Employers were directed to withhold the tax from the periodic wage and salary payments, thus facilitating collection of the levy.[10] In the 1953 revision of the tax rates the spread was reduced to a range of 0.9 percent to 21.5 percent, with the progression extending over twenty-seven steps, becoming less steep at the upper end.[11]

Earnings of persons not subject to the wage and salary tax and the profits of business enterprises, private and socialized, were subject to a more steeply progressive income tax. In 1948 this tax ranged from 5 percent on incomes from 120 to 140 thousand zlotys, the lowest class, to 50 percent on incomes of 5400 thousand zlotys or

[8] Cf. *Dziennik Ustaw*, 1948, No. 29, p. 541; No. 43, p. 873; and No. 50, p. 1036.
[9] *Finanse*, No. 5, 1952, p. 85. See also *infra*, p. 246.
[10] *Dziennik Ustaw*, 1949, No. 7, Item 41.
[11] *Ibid.*, 1953, No. 1, Item 1.

above in the twenty-eighth, or highest, category. An additional 2 to 15 percent was levied as a surtax on incomes ranging from 360 to 400 thousand zlotys in the lowest bracket to 5400 thousand and above in the highest. Reductions up to 25 percent of the basic tax were allowed for income recipients who received nonproperty incomes, while, on the other hand, earnings from real estate and invested funds were burdened with an additional 25 percent of the basic tax.[12] Just as is the case of the wage and salary tax, reductions were allowed as family allowances, and an additional levy above the basic rate was imposed upon childless taxpayers. Cooperative organizations belonging to the Central Cooperative Union benefited from a 25 percent reduction of the tax as computed from the basic schedules, and in no event paid more than one third of their income as tax. Thus, private capitalist incomes were burdened in a discriminatory manner while cooperatives representing the principal means of transition to socialist organization received preferential treatment as part of the continuing state policy aimed at the extinction of the capitalist sector of the economy. State enterprises, unless otherwise provided, paid one half of their profits as tax, but in no case paid less than 10 percent.[13]

Income from land and property taxes is divided between state and local authorities. Although the relative magnitude of this tax is small, its significance in Polish planning is much greater since the tax is one of the principal means of exercising discipline over private agriculture. Since 1947 the land tax has been collected on an increasing scale in the form of agricultural products, principally grain. Typically, the orders of the Council of Ministers prescribing the requirements of deliveries in kind to meet the land tax allowed the smaller farms to pay the levy in cash and gave the tax collector discretion in permitting substitution of other products in place of the usually demanded grain.[14] Up to the time of reintroduction of obligatory sales of agricultural products to the state purchasing agencies in 1951, the payment of land tax in kind and state contracting for agricultural production were the principal means for assuring the state that a dependable share of the agricultural output would be at its disposal.

[12] *Ibid.*, 1948, No. 52, Item 414.
[13] *Ibid*. See also *infra*, pp. 245–48.
[14] *Ibid.*, 1947, No. 11, Item 67; 1948, No. 25, Item 169.

The land tax is graduated progressively. For example, in 1949 it ranged from 2 percent on farms having an income equivalent up to 10 quintals of rye through thirteen stages up to 18 percent on incomes over 250 quintals.[15] At the same time, farmers becoming members of producer cooperative farms were granted tax reductions, amounting to 30 percent on the land to be placed in collective use, while the land tax for the existing collective farms was set near the minimum rate.[16] The state's policy as expressed in the land tax is double-edged: on the one hand it seeks to make the position of the richer peasant a less desirable objective for the ambition of the poorer peasants, while on the other it offers substantial tax relief as an incentive for collectivization, the ultimate aim being the socialization of agriculture in order to effect direct planning of production and distribution of output as in the nationalized industries.

For the present, however, the government uses tax reductions as incentives for the realization of goals set in its economic plans. In order to promote the production of pigs and their sale to state agencies in 1949, reductions of the land tax were allowed in Lublin, Poznań, and Łódź, descending in eleven stages from 50 percent for the delivery of 100 kilograms of live weight from farms with income equivalents up to 30 quintals of rye, to 7 percent for the sale of 700 kilograms from farms with an income equivalent in excess of 250 quintals of rye.[17] Since the tax reductions were differentiated regionally for other areas of Poland, there may have been some intention to influence the location of pig production by this means. It is difficult to appraise the effectiveness of taxation alone in furthering the Polish agricultural plans, but if the outcome of the plans for increasing the pig population be accepted as the measure, then it must be considered a failure, both in the Three-Year Plan and the early years of the Six-Year Plan. Clearly, however, pig production is influenced by the whole complex of relative prices of alternative farm products, the prices of goods bought by peasants, and the conditions of production, particularly the availability and

[15] *Ibid.*, 1949, No. 16, Item 100.

[16] *Ibid.*, Item 101. In 1949 the rate of the land tax on collective farms was 3.5 percent. In 1953 the tax rate on private farms ranged from 10 to 48 percent of the income, while the rate on the more highly socialized collective farms was 3.5 percent and on the less highly socialized, 4.5 percent. Members of joint tillage associations were taxed at the same rate as individual farmers, but received a 30 percent reduction of taxes on land included in the joint effort (*ibid.*, 1953, No. 32, Item 129).

[17] *Ibid.*, 1949, No. 11, Item 70.

prices of feedstuffs. The totality of these factors is by no means an invariant framework for the operation of tax incentives.

The payments by state enterprises into the budget include amortization allowances, surpluses of price equalization funds, and excess working capital. Other sources of revenue include the proceeds of domestic and foreign loans and deposits of insurance organizations. These are considered current revenue and must be kept in mind in evaluating Polish claims of balanced budgets. Since 1949 the income from these sources has been an important factor in covering the planned budget outlays.

Beginning in 1948 and extending through 1951, compulsory saving represented an important source of budget revenue, amounting to about 4 percent of the central budgets up to 1950, and very likely a smaller share thereafter in view of the greater scope of the later budgets. According to the 1948 law establishing the Social Saving Fund, individuals and private enterprises subject to the income or wage and salary taxes and having an income exceeding 240,000 zlotys per year and payers of the land tax on the basis of income exceeding 60 quintals of rye were required to make deposits in the fund according to the source and size of their incomes. The Social Saving Fund initially had four components, namely, the funds obtained from (1) private industry, handicraft, trade, and services, (2) agriculture, (3) hired labor, and (4) public sources. Deposits earned interest or yielded premiums at rates determined by the Minister of Finance and depositors were permitted to withdraw annually 5 percent of the balance of deposits at the end of the preceding year, except in the event of death in the family, maintenance of children in school away from home, and floods, droughts, or similar disasters, when greater withdrawals were allowed. The rates were most steeply progressive for fund (1), rising from 3.7 percent on incomes from 240 to 250 thousand zlotys per year through twenty-one stages up to 18 percent on incomes over 6 million zlotys. The rates of compulsory saving from agricultural income were established annually by the Council of Ministers and could not exceed 50 percent of the levy of the land tax. Wage and salary earners were obliged to save from 1 to 3 percent only, a relatively privileged status. In addition to the permissible withdrawals of savings indicated above, participants in the fund could obtain loans for investment purposes provided the intended investment was included in the state investment plan. In such cases the contemplated investment was required to come up to prescribed technical requirements, and the expenditure of loans granted was subject to control by the banking system to insure that the conditions of the loan were fulfilled.[18] With the shrinkage of the private sector and the imposition of more comprehensive controls over agriculture, the government abolished compulsory saving effective January 1, 1952, for funds (1), (2), and (4) indicated above.[19]

The expenditure side of the budget. Appropriations for financing the national economy became increasingly important in the postwar budgets, rising from about one fourth of the total budgetary expenditures in 1947–48 to more than one half in 1953. These outlays finance most of the new capital investment in the economy, supply additional working capital for expanded production in existing enterprises, and cover the operating losses of state enterprises. In 1949, about four fifths of Polish total gross investment was covered by the investment plan, which in turn depended upon the state budget for about four fifths of its funds.[20] In more recent years the role of the state budget as the primary source of investment funds appears to have increased in keeping with the shrinkage of the private sector and the emphasis placed upon the direct connection of state enterprises with the budget. Investment grants comprise the major part of the outlays under the financing of the national economy. The role of bank credit and of the investor's own funds is small in comparison with the allocations from the state budget; however, the distinction by source of funds within the investment plan is relatively unimportant since the latter controls the outlays from all these sources. The over-all tasks of the national economic plan govern the formulation of the investment plan, which in turn guides the investment activity of the socialized enterprises and of certain private investors that meet the requirements for bank credit under the provisions of the investment plan.

As may be seen from Tables 37 and 38, social and cultural outlays account for the second largest fraction of total budgetary expenditures. The expenditures for food subsidies in the early postwar years may be included in this category. As in the case of material

---

[18] *Ibid.*, 1948, No. 10, Item 74.

[19] *Ibid.*, 1952, No. 12, Item 72.

[20] *Życie Gospodarcze*, March 1–15, 1950, p. 211; *Dziennik Ustaw*, 1949, No. 26, Item 189, p. 574; and *supra*, p. 142. The remaining part of the investment plan is financed by bank credit and the investor's own funds but is under the control of the banks.

production and such services as transportation, the social-cultural activities of the state are an integral part of the national economic plan and are designed to further the execution of the over-all plan in such matters as assuring the required labor skills through the planning of education, freeing women from responsibilities in the home in order to use their labor in other economic activity by the provision of nurseries and preschools for children, and in facilitating control over the attitudes of the population by means of the state monopoly in the field of publication and radio. The distribution of the 1951 appropriation by various social and cultural aims and the shares of the central and local budgets in these activities shown in Table 41 are typical of the later postwar years. General education is predominantly a local activity, and public health services are shared almost equally between the central and local authorities, but in other categories of social and cultural services the role of local authorities is decidedly secondary. "Training of cadres" in Table 41 presumably refers to vocational training and technical education which are under separate headings in the 1952–53 budgets.[21]

The appropriations for national defense showed a lagging tendency with respect to total outlays from 1947 to 1949, but thereafter rose sharply, especially from 1951 to 1952. According to Tables 37

Table 41

SOCIAL AND CULTURAL EXPENDITURES IN THE POLISH CENTRAL
AND LOCAL BUDGETS IN THE 1951 PLAN

(MILLIONS OF ZLOTYS)

Item	Central Budget	Local Budgets	Total[a]
Education	563	1,895	2,458
Science	533	0	534
Training of cadres	2,781	222	3,003
Culture and art	554	159	714
Health	1,401	1,554	2,955
Physical culture and tourism	540	31	572
Social aid	408	170	577
Annuities, pensions, and allowances	5,525		5,525
Total	12,305	4,032	16,336

Source: *Dziennik Ustaw*, 1951, No. 18, Item 145.

[a] The totals in this column in some instances differ from the apparent sum of the items in the other two columns because of rounding.

[21] *Gospodarka Planowa*, April, 1952, p. 19, and *Dziennik Ustaw*, 1953, No. 26, Item 101.

and 38, defense expenditures in 1950 were approximately 10 percent of the total planned budgetary outlays, and while the latter nearly doubled in 1951, principally because of the enlarged scope of the budget, defense allocations increased by about 50 percent, amounting then to about 7 percent of the total. In 1952, however, planned defense outlays increased nearly 77 percent, as against a 21 percent increase in total planned outlays.[22] In the 1953 budget, explicit military expenditures represented 10.8 percent of total planned outlays, as compared to 10.5 percent in 1952. Since defense requirements are competitive with investment, selective cutbacks of outlays in certain other sectors may be required in order to minimize the relative loss to directly productive investment. The apparent absolute decrease in 1952 outlays for social and cultural purposes at the same time that other expenditures increased and the decline in the share of these outlays in the total planned expenditure from about 26 percent in 1952 to 24 percent in 1953 may represent such an accommodation. A comparison of the investment goals of the national economic plans for 1951–52 indicates a fall in the annual rate of increase of gross investment. The 1951 plan contemplated a 30 percent increase in total planned investment funds, whereas the 1952 plan scheduled a 19 percent increase in the so-called limited funds for investment,[23] which represent the overwhelming part of total planned investment outlays.[24]

Judged by a comparison of realized budgetary revenues and expenditures with the planned magnitudes, the Polish budgets in the early postwar years were more in the nature of forecasting rather than operational planning. As may be seen from Table 42, the realized magnitude in every case exceeded the original goals. The discrepancies between plans and realization were in part caused by faulty financial planning which helped to bring about a wage-price inflation, and in part they were a consequence of institutional

[22] A fuller accounting of the Polish defense effort would need to consider the role of the public security forces and possible subsidies in the production and supply of military goods and services.

[23] *Dziennik Ustaw*, 1951, No. 18, Item 146, p. 171; *Gospodarka Planowa*, March, 1952, p. 4.

[24] In 1949, the limited funds, which represent the budgetary grants and repayable bank credits, comprised 94 percent of the total planned investment expenditures (*Wiadomości Narodowego Banku Polskiego* [News of the Polish National Bank], No. 5, 1949, p. 248). By 1951, the limited funds of the state investment plan accounted for about 97.5 percent of the total outlay (*Życie Gospodarcze*, February 1–15, 1951, p. 138).

changes which altered the role of the budget and the credit system. By 1951, the expansion of scope of the state budget lost momentum, and in 1952 the planned revenues and expenditures increased over the preceding year by 14 and 21 percent, respectively. The approximate doubling of the state budget between 1951 and 1953, however, measures only in small part the growth of the national economy. By far the greater part of this increase represents the inflation of prices and wages since the monetary reform of October, 1950. For a time price controls and rationing suppressed the potential inflation, but upon the abolition of rationing in January, 1953, sharp upward revisions of prices and adjustment of wages were necessary for stability with a free market.

Table 42

PLANNED AND REALIZED REVENUES AND EXPENDITURES
IN POLISH STATE BUDGETS, 1946–48

(BILLIONS OF ZLOTYS)

	1946[a]		1947		1948	
Item	*Plan*	*Actual*	*Plan*	*Actual*	*Plan*	*Actual*
Total revenue	49.3	53.7	197.3	223.9	325.4	451.2
Total expenditure	52.7	63.9	197.1	208.9	316.0	406.1

Sources: Planned figures taken from the official budgets and investment plans for the years shown as given in *Dziennik Ustaw*, 1946, Nos. 50, 56; 1947, Nos. 50, 58; 1948, Nos. 1, 22. No account was taken of supplementary appropriations and modifications. The actual results are taken from Table 37 above, and from *Rocznik statystyczny—1949*, pp. 150–51.

[a] For the last nine months of the year only.

Price and Wage Policies

Under the Six-Year Plan, the percentage of national income allocated to total investment, including fixed capital and various material reserves, was expected to increase steadily to a peak of 28 percent in 1955. In practice, however, this peak was reached in 1951, and by 1953 total investment declined to about 25 percent. The revised economic policy for 1954–55 envisions a further decline to about 20 percent in 1955,[25] which is still a relatively high rate. The Polish planners showed an awareness of the inflationary possibilities

[25] *Supra*, p. 141. The Polish national income concept excludes services which are not directly connected with production.

in such a high rate of investment and apparently sought to keep the purchasing power of money stable by appropriate fiscal, price, and wage policies. The plans had expected that productivity of labor would rise sufficiently to permit significant increases in living standards while at the same time assuring a sustained high rate of investment. However, financial planning was not uniformly successful, and increasingly the state has sought to subordinate the private sector to direct controls over production and distribution of output. The postwar period was characterized by inflation, and according to official statements, real wages increased only imperceptibly in the period 1950–53.

Price policies. In 1944 the Polish Committee of National Liberation, in taking over the newly liberated areas, was faced with a choice between thoroughgoing price control and rationing or a free price system. The decision was a compromise featuring a system of low fixed prices for the public sector and free market prices for the remainder of the economy. Initially the prices and wages in the controlled market were pegged at six times the prewar level, whereas in the free market there were no restrictions, and prices in some cases were from 20 to 100 times higher than in the controlled market.[26] In order to compensate for the low wages prevailing in the public sector, the employees were permitted to buy limited quantities of basic necessities at correspondingly low prices with the aim that when both the money wages and the low priced rations were taken into account, the real wage would be the same as for similar work in the free market economy. It was felt that since a large, and possibly even overwhelming, part of the general expenditures of the state were subject to the system of low fixed prices, the bad effects of inflation might thus be more readily avoided. Certainly the requirement for circulating media would be lower with part of the prices and wages thus controlled than with free market prices and wages prevailing universally. After the abolition of compulsory deliveries of agricultural products in the summer of 1946, the government was obliged to purchase such supplies on the free market in order to provide the low-priced rations acting as wage supplements in the controlled sector. At the same time it sold some of the output

---

[26] Wacław Iwaszkiewicz, "Sprawa stabilizacji cen" (The Question of Price Stabilization), *Robotniczy Przegląd Gospodarczy* (Workers' Economic Review), March, 1948, p. 23.

of state industry on the free market and used the profits to finance the transactions for the ration account.

In practice the two-price system led to many complications which impeded economic accounting. Thus, state industry produced goods for both the public and the private sectors and had to base its calculations on both systems of prices. Such services as railroad transportation and mail, which served both sectors, developed a single set of in-between prices which in relation to prewar were higher than the level of the low fixed prices but lower than the free market level. Frequent adjustments of money wages or rations were needed to compensate employees in the public sector for price movements on the free market since the ration failed to cover all the requirements for basic necessities and recourse to the free market was necessary for supplementary supplies. In addition, the government was not uniformly successful in providing the full ration which employees considered as part of the wage so that revisions of money wages or supplements in kind could be demanded.[27]

The price policy enunciated in the first version of the Three-Year Plan as formulated by the Polish National Council in 1946 aimed at the abolition of the two-price system during 1947 except in certain cases where two prices for the same article would be necessary to realize the goals of social and economic policy. In particular, differential pricing could occur when (1) the same article served the needs of different categories of workers, and (2) it was necessary to give the population a certain minimum of necessities at lower than market prices. Elimination of the dual price system was to take place by lowering the prices of the free market,[28] including some free-market prices set by the state, and by an increase in wholesale prices on products of state industry to make them correspond to costs of production.[29] The lowering of state-fixed prices was to occur gradually as supplies became more plentiful. In other respects, the plan set forth the principle that more attractive agricultural prices should be set for certain products, such as pigs, oilseeds, fibers, tobacco, sugar beets, potatoes, and milk. Industrial prices should be governed by the level of costs of production, and

[27] Dr. Edward Rose, "Problem dwoistych cen w Polsce" (The Problem of Dual Prices in Poland), *Życie Gospodarcze*, October, 1946, pp. 726–27.
[28] Free in the sense that there was no limitation on the quantity that could be bought at the existing prices.
[29] *Polish National Economic Plan*, p. 26.

state industry as a whole should be profitable. The relation of agricultural prices to those paid by farmers for industrial goods should be such as to make farming more profitable than in prewar years.[30]

These policy aims were repeated in the revised version of the Three-Year Plan approved by the Polish legislative assembly in August, 1947.[31] Under the 1948 national economic plan, the policy of stabilization of prices of goods and services produced in the state and cooperative enterprises was continued, and at the same time state control over prices on the free market was to be gradually expanded in the sphere of basic goods and services. In order to facilitate price stabilization, the plan envisioned the accumulation of reserves of basic consumer goods. As the supply of basic necessities on the market increased, rationing was to be gradually eliminated.[32] The 1949 economic plan extended the pledge to maintain the stability of the purchasing power of money. Monetary circulation was to be kept on the level essential for financing the national economy while maintaining the proper proportions between the quantity of money and the mass of goods and services.[33] The subsequent annual plans as given in the summary text of laws defining the planning policy and goals contain few specific references to price policy, although the provisions concerning wages and employment, production of consumer and investment goods, and foreign trade implicitly contain elements of price policy.

The Six-Year Plan envisioned a 50 to 60 percent rise in the standard of living of the population, which was to come about in part by increased employment and higher productivity and in part by a reduction of prices on widely used consumer goods. Real wages were expected to rise 40 percent over the 1949 level by the end of 1955.[34]

The liquidation of the system of dual prices progressed gradually by means of reduction of rations, elimination of items from the ration lists, and corresponding increases in money wages until in 1949 the objective of a single price system was substantially achieved. In 1951–52, however, the accelerated rate of investment and greatly increased military expenditures, coupled with partial

[30] *Ibid.*
[31] *Dziennik Ustaw,* 1947, No. 53, Item 285, p. 877.
[32] *Ibid.,* 1948, No. 19, Item 134, p. 357.
[33] *Ibid.,* 1949, No. 26, Item 189, p. 575.
[34] *Ibid.,* 1950, No. 37, Item 344, pp. 443–44.

crop failures, led to renewed rationing of consumer goods. Money wages rose less rapidly than prices, and real wages appeared to have declined.[35]

Rationing was abolished by decree on January 4, 1953, and at the same time wages and prices were revised upward substantially, but unevenly. The decree declared that rationing restricted free buying and therefore reduced the economic incentive for increases in the productivity of labor and lowered the standard of living of the working class.[36] Official opinion expressed at the time of derationing asserted that, among other faults, the rationing system required a costly apparatus for enforcement, failed to take account of tastes of individual consumers, and did not give adequate stimulus for improving the quality of output of the rationed goods.[37] In order to make derationing effective, the planning office declared that it was necessary to await the accumulation of the necessary reserves of consumer goods and the expansion of production to the requisite level.[38] The extent of disproportion between the relative prices under rationing and the valuations of consumers, which the price revision aimed to correct, is indicated in the uneven upward adjustments of prices and compensating increases in wages. For selected items these percentage increases were: intercity plane, rail, and bus transportation—140; coal—100; soap—100; butter—100; gasoline—100; flour—50; cream—50; newspapers—33; electricity and gas—30; phone calls and postage—25; clothing—20; rents—unchanged; wages—12–40; and pensions—25–56.[39] Such wide variation in the adjustments suggests that the planning authorities in the past had been operating with a very faulty set of relative prices, at least with regard to their policy of supply of goods and services. The price relationship between bread and grain before the revisions reportedly was such that bread was being fed to livestock instead of grain.[40] The realignment of prices on agricultural products and industrial goods raised the level on the former relative to the latter, but the peasants benefited from this only to the extent that they

[35] United Nations, Economic Commission for Europe, *Economic Survey of Europe in 1951,* pp. 113–16.

[36] New York *Times,* January 5, 1953.

[37] *Gospodarka Planowa,* February, 1953, p. 16.

[38] *Ibid.* Cf. *supra,* p. 236, the aims of the 1948 national economic plan prior to the derationing of 1949.

[39] New York *Times,* January 5, 1953; Washington *Post,* February 8, 1953.

[40] *Gospodarka Planowa,* February, 1953, pp. 10, 16.

had surpluses above compulsory deliveries which they could sell directly to consumers. On balance it was expected that the share of the peasants in financing industrialization would increase.[41]

According to a Polish official statement, real wages over the period 1950–53 remained practically unchanged, and it is very probable that the level of real wages by 1955 will fall far short of the Six-Year Plan goal of 40 percent increase over 1949. Indeed, the revised goal for 1954–55 called for a 15 to 20 percent increase which, if realized,[42] would mean that about half of the Six-Year Plan goal would be achieved.

The extent to which prices of producer goods circulating among socialized enterprises departed from cost is illustrated by revisions introduced on January 1, 1953, in keeping with an earlier resolution of the Presidium of the Government to the effect that these prices should not lead to continuous deficits by producers and at the same time should not include excessive profits, the intent being that prices should reflect actual costs plus a small planned profit, certain exceptions being allowed.[43] Average prices were reduced by the percentages shown in the following categories: machine tools—3; heavy machines and technical equipment—8; electrical machines— 14; and electrical apparatus—40. In order to remedy the long-standing deficit in the coal and metallurgical industries, prices were raised upward on a selective basis, taking account not only of costs, but also the desirability of rationing particular grades of the products for special uses and preventing scarce items from being used where other more plentiful materials would suffice. Prices of coal were raised an average 33 percent; however, coal for energy purposes was raised only 25 percent, while coking coal was raised on the average about 80 percent. The new price schedule aimed at fixing prices so that the lowest grade coking coal would be priced above the highest grade of coal for energy purposes. Coke prices were raised on the average 50 percent, with the range by qualities extending from 40 to 90 percent. Prices of rolled steel products were raised on the average 40 percent, and prices of iron ores were recalculated on the principle that the cost of pig iron should be the same, other things being equal, for the various grades of ore used.

[41] *Ibid.*, pp. 14–15.

[42] Polish Embassy, Washington, *Press Release*, March 22, 1954, p. 11.

[43] Zbigniew Augustowski, "Ceny środków produkcji" (Prices of Means of Production), *Gospodarka Planowa*, January, 1953, pp. 43–47.

Scrap iron and pig iron prices were adjusted so that increased use of pig iron would not result in a rise in costs of steel production. Although the price increases did not fully eliminate losses in the coal and metallurgical industries, it was expected that attainable cost reductions would make profits possible. Prices were reduced on inorganic chemicals by about 20 percent, on electrotechnical supplies about 30 percent, and on prefabricated units for construction about 10 percent. Generally speaking, prices of raw materials and semimanufactures departed from cost more frequently than prices of machines and equipment.

Inflation in the postwar period. The government was not entirely successful in suppressing inflation in the postwar period, although it did succeed in limiting price increases to modest proportions in comparison with the astronomical inflation after World War I. As may be seen in Tables 43 and 44, a rapid advance in prices occurred in 1947, with industrial prices showing the greatest gain. The inflation was checked during the last half of 1947 and early in 1948, but by 1950, prices were again rising. With the abolition of rationing on January 4, 1953, prices of basic foodstuffs were raised an average of about 50 percent while other prices and wages were raised varying amounts.[44]

Although the official explanation of the causes of the inflation in 1946–47 stressed the excessive purchasing power of the middle class, the great quantity of speculative capital not suitably invested in productive activity, and the cupidity of private merchants, the

Table 43

INDEXES OF FREE MARKET PRICES IN WARSAW, 1945–49

(1945 = 100)

Item	1946	1947	1948	1949[a]
General price index	99.4	144.2	148.8	149.2
Foodstuffs[b]	87.7	107.7	113.2	125.5
Industrial commodities	111.0	180.8	184.4	172.8
Fuels	79.4	112.7	105.0	76.1
Semimanufactures	143.1	236.8	245.6	249.7
Manufactured products	110.5	192.9	202.5	192.7

Source: Statistical Tables of the Institute of the National Economy, Tables 4–5—Supplement to *Gospodarka Planowa*, June, 1949.

[a] First quarter. The series shown in this table was discontinued in the spring of 1949.

[b] Including beverages and tobacco.

[44] *Ibid.*

Table 44

INDEX OF RETAIL PRICES OF GOODS AND SERVICES PURCHASED BY
A WAGE-EARNER'S FAMILY IN WARSAW, 1947–51
(1947 = 100)

Item	1946	1948	1949	1950	1951[a]
Total	77	104	108	118	120
Foodstuffs	83	102	108	118	118
Alcohol and tobacco	104	100	132	141	166
Housing	75	124	132	152	158
Fuel and light	64	92	84	86	91
Clothing and shoes	67	104	96	109	111
Hygiene and health	57	102	121	128	125
Cultural-educational outlays	58	108	96	93	94
Other	51	162	217	221	223

Sources: 1946–48, *Rocznik statystyczny—1949*, p. 108; 1949–51, *Wiadomości Statystyczne* (Statistical News), May, 1951, p. 9. The indexes are based on average prices in socialized and private trade up to the end of 1950, but beginning in 1951 for industrial products, only the prices in socialized trade are considered.

[a] Average for first four months.

basic cause is to be found in the high rate of investment under the plan for industrialization. This resulted in the national wage bill growing faster than the output of consumer goods, while the government failed to tax away or sterilize the excess purchasing power. The deliveries by UNRRA had a strong deflationary impact in 1946 since they provided about 11 percent of the total goods and services available in that year, and moreover, the sale of these by the government provided an important source of income for the state budget. By the end of 1946, however, the deliveries from UNRRA were diminishing, and on May 31, 1947, only about 2.3 percent of the total program of 481.3 million dollars remained unshipped.[45] The expectations of the Polish government for substantial foreign long-term investment loans were not realized, since Poland did not participate in the Marshall Plan and failed to obtain a loan from the International Bank for Reconstruction and Development.

The inflation of 1946–47 gave rise to a series of measures regulating and limiting private trade, subjecting cooperative organizations to the discipline of central planning, and expanding the network of socialized trading establishments. Its outcome was the virtual

[45] United Nations Relief and Rehabilitation Administration, *Operational Analysis Papers, No. 45*, pp. 7, 40, 42.

elimination of private enterprise in trade. In the inflation during 1950, one of the principal tools for eliminating excess purchasing power was the currency reform of October, 1950, which served to diminish the liquid reserves of the peasantry and other groups of the population. During 1951, obligatory sales were reimposed on the peasants. At the beginning of 1953, the government acknowledged the inflation that had occurred by a very substantial upward revision of prices and some wage adjustments.

Agricultural prices and prices paid by farmers. Table 45 suggests that the government sought to encourage the purchase of producer goods, such as plows and fertilizers, by favorable price ratios to farmers and at the same time to discourage the purchase of such items as shoes and soap. The table of course does not present conclusive evidence on this score, since it would be necessary to prepare index numbers based on comprehensive baskets of the commodities exchanged in order to establish the trend in relative prices. Moreover, the comparison with the prewar years can be seriously misleading since in that period the relation of agricultural to industrial prices was extremely variable. If March, 1939, be chosen for comparison with postwar years, as is done in the Polish official statistical yearbook for 1949, the postwar prices of industrial goods in terms of rye appear vastly more favorable to farmers but prices in terms of pork and milk are somewhat less favorable than in Table 45. If the comparison be restricted to the relative pricing of rye, pork, and milk in terms of industrial products, it is clear from Table 45 that pork and milk gained very significantly in purchasing power in relation to rye, which would suggest that the government was carrying out its policy of encouraging the production of animal products.

In spite of the government's declared policy of making agriculture more profitable than in prewar, its price policy cannot be judged successful if evaluated in terms of the marketed surplus voluntarily delivered by farmers at the established prices of the state's procurement agencies. According to the plans, agricultural production should expand by favorable pricing of fertilizers and farm equipment, and the character of production was likewise to be shaped by price manipulation, but individual farmers could not be allowed to become prosperous for, according to the official ideology, this would lead to the regeneration of capitalist enterprises. The government has recognized the failure of its agricultural price and invest-

Table 45

PRICES OF SELECTED INDUSTRIAL PRODUCTS EXPRESSED IN
KILOGRAMS OF RYE AND PORK AND LITERS OF MILK

Item	Unit	1937/38[a]	1946	1947	1948
		IN KILOGRAMS OF RYE			
Plow	unit	141	133	92	120
Superphosphate	100 kg	46	35	25	38
Men's shoes	pair	121	262	241	290
Sugar	10 kg	48	125	60	71
Soap	10 kg	69	159	137	186
Kerosene	10 liters	18	41	15	20
Coal	100 kg	23	15	14	15
		IN KILOGRAMS OF PORK, LIVE WEIGHT			
Plow	unit	33.7	13.0	17.6	17.0
Superphosphate	100 kg	11.1	3.4	4.9	5.3
Men's shoes	pair	29.0	25.8	46.0	40.5
Sugar	10 kg	11.6	12.3	11.5	10.0
Soap	10 kg	16.7	15.7	26.2	26.0
Kerosene	10 liters	4.4	4.1	2.8	2.9
Coal	100 kg	5.6	1.5	2.6	2.2
		IN LITERS OF MILK			
Plow	unit	193	114	118	110
Superphosphate	100 kg	64	30	32	35
Men's shoes	pair	166	225	306	267
Sugar	10 kg	67	107	77	65
Soap	10 kg	96	137	175	172
Kerosene	10 liters	25	36	19	19
Coal	100 kg	32	13	18	14

Sources: Data for 1937/38 are taken from *Mały rocznik statystyczny—1939*, p. 257; for 1946–48, from *Rocznik statystyczny—1949*, pp. 125–26.

[a] August 1, 1937, to July 31, 1938.

ment policies in the revision of its economic plans for 1954–55. In an attempt to spur production, the new policy seeks to increase material incentives to farmers, but it is significant that compulsory deliveries are to be maintained, albeit on a "non-increasing level."

Pricing and cost accounting in state enterprises. The Council of Ministers is the chief authority in establishing prices, but it may delegate its authority in certain instances to ministries, the state planning commission, presidiums of local people's councils, or a special price commission.[46] Retail prices of widely consumed goods and services, prices paid by the state for compulsory deliveries from agriculture, and the prices of basic raw materials and other goods supplied to agriculture are directly established by the Council or under its supervision. The official policy requires that the prices at which goods and services produced by state enterprises are sold on the domestic market as a rule should cover costs and provide revenues for financing state expenditures. It expects that the prices will be such as to assure equilibrium of the existing supply with demand. As a consequence, this price may not be equal to the costs of production, but may be greater or less than the latter depending on the policy of the state with respect to the quantity to be supplied. In some cases the social policy of the state may seek a wide distribution of certain goods or services which might imply that certain enterprises or branches of industry would operate with planned losses, and on the other hand, a restriction of output under the same principle of price setting could assure very high profits. Since prices of final sales on the free market[47] may not be directly related to the costs of a producing enterprise, if the latter is to be kept in operation on a self-sustaining basis, it must be assured the prospect of profitable operation by suitable administrative provisions. The matter of coordination of production and sale of the output of state enterprises was regulated by the following principles established by the Council of Ministers on August 21, 1947:[48]

(1) The production enterprise receives for the sale of its output, regardless of to whom it is sold, so-called factory accounting prices, which are planned magnitudes consisting of the planned costs of production and the prescribed profit margins.

(2) The central sales organization, or sales central, which distributes the products, settles with the production enterprises on the basis of their factory accounting prices, but in order to cover the latter and also the sales commission for the central, the turnover tax, and the cost of maintaining the administrative apparatus of the industry, the sales central receives its

[46] *Dziennik Ustaw*, 1947, No. 61, Item 337; 1953, No. 31, Items 122 and 125.

[47] Free in the sense that the consumer may buy as much as he desires at the existing price.

[48] Zbigniew Augustowski, "Zagadnienie cen i kosztów w przemyśle państwowym" (The Problem of Prices and Costs in State Industry), *Gospodarka Planowa*, July, 1948, p. 310.

own variety of accounting price consisting of the preceding elements.

(3) The difference between the actual sale price realized by the sales central and the accounting price for the sales central flows into a price equalization fund maintained by the ministry in the Polish National Bank. If the difference is negative, it is covered from this account.

(4) The profit earned by an enterprise consists of the difference between the aggregate receipts from sales at the factory accounting prices and the actual costs of production. The actual profit may be greater or less than the planned aggregate profit depending on the actual level of output and costs. The realized profit covers the income tax, provides a plant fund for premiums and other incentives for employees, and augments the enterprise's working capital.

In principle, the factory accounting prices were established individually for each production establishment, or groups of these, and for each separate commodity. However, in practice they were established only for certain groups of articles produced by the given establishment. If the factory accounting prices were set properly, the profit realized by the enterprise would afford a measure of the efficiency of its operation relative to its particular circumstances of production. The device of factory accounting prices made it possible to subsidize high-cost plants through the operation of the price equalization fund. At the beginning of a new accounting period each enterprise submitted to its sales central a price calculation based on its annual production plan. From this calculation the factory accounting price was derived, and after confirmation by the central administration for the given branch of industry, this price was binding on both the production enterprise and the sales central. Although the regulations established by the Council of Ministers envisioned both individual and group factory accounting prices, as late as 1949 these prices were set predominantly on an individual factory basis.[49] This made it difficult to judge the efficiency of the various plants, since, if a given plant succeeded in making its planned profit, this might mean only that the plant's management made a good estimate of the future course of events and would say little about cost

[49] Zdzisław Fedak, "Cena grupowa" (The Group Price), *Życie Gospodarcze,* March 1–15, 1949, p. 204.

economies or efficiency relative to other plants.[50] However, the supervision exercised by the central administration could be expected to restrain managers of enterprises from setting excessively high planned costs. Use of a single factory accounting price somewhat below the average for a group of plants having similar conditions of production would in limited measure be a substitute for the incentive to efficiency afforded by a single market price for firms in a competitive economy. The profit differences in the latter case would correspond to the residue of profit left to the incentive fund and to the plant's working capital in the Polish planned economy.

According to the pricing regulations, the actual price paid by purchasers should be the same for all purchasers of a given commodity regardless of the settlement price realized by the producer. Any difference between the actual uniform procurement prices paid by the enterprises and the actual costs of providing the supplies by the sales centrals should flow through the price equalization fund. However, this solution was not uniformly adopted even by mid-1948.[51] Among other factors which confused the problem of pricing and cost accounting in the state-owned sector were: (1) wages paid partly in cash and partly in the form of low-priced rations, (2) nonuniform amortization principles and too low amortization rates, and (3) subsidies designed to lower the cost of imported raw materials. As a result, it would be difficult to compare the efficiency of various producers.

During 1950–51, the system of factory accounting prices was replaced by a new system of uniform sale prices. In practice under the old system an enterprise would receive a profit despite its level of costs, since profits were calculated as a percentage of costs. In fact, profits would be greater when costs were higher. For this reason the old system was abandoned with the hope that the new system of uniform sale prices would give greater stimulus to cost economics.[52] Concurrently with this change, the role of the distributive centrals was reduced by the new practice of direct contracting between enterprises and by the more direct connection between the financial results of the operation of an enterprise and the state budget.

[50] *Ibid.*

[51] *Gospodarka Planowa,* July 1948, pp. 311–12.

[52] The discussion of prices which follows is based on *Gospodarka Planowa,* June, 1952, pp. 35–36; May, 1954, pp. 33–35; June, 1954, pp. 40–42; and September, 1954, p. 35.

Under the new system an enterprise calculated its planned profit as the difference between the planned uniform sale price on a given commodity applicable to all enterprises and the planned cost plus the turnover tax. Since the turnover tax was to be uniform for all enterprises, the planned profit of an enterprise would depend on the status of its productive equipment. It was expected that with the level of planned profits varying in this manner, the enterprises would have approximately equal opportunities to earn profits above the planned profits through their efforts to lower costs by greater efficiency in the use of their resources. The percentage of "above-plan" profits which entered the enterprise's incentive fund was much higher than the percentage of planned profits entering this fund, and accordingly the incentive for efficiency under the new system was expected to be greater than under the old. The retail trade margin was fixed for the entire trade organization at the outset so as to provide incentive to reduce costs by using the most direct distributive channels. If an entire branch of production operated at a planned loss, its deficit would be covered by a subsidy from the state budget, but an unprofitable enterprise in an otherwise profitable branch would be subsidized through the operation of an equalization fund derived from contributions from profits of the successful enterprises in the same branch.

In practice the new system did not work satisfactorily. In 1953 the turnover tax, which was conceived as a uniform rate applying to a given commodity, in fact varied from enterprise to enterprise. The incentive scheme must have been weakened accordingly. On August 12, 1953, the Presidium of the Government resolved that in all basic branches of large- and medium-scale industry, beginning on January 1, 1954, so-called factory prices, representing the difference between the uniform sale price and the turnover tax, would be introduced for planning purposes. These factory prices would correspond to the Russian "wholesale prices of enterprises." Initially the factory prices were to be used by the export centrals in paying the production enterprises for the value of goods procured for export. Up to January 1, 1954, the centrals paid for such goods at the uniform sale prices, including the turnover tax. In the new system the production enterprise would prepare an invoice showing the value of the goods at factory prices, the value at the uniform sale prices, and the difference comprising the turnover tax. The export central would pay only the amount at the factory prices, but the Polish National Bank would credit the production enterprise with the amount of the turnover tax from a special account. In the case of imports, the foreign trade central in rendering invoices upon domestic purchasers would specify for the bank the amount of the so-called supplementary budget differences, which correspond to the turnover tax. The bank would credit the foreign trade central for the amount of the invoice less these differences. When the bank received payment in the full amount of the invoice, it would transfer the budget differences automatically to the income of the state budget.

The use of factory prices for planning, for settlements between enterprises, and for cost accounting was apparently scheduled for wider application in 1954–55, with the hope that in 1956 all enterprises would be ready to use such prices in the new Five-Year Plan. The provisions of the government's resolution as regards 1954 were only partially carried out as of mid-year. Continued failure to operate with a set of prices adequately reflecting current costs must be regarded as a serious deficiency in Polish economic planning.

The Plant Fund. One of the widely discussed incentives for fulfilling national economic plans, in theory at least, is a form of profit sharing designed to spur individual and group productive effort. As far back as August 14, 1946, the Polish government decreed that the profit earned by a state enterprise should be divided into three parts, namely, (1) from 5 to 15 percent earmarked for increasing the enterprise's working capital or adding to its productive equipment, (2) a group premium for the employees amounting to a share half as great as the first, but which might be increased to the same size as the first share if the quality of production, cost economies, and other factors warranted this, and (3) the residue, which was to be paid into the state investment fund.[53] Subsequent regulations amended the provisions of this decree, and finally they were superseded by the law of February 4, 1950, establishing the Plant Fund for incentives. Whereas the group premiums of the 1946 decree were designed for satisfying the collective social needs of the employees, the provisions governing the Plant Fund established three chief aims:[54] (1) financing cultural, social, and housing investments serving the needs of the employees of the given enterprise,

[53] *Dziennik Ustaw*, 1946, No. 35, Item 216.
[54] *Ibid.*, 1950, No. 6, Item 53.

(2) providing supplements to the budget of social expenditures of the enterprise, and (3) rewarding outstanding employees. The percentage distribution of income of the fund among its various outlays was to be accomplished by the management of the enterprise in agreement with the employees' council in the plant.

The profit earned by a state enterprise consists of two parts, namely, the planned profit, which represents the difference between the planned income of the enterprise and its planned costs, and the above-plan profit, which is the surplus profit above the first part. According to the 1950 law, the income of the Plant Fund was to consist of percentage shares of the two components of the enterprise's profit, and these percentage shares were to be established annually by the Economic Committee of the Council of Ministers. Actual payments into the fund were to be determined by the plant's immediately superior administrative organ with the advice of the bank financing the enterprise. The amounts were to be obtained by applying the percentages established for the year to the profit shown upon the closing of the annual accounts. Where a plant was operating under a plan envisioning a loss instead of a profit, the payments into the Plant Fund were to be percentages of the actual cost reductions in relation to the planned reductions. The law was retroactive to January 1, 1949, and established the quotas for initiating the fund at 1 to 4 percent of the planned profit and 10 to 30 percent of the above-plan profit, excluding windfalls and allowing for cost increases beyond the control of the enterprise. On July 21, 1950, the Economic Committee of the Council of Ministers established the percentage contributions from profits to the account of the Plant Fund at 2 percent of the planned profit and 15 percent of the above-plan profit for enterprises subordinated to the Ministry of Mining and the Ministry of Heavy Industry, and at 1 percent and 10 percent of the planned and above-plan profit, respectively, for all other state industrial enterprises.[55] In March, 1951, the rates applying to the above-plan profit were revised as follows: Ministry of Mining —30 percent; Heavy Industry—20 percent; and Light Industry— 15 percent. At the same time the rates pertaining to planned profit were raised in the Ministries of Mining, Heavy Industry, and Light Industry to 4, 2.5, and 2 percent, respectively.[56] The differentiated

[55] *Przegląd Związkowy* (The Union Review), August, 1950, p. 376.
[56] *Ibid.*, June, 1951, p. 259.

rates indicate the importance attached to the various industries by the planners.

In furthering the official aim of the fund to promote the fulfillment of economic plans, reduce costs, and raise the productivity of labor, an enterprise is allowed to establish the fund only in the event that it fulfills or overfulfills the plan of production as a whole and in the envisioned assortment and attains at least the planned profit. In distributing the fund to various uses, the management of the plant is expected to spend 50 percent for above-plan investments for cultural and social aims and employees' housing, 30 percent for promoting organized labor competition to raise output and improve quality, and 20 percent for premiums for individual employees. Since the total income of the fund cannot exceed 2.5 to 3 percent of the plant's annual wage bill, the amount directly devoted as incentive to individual effort, other than organized labor competition, will be not more than six tenths of 1 percent of the wage bill of the enterprise which is fortunate enough to have a Plant Fund. Total rewards for individuals winning organized labor competitions cannot exceed 20 percent of the fraction of the fund set aside for administering and promoting the competitions, and a single award is expected to come within the limits of 100 to 300 new zlotys.[57] If one takes account of both the maximum total rewards under labor competition and other individual rewards, their maximum share in the recommended distribution of the Plant Fund would amount to 26 percent, or about 0.8 percent of the wage bill if the enterprise succeeds in establishing the maximum permissible fund. Nearly three fourths of the fund is to be designated for collective benefits of the employees.

The performance of the incentive scheme outlined in the 1946 decree and the 1950 law failed by far to come up to expectations. The premiums for 1946 were paid in 1948 to the central administrations and were not distributed to the individual enterprises, and as late as March, 1949, the premiums for 1947 were not even approved.[58] Clearly, if immediacy of reward is important for incentive effect, the scheme failed badly. In 1950 only a small number of enterprises established Plant Funds under the new law. On one

[57] *Ibid.*, p. 260. The average monthly wage of workers in January, 1949, was 15,000 zlotys, or, in view of the 1950 monetary reform, 450 new zlotys (*Gospodarka Planowa*, February, 1949, p. 87).

[58] *Życie Gospodarcze*, March 1–15, 1949, p. 206.

hand, the possibility of having such a fund seems to have failed to arouse enthusiasm in either the plant management or the employees, and, on the other, in frequent instances failure to meet the assortment requirements of the production plan disqualified otherwise eligible enterprises.[59]

A negative reflection on the operation of the incentive schemes and the problem of maintaining high quality production in the socialist sector is given in a government decree of March 4, 1953. This decree established penalties ranging up to 5 years' imprisonment for plant managers or heads of production divisions in plants who sell substandard quality products or products which are obviously unsuited for their designated use. In cases where such products should cause great damage to the state's defense or foreign trade interests, the punishment is 2 to 10 years' imprisonment.[60]

Wage policies. Up to 1949, the Polish wage system consisted of a patchwork of special measures not at all in keeping with the precision one might expect in a centrally planned economy. In the first postwar months the wages of industrial employees consisted of a part of the output of the enterprise which was then sold by the employees or exchanged for other goods. In view of the differing attractiveness of products and the varying conditions of demand for them, this system created many disproportions in relative wages. Money wages in part replaced payments in kind during 1946, but shortages of consumer goods led the government to supply rations of basic necessities to employees in the public sector at low, controlled prices as a form of wage supplement. In mid-1946, cash wages represented about 50 percent of the wage, the rationed goods accounted for about 40 percent, and wages in kind the remaining 10 percent.[61] The rations varied with the importance assigned to various occupations, and heavy work, such as in mining and heavy industry, was favored with larger rations. This system persisted through 1948 with gradual replacement of ration privileges and payments in kind by increased cash wages. Finally, at the beginning of 1949 the government was in a position to implement the wage policy it had enunciated in 1946 at the outset of planning. In brief, this policy called for wages entirely in money, wage changes in pro-

[59] *Przegląd Związkowy,* June, 1951, p. 259.

[60] *Dziennik Ustaw,* 1953, No. 16, Item 63.

[61] Józef Janiak, "O reformie płac" (Concerning the Wage Reform), *Gospodarka Planowa,* February, 1949, p. 85.

portion to changes in productivity of labor, uniform rates to all employees doing similar work under similar conditions and having similar qualifications, elimination of large wage differentials which were not justified economically, and uniform basic social services to all branches of labor.[62]

In 1947, the Three-Year Plan amplified these aims and called for (1) a system of wages that would induce an increase in productivity of labor and a simultaneous reduction of real costs, (2) introduction of wage scales for various occupations based on the required skills, intensity of effort, conditions of work, and degree of responsibility, and (3) use of wage policy as a tool for realizing the desired allocation of labor.[63] Subsequent annual economic plans repeated the intention to increase wages in keeping with advances in the productivity of labor, and the Six-Year Plan set a goal of 40 percent increase in real wages in the socialized economy by 1955 as compared to 1949.[64] This increase was supposed to come about by increasing money wages and at the same time gradually reducing prices of basic necessities.

In spite of the expressed desire of the planning authority to increase labor productivity, the pre-1949 system of mixed cash wages, ration privileges, and payments in kind actually delayed realization of this aim since a very substantial part of the wage, namely the ration privilege, was not very closely connected with individual effort. Although piece-wages were introduced early in the postwar years, they applied only to the cash part of the wage, and in order to popularize the system many abuses were tolerated. In particular, the lack of tested norms led to much confusion, and a race to lower norms so as to raise wages apparently occurred.[65] At this time the labor unions had not yet been subordinated to centralized control, and by their uncoordinated efforts they succeeded in winning for themselves a variety of benefits which contributed to the lack of uniformity in the wage structure. The consolidation of political power in the Polish United Workers' Party at the end of 1948 and the abolition of rationing on January 1, 1949, paved the way for a long overdue wage reform.

---

[62] *Polish National Economic Plan*, pp. 26–27.
[63] *Dziennik Ustaw*, 1947, No. 53, Item 285, p. 876.
[64] *Ibid.*, 1950, No. 37, Item 344, p. 444.
[65] Janiak, *op. cit.*, p. 86.

The new wage system introduced in January, 1949, was based on a determination of these factors:[66]

1. Typical activities requiring similar qualifications, effort, and responsibility, and a suitable ranking for these activities
2. A common minimum wage and the proper wage spread for particular typical activities and positions
3. The bases for supplementary remuneration for work that is harmful to health, strenuous, and dangerous, and principles for granting supplements for leadership and responsibility
4. Systems of remuneration and bases for granting premiums.

Table 46 shows the wage scales established for the principal industries by the wage reform. The minimum wage at the time of the reform was set at 36 zlotys per hour plus an equalization supplement of 6.5 zlotys for all wage categories, making the actual minimum 42.5 zlotys. Wage rates reached the highest levels in the metallurgical, mining, and metalworking industries, which reflected the desire to attract suitable skills into these fields. Supplements for the various reasons listed in (3) above would increase the hourly rates shown in the table.

Table 46

BASIC HOURLY WAGE RATES IN POLISH INDUSTRIES, JANUARY, 1949
(ZLOTYS)

Wage Group	Coal	Metal- lurgical	Metal	Electro- technical	Chemical	Textile
1	36	36	36	36	36	36
2	39	39	39	39	39	38
3	44	44	42	44	44	40
4	47	49	47	49	49	42
5	49	55	52	55	55	44
6	53	61	58	61	61	46
7	55	66	66	66	66	48
8	61	72	74	72	72	50
9	66	79	82	80		53
10	72	87				58
11	78					63
12	84					69

Source: *Gospodarka Planowa*, February, 1949, p. 87.

[66] *Ibid.*, p. 87.

Despite the intention of the reform to level out unjustified disproportions in wages, its requirements were almost immediately amended to perpetuate some of the relative advantages where their elimination would mean an actual reduction in wages for entire groups of workers or enterprises. The eventual elimination of such disproportions was expected to take place as real wages rose by imposing a slower rate of increase for the initially favored groups.[67]

According to Table 46, the wage spread for industrial workers is greatest in the metallurgical industry, ranging from 1 to 2.4, and is rarely less than 1 to 2 in the other industries. However, a complete appraisal of the spread would have to take account of various supplements and incentive payments above the established levels. For clerical, technical, and managerial personnel the spread on January 1, 1949, was from 8,500 zlotys per month, minimum, to about 50,000 maximum, that is, about 1 to 6.[68] Family allowances, the operation of the progressive wage and salary tax, and compulsory savings tend to offset wage differentials. The prewar wage spread for manual workers fluctuated from 1:2.3 in 1928 to 1:3.2 in 1936, and stood at 1:2.9 in 1938,[69] but it is difficult to trace the changes in wage spread over the postwar period before 1949 due to the prevalence of noncash components in wages and various services rendered to employees in lieu of wages. Judged by the status immediately after the wage reform, a modest reduction of differentials appears to have occurred as compared to prewar, but the compromise between equality and differential wages favored the latter.

In an effort to relate wage rates to productivity, remuneration by piece rates was introduced on an ever wider scale in state enterprises. This system was extended even to state farms on June 1, 1951. For a double incentive effect it related wages, for example, to the number of pigs cared for at a fixed rate per head and to the kilograms of weight gained by the animals.[70] Thus the greater the number of animals tended and the greater the gain in weight by the animals, the greater would be the wage earned by the employee. There was, therefore, a direct connection between the compensation paid and the realization of production plans. Progressive piece wage rates which provided increasing rewards per unit as the number

[67] *Robotniczy Przegląd Gospodarczy* (Workers' Economic Review), March, 1949, p. 98.
[68] Janiak, *op. cit.*, p. 87.
[69] *Robotniczy Przegląd Gospodarczy*, July-August, 1947, p. 19.
[70] *Życie Gospodarcze*, August 16–31, 1951, p. 903.

of units increased beyond certain limits were applied in branches of production considered particularly important for the national economy.

The wage policy of the government as reflected in the national wage bill, the price policy on consumer goods, and the various fiscal devices for draining away or sterilizing excess purchasing power are all parts of one of the central problems in financial planning, namely, to assure the government enough resources to carry through its program of planned economic growth while maintaining sufficient incentives for labor and independent producers. The goal of planning the level and spread of wages was to assure an over-all wage bill of suitable structure which after reduction by taxation and various forms of saving would stand in proper relation to the mass of consumer goods at the existing prices and at the same time afford an adequate incentive to effort. Wage differentials and the various schemes of piece rates and premiums, while providing for incentives, could, however, affect the average wage rate in an unplanned manner, which in a situation of growing labor shortage could be expected to be in the direction of excessive growth of the wage bill. A contributing factor to such a growth was the pressure for plan fulfillment which often came about by unplanned additions to the labor force or extension of working hours beyond the customary limits.

Poland's success in managing the national wage bill has been very uneven over the postwar years. In the earlier part of this period, the situation was confused by the existence of wages in kind, wage subsidies under the selective rationing system, varying levels of cash wages depending in part on the strength of local unions or the tardiness of government officials in making revisions, and the varying obligations upon enterprises to supply certain social services to employees. As measured by the inflation which occurred in the postwar period, the total financial policy was not uniformly successful, and confusion on the labor market was one of the chief causes. Real wages fluctuated over the period, rising very sharply though unevenly in 1946 from the low postwar levels, falling somewhat in the first part of 1947, then rising again until in 1949 they were reported above the 1938 level.[71] A part of this increase came

[71] United Nations, Economic Commission for Europe, *Economic Survey of Europe in 1949*, p. 24.

by way of redistribution of the national income to the disadvantage of the middle class,[72] and a part represented gains in productivity. According to official sources, real wages rose only imperceptibly in the period 1950–53, despite the 40 percent increase by 1955 set in the Six-Year Plan. In March, 1954, this goal was reduced to a 15 to 20 percent increase in 1954–55.[73]

Although the Six-Year Plan expected that increases in productivity would precede increases in wages by a very substantial margin, the performance in 1950, the first year of the plan, was the direct opposite of this expectation. According to official results, productivity per worker in industry increased 9.1 percent, while wages in money increased 17 percent.[74] Hilary Minc indicated that this was caused by the universal disregard of discipline in the setting of norms of work and the violation of wage regulations and obligatory norms of employment.[75] This would suggest that the control function by the banking system and other financial apparatus over the execution of the plan still had not been perfected and that employment plans were not realistic. Evidence that wage policy alone has not been successful in allocating labor to various branches of industry and keeping employees on their jobs is found in the array of controls over labor in postwar legislation.[76]

Polish Money and Banking

Currency reforms. Upon liberation of Poland during the years 1944–45, the financial situation was complicated by the presence of four different kinds of currency, namely, reichsmarks in the area that had been annexed to Germany, the occupation zlotys issued by the German authorities in the so-called General Government of Poland, Soviet rubles, and the notes of the Polish National Bank. The last were printed in Moscow and issued by the Lublin government beginning in October, 1944, even though the bank did not come into being until January, 1945. On the basis of the decrees of October 23, 1944, and January 6 and February 5, 1945, the

[72] Hilary Minc, "Kilka uwag o zagadnieniu płac" (A Few Observations on the Wage Problem), *Nowe Drogi*, January, 1948, p. 2.

[73] *Supra*, p. 148.

[74] *Życie Gospodarcze*, May 1–15, 1951, p. 499.

[75] *Ibid.*

[76] *Supra*, p. 70.

occupation zloty was converted at 1:1 for the new zloty notes of the Polish National Bank up to a maximum limit of 500 for persons over eighteen years of age, while remaining quantities of the occupation zlotys were subject to deposit in special accounts from which payments in every case required the special permission of the Ministry of Finance. Such permission was given very rarely and then only to corporate bodies.[77] Reichsmarks were similarly exchanged, but at a less favorable ratio or a lower maximum limit, which varied from 1:1 and a limit of 300 in Białystok, to 1 zloty: 2 reichsmarks and a limit of 500 in the remaining provinces. This conversion drastically reduced the stock of money in circulation and made it possible for the government to finance a major part of its early postwar requirements simply by emission of banknotes in keeping with the expansion of production of goods and services in the economy.

The Polish National Bank established by decree on January 15, 1945, was entrusted with the regulation of money and credit circulation subject to the economic policy of the state. Currency notes may be issued only by the bank, and these constitute the legal tender in Poland. The backing of the currency consists of the estate and revenues of the treasury and the security given for credits granted. The volume of issue of banknotes is limited by the decisions of the Council of Ministers. According to the decree establishing the bank, the entire circulation of money must always be secured and thus should vary with the holdings of gold, foreign exchange, and other resources, including trade bills, collateral for loans, and the obligations of the state treasury within limits established by the Council of Ministers.[78] Although gold and foreign exchange were included in the backing of the currency established by the decree, their relation to the volume of circulation was not indicated, and in practice they were used chiefly to settle foreign claims. In effect, the zloty was established without external connections and could be managed by the Ministry of Finance through the Polish National Bank as the internal needs required.

Poland's second postwar monetary reform, introduced by legislative action on October 28, 1950, apparently was motivated by the

[77] *Quarterly Review of the Polish National Economic Bank,* March-June, 1946, pp. 1–2.
[78] *Ibid.,* p. 3.

resurgence of inflationary forces after a period of stability extending from the last half of 1947 to 1949. According to its provisions,[79] the unit of currency on October 30, 1950, became the new zloty, which was defined as being equal to 0.222168 grams of pure gold. All wages and incomes from labor, pensions, and stipends, as well as all prices for goods and services, were recalculated on the basis of 100 old zlotys equal to 3 new zlotys. Money in circulation was subject to exchange at the ratio of 100 old zlotys to 1 new zloty. All savings kept in banks, savings institutions, and in the Social Saving Fund which concerned the deposits of workers, small and medium peasants, and fishermen were recalculated at the same ratio as prices and wages, but deposits in excess of 100,000 zlotys were subject to conversion at less favorable rates. Private debts were translated at the 100:3 ratio with the exception of debts of small and medium peasants to the so-called village rich, which were recalculated at the 100:1 ratio. Thus, the reform discriminated against the wealthier peasants, persons holding cash reserves, and the remnants of the urban middle class. The prospect of similar reforms in the future would discourage hoarding in favor of immediate spending. Even modest accumulation in banks met with discriminatory conversion ratios.

The new zloty, like the old, remains an internal currency. Although defined in terms of gold, it cannot be freely converted into gold or foreign exchange at rates roughly equivalent to its declared gold value. The law which introduced the reform also prohibited the possession of foreign exchange, gold coins, gold, and platinum, except for useful articles, without the permission of the Polish Foreign Exchange Commission, and it raised the punishment for illegal traffic in these items up to and including the death sentence under trial by summary courts.

The banking system and financial control. The functions of the principal institutions in the financing of economic activity, as envisioned by the legal enactments establishing them, have been set forth briefly in Chapter V. In their planned role, the banks are tools of the national economic plan, allocating short-term and investment credit or grants in accordance with the plan and supervising the

[79] Janusz Malicki, "Reforma systemu pieniężnego (Reform of the Monetary System), *Gospodarka Planowa,* November, 1950, p. 595. The new zloty by its definition becomes equivalent to the Soviet ruble, both being declared equal to the same amount of gold.

activity of enterprises to see that financial discipline is observed. In principle, the quantity and assortment of production in the socialized economy and in each enterprise are determined by the plans, as are the prices of goods, wages, interest rates, and other elements of the cost of production. The credit requirements of enterprises, therefore, would follow from the planned production cycle, the envisioned quantities and prices of inputs and outputs, and the initial working capital of the enterprise.

In practice, however, the planning of production and distribution could not be precise, since not every detail of labor and material cost could be centrally specified, and therefore a certain amount of discretion was exercised on the local level. Since in the socialized enterprises the incentives of ownership are lacking, the management probably would be inclined to make things comfortable by concentrating on the technical side of production and feeling that credits would always be forthcoming to meet the outlays for fixed and working capital. To a certain extent the incentives to management and employees contained in the provisions for the Plant Fund and various premiums were expected to arouse a proprietary spirit, but certainly the postwar experience in this respect left much to be desired. The planners envisioned, therefore, the need for constant surveillance over the activity of enterprises by the banking apparatus. In the Polish economy the banks' control function, therefore, requires a knowledge of the provisions of the production and financial plans of the enterprises as well as an intimate knowledge of the enterprises themselves. In particular, the bank supervising an enterprise is expected to see that its receipts correspond to the goods produced, and that expenditures are supported by invoices, wage lists, and other documentation permitting the bank to follow transactions and judge their conformity to the established plans.[80] The bank oversees the distribution of the profits and the coverage of losses, settlements between an enterprise and the state budget, the conclusion of planned agreements, observance of the obligatory price schedules, observance of limitations on cash transactions, and in general the entire financial operation of the enter-

[80] Witold Trąmpczyński, "Uwagi o roli banków w gospodarce planowej" (Remarks on the Role of Banks in a Planned Economy), *Wiadomości Narodowego Banku Polskiego* (News of the Polish National Bank), August, 1946, pp. 24–27.

prise.[81] Banks are expected to assist in the formulation of financial plans of enterprises and make recommendations for improving their efficiency.

The performance of the banking apparatus and the financial system as a whole during the Three-Year Plan was obscured by the existence of rationing alongside the so-called free market; nevertheless, the accumulation of unexpected budget surpluses, unforeseen yields from various taxes, and the *ad hoc* development of the wage bill gave evidence of the confusion that existed in the initial planning period. Control by banks over the expenditure of the wage fund was only begun in 1949, and their performance since that time left much to be desired. As indicated above, the violation of discipline in establishing norms of work, violation of wage regulations, and excesses above norms of employment appear to have been very widespread.

Delays in submitting approved plans for such things as the wage bill impeded the control work by banks in 1950. It was only by the end of May that the branches of the Polish National Bank could begin to apply sanctions against those enterprises which failed to stay within the limits of their approved wage bills, and the greatest number of suspensions of payments to enterprises came in June and July after an analysis of accounts. The government cannot foreclose its enterprises in the case of failure to stay within the limits of planned costs, and frequently the responsible ministry freed the negligent enterprise from the imposed sanctions even before analyzing the causes of the violation in order that the wages of large groups of employees might not be withheld for an extended period.[82] Complaints were voiced against such practices by management as: (1) changing the planned assortment of production in favor of the items which would assure the greatest profit with the least effort, (2) disregard of quality of production in a drive to fulfill the production plan quantitatively, (3) failure to pay financial obligations promptly, (4) possession of excessive inventories of materials, and (5) using working capital for investment purposes.[83] In

[81] Józef Szyrocki, "O współpracy banku z przedsiebiorstwem" (Collaboration of the Bank with the Enterprise), *Finanse,* 1953, No. 5, p. 57.

[82] Franciszek Stefański, "O przestrzeganiu dyscypliny finansowej" (Concerning the Observance of Financial Discipline), *Życie Gospodarcze,* May 1–15, 1951, p. 502.

[83] *Ibid.,* p. 500.

view of such complaints, the control exercised by banks apparently failed to come up to expectations.

Cash planning, which includes the planning of cash turnovers, the inflow and outflow of cash with respect to banks, and a balance showing the magnitude of cash in circulation, was not introduced in Poland until mid-1950.[84] Under the existing regulations, Polish socialized enterprises are expected to deposit promptly their cash supplies in banks and request cash as needed for specific purposes. However, exceptions are allowed which permit certain economic units, such as rural cooperatives, to cover their expenditures for agricultural procurements from cash receipts from sales. On the outflow side, cash planning is primarily concerned with providing cash for wage bills and for procurements from the private sector and, on the inflow side, with the receipts from socialized trade, taxation, and other payments by the population to the agencies of the state. Since these cash movements are important indexes of physical counterparts in the national economic plan, the absence of an over-all cash plan prior to 1950 is an indication of the incompleteness of financial control in centralized planning. A comparison of actual cash movements with their planned magnitudes may signalize lack of coordination of economic activity and call for remedial action. By the fourth quarter of 1951, the cash plan was setting fixed norms, the so-called limited items, for cash outlays by state enterprises in such areas as: (1) purchase of goods and materials for their own use, (2) payment for services, and (3) miscellaneous expenditures. These quotas were set monthly, and any unused balance could not be carried over to a subsequent period.[85] Although cash planning has improved since its introduction, many defects still remain.

Among over-all criticisms of financial planning, frequent complaints appeared against the undiscriminating formality of planning which failed to set tasks in keeping with the real ability of enterprises. The basic technical and economic indexes appeared too often to be based on averages and were not adapted to the special circumstances of enterprises. One enterprise could exhaust its working capital sooner than foreseen and, unless it was granted credit, it could throw others off their schedules, while another enterprise

[84] *Życie Gospodarcze,* April 21, 1952, p. 470.
[85] *Ibid.,* p. 472.

could have such comfortable circumstances that waste would ensue. Frequently the management of an enterprise drafted its financial plan without directly relating it to production and without consulting the accounting, supply, and production departments. The poor professional level in financial offices was also a source of complaint.[86]

Polish financial planning in the postwar period was not uniformly successful. Contrary to the declared aims of the economic plans, the period was characterized by recurrent wage-price inflation, and the announced goals for real wage increases were not realized. Financial incentives proved inadequate to allocate the factors of production as desired by the plans, and a battery of direct controls over labor and material resources came into existence. Financial supervision over the socialized sector was improved in various details, but the scheme of incentives worked poorly and stern sanctions were established to further the achievement of the plans. Through discriminatory taxation and confiscatory monetary reforms, the socialized sector of the economy was expanded at the expense of private enterprise. By the end of 1953 the Polish financial system had been almost completely transformed to the Soviet model.

[86] *Ibid.*, pp. 462–64.

X

Foreign Economic Relations

THE volume, composition, and direction of foreign trade; investment loans and credits; and exchange of various services are factors which may have a very significant influence upon the course of a country's planned economic development. At the same time, the fulfillment of plans for foreign trade obviously does not lie wholly within the control of the country seeking a planned evolution of economic activity, but is subject to the desires of trading partners, the potential sources of loans and credits, and the world political and economic situation. In the period after World War II Poland's foreign economic relations were strongly conditioned by the country's new political orientation. Economic ties with countries within the Soviet sphere were greatly strengthened while connections with the rest of the world in general deteriorated. The high priority assigned in economic plans to industry and the neglect of agriculture were reflected in the composition of foreign trade. State control over foreign trade became practically complete and was directed toward implementation of national economic plans.

Planning and Organization of Foreign Trade

The organization of foreign trade. From the outset of national economic planning in 1946, foreign trade was a state monopoly exercised either directly by state enterprises or on behalf of the state and under its control by private and cooperative organizations. Private enterprises soon became insignificant in this sector, while cooperatives were transformed into instruments of the state directly subject to the discipline of central planning.

Since July 21, 1944, when the Polish Committee of National Liberation began to function as the government of Poland, the administration of foreign trade rested in various departments and ministries which were split off and recombined in a series of changes which finally culminated in the dissolution of the omnibus Ministry of Industry and Trade on February 10, 1949, in favor of six new ministries including the Ministry of Foreign Trade. The sphere of activity of the latter as defined on March 8, 1949, included:[1]

1. Financial and economic planning in the realm of foreign trade
2. Conduct of trade negotiations, preparation of international trade agreements, and supervision over their execution in understanding with the Ministry of Foreign Affairs and with the participation of other interested authorities
3. Regulation of foreign trade turnovers and effecting settlements from this trade
4. Direction of state and cooperative enterprises engaged in foreign trade and guidance and supervision over the activity of other enterprises in this area
5. Establishment and supervision of foreign trade offices abroad and designation of commercial attachés and other representatives in foreign trade in understanding with the Ministry of Foreign Affairs
6. Matters of foreign trade technique, norms, and standards; fairs and displays; and other matters relating to foreign trade.

Under the supervision of the ministry, the actual trading transactions are carried out by special enterprises called centrals. Up to the end of 1947, these foreign trade centrals appear to have operated inefficiently. Typically, a given central would both import and export a wide selection of commodities which often overlapped with that of other centrals. Confusion, needless complication, and price competitions are alleged to have resulted instead of the envisioned purposeful monopoly in foreign trade.[2] During 1948 a reorganization of the foreign trade enterprises was undertaken, which, with some exceptions, was based on the following principles: (1) segregation of import activities from export by means of separate enterprises for each, (2) concentration of import or export of certain commodities into single centrals so as to prevent an overlap of lists of goods handled, (3) establishment of a direct connection between the foreign trade centrals and the production enterprises in order

[1] *Dziennik Ustaw*, 1949, No. 15, Item 96.
[2] *Gospodarka Planowa*, October-November, 1948, p. 453.

to coordinate export requirements more closely with production possibilities, (4) introduction of a uniform organizational type for the foreign trade central which should thereafter operate on the basis of "economic calculation," that is, act like an independent firm seeking to cover expenditures by income and maximizing profits under the rules imposed by superior administrative units, and (5) transition from the role of middleman acting on a commission basis and using others for actual contacts to the role of direct importing and exporting by the centrals.[3] The foreign trade central when distinct from the central engaged in domestic trade and distribution acquired export commodities from the latter. This double intervention between the domestic producer and the foreign purchaser was criticized as a harmful separation of the requirements of the market from the production possibilities of the producer. Point (3) above aimed at correcting this deficiency by either having a single central serve both the domestic and foreign markets or having an industry specialist attached to the foreign trade central in order to facilitate the adaptation of the industry to the competitive situation on foreign markets.

Prices received by Polish producers of exports and paid by purchasers of imports were to a large extent insulated from world market prices by means of foreign trade accounts maintained by the state in the Polish National Bank or under its control in other banking institutions. In effect, the suppliers of exported goods were paid internal prices which did not necessarily bear any automatic relation to the receipts in foreign currency. Similarly, the domestic prices on imported raw materials and manufactured goods could be divorced from the prices paid abroad.[4] In the import of basic raw materials in the postwar period, the state has paid subsidies into the foreign trade account in order to keep the raw material prices paid by industry on a planned low level. At the same time the foreign trade accounts received the difference between the actual receipts from exports and the costs which included the prices paid to domestic suppliers increased by the costs of export.[5] Such calculations imply a conversion rate between the zloty and foreign currencies, but this rate had primary significance for the state in appraising

---

[3] *Handel Zagraniczny* (Foreign Trade), July, 1948, p. 37 (Supplement to *Życie Gospodarcze,* July 1–15, 1948).

[4] *Wiadomości Narodowego Banku Polskiego,* No. 12, 1946, p. 33.

[5] *Gospodarka Planowa,* July, 1948, pp. 311–12. See also *supra,* pp. 246–47.

the over-all results of foreign trade, and very little significance for the production enterprises. In 1948, the conversion rate between the zloty and the dollar was 400:1 for foreign trade purposes, with other currencies being converted on the basis of this parity. Foreign payments, where required, were made in foreign currencies, the zloty being an internal currency.

Under the regulations in effect in 1948, the tasks of foreign trade centrals included: (1) analyses of foreign markets, (2) maintaining a knowledge of competitive sources of supply, (3) arranging for appropriate transportation of goods, including suitable packaging and insurance, (4) setting prices on goods sold so as to realize maximum profits while taking account of competition of other sellers, (5) assuring payment for goods sold so as to avoid loss while at the same time not making payment conditions too onerous, and (6) liaison with production enterprises to assure that the goods dispatched would correspond to the conditions of sale with regard to quality, assortment, terms of delivery, packing, and transportation.[6] The advice of consular establishments, special trade missions, and trade delegations helped to establish prices, quality, and assortment of export to meet conditions on foreign markets. Among the difficulties experienced by the export centrals, those relating to the establishment of prices and the adaptation of production to the requirements of particular clients were regarded as the most prominent.[7] Reconciliation of centralized economic planning with the requirement of flexibility in production programs to meet changing situations on world markets continued to be an important practical problem in production for export. The export central was required to submit periodically lists of particular requirements for purposes of planning production, regardless of whether or not it possessed orders for these from abroad.[8] Although detailed production programs were drawn up on the basis of expectations listed by the centrals, in practice it was expected that the requirements would change, and much of the Polish planning discussion was devoted to devising efficient coordination of production with the varying foreign market situation.

On September 28, 1949, by decree of the Council of Ministers,

[6] *Handel Zagraniczny*, April, 1948, pp. 9–10. (Supplement to *Życie Gospodarcze*, April 1–15, 1948).

[7] *Ibid.*, October, 1948, p. 52 (Supplement to *Życie Gospodarcze*, October 1–15, 1948).

[8] *Życie Gospodarcze*, July 1–31, 1949, p. 567.

the Polish Chamber of Foreign Commerce came into being. This institution was conceived as an advisory and research body serving to facilitate the work of other organizations in the field of foreign trade. In Polish trade with the Soviet Union and its European satellites, the Chamber was expected to supplement in relatively minor detail the collaboration already established by the Council of Economic Mutual Assistance and various bilateral arrangements. Its work included such matters as establishing model contracts between trade organizations, arbitration, and a joint policy of exhibition of goods. In relation to other countries, the Polish Chamber of Foreign Commerce was expected to carry out research on foreign economic conditions and other matters of interest to foreign trade, and to render advice to trade organizations. Its tasks included problems of foreign trade technique, commercial usages, and arbitration, wherein it would collaborate with analogous foreign bodies. The new Chamber took over the activities in foreign trade which were formerly carried out by the Chambers of Industry and Trade on behalf of private trade and also on behalf of the socialized sector in the absence of its own representative body. The Polish Chamber and its associated Arbitration College were patterned on their Soviet equivalents.[9] The Chamber's membership included the foreign trade centrals, maritime shipping enterprises, the Polish National Bank, the Bank of Trade, the leading Polish insurance companies, and the Association of Importers and Exporters. The prescribed function of the Arbitration College was to resolve civil law disputes in the realm of foreign trade and shipping between Polish persons or firms and their foreign counterparts.[10]

Planning of foreign trade. Polish law defined the foreign trade plan as a constituent part of the over-all national economic plan. As such it entered into the material and financial balances established by the plans for production, consumption, investment, and trade.[11] Deficits of raw materials, finished goods, and equipment which could not be covered by domestic supply were the basis of the plan of imports, while demand conditions on foreign markets and the possibilities for expanding domestic production or restraining consumption determined the composition of exports, which along

[9] *Ibid.*, January 1–15, 1950, pp. 11–12.
[10] *Ibid.*, March 16–31, 1950, p. 290.
[11] *Dziennik Ustaw*, 1947, No. 53, Item 285, pp. 880–83.

with foreign credits were regarded as the principal means for realizing the essential imports. Commitments arising from long-term trade agreements were taken into account in the formulation of annual plans.

Coordination of the requirements of foreign trade with the plans for production has proved troublesome in Polish experience. Instructions for drafting the annual plan for 1951 aimed at removing some of the earlier deficiencies by establishing the following scheme of coordination: (1) the State Commission of Economic Planning establishes the principal aims for foreign trade on the basis of the Six-Year Plan goals and with reference to particular instructions for 1951 as given by the Council of Ministers; (2) on the basis of (1), the Minister for Foreign Trade prepares general postulates concerning the assortment of exports; (3) these postulates are included in the planning instructions passed on to the production ministries by the planning commission; and (4) on the basis of the foreign trade postulates, the Minister for Foreign Trade distributes quantitative goals for imports and exports to the central offices for the administration of foreign trade. These goals are to be accompanied by prescribed levels of trade with principal trade partners and the quantities of leading products to be traded with them. The central offices elaborate details in understanding with the trade centrals, which are the economic units actually engaged in trade, and with the central administrations of industry desiring imports or providing exports.[12] In earlier years, the planning units were obliged to use a series of relatively uncoordinated instructions which they tried to reconcile individually with the various authors.[13]

Polish postwar foreign trade policy was differentiated according to the political orientation of the trading partners. After Poland's failure to obtain extensive investment credits from the United States and the International Bank for Reconstruction and Development, the subsequent failure to participate in the Marshall Plan, and the political consolidation in Poland under the hegemony of the Polish United Workers' Party, the Polish outlook on the path of economic development came ever more closely into alignment with the Soviet precept and the current requirements established

[12] Piotr Czerwiński, "Planowanie handlu zagraniczego na rok 1951" (Planning of Foreign Trade for 1951), *Gospodarka Planowa,* September, 1950, p. 463.

[13] *Ibid.,* p. 467.

by Soviet leadership. Hilary Minc asserted in 1951 that backward countries could industrialize only by means of socialist construction and only when they marched in the ranks directed by the Soviet Union and with its support and aid.[14] Through economic relations within the Soviet orbit, according to Minc, the national economies were interrelated in a planned manner. On the other hand, the state monopoly in foreign trade was regarded as a means of defense against capitalist economies. Poland, in his view, should seek economic relations with the latter only on a selective basis, that is, only to the extent that these relations would facilitate Polish economic development, but at the same time a consistent and systematic effort should be made to avoid any form of dependence upon capitalist countries.[15]

The desire to plan foreign trade effectively and also the necessity to seek balanced trade relations where credits could not be arranged led to the widespread use of bilateral trade agreements in the postwar period.[16] Other factors which served to facilitate the planning of foreign trade in this period included long-term commercial agreements, investment credits over a period of years granted against future deliveries of Polish goods, and treaties providing for economic collaboration within the Soviet sphere.

Polish Postwar Foreign Trade

Foreign trade during 1945–46. The purely commercial transactions by Poland during this period were dwarfed in comparison with the supplies delivered by the United Nations Relief and Rehabilitation Administration. The UNRRA program for Poland totaled over 481 million dollars, distributed as shown in Table 47. Although the direct aid to agricultural and industrial rehabilitation amounted to about 171 million dollars, the over-all effect upon the reconstruction of the Polish economy must be judged far greater. The food, clothing, and health supplies invested in the Polish population were undoubtedly manifested in increased productive capacity of human labor, which after all is to some extent substitutable for imports of capital goods. Moreover, the sale of UNRRA supplies

[14] *Życie Gospodarcze*, October 16–31, 1951, p. 1100.
[15] *Nowe Drogi*, July-August, 1950, pp. 38–39.
[16] Poland also participated in triangular trade with Finland and the USSR. See *infra*, p. 282.

by the Polish government to the population provided a very significant drainage of purchasing power to the advantage of the state budget.

Table 47

UNRRA PROGRAM FOR POLAND

(THOUSANDS OF DOLLARS)

Food	201,725
Clothing, textiles, and footwear	82,700
Medical and sanitation aid	25,800
Agricultural rehabilitation	75,900
Industrial rehabilitation	95,135
Total	481,260

Source: United Nations Relief and Rehabilitation Administration, *Operational Analysis Papers, No. 49*, p. 40.

Of the total UNRRA program, about 92 million dollars worth arrived in 1945, approximately 306 million in 1946, and practically all the rest by the end of June, 1947. Purely commercial trade in millions of dollars, according to prices established in trade agreements, amounted to 34.0 and 139.6 for imports, and 37.8 and 132.8 for exports in 1945 and 1946, respectively. The development of Polish foreign trade was conditioned by transport possibilities in the early postwar years. During 1945, approximately 91 percent of Poland's imports and 93 percent of her exports were exchanged with the Soviet Union. By 1946, trade with the Scandinavian countries and the Russian Zone of Occupation of Germany became significant, but the USSR still accounted for 70 percent of imports and 49 percent of exports in the Polish commercial trade totals.[17] Food, textile fibers, petroleum products, and various raw materials were the principal imports, while among exports, coal and coke predominated, followed by cotton and linen fabrics, iron and steel products, sugar, cement, zinc, and electric energy.[18] By the end of 1946, Poland was beginning to function under national economic plans and thereafter it is possible to compare the realized foreign trade with the goals set in the plans.

Value and composition of foreign trade. According to official Polish data shown in Table 48, Poland's foreign trade increased

[17] *Wiadomości Statystyczne* (Statistical News), Special Volume 1, June, 1947, p. 5.
[18] *Ibid.*, pp. 6–7.

rapidly in the postwar years, both in volume as measured in weight and in value according to prices of 1937. The relatively small increase in imports from 1947 to 1948 reflects the termination of UNRRA deliveries in the former year. Although the volume of UNRRA shipments in 1947 had fallen sharply from the level of the preceding year, the value of the contribution represents about 80 million dollars, or approximately one fourth of the purely commercial imports into Poland during 1947.[19]

The analysis of Poland's foreign trade after 1947 on the basis of Polish statistics becomes increasingly difficult due to the unavailability of official information concerning the value, composition,

Table 48

POLAND'S FOREIGN TRADE, 1938 AND 1947–50

	IMPORT	EXPORT	IMPORT	EXPORT
Year	*In Millions of Metric Tons*		*Index of Value in 1937 Prices*	
1938[a]	3.31	15.60	100.0	100.0
1947	3.12[b]	21.86	128.3[b]	51.4
1948	4.43	31.97	130.5	95.6
1949	5.34	35.22	148.9	120.8
1950	5.83	34.88	196.5	144.3

Source: *Wiadomości Statystyczne* (Statistical News), March, 1951, p. 2.

[a] Prewar boundaries.

[b] Including 264,258 tons of UNRRA deliveries (cf. *Statistical Yearbook of Poland—1948*, p. 105).

and directions of trade. Thus, the 1948 official statistical yearbook contains eighteen pages of tables devoted to foreign trade data for the years 1945 through 1947, including valuations in dollars for the trade totals by countries and considerable detail as to the composition of trade in tons for the total imports and exports and by trade partners. Although this leaves much to be desired, it is relatively bountiful in comparison with the five pages of foreign trade statistics given in the 1949 yearbook. The latter discontinued the breakdown of trade totals by countries and presented a commodity breakdown in terms of broad categories without a detailed listing of principal commodities. Price information, as in the earlier postwar yearbooks, remained scarce, relating mostly to expressions in terms of trade agreement dollars, which may or may not be com-

[19] *Statistical Yearbook of Poland—1948*, p. 103.

parable to world prices and to valuations in terms of prewar zloty prices. Early in 1949, the statistical publications of the Polish Institute for Economic Research were discontinued, and in June, 1951, the indexes on foreign trade published in the *Statistical News* of the Central Statistical Office of Poland were restricted to a series in terms of total weight of imports and exports, discontinuing the index of volume in 1937 prices.

The United Nations Economic Commission for Europe has been able to reconstruct Poland's foreign trade with countries outside the Soviet sphere by the use of the statistics of trading partners. Within the circle of the USSR and its satellites, the reconstruction of trade totals and commodity composition is much more difficult and subject to possibly wide error due to lack of information or failure of official statements to specify the basis of various quantitative estimates. Similarly, trade totals in rubles translated into dollars at the Soviet official rate leave much to be desired.

As may be seen from Table 49, Poland's foreign trade plans for the period 1947–49 were underfulfilled by wide margins as regards imports but were significantly exceeded with respect to exports, except for 1947. Instead of an unfavorable balance of 767 million dollars for 1947–49 anticipated by the Three-Year Plan, with the expectation of approximately equivalent coverage from foreign aid and credits, the realized negative balance was about 149 million dollars, of which about 83 million was covered by UNRRA assistance.

Since the Three-Year Plan expected that about 25 percent of the total planned investment would be covered by imports under foreign credits,[20] the failure to receive these credits and the corresponding failure to realize the planned imports reacted unfavorably upon the course of actual investment. The expansion of exports in 1948 and 1949 above the initially planned goals kept imports from falling lower than they did, but the gain from increased exports was not a net gain since the additional exported goods may be presumed to possess an investment equivalent if used domestically, although not as great as the imports they financed. According to Table 50, the goals of investment for 1947–49 envisioned under the 1946 draft of the National Economic Plan were fulfilled only 69 percent, but those of the revised version in the Three-Year Plan were carried

[20] *Plan odbudowy gospodarczej* (Plan of Economic Reconstruction), p. 87.

Table 49

POLAND'S PLANNED AND REALIZED FOREIGN TRADE, 1947–49
(MILLIONS OF DOLLARS UNLESS OTHERWISE INDICATED)[a]

Item	1947	1948	1949
Imports:			
Goals set in 1946 draft of plan	510	665	775
Three-Year Plan goals	729	738	877
Realized	401	516	632
Realized as percentage of Three-Year Plan	55	70	72
Exports:			
Goals set in 1946 draft of plan	298	400	485
Three-Year Plan goals	338	458	560
Realized	248	533	619
Realized as percentage of Three-Year Plan	73	116	111
Balance of trade:			
Goals set in 1946 draft of plan	−212	−265	−290
Three-Year Plan goals	−391	−280	−317
Realized	−153	17	−13

Sources: Goals of the 1946 draft of plan are taken from *Polish National Economic Plan*, p. 83; Three-Year Plan Goals taken from *Plan odbudowy gospodarczy* (Plan of Economic Reconstruction), p. 147; realized trade totals taken from *Rocznik statystyczny—1949* (Statistical Yearbook—1949), pp. 103–4, for 1947 and 1948. The 1947 total was increased by UNRRA deliveries amounting to 83.4 million dollars in order to make it correspond to the goals set in plans. The realized imports do not include purchases of demobilization supplies, but inclusion of these would not change the totals very significantly since the total credit for such purchases amounted to 50 million dollars from the United States and 6 million pounds sterling from Great Britain. The 1949 trade totals are taken from *Poland of Today*, May, 1950, p. 19, and apparently are an extension of the series for 1947 and 1948 as presented in the Polish official statistical yearbooks, although the totals for the earlier years differ slightly. The data in Table 49 are not fully comparable to those of Table 53. The latter table was compiled primarily from data of Poland's trading partners and gives all totals f.o.b., whereas Table 49 gives the totals *franco* Polish custom boundaries for the Three-Year Plan goals, and f.o.b. for the 1946 draft goals.

[a] The prices in the 1946 draft of the plan for the years 1947–49 refer to the first half of 1946. For the Three-Year Plan goals, the values are expressed in average prices of the first half of 1947. The realized trade totals are in current dollars.

out 95 percent. Without more detailed information it is difficult to appraise the substitutions that must have been made in the scheduled investments during the Three-Year Plan in adjustment to the failure of credit expectations. The communique of the State Commission of Economic Planning announcing the results of the fulfillment of the 1949 national economic plan stated that the investment plan for the year was not fully realized although the investment outlays increased 64 percent over 1948. The highest degree of fulfillment was shown in communications, transportation, and industry, while unsatisfactory results appeared in social and cultural categories and housing.[21]

Table 50

POLAND'S PLANNED AND REALIZED INVESTMENTS, 1947–49
(IN BILLIONS OF ZLOTYS AT 1938 PRICES)

	1947	*1948*	*1949*
1946 draft of the National Economic Plan	2.8	3.2	4.0
Three-Year Plan	1.9	(5.3)	
Realized	1.4	2.2	3.3

Sources: The goals under the 1946 draft of the plan were taken from *Polish National Economic Plan*, p. 73; Three-Year Plan goals from *Plan odbudowy gospodarczej*, p. 88; realized totals from *Życie Gospodarcze*, March 1–15, 1950, p. 211.

The commodity composition of Poland's foreign trade. Table 51, which sets forth the planned and realized imports for 1947–49 and their planned distribution into four large categories of goods, shows that the original expectations of the Three-Year Plan were poorly realized in the field of investment goods. The foreign trade goals for 1948 and 1949 were modified in the plans for these years primarily by the reduction of import goals and an increase of export totals. It is possible to make a rough comparison of the expected investment imports under the Three-Year Plan and the actually realized investment imports by applying the percentage composition of imports to the planned and realized total imports. The actual composition of imports for 1947 is shown in Table 51, and it may be assumed that the realized percentages for investment goods in 1948–49 did not differ very substantially from the planned composition for those years as given in the annual plans. On this basis, disregarding price changes, it is seen that the realized investment imports were about one third of the Three-Year Plan expectations. Although some substitutions could be made from domestic sources, the failure to realize planned imports must have led to serious dislocations of the investment plan.

According to an official Polish source, the realized composition of imports in 1949 was as follows: investment goods—21 percent; raw materials and semimanufactures—63.6 percent; food—8.8 percent;

[21] *Życie Gospodarcze*, February 1–15, 1950, p. 141.

and manufactured consumer goods—6.5 percent.[22] It seems clear from this and from Table 51 that the realized imports of raw materials and semimanufactures missed the 1947 goal by a wide margin. Performance on this score was better in 1948–49, when about 80 to

Table 51

COMMODITY COMPOSITION OF POLAND'S IMPORTS, 1947–49

	1947	*1948*	*1949*
Total imports:			
Three-Year Plan totals, millions of dollars, 1947 prices	729	738	877
Realized, millions of current dollars	318[a]	516	632
Composition as percentages of total imports:			
Food:			
Three-Year Plan	21	3	2
Annual plans	28[a]	10	5
Raw materials and semimanufactures:			
Three-Year Plan	41	51	52
Annual plans	47[a]	65	68
Investment goods:			
Three-Year Plan	34	42	44
Annual plans	25[a]	25[b]	22
Miscellaneous:			
Three-Year Plan	4	4	3
1949 plan			5

Sources: The Three-Year Plan totals and composition are taken from: *Plan odbudowy gospodarczej*, p. 147. The data for the realized imports are from Table 49, above. Data for the annual plans of 1948 and 1949 are taken from *Dziennik Ustaw*, 1948, No. 19, p. 355, and 1949, No. 26, p. 570.

[a] These figures are realized imports for 1947 and do not include UNRRA deliveries. The percentage composition of imports for 1947 refers to the realized trade (*Gospodarka Planowa*, October-November, 1948, p. 450). The "annual plan" entry for food for 1947 refers to consumer goods, including food.

[b] Including miscellaneous imports, which probably amount to about 4 percent of total imports.

90 percent of the Three-Year Plan goal was realized in current value. Food and miscellaneous imports in 1948–49 significantly exceeded the planned goals.

The commodity composition of Poland's foreign trade, 1937 and

[22] Statement of the Minister of Foreign Trade, *Życie Gospodarcze*, May 1–15, 1950, p. 412.

1947–50, is shown in Table 52 in 1937 prices. Unfortunately, Polish statistics fail to indicate the composition within the broad categories listed, or to give the value in current prices. Nevertheless, a general impression of the character of foreign trade can be gained from this table and from supplementary sources, including the goals set in the national economic plans. Imports in the postwar period increased markedly in (1) mineral products, which include primarily iron and manganese ores and petroleum products, (2) chemicals, including fertilizers, (3) machinery and equipment, including transportation equipment, and (4) various precision equipment. Textile fibers, rubber, wood and paper products, metals and metal products, hides and leather, and grain and other plant products are other important items in postwar imports.

According to the Three-Year Plan, coal and coke were expected to account for 60 to 63 percent of the total planned dollar value of exports, with the share increasing slightly from 1947 to 1949.[23] The actual percentage share of coal and coke in the total value of Polish exports since 1945, however, steadily declined as follows: 1945—77 percent; 1946—62 percent; 1947—54 percent; 1948—51 percent; and 1949—46 percent.[24] At the same time, the absolute value of coal exports shows a steady increase in this period. In 1949, Poland exported 32.3 million tons of coal.[25] By applying the planned percentage share of coal and coke to the total value of planned exports in 1947–49 shown in Table 49, and comparing the results with a similar calculation of realized shares in the actual exports, it appears that Poland's expectations of returns from coal exports fell short of the goal in 1947 by about one third. In 1948, actual performance came close to coinciding with the planned goal, but in 1949 it fell short again, this time by about one fifth.

According to a Polish official source, the 1949 composition of exports, apparently in current prices, was as follows: coal and coke— 46 percent; agricultural and food products—20 percent; raw materials and semimanufactures—17.8 percent; and industrial products —16.2 percent,[26] which corresponds closely to the goals of the 1949

[23] *Plan odbudowy gospodarczej*, p. 147.

[24] *Życie Gospodarcze*, April 16–30, 1949, p. 336; May 1–15, 1950, p. 413. Data are apparently based on current prices.

[25] United Nations, Economic Commission for Europe, *Economic Bulletin for Europe*, Second Quarter, 1951, Vol. 3, No. 2, p. 86.

[26] *Życie Gospodarcze*, May 1–15, 1950, p. 413.

Table 52

COMMODITY COMPOSITION OF POLAND'S FOREIGN TRADE, 1937 AND 1947–50

(MONTHLY AVERAGE IN MILLIONS OF ZLOTYS, 1937 PRICES)

Category of Goods	IMPORTS					EXPORTS				
	1937ᵃ	1947	1948	1949	1950	1937ᵃ	1947	1948	1949	1950
Total	104.5	149.1	151.8	173.2	228.5	99.6	50.8	94.6	119.5	137.7
Plant products	9.0	12.3	10.4	6.9	11.1	11.6	0.5	3.2	14.6	4.8
Live animals and animal products	2.8	7.0	1.9	4.9	2.1	17.0	0.8	7.0	8.3	18.0
Mineral products	5.1	7.3	15.1	17.6	23.5	19.5	32.4	44.5	48.2	47.9
Waxes, fats, vegetable and animal oils, not elsewhere included	1.8	1.0	1.0	2.0	3.1	0.8	0.0	0.2	0.0	0.2
Processed food products; tobacco	3.6	12.6	2.4	2.7	4.4	7.5	1.6	3.2	4.2	6.1
Chemicals and pharmaceuticals; dyes	5.6	11.3	9.0	20.3	27.9	2.9	1.5	3.0	3.9	8.9
Hides, furs, leather products	8.0	5.1	10.1	8.1	7.7	2.6	0.1	0.1	0.1	0.6
Textile raw materials and products	29.0	23.7	28.0	29.0	30.3	7.4	5.6	9.8	12.1	12.8
Rubber and its substitutes; products thereof	1.9	3.2	5.3	5.5	6.6	0.1	0.0	0.0	0.0	0.1
Wood, cork, products thereof, basketware	0.5	0.8	3.4	3.3	4.4	16.8	0.3	1.1	4.0	4.9
Paper and paper products	2.2	1.4	2.4	2.4	4.2	0.7	0.1	6.3	1.3	1.0
Stone, ceramic, and glass products	1.1	0.3	0.7	1.3	1.5	0.2	1.3	2.6	2.7	2.5
Base metals and products thereof	16.9	8.5	15.1	16.5	19.6	11.5	5.9	11.0	12.5	11.9
Machinery and apparatus, electrotechnical equipment	9.8	14.8	20.7	33.2	44.6	0.6	0.2	0.9	1.9	2.6
Transportation equipment	3.5	29.5	22.0	14.9	28.7	0.1	0.2	0.7	5.2	12.9
Balances, precision equipment, typewriters, clocks, musical instruments	2.4	4.9	3.6	3.9	7.7	0.1	0.1	0.7	0.3	0.3
Other finished products	1.2	5.3	0.6	0.6	0.9	0.6	0.0	0.1	0.1	0.3

Source: *Wiadomości Statystyczne*, March, 1951, p. 11.

ᵃ Prewar boundaries.

national economic plan. Polish postwar export policy, as formulated at the outset of the Three-Year Plan, aimed at the export of highly processed agricultural products and certain manufactured consumer goods even during the period of great scarcity of these items on the domestic market in order to acquire foreign markets or reestablish prewar contacts. Textiles, chemicals, lumber and wood products, base metals and their products, and transportation equipment were among the more important categories of actual exports but were secondary to coal, coke, and agricultural products. As may be seen from Table 52, the most significant changes from the prewar composition of exports consist of the greatly increased importance of coal, coke, transportation equipment, chemicals, and to a lesser degree textiles, and of the diminished importance of agricultural products and lumber.

Directions of Poland's foreign trade. The network of Poland's foreign trade in 1938 and 1948–50 is shown in Table 53, and the share of the Soviet Union and eastern Europe in Polish trade totals is given in Table 54. Immediately after World War II, due primarily to the disorganization of European transportation, the Soviet Union and the Scandinavian countries accounted for the major part of Polish trade. Poland actively sought trade partners and soon reestablished commercial connections with the principal trading countries of the world. However, in contrast to prewar, the Soviet Union became and remained Poland's leading trade partner. Following the heightened international tension in 1947–48 which divided Europe into two hostile camps, Polish trade as a matter of policy was increasingly oriented toward the USSR and its satellites. The declining share of the USSR and the Soviet satellites in Poland's foreign trade which was prominent from 1945 to 1947 was reversed in 1948–49 with the introduction of the Marshall Plan in western Europe and the formation of the Council of Economic Mutual Assistance in the Soviet sphere. Under Soviet pressure Poland reversed her decision to participate in the plan for European recovery proposed by Secretary of State Marshall in June, 1947, and instead became more closely tied to the USSR and its satellites through credits from the USSR and long-term trade agreements in the Soviet orbit. The appearance of the Council of Economic Mutual Assistance in January, 1949, symbolizes the progressive consolidation of an economic bloc headed by the Soviet Union.

Table 53

NETWORK OF POLAND'S FOREIGN TRADE, 1938 AND 1948–50
(MILLIONS OF DOLLARS IN CURRENT PRICES, F.O.B.)

Geographic Area	EXPORTS				IMPORTS				BALANCE			
	1938	1948	1949	1950	1938	1948	1949	1950	1938	1948	1949	1950
European Countries:												
United Kingdom	41	35	50	49	26	29	32	19	15	6	18	30
France	9	32	38	12	9	10	35	16	0	22	3	−4
Netherlands	10	12	25	7	7	6	19	9	3	6	6	−2
Belgium-Luxemburg	10	8	8	7	10	12	12	8	0	−4	−4	−1
Switzerland	5	12	6	7	5	8	12	11	0	4	−6	−4
Italy	12	17	31	17	6	18	14	16	6	−1	17	1
Denmark	3	36	31	25	2	13	16	8	1	23	15	17
Sweden	14	67	47	36	9	40	31	32	5	27	16	4
Norway	3	19	15	11	2	12	13	7	1	7	2	4
Finland	4	32	18	26	1	8	9	9	3	24	9	17
Germanya	44	42	100	81	48	31	55	136	−4	11	45	−55
Austria	11	19	19	20	8	3	11	9	3	16	8	11
Yugoslavia	1	22	9	...d	2	26	5	...	−1	−4	4	...
USSR	2	111	135	146	3	118	225	337	−1	−7	−90	−191
Czechoslovakia	8	40	50	85	7	53	50	81	1	−13	0	4
Rumania	2	5	13	22	2	6	13	22	0	−1	0	0
Hungary	2	4	12	36	1	4	12	36	1	0	0	0
Bulgaria	3	7	12	12	3	6	12	15	0	1	0	−3
Other areas:												
USA and dependencies	13	1	3	11	27	55	23	9	−14	−54	−20	2
Latin American countries	9	3	4	1	17	16	21	10	−8	−13	−17	−9
Overseas sterling areab	4	...	2	4	20	6	46	44	−16	−6	−44	−40
Summary:												
USSR and East Europec	17	167	222	301	16	187	312	491	1	−20	−90	−190
Other European countries	173	356	406	305	138	218	269	284	35	138	137	21
Rest of world	33	8	15	25	77	93	106	69	−44	−85	−91	−44
World total	223	531	643	631	231	498	687	844	−8	33	−44	−213

Source: United Nations, Economic Commission for Europe, *Economic Bulletin for Europe*, Second Quarter, 1950 and 1951, Tables XXI and XXII, respectively. See this source for methods used.   b Including British colonies.

a Includes East Germany in the postwar period.   d ... = nil or less than one-half million dollars.

c East Europe in this table includes Bulgaria, Rumania, Hungary, and Czechoslovakia.

According to Poland's declared policy, trade relations within the Soviet sphere must be based upon the economic plans of the participating countries. The Six-Year Plan postulates the construction of the foundations of socialism in Poland upon Socialist solidarity and mutual aid within the Soviet sphere.[27] Poland's trade with the USSR and eastern Europe became increasingly important after 1948, and in 1952 it represented about two thirds of the total foreign trade.

Poland's postwar imports from the Soviet Union consist primarily of industrial raw materials and investment goods. According to the 1950 plan for imports, for example, the USSR would supply Poland with 80 percent of her cotton imports, 65 percent of iron ore, 100 percent of manganese ore, and 50 percent of ferro-alloys.[28] Investment goods to be received from the USSR during the Six-Year Plan were expected to account for about 50 percent of the total imported from all sources.[29] Imports from the USSR include, besides the items mentioned, nonferrous metals, synthetic rubber, petroleum products, ball bearings, machine tools, tractors and motor vehicles, construction machinery, agricultural equipment, and certain varieties of grain. On the other hand, Poland's exports to the Soviet Union include coal, coke, metallurgical products, textiles, metal products, chemicals, glass, paper, sugar, locomotives, railway wagons, and other industrial products.[30]

Soviet-Polish economic relations are difficult to analyze because of the lack of detailed information concerning quantities and prices and the role of reparations deliveries. The totals of trade agreements as given in dollars or rubles afford an approximate indication of the magnitude of commercial trade but do not disclose the relative prices of the bartered commodities. The zloty totals, on the other hand, even when available, indicate the settlements with domestic buyers and sellers and are subject to the state's policy either to subsidize or to limit the use of particular imported goods.[31] A full ac-

---

[27] *Dziennik Ustaw*, 1950, No. 37, Item 344, p. 429.
[28] Stanisław Gall, "Import Polski ludowej" (Import of People's Poland), *Życie Gospodarcze*, May 1–15, 1950, p. 416.
[29] *Życie Gospodarcze*, October 16–31, 1951, p. 1106.
[30] *Ibid.*, April 1–15, 1951, p. 422.
[31] Cf. House Select Committee on Foreign Aid, *Final Report on Foreign Aid*, 80th Congress, House Report No. 1845, May 1, 1948, p. 398. In 1946 the accounts for Polish-Soviet trade were as follows according to terms of settlement: (1) in "trade agreement dollars," Poland's imports and exports were valued at 98.2 and 65.6 million dollars, respectively, and (2) in zlotys, the totals were 7.4 and 8.6 billion for imports and exports, respectively. Thus, in dollars, the Polish deficit was about 32 million, whereas, in zlotys, the balance was favorable by 1.2 billion.

count of Soviet-Polish exchanges would have to take account of Polish deliveries of coal at special low prices to the USSR in exchange for 15 percent of the reparations realized by the Soviet Union from the zones of occupation of Germany. The reparations coal quotas were originally set at 8 million tons for 1946, 13 million tons in each subsequent year through 1950, and 12 million tons annually thereafter until the end of the occupation of Germany. However, in March, 1947, the scheduled deliveries were reduced by half,[32] and with the announced termination of reparations from East Germany beginning on January 1, 1954, Polish deliveries of coal on the reparations account presumably would be correspondingly adjusted.[33]

Table 54

POLAND'S FOREIGN TRADE WITH THE USSR AND EASTERN EUROPE, 1938–50
(PERCENTAGE SHARES IN POLISH IMPORTS AND EXPORTS, CURRENT PRICES)

	USSR		EASTERN EUROPE[a]	
Year	*Imports*	*Exports*	*Imports*	*Exports*
1938	1.3	0.9	7.0	8.0
1945	90.6	92.8	90.6	93.3
1946	69.4	46.0	72.1	51.7
1947	25.1	28.4	30.7	37.3
1948	23.7	20.9	37.5	31.5
1949	32.8	21.0	45.4	34.5
1950	39.9	23.1	58.2	47.7

Sources: Data for 1938 and 1948–50 taken from United Nations, Economic Commission for Europe, *Economic Bulletin for Europe*, Vols. 2 and 3, No. 2, for 1950 and 1951, Tables XXI and XXII, respectively. Data for 1945–47 taken from *Statistical Yearbook of Poland—1948*, pp. 103–4.

a Includes the USSR, Czechoslovakia, Hungary, Rumania, and Bulgaria.

Besides the USSR, Poland's chief trade partners in eastern Europe are the Soviet Zone of Occupation of Germany and Czechoslovakia. The former accounted for about four fifths of the total trade for 1949–50 shown for Germany in Table 53.[34] Hungary and Rumania

---

[32] Margaret Dewar, *Soviet Trade with Eastern Europe, 1945–1949*, pp. 39–40. Dewar cites a statement by Stanisław Mikołajczyk, formerly a minister in the Polish government but now in exile, giving 1.25 dollars per ton as the Soviet price for these deliveries.

[33] New York *Times*, August 24, 1953.

[34] United Nations, Economic Commission for Europe, *Economic Bulletin for Europe*, Second Quarter, 1951, Vol. 3, No. 2, p. 93.

increased their trade turnovers with Poland severalfold in 1948–50, while Bulgaria's trade with Poland approximately doubled, and Yugoslavia's practically disappeared.

According to a Russian source, the share of the Soviet orbit countries, including Communist China, in Poland's total foreign trade turnover rose from about 43 percent in 1949 to 67 percent in 1952.[35] Russia's share alone was about 32 percent of Poland's total turnover in 1952.[36]

Poland's trade with European countries outside the Soviet sphere declined in relation to the growth of her over-all trade, and in 1950 it fell in an absolute sense as compared to 1949. United States exports to Poland show a sharp decline from 1948 to 1950 as a consequence of the licensing of exports to the Soviet sphere following the increased international tension in this period. Polish export to the European countries outside the Soviet sphere, as measured in current prices, f.o.b., dropped from about 325 million dollars in 1949, to 254 million in 1950, recovered to about 337 million in 1951, and declined to 258 million in 1952. Polish imports from these countries showed a similar evolution, ranging from 218 million dollars, f.o.b., in 1949 to 167 million in 1950, then rising to 211 million in 1951, and falling to 172 million in 1952.[37]

Although political factors are important in explaining the decline of Poland's trade with countries outside the Soviet sphere, a number of economic considerations also contributed to this decline. These include the postwar lag in agricultural and forestry production, absorption of some traditional exports by the home market in connection with the industrialization of the country, and difficulties imposed by the bilateral character of postwar trade. Poland's failure to meet scheduled deliveries of coal and coke to the Scandinavian countries in the fall of 1952, for example, led to exhaustion of swing credits and an interruption of trade. Under the requirement of bilateral balancing it has been found difficult at times to find acceptable commodities to exchange for the offerings of trade partners. The behavior of the Polish foreign trade monopoly in the pricing of coal also contributed to reduction of the volume of exchanges.

[35] *Vneshnyaya Torgovlya* (Foreign Trade), 1953, No. 3, p. 6.
[36] *Ibid.*, 1953, No. 11, p. 18.
[37] United Nations, Economic Commission for Europe, *Economic Bulletin for Europe*, Second Quarter, 1951, Vol. 3, No. 2, p. 58; *ibid.*, Second Quarter, 1952, Vol. 4, No. 3, p. 55; *ibid.*, First Quarter, 1953, Vol. 5, No. 2, p. 28.

This monopoly pursued a flexible price policy varying with the degree of dependence of western Europe on American coal and aimed at aligning the export price of Polish coal with the landed cost of American coal. Such pricing in accordance with the marginal cost of coal to western Europe brought substantial gains to Poland during 1951 when there was a relative scarcity of shipping, but with the collapse of the shipping boom in 1952 and increased availability of British coal, Polish reluctance to reduce prices led to a decline in volume of exports of Polish coal. By October of 1952, however, Poland had reduced prices on export coal by about 40 percent from the peak earlier in the year.[38] Partly as a result of such price policy and partly because of increased domestic coal requirements and the needs of other countries in the Soviet bloc, Poland's exports of coal to western Europe declined from 11.8 million tons in 1949 to 9.9 and 7.0 million in 1951 and 1952, respectively.[39] Poland's total exports of coal in 1950 were estimated at 32 million tons,[40] of which about 10 million tons went to western Europe.

Important exceptions to the bilateral character of Poland's foreign trade include Polish participation in a transferable sterling group and the triangular trade arrangements with Finland and the USSR. The positive balance realized by Poland in her trade with the United Kingdom helped to finance the deficit incurred in trade with the overseas sterling areas. In triangular trade with Finland and the Soviet Union, Poland delivered sugar, coal, iron and steel, machinery, and textiles to Finland to cover Finnish counterpart deliveries to the USSR and the latter's shipments to Poland.[41]

Machinery, metals, metal products, transport equipment, and raw materials were the principal postwar Polish imports from western Europe. The share of machinery in these imports, as measured by constant prices, rose from about one fifth in 1948 to over one third in 1950.[42] Polish exports to western Europe in 1950 were dominated by coal, which accounted for over half of the total value. Next in order of importance were meat, timber, eggs, grain products, metals and metal products, chemicals, and textiles. Food products and raw

---

[38] *Ibid.*, Second Quarter, 1952, p. 43.

[39] *Ibid.*, pp. 42, 46; and Vol. 5, No. 1, Second Half, 1952, p. 21.

[40] United Nations, Economic Commission for Europe, *Quarterly Bulletin of Coal Statistics*, No. 1, 1952, p. 17. Estimate represents total, ton for ton, of coal, lignite, and coke. Hard coal alone was 26.5 million tons.

[41] *Ibid.*, pp. 73, 75.

[42] *Ibid.*, Second Quarter, 1951, p. 60.

materials represented about nine tenths of the total value in current prices.[43] Trade with countries outside Europe was relatively unimportant insofar as it concerns Polish exports, but accounted for about one fifth of total imports in 1948, and less than one twelfth in 1950. Wool, rubber, and other products of overseas sterling areas were the principal items in this trade. The course of Poland's trade with countries outside the Soviet sphere suggests that this trade will be pursued only insofar as it contributes to Polish plans of economic development.

In contrast with the developments in the interwar period, Poland's postwar foreign trade was redirected increasingly across land frontiers, corresponding to the status before World War I. The Six-Year Plan aimed at tripling the carrying capacity of the Polish merchant fleet, and set the 1955 goal of total commodity transport by this fleet at 5.7 million tons.[44] Poland's growing merchant fleet is expected to contribute toward the self-sufficiency of Soviet bloc shipping, the requirements for which have also grown because of the expansion of trade with China.

Foreign Economic Agreements

Foreign credits. As has been stated above, the aid extended by the United Nations Relief and Rehabilitation Administration during 1945–47 was the principal external factor in the recovery of the Polish economy after World War II. The contribution of the United States through UNRRA and other grants amounted to 349 million dollars.[45] Credits and loans granted to Poland since 1946 to the end of the Three-Year Plan in 1949 total approximately 674 million dollars.[46] Of this total, 90 million dollars were United States credits granted on April 24, 1946, consisting of 40 million dollars from the Export-Import Bank for the purchase of railway and mining equipment and 50 million dollars for the purchase of U.S. war surplus property. Approximately 106 million dollars of medium-term credits for the purchase of raw materials and investment goods was made available in 1947–49 by the following European countries in the amounts indicated: Sweden—34 million dollars; Norway—8 million

[43] *Ibid.*, p. 62.
[44] *Dziennik Ustaw*, 1950, No. 37, p. 443.
[45] House Select Committee, *op. cit.*, p. 403.
[46] *Études et Conjoncture*, September-October, 1949, p. 74.

dollars; Denmark—15 million dollars; France—15 million dollars; and Great Britain—34 million dollars.[47] The Soviet Union granted a loan in gold on March 5, 1947, amounting to 27.885 million dollars, repayable in commodities over a period of ten years beginning in 1950, and a credit established by agreement on January 26, 1948, for the delivery of investment goods worth 1,800 million rubles to Poland over a period of eight years. Imports under this agreement were to be paid for by Polish exports to the USSR successively in the five years following each delivery from the Soviet Union.[48] In view of the terms for deliveries and repayment, the net outstanding credit at any given time under this agreement will be much smaller than the publicized 1,800 million rubles. It is not known how deliveries will be staged, but assuming an average annual delivery of investment goods by the USSR to the amount of 225 million rubles over eight years and Polish repayment of each such annual contingent by counter deliveries amounting to 45 million rubles annually in the succeeding five years, the net indebtedness of Poland to the USSR would range from 225 million rubles in the first year to a peak of 675 million in the fifth through the eighth years, and then decline rapidly to 45 million rubles in the twelfth year.

Poland's request for a loan of 600 million dollars from the World Bank of Reconstruction and Development was refused early in 1947, and moreover, under Soviet pressure, Poland refused to participate in the Marshall Plan. As a consequence of the failure of credit expectations, the Three-Year Plan goals for imports, especially of investment goods, were underfulfilled by wide margins.[49]

On July 2, 1950, Poland and the USSR announced a new credit agreement for the years 1953–58, which provided additional credits to Poland to the extent of 400 million rubles[50] to cover deliveries of industrial equipment. Under the provisions of trade agreements extending to 1958, the share of capital goods was expected to expand

[47] *Ibid.*

[48] *Gospodarka Planowa,* January, 1949, pp. 21–22. The 1,800 million rubles equal 450 million dollars at the Soviet official rate of exchange.

[49] *Supra,* p. 273.

[50] This is equivalent to 100 million dollars at the Soviet official rate of exchange, but the purchasing power equivalent depends on the particular list of scheduled Polish imports of investment goods and the prices charged for these by the USSR. The ruble appears to be highly overvalued with respect to the dollar at the official rate as concerns consumer goods, but not necessarily so as regards capital goods. Very little is known concerning the prices used in Soviet-Polish trade.

to 40 percent of the total Soviet exports to Poland.[51] The USSR was expected to be Poland's chief source of investment imports under the Six-Year Plan. An accurate appraisal of the net Soviet assistance to Poland would have to take account of Polish deliveries of reparations coal, the prices used in Polish-Soviet commercial exchanges, and the drain imposed on the Polish economy by rearmament at Soviet behest. On balance these factors might completely offset Soviet aid to Poland.

Economic agreements. A major part of Poland's postwar foreign trade is carried on under bilateral clearing agreements. Initially the trade agreements were for short periods, up to a year, but by 1949, long-term trade agreements were becoming more common, particularly within eastern Europe. Such agreements provided a firmer basis for economic planning than short-term arrangements or completely unscheduled trade. Among the countries which have concluded long-term trade agreements with Poland are Great Britain, the USSR, Argentina, Italy, Switzerland, and countries of eastern Europe. The following agreements are illustrative:

1. A five-year agreement with the USSR covering 1948–52, and a second agreement for 1953–58. The first provided for a commodity exchange totaling one billion dollars, while the second anticipated a 60 percent increase in trade turnover above the annual average attained in 1948–50.[52]

2. A five-year agreement with Great Britain covering the period 1949–53 and calling for a total exchange in excess of one billion dollars. From the Polish side, it specified deliveries of eggs, bacon, poultry, fish, and other goods against British deliveries of rubber, wool, and other materials from Commonwealth sources. Britain provided credit guarantees for Polish purchases of wool on short-term credit, and an existing 6 million pound sterling credit for the purchase of capital equipment was converted into a revolving credit within the five-year period.[53]

Using the medium-term credits granted by the Soviet Union, Sweden, Great Britain, France, and Switzerland, Poland has been

---

[51] *Poland of Today*, August, 1950, p. 3; *Życie Gospodarcze*, July 16–31, 1950, p. 706. The credit was to be repaid by Polish exports in later years, presumably in a manner similar to the 1948 credit, but details of the terms were not announced.

[52] *Poland of Today*, August, 1950, p. 3.

[53] *Ibid.*, February, 1949, p. 12.

able to contract for the purchase of industrial equipment and other investment goods to be paid for by subsequent deliveries of Polish goods. In some cases the credits were renewable within the established period of the accord.

Within eastern Europe, Poland is bound by treaties of mutual assistance to the USSR, Czechoslovakia, Hungary, Rumania, and Bulgaria. These treaties have economic significance which follows from the general pledges by the contracting parties to collaborate in a spirit of amity in the development of economic relations. In addition to the mutual assistance treaties which run for twenty years, Poland is bound by agreements for economic cooperation with Czechoslovakia, Hungary, Rumania, and Bulgaria, which were concluded during 1946–49, to run in each case for five years. A similar agreement was signed with East Germany in 1950.

Among the most important of these accords were the Polish-Czechoslovak agreements for economic collaboration. Their basic aim was to establish a division of labor within given fields of production. The executive organs regulating the collaboration were headed by the Polish-Czechoslovak Economic Council, which possessed eight commissions, namely, for trade, investment, finance, communications, industry, agriculture, scientific and technical matters, and planning and statistics.[54] Each commission was divided into committees, and the latter into subcommittees, all of which had mixed membership. For example, the commission for industry had among others a committee for the metal industry, which in turn had numerous subcommittees dealing with the principal branches of the industry, such as motors, railway equipment, heavy machines, and agricultural equipment.

At the basis of the planned collaboration was the principle that mass production of a given type of product should take place in a single country so as to realize the advantages of large-scale production, certain exceptions being allowed. The specialization in production could extend to particular parts of a given machine which could then be assembled in either or both countries. By the end of 1948, agreements had been reached to allocate the production of various types of machine tools, presses, locomotives, office machines, optical equipment, textile machines, and many other metal products.

[54] Henryk Wencel, "Współpraca Polsko-Czechoslowacka" (Polish-Czechoslovak Cooperation), *Życie Gospodarcze,* December 16–31, 1948, pp. 962–63.

Standardization of parts for motor vehicles and other products, joint research and testing facilities, and joint construction and operation of shipyards and other industrial establishments were envisioned under the program. The projected collaboration appeared most far-reaching in the motor vehicle industry.[55] After the formation of the Council of Economic Mutual Assistance early in 1949, the reports of Polish-Czechoslovak collaboration became less informative and received less prominence than formerly.

It is difficult to quantify the extent of economic cooperation springing from the Polish-Czechoslovak agreements, since the growth of trade between the two countries reflects other factors, such as the vacuum created immediately after the war by the prostration of Germany and the East-West trade stalemate later. It is clear, however, that cooperation among the planned socialist economies of eastern Europe can create limited economic complementarities that otherwise might not appear.

On January 25, 1949, the Soviet Union, Poland, Czechoslovakia, Hungary, Rumania, and Bulgaria announced the formation of the Council of Economic Mutual Assistance. Official aims of the Council included an exchange of economic experience, mutual extension of technical assistance, and mutual aid with respect to raw materials, food, machinery, and industrial equipment.[56] Officially, the Council is an open organization which any nation may join provided it subscribes to the principles of the Council and seeks to participate in extensive economic cooperation with the countries listed above. However, in response to Yugoslavia's protest over not being invited to join, the reply of the Polish government pointed out that admission would be countenanced only if Yugoslavia would change its policy toward the USSR and other members of the Council and return to the former policy of friendship.[57] In effect, therefore, the Council is restricted to the USSR and its satellites.

In describing economic cooperation within the Soviet sphere, Hilary Minc, at that time the chairman of the Polish Commission of Economic Planning, stated that each country, in introducing its plan for industrialization, creates and expands first of all those branches of industry, especially heavy industry and machine build-

---

[55] *Ibid.*
[56] *Gospodarka Planowa,* February, 1949, pp. 64–65.
[57] *Życie Gospodarcze,* March 1–15, 1949, p. 199.

ing, for which it possesses the most favorable conditions, and which are the most essential both to the given country and to other friendly states.[58] The coordination of economic objectives within the Soviet sphere would appear to be one of the chief functions of the Council of Economic Mutual Assistance. Such coordination seems to be effected primarily by long-term trade agreements covering the periods of the long-term production plans.

In the emerging pattern of postwar trade in eastern Europe, the strongest connections are those of each satellite with the USSR, and on the next level are the ties among the satellites and between them and the rest of the countries of the world. The growth of trade among the countries of eastern Europe has been furthered by the improvement of the transport system, the adoption of Soviet industrial standards and measures, and coordination of planning by means of trade agreements. Despite the intensification of trade among the countries of eastern Europe, the volume of trade there appears to be rather small as compared to the level attained between most countries of western Europe.[59]

The autarkic policies being followed in eastern Europe with regard to the development of basic industries seem to run counter to the declared aim of these countries to develop a high degree of economic cooperation. Each of these countries seeks to achieve rapid increases in the output of coal, electric power, and steel, although the resource endowment of the area would indicate specialization of production. The autarkic policies also seem to include the development of the engineering industries on an all-round basis, as is shown in production plans for such products as motor vehicles, electric motors, and machine tools. It is possible, however, for specialization to occur by types of output within the broad categories mentioned above.[60] Hilary Minc gave an example of such specialization planned for 1954–55 in tractor production in which Poland would produce all her requirements for medium tractors and a surplus for export against imports of other types of tractors. The revised economic policies introduced in the European satellites during 1953 in general tend to reduce the emphasis on autarky shown in earlier plans

---

[58] Hilary Minc, "Owocna współpraca wolnych narodów" (Fruitful Cooperation of Free Nations), *Życie Gospodarcze*, October 16–31, 1951, p. 1101.

[59] United Nations, Economic Commission for Europe, *Economic Survey of Europe since the War*, p. 217.

[60] *Ibid.*

in favor of a higher degree of economic integration within the Soviet sphere.[61]

While Poland's economic relations with countries in the Soviet sphere have become more intimate, contacts with the rest of the world have suffered. Poland has withdrawn from participation in the World Bank for Reconstruction and Development, the International Monetary Fund, and the United Nations Food and Agricultural Organization. The percentage of Poland's total foreign trade that is accounted for by the countries outside the Soviet sphere has declined from about 93 percent in 1937 [62] to about 33 percent in 1952.[63]

[61] Polish Embassy, Washington, *Press Release,* March 22, 1954, pp. 20, 27.

[62] United Nations, Economic Commission for Europe, *Economic Survey of Europe since the War,* p. 216.

[63] *Vneshnyaya Torgovlya* (Foreign Trade), No. 3, 1953, p. 6.

XI

Conclusion

TWO factors stand out in a comparison of Poland's prewar and postwar development. First, the physical environment within which economic activity takes place was changed as a result of World War II and the subsequent boundary revisions and populations changes, and second, the matrix of social organization, policy, and control was drastically altered by the Communist-dominated postwar governments. Poland's population in the postwar period was reduced from prewar by about one third, and although the country's area was reduced by about one fifth, the assortment of natural resources and installed productive capacity was such that by regaining prewar production within present boundaries Poland could equal the prewar agricultural output in prewar boundaries and increase industrial production by more than half. With a smaller total population, this implied excellent prospects for full employment, substantially increased production per capita, and good cause to expect a much higher scale of living.

The Polish economy had moved a long way toward centralization of control before 1939. Its heritage from the years of partition, World War I, and the Russo-Polish War included a wide array of government controls and direct participation in production and distribution. Subsequently, in seeking to establish economic unity, provide for national defense, and insure fuller employment, the government expanded its intervention in the economy, and by 1937 it had embarked on economic planning on a broad basis. In contrast to the postwar development, however, this effort was but a partial approach to planning. Moreover, the government did not aim at complete socialization of production. Instead it sought to create a framework within which private and state enterprise could collaborate, the state taking over in areas where private domestic venture was lacking.

After World War II, the legal forms governing economic activity were progressively recast into a pattern permitting highly centralized control and planning. At the same time a dictatorial government dedicated to a policy of rapid industrialization proceeded to implement its plans with ruthless zeal. The catalogue of laws, decrees, and administrative measures which regulate economic activity stem from a central conviction that planned economic development must follow the pattern pioneered in the USSR, both with respect to the character of development and the institutional means by which resources are directed to this goal.

Viewed against the background of physical possibilities, the extent of public control, and the priorities established by the government, the impressive growth in industrial production achieved in the postwar period is not surprising. Practically all of the industrial sector has passed into state ownership, and the same is true of forestry, transportation, communications, trade, and the services of finance. The nation's agriculture by the end of 1953 was about one-fifth socialized, and the remainder operated within a tight framework of regulations governing compulsory deliveries of products to the state and of dependence upon the socialized sector for the supply of equipment, construction materials, fertilizers, and other production requirements. By means of its comprehensive controls, the government was able to shift labor from agriculture and services to socialized industry. In this endeavor the government supplemented its policy of differential wages according to planned priorities with an array of direct controls over labor and the professions, and it geared the nation's educational system to the requirements of the planned economy. As a matter of policy, the government largely replaced private saving by public saving, and it allocated the resources freed by enforced abstinence from consumption primarily to industrial expansion. Through its direct control over production and trade the government was able to implement its allocations.

Under the government's priorities agriculture failed to meet its goals, but under the expanded state controls it was nevertheless obliged to provide the necessary supplies for the urban population and the raw material needs of industry. Agriculture rated a low priority for investment, and its labor force already reduced by war was further diminished by recruitment for industry. In addition the individual private farmer was subjected to onerous schedules of compulsory deliveries, restricted opportunities for free sale of his surplus above these deliveries, discriminatory taxation and compulsory deliveries favoring the socialized farms, and other pressures for collectivization of production. After a period of fairly rapid recovery up to 1950, agricultural production leveled off and declined under this regimen.

The failure of the population to realize a substantial increase in the scale of living is implicit in the stagnation of agriculture and the relatively low priorities assigned to the production of consumer goods and services. This failure is acknowledged in Polish official statements which assert that at the end of 1953 real wages in non-agricultural employment had changed only imperceptibly as compared with 1949, but that increased employment made possible an increase of about 15 to 20 percent in urban and rural per capita real income. Even if this claim be granted, when measured against the Six-Year Plan goal of 60 percent increase in the scale of living by 1955, it is a significant admission of failure. If the revised goals for 1955 are realized, only about one half of the original planned increase in consumption would be achieved.

Poland's postwar rate of growth of industrial production was particularly rapid due to a combination of unusual factors. This growth started from very low postwar levels and proceeded rapidly during the period of reconstruction when relatively small capital investments could activate relatively large increments of productive capacity. Expansion in this early period was aided by assistance from the United Nations Relief and Rehabilitation Administration to the extent of about 481 million dollars and by foreign loans. In re-establishing and expanding production, Poland was able to profit from the accumulated technological advances realized in other countries. As this backlog is used up, Poland's rate of expansion will tend to diminish. Expanding industry, moreover, was able to draw labor from agriculture and services and to introduce a higher percentage of women into the labor force. Successive additions from these sources, however, became increasingly more difficult to realize. The activation of reserves of labor was paralleled by mobilization of industrial capital, natural resources, urban housing, and other material means for the achievement of planned industrialization. The working out of these unusual factors is reflected in the declining rate of growth of industrial production. Future gains will depend more on increases in output per worker made possible by new skills and new investment in production facilities and less upon new additions to the labor force and a higher rate of exploitation of existing capital.

Recognition of the depressive effect its policies had produced in agriculture and upon worker morale in the socialized sector at first led the government to increase the rigor of its controls over the economy. Laws were passed aiming at increased labor discipline, reduced labor turnover, and increased compulsory deliveries from agriculture. In 1953, however, following the lead of the USSR and several of its satellites in eastern Europe, Poland revised her economic policies. Under the new plans for 1954–55, absolute investment is to be kept constant at the 1953 level, thus permitting consumption and other uses of the national product to increase with the anticipated gains in total output. Investment priorities and labor policies would be altered to expand the production of manufactured consumer goods and agricultural products. If the new plans are realized, the Six-Year Plan will be overfulfilled in industry, but agricultural production and levels of consumption will still be far below the original goals.

Despite the changes introduced by the new policies, the Polish economy remains basically oriented toward further development of heavy industry. Socialization of agriculture likewise remains a continuing objective to be pursued in 1954–55 as vigorously as in 1953. At the same time, in the interest of expanding production, the government assured the peasants that compulsory deliveries would not be further increased and that they could dispose of their increased production without restraint. The revised policies generally should permit the government to remove some of the disproportions its earlier priorities had introduced among the sectors of the economy and to adjust to a lower rate of growth implicit in the playing out of the unusual growth factors operating in the earlier postwar years.

Developments in Polish postwar economic organization and policy closely parallel the Soviet experience. Similarities between institutional arrangements of the two economies are becoming ever closer as the legal enactments to transform Polish society take effect. From 1946 to 1949 Poland passed through a state of evolution broadly corresponding to the period of the New Economic Policy in Russia.[1] Following a brief period of recovery, the state proceeded to elimi-

---

[1] See the account of Soviet development in Harry Schwartz, *Russia's Soviet Economy*.

nate the remaining elements of private enterprise in the nonagricultural sector of the economy, excepting handicrafts. Beginning in 1948, Polish planning proceeded more and more by reference to current Soviet practice. In 1949 the Central Board of Planning was replaced by the State Commission of Economic Planning, which is the Polish equivalent of Gosplan in more than name alone. Shortly thereafter, both the government and the economic administration in Poland were reorganized to correspond more closely to the Soviet model.

The Soviet model was similarly applied in the reform of the banking and financial system, the planning of the supply of labor to industry and professions, and in the revision of the methodology and techniques of planning and control both on the aggregative levels and within enterprises. In fact, there are very few areas of economic activity that have not been subjected to controls currently in effect in the USSR. Agriculture is the significant exception, but socialization of production has already engulfed about one fifth of this sector and further collectivization remains a firm goal for the future. Progress in socializing agriculture has been relatively slow, possibly in keeping with the slowly expanding supply of farm machinery or possibly in the light of the disastrous effect of forced all-out collectivization in the Soviet Union. The incentives which the Polish government is offering to promote the formation of collective farms favor the type which most closely resembles the Soviet kolkhoz.

Many of the Polish approximations to the Soviet model are not as close as the formal measures introducing them would suggest. It takes time to educate the bureaucracy and to overcome the resistance of the population. A study of Polish economic literature shows that even two or more years after particular measures have been introduced, they have not completely permeated the economic organization. Most of the formal divergences from the Soviet pattern belonging to the earlier postwar years were progressively removed up to the end of 1953. On the operational level undoubtedly there are deviations from the official regulations in Poland just as there are in the USSR, either to accomplish more directly some of the production goals of the enterprise or to gain some personal advantage.

The close correspondence between the institutions, techniques, and goals of planning in Poland and the Soviet Union is not accidental; instead it springs from Soviet domination over Poland exercised through the subservient (Communist) Polish United Workers' Party. One does not need to impute this subordination to the Polish Communist leaders; they publicly acknowledge the leading role of the Communist Party of the Soviet Union in the determination of basic lines of foreign and domestic policy for the countries of "people's democracy." The social science of Lenin and Stalin is invoked in practically every public discussion of economic policy. Indeed, the techniques of social control and economic management gained from Russia may well be considered Poland's chief import from that country. One may question whether the application of the Soviet model for economic development was appropriate for the Polish environment, but at the same time one must take into account the fact that the decision was not Polish, but Russian. The relevant question, therefore, would be whether the Soviet Union acted wisely in imposing the norms of its experience on the Polish economy, or, alternatively, whether the result was for the good of Poland.

Whether the result is for the good of the Poles must depend on the valuations to be taken as a standard. Clearly, Poland has experienced a rapid industrial expansion since World War II. Although much of this growth is due to the territorial gains from Germany, the techniques of social control imported from the Soviet Union have made possible centralized planning of economic activity and have enforced abstinence from current consumption to make possible extensive investment in new industrial capacity. In addition, these methods of control have provided the labor necessary to man the industrial capacity taken over by the state. Obviously the volume of industrial production is not the only criterion of national welfare. In a country with such low levels of consumption as Poland, the output of agriculture could be the most immediate source of a higher level of living. Performance in this slighted sector of production was very disappointing, and accordingly the consumption goals of the Six-Year Plan had to be abandoned. But the forfeit of a currently higher scale of living was not the only cost of Poland's industrialization. Clearly the host of laws, decrees, administrative orders, and regulations designed to channel the country's efforts toward the government's goals and the burden of an expanded bureaucracy to enforce them represent a loss of personal freedom as well as a consumption of resources that could be used for directly productive purposes.

The use of force to impose the Communist program for Poland, however, makes it clear that the wishes of the population differ from those of the planners. The latter not only decide the aggregate rate of investment but also in large measure designate the specific forms this investment shall take. Within the share of the national product provided for consumption, the planners' choice of the assortment of consumer goods has attempted to take account of consumers' preferences, but performance on this score left much to be desired even by the standards set by the planners. Given a desire by the Poles to govern their econonomic destiny by democratic means, then the Soviet model clearly is inappropriate for Poland. Attempts aimed at a large measure of decentralized decision making within the broad framework of the state's economic policy were effectively blocked by the consolidation of political power in Communist hands. The Communists ruled out any compromise between the Soviet model and the mixed economies of the West.

The Communists' insistence upon the Soviet model of a highly centralized planned economy perhaps can best be understood in terms of the requirement of effective control. In the Russian view this model had demonstrated its efficiency in assuring political control and in mobilizing productive resources for the development of industry and for military strength. Its extension into eastern Europe serves the same purpose. For the Polish Communists the rapid transition to the Soviet pattern surely must have outweighed the finer considerations of economic efficiency. Their performance apparently was evaluated not only in terms of the magnitude of production and the related costs but also in terms of the institutional adaptations to the Soviet model.

Even within the socialized sector the possible gain in efficiency that could arise from decentralization of decision making must have been weighed against the loss in centralized control that it would necessitate. Despite its apparent inefficiency as compared to schemes of automatic allocation of resources to production and of distribution of the product under prices acting as parameters in various adaptations of a perfectly competitive economy, the Soviet model possesses the advantage of rapid accommodation to the planners' objectives. Within their framework of centralized planning and control, the Polish planners have given some attention to stimulating efficiency. Modifications of the price system and of the scheme of distribution of profits have been directed toward this end. The tardiness shown in selecting prices adequately reflecting costs of production, however, must have hindered realistic planning. The entire postwar period was characterized by both open and disguised inflation, rationing, price control, monetary reforms, and revisions of prices and wages which bear witness to faulty financial planning. These manifestations were primarily the result of the government's policy of a high rate of investment in producer goods industry and of other high public expenditures coupled with inadequate reduction of the population's purchasing power through taxation or other fiscal devices. Perhaps in such circumstances highly centralized planning featuring direct controls over economic activities is rational from the viewpoint of the planners. It permits at least a rough approximation to their principal objectives.

The evolution of centralized planning illustrates the tendency of direct economic controls to spread to ever wider areas of activity. Given the conflict between the preferences of the population and the independent producers expressed through the market and the desires of the planning authority manifested in a given direct control, it could be expected that the market would seek to circumvent the control and that the planning authority would try to thwart such action by the introduction of new direct controls. In the case of Poland such tendencies were powerfully augmented by the Soviet example. Indeed the series of piecemeal extensions of state control can be regarded as the progressive application of a well-established ideology and its fully developed pattern of action.

It might appear that the autarkic development being followed by Poland would not be in keeping with Russian aims for integration of the country into an expanded Soviet economy. Such a development, however, does not differ from the policy prescribed by the USSR for development of its own regions. In both cases, the prescription calls for as much self-sufficiency as possible for a given region, and at the same time it demands a specialized role for the region based on its assortment of productive resources. Polish official statements stressing economic collaboration within the Soviet bloc were reiterated with added emphasis in connection with the revision of economic plans for 1954–55. Such increased cooperation was expected to result in cost economies through specialization and division of labor. The growth of Polish trade with Soviet orbit countries indicates that it is possible for economic planning to create complementarities among economies which are basically similar in structure. Increased trade on a much wider geographic basis would yield even greater economic advantages, but such a practice would not be compatible with the aim of self-sufficiency within the Soviet bloc.

From the Russian point of view the rapid adoption of the Soviet model of economic organization and planning in Poland must be regarded as highly desirable since it paves the way for possible incorporation of the country into the USSR. Even if Soviet policy did not aim at formal annexation, an industrially developed Poland under a Communist government responsive to Soviet control would represent an important increment to Russia's military potential. In any case, Communist control would prevent Poland from joining possible adversaries.

Appendix A: Sources of Tables 10 and 13

TABLE 10

THE ABSOLUTE figures and index for 1938–49 and 1955 are taken from Kazimierz Secomski, *Podstawowe zadania planu sześcioletniego* (Basic Tasks of the Six-Year Plan), p. 22. Although Secomski indicates that "fixed prices" (see *supra*, p. 136) were used, a statement in the text of the Six-Year Plan law, *Dziennik Ustaw*, 1950, No. 37, p. 443, gives the 1955 goal as 5,300 billion zlotys in prices of 1950, or an increase of 112 percent over 1949. It would appear, therefore, that the index between 1949 and 1955 is based on 1950 prices, and that the absolute figure for 1955 in Table 10 is obtained simply by applying the 112 percent increase to the 1949 absolute figure in "fixed prices." *Życie Gospodarcze*, February 1–15, 1951, p. 132, and *Gospodarka Planowa*, February, 1952, p. 9, February, 1953, p. 5, and March, 1954, p. 6, give percentage increases over the preceding years. An increase of 21 percent for 1950 is reported without an indication of the prices used, although the goal in the 1950 plan law is in "fixed prices." The increases for 1951, 1952, and 1953, respectively, are reported as 12, 10, and 10 percent in "comparable prices." No definition is given for these prices. In the absence of better information, Table 10 was constructed with the linkages indicated.

TABLE 13

Item 1, national income, is taken from Table 10.

Item 2, index of industrial production, 1937–49 inclusive, is taken from *Wiadomości Statystyczne* (Statistical News), May, 1950, p. 1; and the index for 1953 is taken from Polish Embassy, Washington, *Press Release*, March 22, 1954, p. 8, which gives the output 118 percent above 1949. The 1955 goal is taken from *Nowe Drogi*, July-August, 1950, p. 11. An alternative calculation based on Polish official sources, taking 1949 = 100, yields 231.4 as the *all industry* index for 1955, instead of 225.9 as given in the table. In view of the rounding of percentage figures in the Polish sources, this difference is not regarded as a significant discrepancy. The alternative calculation is based on data for socialist industry given in *Dziennik Ustaw*, 1950, No. 37, p. 344, and the data given *supra*, p. 156. The planned advance in *all socialist industry* shown in the indexes 1949 = 100, 1955 = 258, is offset by the decline in the private sector of industry represented by 1949 = 100, 1955 = 20.

Item 3, index of production of large- and medium-scale state industry, 1937 and 1949, is taken from the law of the Six-Year Plan, *Dziennik*

Ustaw, 1950, No. 37, Item 344, p. 427. Value of the index for 1947 is obtained by converting absolute values given for 1947–49 in fixed prices by Kazimierz Secomski, *Podstawowe zadania planu sześcioletniego,* p. 32, into relatives using the already established value of the index for 1949 as the point of departure. The goal for 1955 for this series is taken from the Six-Year Plan, p. 430, by applying the percent of increase given therein to the 1949 level. The indexes for producer and consumer goods industries are derived from the large- and medium-scale industry index by applying to it the shares of the two components of output in the total output of the industry, 1937–49, and extending this by the percent of increase for the components by the end of 1955. The percentage shares of the two components in the output of large- and medium-scale industry for the years in question were taken as follows:

	1937	1949	1955
Producer goods	50.6	59.1	63.5
Consumer goods	49.4	40.9	36.5

In the above series of percentage shares, the figures for 1949 and 1955 appear in *Nowe Drogi,* July-August, 1950, p. 12. The 1937 shares are estimates. The law of the Six-Year Plan, p. 427, as cited above, gives the percentage shares of producer goods and consumer goods for 1938 and 1949 in the gross output of *all industry and handicraft* and *large- and medium-scale industry* as follows:

	ALL INDUSTRY AND HANDICRAFT		LARGE- AND MEDIUM-SCALE INDUSTRY
	1938	*1949*	*1949*
Producer goods	47	54	59.1
Consumer goods	53	46	40.9

In the light of the relationship of the shares for producer goods and consumer goods in the two aggregates for 1949, the 1938 percentage share of producer goods in *large and medium-scale industry* was estimated at 51.4, and for consumer goods the share was taken at 48.6 percent. The 1937 shares in *large- and medium-scale industry* were then estimated at 50.6 percent for producer goods and 49.4 percent for consumer goods in an adjustment for the relative gain of producer goods from 1937 to 1938 as shown in Table 4 above.

Item 4, the index of agricultural production, is calculated from the following absolute series of the gross value of output in billions of 1937 zlotys:

	1937	1947	1949	1955 *(goal)*
Value	11.2	6.6	9.6	14.4

The 1955 goal is given in absolute terms in "fixed prices" and as a percentage of 1949 in the law of the Six-Year Plan, p. 439. This leads to the 1949 absolute figure. The 1937 figure follows from the absolute goal of 1955 and the percent of increase over 1937 given in *Nowe Drogi,* July-August, 1950, p. 22. The 1947 figure is taken from Główny Urząd Statystyczny (Central Statistical Office, *Dochód narodowy polski—1947* (Polish National Income—1947), p. 26. In view of the above construction and sources, the 1947 figure is in 1937 prices and the data for other years in the "fixed prices" based on 1937 prices. The Polish Embassy, *Press Release,* March 22, 1954, p. 8, reports the 1953 agricultural output "a mere 10 percent" over 1949.

Item 5, 1937–49, is taken from *Wiadomości Statystyczne* (Statistical News), May, 1950, p. 1, by converting the absolute figures in ton-kilometers into the index. The 1955 figure as given in the Six-Year Plan, p. 442, in tons, is converted into ton-kilometers according to the proportion of tons to ton-kilometers in the 1948–49 experience as given in *Wiadomości Statystyczne,* May, 1950, p. 1.

Item 6, in absolute figures, is derived from the following sources and then converted into the index: the 1937 figure appears in *Mały rocznik statystyczny—1938,* p. 19; 1947 and 1949 figures are given in *Rocznik statystyczny—1949,* p. 14; and the figure for 1953 is given by the Polish Embassy, *Press Release,* March 22, 1954, p. 13, as over 26.5 million.

Appendix B: Sources of Tables 21–25

THE PRINCIPAL SOURCES used in compiling Tables 21–25 are listed below. For convenience in making reference, only the number of the source and the location within it are cited.

(1) *Mały rocznik statystyczny—1939* (Little Statistical Yearbook—1939)
(2) *Statistical Yearbook of Poland—1947*
(3) *Statistical Yearbook of Poland—1948*
(4) *Rocznik statystyczny—1949* (Statistical Yearbook—1949)
(5) United Nations, Economic Commission for Europe, *Economic Survey of Europe*, 1948–51 (four numbers)
(6) *Dziennik Ustaw* (Journal of Laws), 1946–50
(7) *Życie Gospodarcze* (Economic Life), a periodical
(8) *Wiadomości Statystyczne* (Statistical News), an official government publication
(9) *Nowe Drogi* (New Ways), July-August, 1950
(10) *Gospodarka Planowa* (Planned Economy), a monthly periodical

TABLE 21

Coal: 1913, source (1), p. 148; 1938, source (1), p. 128; 1947–48, source (4), p. 47; 1949 and 1955 goal, source (9), p. 14; 1950–51, source (7), February 9, 1952, p. 166, using the percentage increases given therein. 1952, source (10), March, 1954, p. 3, by applying the percentage of increase to the 1953 base. 1953, Polish Embassy, Washington, *Press Release,* March 22, 1954, p. 6.

Lignite: 1913, source (1), p. 148; 1938 and 1948–50, source (5), *Survey* for 1950, p. 62; 1947, source (4), p. 45; 1955 goal, source (6), 1950 Journal, No. 37, p. 430; 1951 goal, source (6), 1951 Journal, No. 18, p. 170; 1952, source (10), February, 1953, p. 2, by applying stated percentage increase to the 1951 base; 1953, source (10), March, 1954, p. 3, by applying stated percentage increase to the derived 1952 figure.

Coke: 1938, 1947, and 1948, source (4), p. 2; 1949, source (8), May, 1950, p. 3; 1950, source (8), March, 1951, p. 3; 1951, source (10), February, 1952, p. 4, by applying the stated percentage increase to the 1950 base; 1952 and 1953, source (10), February, 1953, p. 2, and March, 1954, p. 3, by applying the stated percentage of increase to the derived 1951–52 figures; 1955 goal, source (6), 1950 Journal, No. 37, p. 435.

Crude petroleum: 1913, source (1), p. 148; 1938 and 1948–50, source (5), *Survey* for 1950, p. 172; 1947, source (3), p. 76; 1951, computed from the 1950 base by use of percentage relationships stated in source (6),

1951 Journal, No. 18, p. 170, and source (10), February, 1952, p. 4; 1952, source (10), February, 1953, p. 2, by applying the given percentage of increase to the computed 1951 base; 1955 goal, source (6), 1950 Journal, No. 37, p. 430.

Electric power, capacity: 1925 source (1), p. 127; 1938 and 1948–50, source (5), *Survey* for 1950, p. 171; 1947, source (3), p. 78; 1955 goal, source (6), 1950 Journal, p. 432.

Electric power, production: 1925 and 1938, source (1), p. 127; 1947–48, source (4), p. 51; 1955 goal, source (6), 1950 Journal, p. 430; 1953, given as absolute figure, Polish Embassy, *Press Release,* March 22, 1954, p. 6. For 1949–52, computed from the 1953 figure by working backward, using the percentage increases over the preceding year given in source (10), March, 1954, p. 3; source (10), February, 1952 and 1953, p. 2 and p. 4, respectively; and source (7), February 1–15, 1951, p. 178.

TABLE 22

Iron ore: 1913, source (1), p. 148; 1938 and 1948–50, source (5), *Survey* for 1950, p. 174; 1947, source (4), p. 47; 1951, source (10), February, 1952, by applying the percentage increase stated in the source to the 1950 base; 1952 and 1953, source (10), February, 1953, p. 2, and March, 1954, p. 3, by applying the percentage of reported increase to the 1951 figure; 1955 goal, source (6), 1950 Journal, p. 432. The metallic content of the ores was given as 34 percent in source (5) and was applied to the other years as well.

Pig iron: 1913, source (1), p. 149; 1938 and 1948–50, source (5), 1950 *Survey,* p. 174; 1947, source (3), p. 79. For 1951–53, source (10), February, 1952, p. 5; February, 1953, p. 2; and March, 1954, p. 3; by applying the stated increases to the 1950 figure. For 1955 goal, source (6), 1950 Journal, No. 37, p. 430.

Crude steel: 1913, source (1), p. 149; 1938 and 1948–50, source (5), 1950 *Survey,* p. 63; 1947, source (3), p. 79. For 1951–53, source (10), February, 1952, p. 5; February, 1953, p. 2; and March, 1954, p. 3; by applying the stated percentage increases to the 1950 figure. For 1955 goal, source (6), 1950 Journal, No. 37, p. 430.

Crude zinc: 1913, source (1), p. 149; 1938, source (1), p. 129; 1947, source (3), p. 79. For 1948–50, by applying the reported annual percentage increases to preceding years, beginning with the firm figure for 1947, source (7), February 1–15, 1949, p. 136; February 1–15, 1950, p. 139; and February 1–15, 1951, p. 178. For 1951–53, in the same manner as before, source (10), February, 1952, p. 5; February, 1953, p. 2; and March, 1953, p. 3. For 1955 goal, source (6), 1950 Journal, No. 37, p. 430.

TABLE 23

Index of production of chemical industry: Source (9), October, 1953, p. 43, reports 1953 output 2.5 times 1949 level or 4.3 times prewar. Source

(6), 1950 Journal, No. 37, p. 435, gives 1955 goal 3.5 times the 1949 output. The rough index is derived from these data.

Sulfuric acid: 1913, information not available; 1938 and 1948–50, source (5), 1950 *Survey,* p. 175; 1951 goal, source (6), 1951 Journal, No. 18, p. 170; 1955 goal, source (6), 1950 Journal, No. 37, p. 431.

Caustic soda: 1938 and 1948–50, source (5), 1950 *Survey,* p. 175; 1951, source (10), February, 1952, p. 4, by applying the percentage increase stated to the 1950 base; 1952 plan, source (10), March, 1952, p. 3; 1955 goal, source (6), 1950 Journal, No. 37, p. 431.

Calcium carbide: 1938 and 1948–49, source (5), 1950 *Survey,* p. 175; 1950, source (8), March, 1951, p. 4.

Fertilizers: 1938 and 1948–49, source (5), 1950 *Survey,* p. 176; 1955 goal, source (6), 1950 Journal, No. 37, p. 437.

Dyes and tires: 1937 and 1947–48, source (4), p. 48; 1949, source (8), May, 1950, p. 4; 1950, source (8), March, 1951, p. 4.

TABLE 24

Tractors: 1938 and 1948–50, source (5), 1950 *Survey,* p. 185; 1947, source (7), May 1–15, 1947, p. 324; 1951, source (10), February, 1952, p. 5, by applying the reported percentage of annual increase to the 1950 base; 1955 goal, source (6), 1950 Journal, No. 37, p. 430.

Woodworking and metalworking machine tools: The average weight of the woodworking tools for the years 1937 and 1947–48 was estimated at 1.4 tons on the basis of numbers produced and total weight of both varieties of tools for the first eight months of 1949, as given in source (8), November 20, 1949, p. 258, and May, 1950, p. 3. This factor was used in converting the number of woodworking tools for the years 1937–48 into tons. Since the proportion of woodworking tools to the total weight in the first eight months of 1949 was about 5 percent, and this does not appear subject to much variation in the period considered, the possible error in the total weights of both varieties is not likely to be very substantial. For 1937–48, source (4), p. 48; 1949–50, source (8), May, 1950, p. 3, and March, 1951, p. 3; 1951, source (10), February, 1952, p. 5, by applying the reported percentage increase to the 1950 base; 1955 goal, source (6), 1950 Journal, No. 37, p. 433, by applying the planned fourfold increase to the 1949 base.

Agricultural machines and implements: 1937 and 1947–48, source (4), p. 47; 1949–50, source (8), May, 1950, p. 3, and March, 1951, p. 3; 1951, source (10), February, 1952, p. 4, by applying the reported percentage of annual increase to the 1950 base.

TABLE 25

Bicycles: 1937 and 1947–48, source (4), p. 48; 1949–50, source (8), May, 1950, p. 3, and April, 1951, p. 5; 1951, source (10), February, 1952, p. 5, by applying the reported percentage increase to the 1950 base.

Shoes: 1937 and 1947–48, source (4), p. 50; 1949–50, source (8), May, 1950, p. 5, and April, 1951, p. 7. For 1951–53, by applying the reported annual percentage increases as given in source (10), February, 1952, p. 4; February, 1953, p. 2; and March, 1954, p. 3.

Cotton and wool cloth: 1937, source (6), 1948 Journal, No. 19, p. 349; 1947–48, source (4), p. 45; 1953, source (9), October, 1953, p. 44. For 1949–52, derived from the 1953 figure by working backward, using the reported annual percentage increases as given in source (10), March, 1954, p. 3; February, 1953, p. 2; February, 1952, p. 4; and in source (7), February 1–15, 1951, p. 178.

Bibliography

Public Documents: Poland

Centralny Urząd Planowania (Central Board of Planning). Narodowy plan gospodarczy (National Economic Plan). Warsaw, 1946. Also published in English as The Polish National Economic Plan.

—— Plan odbudowy gospodarczy (Plan of Economic Reconstruction). Warsaw, 1947.

—— Some Facts Concerning the Polish Economy. Warsaw, 1947.

Dziennik Ustaw Rzeczypospolitej Polskiej (Journal of Law of the Polish Republic). Vols. 1945–53. Warsaw, 1945–53.

Główny Urząd Statystyczny (Central Statistical Office). Dochód narodowy polski—1947 (Polish National Income—1947). Warsaw, 1949.

—— Mały rocznik statystyczny (Little Statistical Yearbook). Vols. 1930–39. Warsaw, 1930–39. Also published in English as Concise Statistical Yearbook of Poland.

—— Rocznik statystyczny (Statistical Yearbook). Vols. 1947–49. Warsaw, 1948–50. Also published in English as Statistical Yearbook of Poland.

—— Wiadomości Statystyczne (Statistical News). Vols. 1945–51. Warsaw, 1945–51.

Krajowa Rada Narodowa (The National Council). Sprawozdanie stenograficzne z posiedzeń krajowej rady narodowej w dn. 31 grudnia 1944 r. oraz 2 i 3 stycznia 1945 r. (Stenographic Report of Sessions of the National Council, December 31, 1944, and January 2–3, 1945). Warsaw: Czytelnik, 1946.

Ministry of Foreign Affairs, Press and Information Department. Information on Poland. Warsaw, n.d.

Monitor Polski (The Polish Monitor). Vols. 1948–52. Warsaw, 1948–52.

Public Documents: Other Nations

Germany, Statistisches Amt. Statistisches Jahrbuch für das Deutsches Reich. Vols. 1934–37. Berlin: Puttkammer und Muhlbrecht, 1935–38.

United Nations, Economic Commission for Europe. Economic Bulletin for Europe. Vols. 1950–53. Geneva, 1950–53.

—— Economic Survey of Europe. Vols. 1948–53. Geneva, 1949–54. The 1952 volume appeared under the title Economic Survey of Europe since the War.

—— Quarterly Bulletin of Coal Statistics. No. 1, 1952.

United Nations, United Nations Relief and Rehabilitation Administration. Operational Analysis Papers. Nos. 35, 44, 45. London, 1946–47.

United States Congress, House of Representatives. House Select Committee on Foreign Aid. Final Report on Foreign Aid. House Report 1845, 80th Congress. Washington: Government Printing Office, 1948.

United States Department of Commerce, Office of International Trade. International Reference Service, Vol. V, No. 33. Washington: Government Printing Office, 1948.

Works in Polish

Andrzejewski, Adam. "Ku gospodarce planowej na odcinku mieszkaniowym" (Toward Planned Economy on the Housing Sector), *Gospodarka Planowa,* September, 1948.

Aniola, Jan. "Rola Nowej Huty w postępie technicznym hutnictwa" (Role of Nowa Huta in the Technological Progress of Metallurgy), *Gospodarka Planowa,* July, 1951.

Augustowski, Zbigniew. "Ceny środków produkcji" (Prices of the Means of Production), *Gospodarka Planowa,* January, 1953.

——— "Zagadnienie cen i kosztów w przemyśle państwowym" (The Problem of Prices and Costs in State Industry), *Gospodarka Planowa,* July, 1948.

Baranow, J. "Umowa gospodarcza jako środek wykonania planów państwowych" (The Economic Agreement as a Means of Executing State Plans), *Życie Gospodarcze,* January 1–15, 1950.

Berezowski, Stanisław. "Regionalizacja gospodarcza w Polsce ludowej" (Economic Regionalization in People's Poland), *Życie Gospodarcze,* December 1–15, 1951.

Bierut, Bolesław. "O odchyleniu prawicowym i nacjonalistowym w kierownictwie partii i o sposobach jego przezwyciężenia" (Concerning Rightist and Nationalist Deviation in the Leadership of the Party and Methods of Overcoming It), *Nowe Drogi,* September-October, 1948.

——— "Zadania partii . . ." (Tasks of the Party . . .), *Nowe Drogi,* October, 1953.

Binstein, Ignacy. "PGR ośrodkami wyższej formy gospodarowania na roli" (State Farms as Centers of Superior Forms of Farm Economy), *Życie Gospodarcze,* September 1–15, 1950.

Bobrowski, Czesław. "Ekonomika i polityka w planie odbudowy" (Economics and Politics in the Plan of Reconstruction), *Przegląd Socjalistyczny,* October, 1946.

——— "Kolejny etap" (The Next Stage), *Przegląd Socjalistyczny,* September, 1946.

Bojarski, Pawel. "Gospodarka mięsna na nowym etapie rozwoju" (The Meat Economy on a New Stage of Development), *Życie Gospodarcze,* April 21, 1952.

Bolewski, Andrzej. "Zagadnienie węgli koksujących w Polsce" (The Problem of Coking Coals in Poland), *Hutnik,* January, 1950.

Borejdo, Ignacy. "Hutnictwo w planie 6-letnim" (Metallurgy in the Six-Year Plan), *Hutnik,* September-October, 1950.

Brach, Ignacy. "Przemysł metalowy w planie trzyletnim" (The Metal Industry in the Three-Year Plan), *Życie Gospodarcze,* June 27, 1946.

Brzoza, Anatol. "Statuty spółdzielni produkcyjnych" (Statutes of Producer Cooperatives), *Nowe Drogi,* May-June, 1949.

Czerwiński, Piotr. "Planowanie handlu zagranicznego na rok 1951" (Planning Foreign Trade for 1951), *Gospodarka Planowa,* September, 1950.

Dietrich, Tadeusz. "Gospodarka wielosektorowa" (The Many-sectored Economy), *Przegląd Socjalistyczny,* January, 1947.

Dziewicki, L., and J. Wagner. "Elektro-energetyka w walce o pokrycie zapotrzebowania na energie w 1948 r." (Electric Energy in the Struggle for Meeting Energy Requirements in 1948), *Życie Gospodarcze,* February 1–15, 1949.

Fedak, Zdzisław. "Cena grupowa" (The Group Price), *Życie Gospodarcze,* March 1–15, 1949.

Fihelowa, Janina. "Drogi rozwojowe drobnej wytwórczości w mieście" (Paths of Development of Small-Scale Production in Towns), *Życie Gospodarcze,* February 1–15, 1950.

Fonar, Adam. "Nowa organizacja państwowego przemysłu terenowego" (New Organization of State-owned Local Industry), *Życie Gospodarcze,* April 16–30, 1951.

Gall, Stanisław. "Import Polski ludowej" (Import of People's Poland), *Życie Gospodarcze,* May 1–15, 1950.

Gibuła, Tadeusz. "Uporządkowanie gospodarki finansowej w spółdzielniach" (Setting in Order the Financial Economy in Cooperatives), *Społem,* April 5, 1949.

Grzedzielski, Jan. "Usprawnienie organizowania narad wytwórczych" (Making Efficient the Organizing of Production Conferences), *Życie Gospodarcze,* March 16–31, 1951.

Grzelak, Henryk. "Zamknięcia roczne w spółdzielniach produkcyjnych (Annual Closing of Accounts in Producer Cooperatives), *Życie Gospodarcze,* January 28, 1952.

Instytut Ekonomiki Rolnej (Institute of Agricultural Economics). *Wieś w liczbach* (The Village in Figures). 2d ed. Warsaw: Państwowe Wydawnictwo Rolnicze i Leśne, 1952.

Iwaszkiewicz, Wacław. "Sprawa stabilizacji cen" (The Problem of Price Stabilization), *Robotniczy Przegląd Gospodarczy,* March, 1948.

Jabłoński, Eugeniusz. "Polskie prawo arbitrażowe" Polish Arbitration Law), *Przegląd Ustawodawstwa Gospodarczego,* July-August, 1949.

Janiak, Józef. "O reformie płac" (Concerning the Wage Reform), *Gospodarka Planowa,* February, 1949.

Keh, Zygmunt. "Przemysł budowy maszyn ciężkich w drugim roku planu 6-letniego" (Heavy Machine Building Industry in the Second Year of the Six-Year Plan), *Życie Gospodarcze,* November 1–15, 1951.

Kizler, Jan. "Reforma bankowa" (Banking Reform), *Życie Gospodarcze,* April 1–15, 1951.

Korolewicz, M. "Problematyka paliw płynnych w planie sześcio-letnim" (The Liquid Fuel Problem in the Six-Year Plan), *Gospodarka Planowa,* February, 1949.

Kozak, Władysław. "Wytyczne polityki kontraktowania produkcji roślinnej w 1952 roku" (Principles of Contracting Policy for Plant Crops in 1952), *Życie Gospodarcze,* February 9, 1952.

Krajewski, Roman. "Przegląd polskich złóż rudnych z uwagi na ich znaczenie gospodarcze" (Review of Polish Ore Deposits with Regard to Their Economic Significance), *Hutnik,* July-August, 1947.

Lange, Oskar. "Gospodarcze podstawy demokracji w Polsce" (Economic Bases of Democracy in Poland), *Przegląd Socjalistyczny,* March, 1947.

——— "Od lewicy socjalistycznej do Marksizmu-Leninizmu" (From the Socialist Left to Marxism-Leninism), *Robotnik,* September 29, 1948.

——— "Polskie gospodarstwo narodowe w drugim roku planu 6-letniego" (The Polish National Economy in the Second Year of the Six-Year Plan), *Ekonomista,* Second Quarter, 1951.

——— "Wspólna partia—wspólna ideologia" (A Mutual Party—A Mutual Ideology), *Nowe Drogi,* May-June, 1948.

Lesz, Mieczysław. "Przemysł metalowy osiągnął przedwojenny poziom wytwórczości" (The Metal Industry Has Attained the Prewar Level of Production), *Życie Gospodarcze,* January 15, 1947.

Lipiński, Edward (ed.). *Koniunktura Gospodarcza Polski, Miesięczne Tablice Statystyczne* (Economic Conditions in Poland, Monthly Statistical Tables), Special Issue, December, 1938. Warsaw: Institute for Research on Economic Conditions and Prices, 1939.

Lipski, Tadeusz. "Węgiel decydującym czynnikiem . . ." (Coal the Decisive Factor . . .), *Życie Gospodarcze,* March 16–31, 1950.

Malicki, Janusz. "Reforma systemu pieniężnego" (Reform of the Monetary System), *Gospodarka Planowa,* November, 1950.

Malisz, Bolesław. "Aktywizacja terenow nieuprzemysłowionych" (Activization of Non-industrialized Areas, *Życie Gospodarcze,* December 1–15, 1951.

——— Rozmieszczenie sił wytwórczych w planie 6-letnim" (Location of Productive Forces in the Six-Year Plan), *Gospodarka Planowa,* October, 1950.

Minc, Bronisław. "Program produkcji narodowego planu gospodarczego" (The Program of Production of the National Economic Plan), *Gospodarka Planowa,* February, 1952.

——— "W sprawie rozstawienia sił w gospodarce Polski ludowej" (Concerning the Distribution of Forces in the Economy of People's Poland), *Nowe Drogi,* November, 1953.

——— "Zmiany w metodologii planowania na r. 1952" (Changes in Methodology of Planning for 1952), *Gospodarka Planowa,* July, 1951.

Minc, Hilary. "Charakter i tendencje rozwojowe naszego przemysłu" (Character and Developmental Tendencies of Our Industry), *Nowe Drogi,* May, 1947.

——— "Kilka uwag o zagadnieniu płac" (A Few Observations on the Wage Problem), *Nowe Drogi,* January, 1948.

——— "O bieżących zadaniach partii w zakresie polityki gospodarczej i społecznej wsi" (About the Current Tasks of the Party in the Sphere of Social and Economic Policy of the Village), *Nowe Drogi,* September-October, 1948.

——— "O właściwe metody planowania w Polsce" (Concerning Proper Methods of Planning in Poland), *Nowe Drogi,* March, 1948.

——— Osiągnięcia i plany gospodarcze (Economic Plans and Fulfillments). Warsaw: Książka i Wiedza, 1949.

——— "Owocna współpraca wolnych narodów" (Fruitful Cooperation of Free Nations), *Życie Gospodarcze,* October 16–31, 1951.

——— "Sześcioletni plan rozwoju gospodarczego" (The Six-Year Plan of Economic Development), *Nowe Drogi,* July-August, 1950.

Mokrzyński, Józef. "Aktualne problemy przemysłu naftowego" (Current Problems of the Petroleum Industry), *Życie Gospodarcze,* September 16–30, 1947.

Moskwa, Rajmund. "Przemysł chemiczny na tle wykonania pierwszego roku planu 6-letniego" (The Chemical Industry on the Background of Fulfillment of the First Year of the Six-Year Plan), *Życie Gospodarcze,* December 1–15, 1950.

Niczman, Marian. "Nowy statut wzorcowy" (New Model Charter), *Społem,* April 20, 1949.

Niekrasow, Professor Mikołaj. "Zasady lokalizacji socjalistycznego przemysłu" (Principles of Location of Socialist Industry), *Życie Gospodarcze,* November 1–15, 1951.

Orłowski, Mirosław. "Problem rolnictwa" (The Problem of Agriculture), *Życie Gospodarcze,* August 30, 1946.

Pilawski, Bronisław. "Plan techniczno-przemysłowo-finansowy na rok 1952" (The Technical-Industrial-Financial Plan for 1952), *Życie Gospodarcze,* January 14, 1952.

Pirożyński, Zbigniew. "Podstawowe zasady przebudowy systemu budżetowego" (Basic Principles of the Transformation of the Budget System), *Życie Gospodarcze,* May 16–31, 1950.

——— System budżetowy Polski ludowej (The Budget System of People's Poland). Warsaw: Polskie Wydawnictwa Gospodarcze, 1952.

Raczyński, Kazimierz. "Przemysł maszyn rolniczych . . ." (The Agricultural Machinery Industry . . .), *Życie Gospodarcze,* April 16–30, 1951.

Rapaczyński, Kazimierz. "Budżet pokoju Polski ludowej" (The Budget of Peace of People's Poland), *Gospodarka Planowa,* April, 1952.

Rataj, Julian. "Budżet państwowy na rok 1951" (The State Budget for 1951), *Życie Gospodarcze,* April 16–30, 1951.

Róg, Stanisław. "Ceny niezmienne" (Fixed Prices), *Życie Gospodarcze,* July 1–31, 1949.

Rościszewski, Witold. "Gospodarka zbożowa" (The Grain Economy), *Życie Gospodarcze,* September 16–30, 1949.

Rose, Dr. Edward. "Problem dwoistych cen w Polsce" (The Problem of Duel Prices in Poland), *Życie Gospodarcze,* October, 1946.

Sadulski, Michał. "Doświadczenia przebudowy rolnictwa" (Experience in the Transformation of Agriculture), *Życie Gospodarcze,* May 1–15, 1950.

Secomski, Kazimierz. "Plan inwestycyjny na rok 1949" (Investment Plan for 1949), *Życie Gospodarcze,* February 16–28, 1949.

———— "Plan inwestycyjny na rok 1951" (Investment Plan for 1951), *Życie Gospodarcze,* February 1–15, 1951.

———— "Plan inwestycyjny na rok 1953" (The Investment Plan for 1953), *Inwestycje i Budownictwo,* February, 1953.

———— Podstawowe zadania planu sześcioletniego (Basic Tasks of the Six-Year Plan). Warsaw: Polskie Wydawnictwa Gospodarcze, 1950.

Sikora, Marian. "Wielkie budowle socjalizma" (Great Constructions of Socialism), *Życie Gospodarcze,* December 16–31, 1951.

Sokołowski, Jan. "Rozszerzenie zasięgu planowania w planie roku 1949" (Broadening the Scope of Planning in the 1949 Plan), *Gospodarka Planowa,* September, 1948.

Stefański, Franciszek. "O przestrzeganiu dyscypliny finansowej" (Concerning the Observance of Financial Discipline), *Życie Gospodarcze,* May 1–15, 1951.

Szmidt, Wojciech. "Państwowe ośrodki maszynowe" (State Machine Centers), *Życie Gospodarcze,* March 1–15, 1951.

Szyr, Eugeniusz. "Inicjatywa prywatna w planie trzyletnim" (Private Initiative in the Three-Year Plan), *Nowe Drogi,* January, 1947.

———— "Węzłowe zagadnienia naszej polityki gospodarczej" (Key Problems of Our Economic Policy), *Nowe Drogi,* May-June, 1948.

Szyrocki, Józef. "O współpracy banku z przedsiebiorstwem" (Collaboration of the Bank with the Enterprise), *Finanse,* No. 5, 1953.

Szyszkowska, Anna. "Województwo Białostockie w planie 6–letnim" (The Bialystok Province in the Six-Year Plan), *Gospodarka Planowa,* March, 1951.

Taban, Bronisław. "Powstaje nowa socjalistyczna i pokojowa chemia" (A New Socialist and Peacetime Chemistry Is Rising), *Życie Gospodarcze,* August 1–15, 1951.

Tkaczow, Stanisław. "Państwowe gospodarstwa rolne w 1952 r." (State Farms in 1952), *Gospodarka Planowa,* February, 1952.

Trąmczyński, Witold. "Uwagi o roli banków w gospodarce planowej" (Remarks on the Role of Banks in a Planned Economy), *Wiadomości Narodowego Banku Polskiego,* August, 1946.

Trawiński, Tadeusz. "Bilans przemysłu naftowego za rok 1948" (The Balance Sheet of the Petroleum Industry for 1948), *Życie Gospodarcze,* January 15–31, 1949.

Wencel, Henryk. "Współpraca Polsko-Czechoslowacka" (Polish-Czechoslovak Cooperation), *Życie Gospodarcze,* December 16–31, 1948.

Werfel, Roman. "O wyjaśnienie zasadniczych zagadnień" (About the Elucidation of Fundamental Problems), *Nowe Drogi,* January, 1948.

Zaleski, Roman. "Uwagi o sposobie opracowania narodowego planu . . ." (Observations about the Manner of Preparing the National Plan . . .), *Gospodarka Planowa,* April, 1953.

Zambrowski, Roman. "Aktualne zadania partii na wsi" (The Party's Current Tasks in the Village), *Nowe Drogi,* March-April, 1949.

Żebrowski, Adam. "Uwagi o planowaniu terenowym w drobnym przemyśle" (Remarks on Local Planning in Small-Scale Industry), *Gospodarka Planowa,* August, 1951.

Złotnicki, Grzegorz. "Przestawienie asortymentowe w przemyśle dla zaspokojenia potrzeb wsi" (Shifts in Assortment in Industry for Satisfying the Needs of the Village), *Życie Gospodarcze,* January 26, 1952.

Zralek, Stanisław. "Z doświadczeń budownictwa Nowej Huty" (From the Experience of Building Nowa Huta), *Życie Gospodarcze,* January 1, 1952.

Polish Journals and Newspapers

Ekonomista (The Economist).

Finanse (Finances).

Gospodarka Planowa (Planned Economy).

Handel Zagraniczny (Foreign Trade) (Supplement to *Życie Gospodarcze*).

Hutnik (Metallurgist).

Inwestycje i Budownictwo (Investments and Construction).

Nafta (Petroleum).

Nowe Drogi (New Ways).

Nowe Rolnictwo (New Agriculture).

Przegląd Socjalistyczny (Socialist Review).

Przegląd Techniczny (Technical Review).

Przegląd Ustawodawstwa Gospodarczego (Review of Economic Legislation) (Supplement to *Życie Gospodarcze*).

Przegląd Związkowy (The Union Review).

Przemysł Chemiczny (The Chemical Industry).

Robotniczy Przegląd Gospodarczy (Workers' Economic Review).

Robotnik (The Worker).

Społem (Together).

Statistical Tables of the Institute of the National Economy (Supplement to *Gospodarka Planowa*).

Ustawodawstwo Gospodarcze (Economic Legislation) (Supplement to *Życie Gospodarcze*).

Wiadomości Hutnicze (Metallurgical News).
Wiadomości Narodowego Banku Polskiego (News of the Polish National Bank).
Życie Gospodarcze (Economic Life).

Other Sources

Annals of the American Academy of Political and Social Science.
Bergson, Abram. "The Fourth Five Year Plan: Heavy Versus Consumers' Goods Industries," *Political Science Quarterly,* June, 1947.
Bergson, Abram (ed.). Soviet Economic Growth. Evanston: Row, Peterson and Company, 1953.
Birmingham Information Service on Slavonic Countries. Poland: Monograph No. 3, Poland's New Codes of Law. Birmingham: University of Birmingham, 1937.
—— Poland: Monograph No. 4, National Income of Poland. Birmingham: University of Birmingham, 1937.
Buell, Raymond Leslie. Poland: Key to Europe. New York: Alfred A. Knopf, 1939.
Christian Science Monitor.
Ciechanowski, Jan. Defeat in Victory. London: Victor Gollancz, Ltd., 1948.
Clark, Colin. The Conditions of Economic Progress. London: Macmillan and Co., Ltd., 1951.
Dewar, Margaret. Soviet Trade with Eastern Europe, 1945–1949. London: Royal Institute of International Affairs, 1951.
Domanus, Joseph. "Production of Electricity in Poland," *Poland of Today,* December, 1946.
Economist (London).
Études et Conjoncture.
Gorecki, Roman. Poland and Her Economic Development. London: George Allen and Unwin, Ltd., 1935.
Gurian, Waldemar (ed.). The Soviet Union. Notre Dame: University of Notre Dame Press, 1951.
Jasny, Naum. The Socialized Agriculture of the USSR. Palo Alto: Stanford University Press, 1949.
Kertesz, Stephen. "The Method of Soviet Penetration in Eastern Europe," in The Soviet Union. Edited by Waldemar Gurian. Notre Dame: University of Notre Dame Press, 1951.
Kulischer, Eugene M. "Population Changes behind the Iron Curtain," *Annals of the American Academy of Political and Social Science,* September, 1950.
Lane, Arthur Bliss. I Saw Poland Betrayed. Indianapolis: Bobbs-Merrill Co., 1948.
Lange, Oskar. "Cooperatives in Poland," *Poland of Today,* November, 1949.

Lange, Oskar, and Fred M. Taylor. On the Economic Theory of Socialism. Edited by Benjamin E. Lippincott. Minneapolis: The University of Minnesota Press, 1938.

Lesniewski, V., and W. Ponikowski. "Polish Agriculture," in Agricultural Systems of Middle Europe. Edited by O. S. Morgan. New York: The Macmillan Company, 1933.

Mikołajczyk, Stanisław. The Rape of Poland. New York: McGraw-Hill Book Company, Inc., 1948.

Moore, Wilbert E. Economic Demography of Eastern and Southern Europe. Geneva: League of Nations, 1945.

Morgan, O. S. (ed.). Agricultural Systems of Middle Europe. New York: The Macmillan Co., 1933.

National Committee for a Free Europe. Poland in the Year 1951, Part I. New York.

New York *Times.*

Poland of Today.

Polish Cooperative News Service.

Political Science Quarterly.

Press Release (Polish Embassy, Washington).

Quarterly Review of the Polish National Economic Bank.

Rosada, Stefan, and Jozef Gwozdz. Forced Labor and Confinement without Trial in Poland. Washington: National Committee for a Free Europe, Inc., 1952.

Schwartz, Harry. Russia's Soviet Economy. New York: Prentice-Hall, Inc., 1950.

The Soviet-Yugoslav Dispute. London: Royal Institute of International Affairs, 1948.

Stettinius, Edward R., Jr. Roosevelt and the Russians: The Yalta Conference. New York: Doubleday and Company, Inc., 1949.

Táborský, Eduard. "Government in the 'People's Democracies,'" *Annals of the American Academy of Political and Social Science,* September, 1950.

Times (London).

Vneshnyaya Torgovlya (Foreign Trade).

Washington *Post.*

Wellisz, Leopold. Foreign Capital in Poland. London: George Allen and Unwin, Ltd., 1938.

Zweig, Ferdynand. Poland between Two Wars. London: Secker and Warburg, 1944.

Index

Administration of planned economy, 77–104; central authorities, 78–87; sphere of activities of industrial ministries, 81–82; intermediate and lower levels of, 87–94; procedures and supervision in socialized sector, 94–104

Agrarian reforms, *see* Land reforms

Agricultural Bank, 97, 99

Agricultural commodities, production in Poland's old and new territories, 30 *tab.*, 31 *tab.;* government policies with respect to trade in, 19, 56, 61, 192; compulsory deliveries of, 51, 188, 191, 192, 193–96; marketable surplus, problem of, 191–94; state contracting for, 197, 198 *tab.;* land tax payments in, 227; realignment of prices on, 237–38; prices of, in relation to industrial prices, 241–42; foreign trade in, 275, 276 *tab.*

Agricultural cooperatives, 201

Agricultural machinery, production of, 157, 183 *tab.;* machinery stations, 203–6; UNRRA aid in, 206

Agriculture, problems of surplus agrarian population, 7, 10, 15, 16, 18, 138, 187, 189; problems of, in interwar period, 10, 15–19; employment in, 10 *tab.*, 144–45; investment in, 11 *tab.*, 142 *tab.*, 144, 167, 188, 191; land tenure problems and feudal survivals, 16–17; in former German areas, 17, 190–91; state control in, 17–19, 56, 59–62; postwar changes in land utilization, 28–31; war losses estimated in, 32; socialization of, 49–50, 119, 153, 188, 191–92, 198–203, 291, 293, 294; policy changes in field of (1954–55), 51, 118; percentage of socialization of, 62, 291; functions of Agricultural Bank, 97, 99, taxation in, 115, 188, 201, 203, 227–28; Cominform prescriptions in the field of, 115; elimination of kulaks and collectivization of, 115–16; gross output for Six-Year Plan, 117 *tab.;* relationship between industry and, 119, 124; plans of production (1952), 122; shares of, in national income and in national product, 137, 139–40; under Six-Year Plan, 147 *tab.*, 148, 149 *tab.*, 152–53, 158 *tab.;* under Three-Year Plan, 150; mechanization of, and petroleum requirements, 173; distribution of privately owned farm lands, 190 *tab.;* marketable surplus, problem of, 191; contracting and regionalization of production, 196–98; machine and tractor stations, 203–6; UNRRA aid to, 206, 269 *tab.;* production problems, 206–10; rural electrification, 208; plans and performance in, 210–17; compulsory savings from agricultural income, 229; price policies, 235–36, 241–42; *see also* Agricultural commodities; Collective farms; Land reforms; Private farms; State farms.

Agriculture, Ministry of, 80, 87

Allocation of raw materials, 56, 107

Aluminum, production of, 178

Animal products, compulsory deliveries of, 195–96; state contracting for, 197, 198 *tab.;* Six-Year Plan goals, 211; foreign trade in, 276 *tab.*

Arbitration, economic: state system of, 100–102

Arbitration commissions, 100–102

Area, changes in Poland's, 21–24

Association of Importers and Exporters, 266

Audit, state: legal provisions concerning, 95

Autarkic policy, in capital goods industries, 158; in eastern Europe, 288–89

Balance of trade, 272 *tab.*, 278 *tab.*

Balance sheet of the national economy, 124

Banking system, state control over, 3, 14, 52, 66; socialized financial institutions in, 50; and financial control, 82, 257–61; credit cooperatives, 98; reform (1948), 98; role of, in economic planning, 98–100, 257–58; credits to industry, 143; Polish National Bank, functions of, 256

Bank of Cooperative Societies, 97

Bank of Poland, 4, 5, 15

Bank of the Cooperative Economy, 97, 98

Bank of the Polish Welfare Fund, 99